The ECT Handbook

Fourth Edition

The ECT Handbook

Fourth Edition

Edited by
I Nicol Ferrier
University of Newcastle upon Tyne

Jonathan Waite
University of Nottingham

CAMBRIDGE
UNIVERSITY PRESS

University Printing House, Cambridge CB2 8BS, United Kingdom

One Liberty Plaza, 20th Floor, New York, NY 10006, USA

477 Williamstown Road, Port Melbourne, VIC 3207, Australia

314–321, 3rd Floor, Plot 3, Splendor Forum, Jasola District Centre,
New Delhi – 110025, India

79 Anson Road, #06-04/06, Singapore 079906

Cambridge University Press is part of the University of Cambridge.

It furthers the University's mission by disseminating knowledge in the pursuit of
education, learning, and research at the highest international levels of excellence.

www.cambridge.org
Information on this title: www.cambridge.org/9781911623168
DOI: 10.1017/9781911623175

© Royal College of Psychiatrists 1995, 2005, 2013, 2019

This book was previously published by The Royal College of Psychiatrists.
First published 1995, The Royal College of Psychiatrists
Second edition 2005, The Royal College of Psychiatrists
Third edition 2013, The Royal College of Psychiatrists
This fourth edition published by Cambridge University Press 2019
Reprinted 2020

Printed in the United Kingdom by TJ International Ltd., Padstow Cornwall

A catalogue record for this publication is available from the British Library.

Library of Congress Cataloging-in-Publication Data
Names: Ferrier, I. Nicol. | Waite, Jonathan, editor.
Title: The ECT handbook / edited by I. Nicol Ferrier, University of Newcastle
    upon Tyne, Jonathan Waite, University of Nottingham.
Description: Fourth edition. | Cambridge, United Kingdom ; New York,
    NY : Cambridge University Press, 2020. | Revision of: ECT handbook /
    Royal College of Psychiatrists. Special Committee on ECT. 1995. |
    Includes bibliographical references and index.
Identifiers: LCCN 2019011492 | ISBN 9781911623168 (paperback)
Subjects: LCSH: Electroconvulsive therapy–Handbooks, manuals, etc. |
    BISAC: PSYCHOLOGY / Mental Health.
Classification: LCC RC485 .R69 2020 | DDC 616.89/122–dc23
LC record available at https://lccn.loc.gov/2019011492

ISBN 978-1-911-62316-8 Paperback

....

Contents

List of Contributors   vii
Preface to the Fourth Edition   xi

1. **The Place of ECT and Related Treatments in Contemporary UK Psychiatry**   1
   I Nicol Ferrier

2. **Mechanism of Action of ECT**   13
   Philip J Cowen

3. **ECT in the Treatment of Depression**   24
   I Nicol Ferrier

4. **ECT in Mania (and Mixed States)**   32
   R Hamish McAllister-Williams

5. **Electroconvulsive Therapy for Bipolar Disorder Depression**   38
   Ute Kessler

6. **ECT in Older Adults**   44
   Stuart Watson, Jane Newby and Phil Laws

7. **ECT in People with an Intellectual Disability**   50
   Peter Cutajar and Jo Jones

8. **ECT in Pregnancy and Postnatally**   63
   Alain Gregoire and Joanne Spoors

9. **Electroconvulsive Therapy in Children and Adolescents**   67
   Rosalind Y K Oliphant, Eleanor M Smith and Aditya N Sharma

10. **The Use of ECT in the Treatment of Schizophrenia**   74
    Richard Braithwaite

11. **The Use of ECT in the Treatment of Catatonia**   85
    Richard Braithwaite

12. **ECT in Neuropsychiatric Disorders**   96
    Jasvinder Singh and David Andrew Cousins

13. **Cognitive Side-Effects of ECT**   109
    Martha Finnegan and Declan M McLoughlin

14. **Non-cognitive Adverse Effects of ECT**   121
    Jonathan Waite

15. **Transcranial Magnetic Stimulation**   129
    Alex O'Neill-Kerr and Sudheer Lankappa

16. **Neurosurgery for Mental Disorder**   140
    Keith Matthews and Christine A Matthews

17. **Ketamine for Psychiatric Disorders**   149
    Rupert McShane

18. **The ECT Accreditation Service (ECTAS)**   161
    Jill Emerson

19. **The Scottish ECT Accreditation Network (SEAN)**   164
    Linda Cullen and Alistair Hay

20. **Medical Training for Psychiatrists in ECT**   168
    Vimal Sivasanker and Ian O Nnatu

21. **Nursing Care of the Patient Receiving ECT and the Roles of the ECT Nurse**   173
    Kara Hannigan

22. **Practical Aspects of ECT** 183
Ross A Dunne, Alex O'Neill-Kerr, Declan M McLoughlin and Jonathan Waite

23. **Anaesthesia for Electroconvulsive Therapy** 202
Godfrey M Bwalya, Rahul Bajekal and Jonathan Waite

24. **Dental Issues Related to ECT** 211
Denis Martin, revised by Basel Switzer

25. **Interactions between ECT and Prescribed Medication** 218
Ian M Anderson

26. **Seizure Monitoring in ECT** 234
David M Semple and Ryan Alexander Devlin

27. **Safe ECT Practice in People with a Physical Illness** 247
Jonathan Waite

28. **Capacity, Consent and the Law** 254
Jonathan Waite

29. **Patients', Carers' and the Public's Perspectives on ECT and Related Treatments** 267
Jonathan Waite

Index 274

Contributors

Ian M Anderson
Honorary Professor of Psychiatry, Division of Neuroscience and Experimental Psychology, University of Manchester and Manchester Academic Health Science Centre, UK

Rahul Bajekal
Consultant Anaesthetist, Royal Victoria Infirmary, Newcastle upon Tyne, UK

Richard Braithwaite
Consultant Psychiatrist, St Mary's Hospital, Isle of Wight, UK

Godfrey M Bwalya
Consultant Anaesthetist, Spire Hull and East Yorkshire, Anlaby and Honorary Senior Clinical Tutor, Hull York Medical School, UK

David Andrew Cousins
MRC Clinician Scientist, Institute of Neuroscience, Newcastle University, UK

Philip J Cowen
MRC Clinical Scientist, University Department of Psychiatry, Warneford Hospital, Oxford, UK

Linda Cullen
National Clinical Coordinator, Scottish ECT Accreditation Network, Scottish Healthcare Audits, NHS, National Services Scotland, UK

Peter Cutajar
Consultant Psychiatrist, Nottinghamshire Healthcare NHS Foundation Trust, UK

Ryan Alexander Devlin
ST5 Registrar in General Adult Psychiatry, University Hairmyres Hospital, East Kilbride, UK

Ross A Dunne
Consultant Old Age Psychiatrist, Manchester ECT Lead, Greater Manchester Mental Health Trust, UK

Jill Emerson
Former Lead Psychiatrist, Devizes and former Chair of The ECT Accreditation Service Accreditation Committee

I Nicol Ferrier
Chair, Royal College of Psychiatrists' Committee on ECT and Related Treatments, London and Emeritus Professor of Psychiatry, Institute of Neuroscience, Newcastle University, UK

Martha Finnegan
Research Registrar, Department of Psychiatry and Trinity College Institute of Neuroscience, Trinity College Dublin, St Patrick's University Hospital, Dublin, Ireland

Alain Gregoire
Consultant Perinatal Psychiatrist and Chair Maternal Mental Health Alliance, Southampton, UK

Kara Hannigan
ECT Clinic Manager, Cardiff and Vale University Health Board, UK

Alistair Hay
Chairman, Scottish ECT Accreditation
Network (SEAN), Inverness, UK

Jo Jones
Consultant Psychiatrist, Nottinghamshire
Healthcare NHS Foundation Trust, UK

Ute Kessler
Head of ECT Service, Haukeland
University Hospital, Bergen, and Associate
Professor, University of Bergen, Norway

Sudheer Lankappa
Consultant Psychiatrist, Nottinghamshire
Healthcare NHS Foundation Trust and
Honorary Clinical Associate Professor,
School of Medicine, University of
Nottingham, UK

Phil Laws
Clinical Director of Quality and Patient
Safety, Consultant in Intensive Care
Medicine and Anaesthesia, The Newcastle
Upon Tyne Hospitals NHS Foundation
Trust, UK

Denis Martin
Retired Psychiatrist and Dental Surgeon,
Gloucester, UK

Christine A Matthews
School of Medicine, University of
Dundee, UK

Keith Matthews
Professor of Psychiatry and Head of
Discipline – Psychology, Schools of Medicine
and Social Sciences, University of Dundee, UK

R Hamish McAllister-Williams
Professor of Affective Disorders, Northern
Centre for Mood Disorders, Institute of
Neuroscience, Newcastle University and
Northumberland, Tyne and Wear NHS
Foundation Trust, UK

Rupert McShane
Consultant Psychiatrist, Oxford Health
NHS Foundation Trust, UK

Declan M McLoughlin
Research Professor of Psychiatry,
Department of Psychiatry and Trinity
College Institute of Neuroscience,
Trinity College Dublin, St Patrick's
University Hospital, Dublin,
Ireland

Jane Newby
Consultant in Old Age Psychiatry
and ECT Lead, Northumberland,
Tyne and Wear NHS Foundation
Trust, UK

Ian O Nnatu
Consultant Psychiatrist, Charing Cross
Hospital and Honorary Senior Clinical
Lecturer, Imperial College London, UK

Alex O'Neill-Kerr
Medical Director, Consultant Psychiatrist,
Lead Consultant, The Centre for
Neuromodulation, Northamptonshire
Healthcare NHS Foundation Trust, UK

Rosalind Y K Oliphant
Child and Adolescent Psychiatry Specialist
Registrar, Children and Young People's
Services, Northumberland, Tyne and Wear
NHS Foundation Trust, UK

David M Semple
Consultant Psychiatrist, University
Hospital Hairmyres, East Kilbride and
Honorary Fellow, Division of Psychiatry,
University of Edinburgh, UK

Aditya Narain Sharma
Clinical Senior Lecturer in Child and
Adolescent Psychiatry, Academic
Psychiatry, Institute of Neuroscience,
Newcastle University, UK

Jasvinder Singh
Consultant Neuropsychiatrist,
Northumberland, Tyne and Wear NHS
Foundation Trust, UK

Vimal Sivasanker
Consultant Psychiatrist, Hertfordshire
Partnership University NHS Foundation
Trust and Vice Chair of the Royal College of
Psychiatrists ECT Committee, London, UK

Eleanor M Smith
Consultant Child and Adolescent
Psychiatrist, Northumberland, Tyne and
Wear NHS Foundation Trust, UK

Joanne Spoors
Consultant Perinatal Psychiatrist,
Hampshire, Portsmouth, Isle of Wight and
Farnham Perinatal Mental Health
Service, UK

Basel Switzer
Consultant Psychiatrist, Herdmanflat
Hospital, Haddington, East Lothian, UK

Stuart Watson
Clinical Senior Lecturer, Newcastle
University and Honorary Consultant,
NTW NHS Mental Health
Foundation Trust

Jonathan Waite
Honorary Senior Fellow, Institute of
Mental Health, University of
Nottingham, UK

Preface to the Fourth Edition

This new edition of *The ECT Handbook* comes six years after the publication of the third edition. In the intervening period there have been no major changes in the practice of electroconvulsive therapy, but continuing research has provided good new evidence on the optimal use of ECT in the treatment of mental disorders.

This edition of *The ECT Handbook* contains new chapters on ECT for bipolar depression, ECT in pregnancy and postnatally, ECT in children and adolescents and on the use of ketamine in treatment resistant depression. Many of the other chapters have been completely re-written by new authors and all have been substantially revised to include new evidence published until the end of 2018. There have been further developments to try to resolve the question about whether unilateral or bilateral ECT should be the initial technique when ECT is used in the treatment of depression and these are considered in Chapter 3. Other important new research has been conducted in the use of ECT in the treatment of bipolar depression and resistant schizophrenia and this is discussed in Chapters 5 and 10.

We had expected a major revision of the guidance on the management of depression from the National Institute of Health and Care Excellence (NICE) to be published before this volume in 2018 but its publication has been delayed. There has been a significant change in mental health law in Northern Ireland, which may have implications for other legislatures, but this has not come into force at the time that *The ECT Handbook* goes to print.

As editors we have been fortunate to assemble an excellent team of contributors and we are immensely grateful for their efforts in producing and revising their drafts. We are especially appreciative of the support we have received from Stella Galea at the Royal College of Psychiatrists who has kept the project on track with consummate efficiency. We thank the anonymous reviewers for their helpful comments on earlier drafts and Anna Whiting, Charlotte Brisley and their team at Cambridge University Press for their hard work and skill in the production of the Handbook.

The Place of ECT and Related Treatments in Contemporary UK Psychiatry

I Nicol Ferrier

The previous edition of The ECT Handbook was produced in 2013 and was well received. The current edition updates the 2013 one and attempts to find a similar balance between outlining the scientific literature relating to ECT and related treatment modalities and pragmatic and practical advice on their place in management and delivery in a UK context. This chapter concentrates on the guidelines in the UK for the use of ECT and related treatments. The recommendations of NICE for the use of ECT and related treatments are outlined first, followed by position statements from the Committee. Any differences (which are usually minor and of emphasis rather than substance) are highlighted. The position statements were generated in 2017 and have been ratified by the College. They can be found on the Royal College of Psychiatrists' website at:

www.rcpsych.ac.uk/workinpsychiatry/committeesofcouncil/ectandrelatedtreatments.aspx

Evidence supporting these position statements can be found in individual chapters of the Handbook.

The use of ECT has fallen across the UK in the last few decades although there is some evidence that, in the last few years, the numbers of courses administered each year is falling much more slowly (Buley *et al.*, 2017; SEAN, 2016). There are a myriad of reasons why the numbers of patients receiving ECT have fallen: some relate to attitudes of patients and of staff, others relate to the problems of delivering it in the current service framework. These issues are discussed more fully in subsequent chapters of this Handbook. Paradoxically the evidence base for the efficacy and safety of ECT continues to grow. The Committee feels that it is a valuable treatment that is either not considered at all or left until too late, in the management of many complex and severe cases. The position statement relating to ECT outlines the kind of patients for whom the College believes ECT should be considered. Despite the strong evidence for ECT, it is likely it will continue to be used only for a minority of patients with complex and severe mental illnesses so it is gratifying, given the scale of the clinical problem, that research on other potential physical treatment modalities for some of these patients is active. The position statements, together with the relevant National Institute for Health and Care Excellence (NICE) guideline recommendations, on ECT and the most prominent related treatments are given below, focusing on their use in depression. There are a variety of international guidelines on ECT and other modalities and the College's position is broadly in line with the rest of the world.

ECT

Depression

NICE Guidelines on Use of ECT in Depression

The 2009 NICE Guideline for Depression (CG90, NICE, updated 2016) made the following recommendations about ECT:

1.10.4.1 Consider ECT for acute treatment of severe depression that is life-threatening and when a rapid response is required, or when other treatments have failed.

1.10.4.2 Do not use ECT routinely for people with moderate depression but consider it if their depression has not responded to multiple drug treatments and psychological treatment.

1.10.4.3 For people whose depression has not responded well to a previous course of ECT, consider a repeat trial of ECT only after:

- reviewing the adequacy of the previous treatment course and
- considering all other options and
- discussing the risks and benefits with the person and/or, where appropriate, their advocate or carer.

1.10.4.4 When considering ECT as a treatment choice, ensure that the person with depression is fully informed of the risks associated with ECT, and with the risks and benefits specific to them. Document the assessment and consider:

- the risks associated with a general anaesthetic
- current medical comorbidities
- potential adverse events, notably cognitive impairment
- the risks associated with not receiving ECT.

The risks associated with ECT may be greater in older people; exercise particular caution when considering ECT treatment in this group.

1.10.4.5 A decision to use ECT should be made jointly with the person with depression as far as possible, taking into account, where applicable, the requirements of the Mental Health Act 2007. Also be aware that:

- valid informed consent should be obtained (if the person has the capacity to grant or refuse consent) without the pressure or coercion that might occur as a result of the circumstances and clinical setting
- the person should be reminded of their right to withdraw consent at any time
- there should be strict adherence to recognised guidelines about consent, and advocates or carers should be involved to facilitate informed discussions
- if informed consent is not possible, ECT should only be given if it does not conflict with a valid advance decision, and the person's advocate or carer should be consulted.

1.10.4.6 The choice of electrode placement and stimulus dose related to seizure threshold should balance efficacy against the risk of cognitive impairment. Take into account that:

- bilateral ECT is more effective than unilateral ECT but may cause more cognitive impairment

- with unilateral ECT, a higher stimulus dose is associated with greater efficacy, but also increased cognitive impairment compared with a lower stimulus dose.

1.10.4.7 Assess clinical status after each ECT treatment using a formal valid outcome measure, and stop treatment when remission has been achieved, or sooner if side effects outweigh the potential benefits.

1.10.4.8 Assess cognitive function before the first ECT treatment and monitor at least every three to four treatments, and at the end of a course of treatment.

1.10.4.9 Assessment of cognitive function should include:

- orientation and time for reorientation after each treatment
- measures of new learning, retrograde amnesia and subjective memory impairment carried out at least 24 hours after a treatment.

If there is evidence of significant cognitive impairment at any stage consider, in discussion with the person with depression, changing from bilateral to unilateral electrode placement, reducing the stimulus dose or stopping treatment depending on the balance of risks and benefits.

1.10.4.10 If a person's depression has responded to a course of ECT, antidepressant medication should be started or continued to prevent relapse. Consider lithium augmentation of antidepressants.

Royal College of Psychiatrists' Position Statement on ECT for Depression

The Royal College of Psychiatrists similarly holds that ECT is a well-established and safe treatment option for depressed patients who have an inadequate response to, or poor tolerability of, antidepressant treatment. The College concurs with NICE's recommendations for consent and monitoring of ECT. The position statement broadly agrees with NICE's recommendations but is more robust in its recommendations regarding the elderly, more explicit on the place of ECT in management and more up to date regarding the evidence on cognitive side effects. The evidence supporting these assertions is outlined in Chapter 3. Whilst the current evidence base for ECT in depression is not sufficiently detailed to allow certainty about the sequencing of ECT within a patient's management plan, it is sufficiently robust to be confident about efficacy in the clinical situations outlined below. The Committee's position statement recommends:

ECT as a first-line treatment for patients (including the elderly):

- where a rapid definitive response for the emergency treatment of depression is needed
- with high suicidal risk
- with severe psychomotor retardation and associated problems of compromised eating and drinking and/or physical deterioration
- who suffer from treatment-resistant depression that has responded to ECT in a previous episode of illness
- who are pregnant with severe depression and whose physical health or that of the foetus is at serious risk
- who prefer this form of treatment.

ECT as a second-line treatment for patients (including the elderly):

- with treatment-resistant depression
- who experience severe side-effects from medication

- whose medical or psychiatric condition, in spite of other treatments, has deteriorated to an extent that raises concern.

Chapter 3 reviews the evidence about ECT in the treatment of unipolar depression.

Bipolar Disorder
Mania

The NICE Technology Appraisal Guidance on the Use of Electroconvulsive Therapy (ECT) (TA59) was first published in 2003. It was updated in 2009 (NICE, 2009) and, in 2014, NICE decided there was no new evidence which met NICE standards and left the appraisal unchanged. Recommendation 1.1 of TA59 states that it is recommended that electroconvulsive therapy (ECT) is used only to achieve rapid and short-term improvement of severe symptoms after an adequate trial of other treatment options has proven ineffective and/or when the condition is considered to be potentially life-threatening, in individuals with a prolonged or severe manic episode.

The NICE clinical guideline on bipolar disorder (CG185; NICE, 2014) makes no changes to the recommendation of TA59 except to advise stopping or reducing lithium or benzodiazepines before giving ECT, monitoring the length of fits carefully if the patient is taking anticonvulsants and monitoring mental state carefully for evidence of switching to the opposite pole.

The Royal College of Psychiatrists' position statement concurs with this and indicates that ECT should be a second line treatment for those patients with persistent or life-threatening symptoms in severe or prolonged mania.

Bipolar Depression

The NICE clinical guideline on bipolar disorder (CG185; NICE, 2014) made no recommendations about the use of ECT in bipolar depression. However, more recently, a randomised controlled trial (RCT) from Norway showed improved outcomes when patients with treatment-resistant bipolar depression who had failed to respond to antidepressants were given a course of unilateral ECT (Schoeyen et al., 2015). The Committee's position statement reflects this new evidence and states that ECT should be considered in some circumstances for patients with bipolar depression.

Chapters 4 and 5 review the evidence about ECT in the treatment of the various phases of bipolar disorder.

Schizophrenia

Recommendation 1.9 of the NICE Technology Appraisal Guidance on the Use of Electroconvulsive Therapy (TA59; NICE, 2009) states that 'The current state of the evidence does not allow the general use of ECT in the management of schizophrenia to be recommended' and the Committee's position statement concurs with that view. However it may have a place in the management of some patients. A recent systematic review and meta-analysis assessed the proportion of patients with Treatment Resistant Schizophrenia (TRS) that responded to ECT augmentation of clozapine and concluded that ECT may be an effective and safe augmentation strategy in TRS. A higher number of ECT treatments may be required than is standard for other clinical indications (Lally et al., 2016). In the light of this the position statement indicates that ECT should be considered in some circumstances for patients with TRS.

Catatonia

Recommendation 1.1 of the NICE Technology Appraisal Guidance on the Use of Electroconvulsive Therapy (TA59; NICE, 2009) recommends that ECT is used only to achieve rapid and short-term improvement of severe symptoms after an adequate trial of other treatment options has proven ineffective and/or when the condition is considered to be potentially life-threatening in individuals with catatonia. NICE also states (recommendation 1.7) that:

> A repeat course of ECT should be considered under the circumstances indicated in 1.1 only for individuals who have catatonia or mania and who have previously responded well to ECT. In patients who are experiencing an acute episode but have not previously responded, a repeat trial of ECT should be undertaken only after all other options have been considered and following discussion of the risks and benefits with the individual and/or where appropriate their carer/advocate.
>
> (NICE TA59, 1.7, 2009)

The College's position statement is more robust and states that ECT may be considered as a first line treatment in life threatening catatonia and that it is effective in less severe cases of catatonia that have not responded to medication, where it is a second line treatment.

Chapters 10 and 11 review the evidence about ECT in the treatment of schizophrenia and catatonia.

Severe mental illness in pregnancy and the puerperium

In 2014 the NICE Guidelines for antenatal and postnatal mental health were published (CG192; NICE, 2014). It was recommended that ECT be considered for pregnant women with severe depression, severe mixed affective states or mania, or catatonia, whose physical health or that of the foetus was at serious risk. The Guideline stated that if a pregnant woman with bipolar disorder developed mania while taking prophylactic medication, the dose of the prophylactic medication and adherence should be checked, the dose increased if the prophylactic medication was an antipsychotic and the medication changed to an antipsychotic if she was taking another type of prophylactic medication. If there was no response and the woman had severe mania, lithium should be considered and then ECT considered if there was no response to lithium.

Anderson and Reti (2009) reviewed the use of ECT in pregnancy in 339 published cases. They reported at least partial response of depressive symptoms in 84% of cases and concluded that the risks to foetus and mother are low. There is evidence that depression may respond better to ECT in the post-natal period than in other circumstances, with more rapid and complete remission of mood and psychotic symptoms (Reed et al., 1999). These observations led the Committee to indicate in its position statement that ECT should be used as first line treatment in women who are pregnant with severe depression, or severe mixed affective states, mania or catatonia and whose physical health or that of the foetus is at serious risk. ECT should be considered in some circumstances for those women with post-natal psychosis.

Chapter 8 reviews the evidence about ECT in the treatment of severe mental illness in pregnancy and in the puerperium.

Transcranial Magnetic Stimulation

Transcranial Magnetic Stimulation (TMS) is a non-invasive technique used to stimulate neuronal tissue. This technique involves placement of an electromagnetic coil to deliver a rapidly changing magnetic field which alters the electrical properties of the cortical neurons. Repetitive Transcranial Magnetic Stimulation (rTMS) is a relatively new treatment modality for psychiatric disorders where the stimulus train is repeated at pre-set intervals.

The most recent NICE interventional procedure guidance (IPG542; NICE, 2015) on rTMS for depression recommends that rTMS may be used for depression with normal arrangements for clinical governance and audit. It states:

- The evidence on repetitive transcranial magnetic stimulation for depression shows no major safety concerns. The evidence on its efficacy in the short term is adequate, although the clinical response is variable. Repetitive Transcranial Magnetic Stimulation for depression may be used with normal arrangements for clinical governance and audit.
- During the consent process, clinicians should, in particular, inform patients about the other treatment options available, and make sure that patients understand the possibility the procedure may not give them benefit.

NICE recommends rTMS for the treatment of depression but the evidence cited in the IPG comes from RCTs and meta-analyses of patients with both primary depressive disorder and treatment resistant depression (TRD). The Committee's position statement therefore opined that rTMS could also be considered in patients with TRD and in those with severe depression who do not want to consider, or have contraindications to, the use of ECT. However it was noted that a meta-analysis (Slotema et al., 2010) found that rTMS was not as effective as ECT. This was confirmed in a subsequent meta-analysis by Chen and colleagues although they also found that TMS was better tolerated than ECT (Chen et al., 2017). Hence it should not be considered as a replacement for ECT unless acceptability or tolerability issues dictate this. It was also pointed out that while there are no contraindications for concomitant use of rTMS and neurotropic medications, clinicians should be aware of medications which reduce seizure threshold as there may be a theoretical risk of inducing seizure during stimulation for these patients. Most studies of rTMS involve working age adults hence there is limited safety and efficacy data in child and adolescent populations and pregnant women. The position statement concluded that there should be a protocol in place in each treatment unit which is approved by the local trust governance process. There should also be procedures and policies to ensure the smooth running of the unit and a clear role and responsibility for prescribing clinicians and treating clinicians should be established. A qualified nurse with adequate training and competencies can administer the rTMS and monitor for side-effects during the treatment. They can also assess the patients' progress using appropriate rating scales. The College will look to develop a national training programme for TMS practitioners which will include assessment of competencies and accreditation for rTMS centres along similar lines to ECTAS accreditation.

Chapter 15 reviews the evidence about rTMS in the treatment of depression and outlines the training required for practitioners who wish to deliver rTMS.

Ketamine

There are currently no NICE recommendations on the use of ketamine infusions for the management of depression. Despite clinical trials showing rapid improvement in mood after ketamine infusion, there are still significant gaps in our knowledge about dosage levels, treatment protocols and the effectiveness and safety of long-term use (see Chapter 17). Before ketamine can be recommended for use in clinical practice, extensive research is required to understand how to optimally use ketamine for treating depression. The Royal College of Psychiatrists has concerns for patient safety and hence recommends mental health practitioners to proceed with caution when treating patients with ketamine.

Ketamine is currently approved as an anaesthetic drug by the Medicines and Healthcare Products Regulatory Agency (MHRA) but is not currently approved for use in treating depression.

The antidepressant properties of ketamine were first described over a decade ago (Berman *et al.*, 2000). Since then, ketamine administration has been assessed in treatment of resistant depression, bipolar depression and in ECT induction. Supportive evidence showing rapid antidepressant effect of ketamine has encouraged some clinicians to use 'off label' ketamine in treating patients with depression.

Research investigating the antidepressant effects of ketamine has consistently reported rapid and robust improvement in suicidal depressive symptoms in patients with bipolar disorder. Significant reduction is also seen in depressive symptoms in patients suffering from treatment resistant depression (McGirr *et al.*, 2015). However, most researchers have measured the effects of ketamine for only 72 hours after infusion although there have been a few studies that have shown persistence of the effect for 15–28 days (Singh *et al.*, 2016; Hu *et al.*, 2016). Therefore information about the long-term effects of ketamine prescribed in patients with depression is limited. There is also limited information on ketamine dose-response relationship and the optimal mode of administration (Katalinic *et al.*, 2013).

In the absence of a strong evidence base, there are risks associated with treating depression with ketamine at this stage. Use of low dose ketamine (up to 0.5mg/kg) can produce a variety of psychotomimetic, cognitive or physical adverse effects.

The most common physical adverse effects of ketamine are dizziness, blurred vision, headache, nausea or vomiting, dry mouth, poor coordination, poor concentration and restlessness. These effects have mostly been restricted to the time of administration, usually resolving within 60 minutes. In some studies participants reported transient elevation in blood pressure and heart rate during the period of ketamine infusion and the effect lasted for 80 minutes after dosing. Additionally, ketamine is known for producing psychotomimetic effects, such as hallucinatory behaviour, suspiciousness/paranoia, disorganised thought, unusual thought, blunted affect and emotional withdrawal. There is no clear evidence showing long-term psychotomimetic effect of ketamine when used in repeated doses in depression treatment. Hepatotoxicity and bladder dysfunction have been reported after repeated use of ketamine (Katalinic *et al.*, 2013).

In the light of the above information (which is discussed in further detail in Chapter 17), the Committee's position statement recommended that:

- The use of ketamine for the treatment of depression is considered a novel treatment.
- Ketamine should be used under research trial conditions that include oversight by an institutional research or clinical ethics committee and careful monitoring and reporting of outcomes.

- For persons with treatment resistant depression who are not participating in a research trial but are able and willing to consent to treatment with ketamine, the treating psychiatrist should consider such treatment as a novel or innovative treatment, which should include discussion with peers (preferably including a second opinion) and institutional review by the relevant NHS Trust Drugs and Therapeutic Committee or its equivalent.
- People considering ketamine as a treatment and their carers should be provided with clear information and an explanation that this is a novel treatment. This should include a detailed explanation of the current evidence and potential risks, and be documented in the clinical notes.
- Ketamine treatment for depression occurring outside formal research studies should be collated across centres using a regular mood monitoring framework.
- Practice outside these recommendations should not occur.

Further information on ketamine can be found in Chapter 17. Its use in anaesthesia for ECT is considered in Chapter 23.

Transcranial Direct Current Stimulation

Transcranial direct current stimulation (tDCS) is a novel neuro-modulatory treatment modality for depression and represents a potential alternative to existing pharmaco-logical/psychological treatment options. tDCS is a non-invasive brain stimulation modality, which changes cortical tissue 'excitability' as a result of applying a weak (0.5–2mA) direct current via scalp electrodes overlying targeted cortical areas. In contrast to other neuro-stimulation modalities, tDCS does not directly trigger action potentials in neuronal cells, but instead changes overall tissue excitability, and therefore may be more aptly regarded as a 'neuro-modulatory' rather than a neuro-stimulatory approach.

In 2015, NICE made the following recommendations in its interventional procedure guidance on tDCS for depression (IPG 530; NICE, 2015):

1. The evidence on tDCS for depression raises no major safety concerns. There is evidence of efficacy but there are uncertainties about the specific mode of administration, the number of treatments needed and the duration of effect. Therefore, this procedure should only be used with special arrangements for clinical governance, consent and audit or research.
2. Clinicians wishing to do tDCS for depression should inform the clinical governance leads in their NHS trusts, and ensure that patients understand the uncertainty about the procedure's efficacy and provide them with clear written information – the use of information for the public published by NICE is recommended: www.nice.org.uk/guidance/IPG530/InformationForPublic.
3. Audit and review is recommended of clinical outcomes of all patients having tDCS for depression (NICE developed an audit tool: www.nice.org.uk/Guidance/IPG530/Resources).

A meta-analysis of tDCS for the treatment of major depressive episodes identified 10 RCTs (n = 393) of tDCS, either as monotherapy or as adjunctive treatment alongside antidepressant medication and/or Cognitive Control Training (CCT) (Meron et al., 2015). tDCS was superior to sham tDCS. Adjunctive antidepressant medication and cognitive control training negatively impacted on the treatment effect. However, the pooled log odds ratios (LOR) for response and remission were statistically non-significant. There were no statistically significant differences in the dropout rates due to adverse effects between the active and sham tDCS treatment groups.

Based on this evidence, the following conclusions were drawn in the Committee's position statement in 2016:

1. tDCS may represent an effective treatment option for patients presenting with major depressive episodes.
2. tDCS offers a generally acceptable tolerability profile, which may make it a useful alternative to antidepressant medication in patients who do not wish to take medication and for those who cannot tolerate antidepressant medication.
3. The current body of evidence does not support the use of tDCS in treatment resistant depression.
4. The current body of evidence does not support the use of tDCS as an add-on augmentation treatment for depressed patients who are already taking an antidepressant or undergoing cognitive control training.
5. Further research is needed, in particular, involving larger sample sizes over longer periods of treatment.

However two large randomised clinical trials have recently presented results showing either modest or negative tDCS efficacy (Brunoni *et al.*, 2017; Loo *et al.*, 2018) and a recent systematic review concluded that robust efficacy has not been consistently demonstrated (Borrione *et al.*, 2018). tDCS is not discussed further in this Handbook due to the early stage of the research and associated uncertainty. For further details, please refer to the referenced NICE guideline and the cited 2018 systematic review.

Neurosurgery for Mental Disorder

The College position statement on neurosurgery for mental disorder (NMD) is that, for carefully selected patients, with difficulties in specific symptom domains – specifically those with Depressive Disorders and Obsessive Compulsive Disorders – neurosurgical therapies may reasonably be considered. In each individual case, consideration of the appropriateness of offering any form of NMD must balance the risks and benefits of surgery with the risks and benefits of continuing with 'treatment as usual' and should also acknowledge patient preference.

The evidence base to support this College position is derived from an accumulated literature comprising open case series evaluations, some of prolonged duration and high quality. There is limited evidence from randomized, controlled trials, but this is available for some lesion surgical approaches and for deep brain stimulation (DBS) for obsessive compulsive disorder (OCD).

The position statement set out the core principles for ethical, safe and effective NMD. These are:

1. NMD procedures must only ever be performed with a specific therapeutic intention, i.e. for symptom relief and restoration of function.
2. NMD provision (lesion procedures **and** invasive stimulation methods) should be subject to ethical and clinical governance oversight by an independent body. Special attention must be paid to the processes of patient advocacy, the assessment of capacity and the nature of informed consent.

3. NMD should only be provided by neurosurgeons familiar in functional stereotactic surgery within specialist centres, and the clinical programme should be led by experienced psychiatrists with relevant expertise in the target disorders.
4. All patients who are considered as candidates for NMD must be informed that neurosurgery is only one component of a more comprehensive psychiatric management plan that will also include attention to wider aspects of psychological, social and occupational functioning.
5. Relevant mental health legislation (there are regional variations within the UK) must be adhered to.
6. Candidates for all forms of NMD (including lesion procedures and invasive stimulation methods) must be robustly evaluated by clinicians with specific expertise in the management of the target disorder and confirmed to meet consensus criteria with respect to the severity and refractoriness of the presenting condition.
7. Patient selection procedures and any discussions about possible NMD should be conducted by experienced multidisciplinary teams with close working between – as a minimum – stereotactic and functional neurosurgeons, psychiatrists, mental health nurses and expert psychological therapists. Where DBS is the surgical method proposed, this must also involve neurologists and specialist nurses familiar with the management of DBS systems and their programming.
8. Comprehensive pre- and post-operative evaluation – with specific attention to disorder-specific symptom outcomes, cognition, social and interpersonal functioning and health-related quality of life measures – must take place, with an identified mechanism for reporting the immediate and longer-term outcomes within a robust clinical governance structure.
9. Post-operative care plans should be developed collaboratively, should cover a period of at least 12 months, and should include the full participation of locality mental health services. Surgery should not take place unless a detailed, collaborative, patient-centred post-operative care plan has been agreed.

The position statements on individual NMD treatments are briefly set out below. Further details are available in Chapter 16.

Ablative neurosurgery (the creation of small targeted lesions by focal applications of radiofrequency induced heat, by radiation or by ultrasound) is the form of NMD with the strongest evidence base and longest reported follow-up. In particular, this relates to the two procedures most commonly offered as treatments for patients with otherwise refractory and disabling depression and OCD – anterior cingulotomy and anterior capsulotomy. Both procedures have been considered as representing acceptable, safe and effective established clinical practice in the UK for many years, including following review by independent, multidisciplinary, expert groups. The position statement takes the view that the delivery of safe and effective ablative NMD – subject to the general caveats above – represents an important element of the ethical and optimised management of patients with chronic, otherwise treatment refractory depression and OCD. There is currently no compelling evidence to support ablative NMD for any other psychiatric indication.

DBS is a surgical approach whereby deep structures of the brain can be directly stimulated electrically using permanently implanted electrodes and an externally pro-grammed, implantable pulse generator. Recent pivotal blinded controlled comparisons of active DBS with sham stimulation have failed to demonstrate efficacy for the two most commonly performed DBS surgeries for refractory depression (Dougherty *et al.*, 2015; Holtzheimer *et al.*, 2017). There has been no such blinded, sham controlled study reported for the treatment of OCD using DBS. The College position statement therefore considers that all DBS procedures for all psychiatric indications should continue to be viewed as investigational and therefore should not be performed unless as part of an ethically approved research protocol.

Vagus nerve stimulation (VNS) is a surgical approach whereby the cervical (neck) portion of the left vagus nerve can be directly stimulated electrically using an electrode implanted around the vagus nerve in the neck and an externally programmed, implantable pulse generator. However a pivotal blinded controlled comparison of active VNS with sham stimulation failed to demonstrate efficacy (George *et al.*, 2005). This is reflected in the 2009 NICE recommendations on VNS (IPG330; NICE, 2009) which recommend that VNS should be used only with special arrangements for clinical governance, consent and audit or research and only in patients with treatment-resistant depression.

The most recent VNS report is a long-term registry based study comparing the observational outcomes at up to five years for 494 patients with VNS and 301 patients managed as treatment as usual (Aaronson *et al.*, 2017). These authors reported improved response and remission rates in the VNS treated group. However, the observational study design does not permit strong inferences about potential efficacy. The position statement considers that VNS for all psychiatric indications, including depression, should continue to be viewed as investigational and therefore should not be performed unless as part of an ethically approved research protocol.

References

Aaronson S T, Sears P, Ruvuna F *et al.* (2017) A 5-year observational study of patients with treatment resistant depression treated with vagus nerve stimulation or treatment as usual: comparison of response, remission and suicidality. *Am J Psychiatry*, 174, 640–8.

Anderson E L, and Reti I M (2009) ECT in pregnancy: a review of literature from 1941 to 2007. *Psychosomatic Med*, 71, 235–42.

Berman R M, Cappiello A, Anand A, *et al.* (2000) Antidepressant effects of ketamine in depressed patients. *Biol Psychiatry*, 15, 351–4.

Borrione L, Moffa A H, Martin D *et al.* (2018) Transcranial direct current stimulation in the acute depressive episode: a systematic review of current knowledge. *J ECT*, 34, 153–63.

Buley N, Copland E, Hodge S *et al.* (2017) A further decrease in the rates of administration of ECT in England. *J ECT*, 33, 198–202.

Brunoni A R, Moffa A H, Sampaio-Junior B, *et al.* (2017) Trial of electrical direct-current therapy versus escitalopram for depression. *N Engl J Med*, 376, 2523–33.

Chen J J, Zhao L B, Liu Y Y, Fan S H, Xie P (2017) Comparative efficacy and acceptability of electroconvulsive therapy versus repetitive transcranial magnetic stimulation for major depression: a systematic review and multiple-treatments meta-analysis. *Behav Brain Res*, 320, 30–6.

Dougherty D D, Rezai A R, Carpenter L L *et al.* (2015) A randomized sham-controlled trial of deep brain stimulation of the ventral capsule/ventral striatum for chronic treatment resistant depression. *Biol Psychiatry*, 78, 240–8.

George M S, Rush A J, Marangell L B *et al.* (2005) A one year comparison of vagus nerve stimulation with treatment as usual for treatment resistant depression. *Biol Psychiatry*, 58, 364–73.

Holtzheimer P, Husain M M, Lisanby S H *et al.* (2017) Subcallosal cingulate deep brain stimulation for treatment-resistant depression: a multi-site, randomized, sham controlled trial. *The Lancet Psychiatry*, 4, 839–49.

Hu Y D, Xiang Y T, Fang J X *et al.* (2016) Single i.v. ketamine augmentation of newly initiated escitalopram for major depression: results from a randomized, placebo-controlled 4-week study. *Psychol Med*, 46, 623–35.

Katalinic N, Lai R, Somogyi A, *et al.* (2013) Ketamine as a new treatment for depression: a review of its efficacy and adverse effects. *Aust N Z J Psychiatry*, 47, 710–27.

Lally J, Tully J, Robertson D, *et al.* (2016) Augmentation of clozapine with electroconvulsive therapy in treatment resistant schizophrenia: a systematic review and meta-analysis. *Schizophr Res*, 171, 215–24.

Loo C K, Husain M M, McDonald W M, *et al.* (2018) International randomized-controlled trial of transcranial direct current stimulation in depression. *Brain Stimul*, 11, 125–33.

McGirr A, Berlim M T, Bond D J, *et al.* (2015) A systematic review and meta-analysis of randomized controlled trials of adjunctive ketamine in electroconvulsive therapy: efficacy and tolerability. *J Psychiatr Res*, 62, 23–30.

Meron D, Hedger N, Garner M, Baldwin D S (2015) Transcranial direct current stimulation (tDCS) in the treatment of depression: systematic review and meta-analysis of efficacy and tolerability. *Neurosci Biobehav Rev*, 57, 46–62.

National Institute for Health and Care Excellence. (2009) Technology appraisal guidance: Guidance on the use of electroconvulsive therapy. (TA59)

National Institute for Health and Care Excellence. (2009) Interventional procedures guidance: Vagus-nerve stimulation for treatment resistant depression. (IPG330)

National Institute for Health and Care Excellence. (2014) Bipolar disorder: Assessment and management. (CG 185)

National Institute for Health and Care Excellence. (2014) Antenatal and postnatal mental health: clinical management and service guidance. (CG192)

National Institute for Health and Care Excellence. (2015) Interventional procedure consultation document: Repetitive transcranial magnetic stimulation for depression. (IPG542)

National Institute for Health and Care Excellence. (2015) Interventional procedure consultation document: Transcranial direct current stimulation (tDCS) for depression. (IPG530)

National Institute for Health and Care Excellence. (2016) Depression: The Treatment and Management of Depression in Adults. (Updated Edition CG90)

Reed P, Sermin N, Appleby L, Faragher B (1999) A comparison of clinical response to electroconvulsive therapy in puerperal and non-puerperal psychoses. *J Affect Disord*, 54, 255–60.

Schoeyen H K, Kessler U, Andreassen O A, *et al.* (2015) Treatment-resistant bipolar depression: a randomized controlled trial of electroconvulsive therapy versus algorithm-based pharmacological treatment. *Am J Psychiatry*, 172, 41–51.

Singh J B, Fedgchin M, Daly E J *et al.* (2106) A double-blind, randomized, placebo-controlled, dose-frequency study of intravenous ketamine in patients with treatment-resistant depression. *Am J Psychiatry*, 173, 816–26.

Slotema C, Blom J, Hoek H *et al.* (2010) Should we expand the toolbox of psychiatric treatment methods to include repetitive transcranial magnetic stimulation (rTMS)? A meta-analysis of the efficacy of rTMS in psychiatric disorders. *J Clin Psychiatry*, 71, 873–84.

Mechanism of Action of ECT

Philip J Cowen

Introduction

Electroconvulsive therapy (ECT) possesses several key therapeutic actions, having anti-depressant, anti-manic and antipsychotic effects. The adverse effects of ECT, particularly loss of autobiographical memories, are also of great clinical importance. Whether the same 'mechanism' underpins all these properties is unknown. Most information about the mechanistic effects of ECT has been obtained in relation to the treatment of depression and the current review will focus on this area.

When Anderson and Fergusson (2013) reviewed the mechanism of action of ECT for the previous handbook, they pointed out that for ethical and practical reasons, research on the neurobiology of ECT lagged behind that of other treatment modalities, particularly antidepressant medication. They also argued that studies of the mode of action of ECT needed to be updated to take account of current formulations of the pathophysiology of depression, which continues to be the major treatment indication for ECT. In this respect, an important conceptual change over the last few years has been a move away from 'single neurotransmitter' theories of depression, as reflected, for example, in the monoamine hypothesis, to the view that clinical depression is a 'system' disorder due to dysfunctioning neural networks (Cowen and Browning, 2015). Accompanying this has been an effort to develop an understanding of the neuropathology of depression at both the anatomical and cellular levels, the latter being informed by concepts such as synaptic plasticity and neurogenesis. A brief review of this work will be followed by a summary of studies that have investigated the effects of ECT on these various processes.

Current Concepts of the Pathophysiology of Depression

Developments from Brain Imaging

The study of depression has been transformed by the availability of brain imaging method-ologies, particularly the non-invasive technique of Magnetic Resonance Imaging (MRI). Functional MRI (fMRI) has led to the identification of a distributed neural circuitry that underpins depressive symptomatology involving brain regions such as medial prefrontal cortex, anterior cingulate cortex, amygdala and ventral striatum (Price and Drevets, 2012). More recent studies have used 'resting state' fMRI to examine activity in the functional brain networks that become apparent when participants rest quietly in the camera. There has been particular interest in the 'default mode network', a network linking cortical regions such as medial prefrontal cortex, the anterior and posterior cingulate cortex and medial and lateral areas of parietal and temporal cortex (Sheline et al., 2009), which is involved in inner attention and self-reflection, and is often overactive in depressed patients. This overactivity has been proposed to correlate with depressive ruminative thinking and impaired perform-ance on cognitive tasks (Kaiser *et al.*, 2015). Sheline *et al.* (2010) demonstrated that the default mode network and two other networks, the affective network and the cognitive control network, all show increased intrinsic resting state connectivity in depressed patients and share elevated connectivity to a common area that links them, in the dorsal medial prefrontal cortex.

Contrary to the notion that depression is a reversible biochemical disorder, structural brain imaging, predominantly now carried out with MRI, has shown anatomical deficits in patients with depression. The most consistent findings from meta-analyses are decreased hippocampal volume, enlargement of the lateral ventricles (though this is predominantly in elderly patients with depression), decreased volume in basal ganglia structures and decreased grey matter volume in anterior brain areas including frontal cortex, orbitofrontal and cingulate cortex. As might be expected, the extent of these deficits correlates with the length and severity of the depressive disorder (Arnone *et al.*, 2012).

Cellular Pathology

The origin of the structural deficits seen with MRI is unclear, but might be related to the cellular neuropathological abnormalities that have been described in post-mortem studies of depression, such as loss of interneurons and glial cells in anterior brain regions (see Oh *et al.*, 2012). The *neurotrophic hypothesis* of depression suggests that stress (perhaps mediated by cortisol hypersecretion) can lead to atrophy and death of neurons and down-regulation of adult neurogenesis, particularly in the hippocampus (Duman and Voleti, 2012). Generally, depression is associated with decreased elaboration of neuro-trophins such as brain derived neurotrophic factor (BDNF) which facilitates synaptic plasticity and neurogenesis (Martinowich *et al.*, 2007). Many conventional antidepres-sants increase BDNF production, as well as neurogenesis, in animal experimental studies (Harmer *et al.*, 2017).

Amino Acid Neurotransmitters

Glutamate and γ-aminobutyric acid (GABA) are the principal excitatory and inhibitory neurotransmitters in the brain respectively and thereby play a critical role in regulating the excitability of cortical networks. The brain concentration of both these neurotransmitters can be measured using magnetic resonance spectroscopy (MRS) and there have been numerous studies in depressed patients. While the data have some incon-sistencies, meta-analyses suggest that levels of GABA are diminished in depression, as are those of glutamate, particularly in anterior brain regions (Schur *et al.*, 2016; Arnone *et al.*, 2015). The role of glutamate has attracted further interest because of the acute antidepres-sant effect of sub-anaesthetic doses of ketamine, a dissociative anaesthetic which blocks a subtype of glutamate receptor called the N-methyl-D-aspartate (NMDA) receptor (McGirr *et al.*, 2015). Administration of ketamine in animals leads to an acute increase in glutamate which is proposed to underpin its rapid antidepressant effects, perhaps through indirect stimulation of the α-amino-3-hydroxy-5-methyl-4-isoxazolepropionic acid (AMPA) recep-tor subtype of glutamate receptor (Newport *et al.*, 2015).

Inflammation

Another process that has been related to depression, and that acts at a system level, is that of inflammation. There is now reliable evidence that a subgroup of depressed patients have evidence of peripheral inflammation as judged by markers such as C-Reactive Protein (CRP) and interleukin-6 (IL-6) (Raison and Miller, 2011). There is also tentative evidence for central inflammation in depression as judged by activation of microglia, visualised through Positron Emission Tomographic imaging (PET) (Setiawan *et al.*, 2015). Whether or not anti-inflammatory treatments will be clinically useful in alleviating depression in patients with evidence of inflammation remains to be established but there are promising initial results (Raison *et al.*, 2013). Inflammation appears to be more prevalent in patients with treatment-resistant depression (Carvalho *et al.*, 2013) and therefore might be expected to be relatively common in depressed patients receiving ECT.

Therapeutic Efficacy of ECT in Relation to Mechanism

Meta-analytic summaries suggest that ECT is more effective than antidepressant medication in the treatment of depression (UK ECT Group, 2003). Moreover, ECT is effective in a substantial proportion of patients who have not responded to several trials of antidepressant treatment (Cowen and Anderson, 2015). Therefore, while it makes sense to look for parallels between the mechanisms of ECT and antidepressant drugs, it is also important to search for neurobiological changes that apparently distinguish ECT and that may, therefore, underpin its superior efficacy.

Recent studies have indicated that while a seizure is a necessary part of the effectiveness of ECT in depression, the dose of electrical current applied is also a significant factor in determining outcome (Sackheim *et al.,* 2000). Thus, particularly with right unilateral electrode placement, the amount by which the applied current exceeds seizure threshold seems to have an important bearing on treatment efficacy. The general view has been that bilateral administration of ECT is overall somewhat more effective than right unilateral treatment, but this does not appear to be the case when right unilateral treatment is given at high doses (UK ECT group, 2003; Kolshus *et al.,* 2017).

ECT and Structural Imaging

As noted above, depression is reliably associated with smaller hippocampal volume and there is some evidence that antidepressant medication, given for several weeks, can increase hippocampal volume measured by serial MRI (Arnone *et al.*, 2013). It is therefore of great interest that two meta-analyses have shown that ECT also increases hippocampal volume, in some studies quite substantially (Wilkinson *et al.*, 2017; Takamiya *et al.*, 2018). Whether the extent of this increase correlates with therapeutic outcome is unclear; however, a low hippocampal volume at the start of treatment may predict a better antidepressant response (Joshi *et al.*, 2016). The mechanisms behind the increase in hippocampal volume remain speculative but could be related to neurogenesis as well as an increase in the number of glial cells; both these changes have been reported in animal experimental studies of repeated electroconvulsive shock (ECS) (Bouckaert *et al.*, 2014). Volumes of the amygdala are also increased bilaterally by ECT (Takamiya *et al.*, 2019) but again the mechanism and possible clinical correlates remain to be established. In patients undergoing ECT, serum BDNF levels tend to increase through treatment, consistent with a neurotrophic action of ECT, as far as this peripheral measure of BDNF can be taken as an index of central BDNF synthesis (Rocha *et al.*, 2016).

The hippocampus plays an important role in learning and memory and particularly in relating remembered experience to context (Davachi, 2006). Changes in hippocampal function through neurogenesis and synaptic plasticity could therefore be important in modifying the depressive memory biases to which depressed patients are particularly subject. It is also possible that changes in hippocampal circuitry might underlie the autobiographical memory problems associated with ECT treatment in some patients (Wilkinson *et al.*, 2017).

ECT and Functional Imaging

In the treatment of depression with antidepressant medication, a systematic review found that the therapeutic response correlated with increases in 'resting state' connectivity between frontal and limbic regions suggesting enhanced descending control over circuitry involved in emotional processing during successful treatment. Treatment resistance to antidepressants was associated at baseline with increased connectivity both within the default mode network system and its connections to other structures. Antidepressant treatment diminished connectivity in the posterior portion of the default mode network (Dichter *et al.*, 2015). Several papers have examined the effect of ECT on 'resting state' network connectivity using fMRI. The results have been somewhat variable, presumably due to differing methodologies of resting state analysis and heterogeneity of patient groups. Generally, decreases in functional connectivity are observed in the default mode network (Thomann *et al.*, 2017) with ECT, although an increase in the connectivity of right hippocampus to temporal cortex was seen in patients receiving right unilateral ECT (Abbott *et al.*, 2014). Perrin *et al.* (2012) found that ECT led to significantly reduced connectivity between medial cortical structures and other cortical areas including angular gyrus, and somatosensory association cortex. This effect was exerted primarily through an action of ECT on the left dorsolateral prefrontal cortex which generated the widespread decrease in cortical connectivity caused by ECT treatment. The cortical changes in connectivity produced by ECT were much more widespread than those reported with antidepressant medication. Moreover, unlike antidepressant medication, ECT did not alter connectivity in subcortical structures (Perrin *et al.*, 2012).

ECT, GABA and Glutamate

ECT works in depression by producing seizures. This triggers a number of adaptive mechanisms which act to increase seizure threshold through a course of treatment and the extent of the increase in seizure threshold may correlate with improvement in depressive symptomatology (Sanchez Gonzalez *et al.*, 2009). GABA and glutamate are known to be involved in the regulation of seizure threshold and GABA activity is facilitated by many different kinds of anticonvulsants (Czuczwar and Patsalos, 2001). Indeed, an early theory of the antidepressant mechanism of ECT suggested an important role for elevated GABA function (Sanchez Gonzalez *et al.*, 2009). However, the fact that GABA promoting medications such as benzodiazepines are not reliable antidepressant agents, suggests that a simple connection between increased cortical GABA function and the antidepressant action of ECT is not plausible. However, conceivably increases in GABA activity could play a role in the anti-manic effects of ECT, because the anticonvulsant drug, valproate, which facilitates GABA function, is an effective anti-manic agent (Löscher, 2002; Yildiz *et al.*, 2015).

There is some evidence that antidepressant medication can increase levels of cortical GABA, though the effects on MRS glutamate are inconsistent (Sanacora *et al.*, 2002; Godlewska *et al.*, 2015). One study found that a course of ECT produced a significant increase in GABA levels in occipital cortex (Sanacora *et al.*, 2003). Interestingly, successful treatment of depression with cognitive behaviour therapy did not achieve this effect (Sanacora *et al.*, 2006), suggesting that the increase in GABA following ECT is not simply a consequence of improvement in depressed mood. Glutamate has been little studied in patients receiving ECT. Pfleiderer *et al.* (2003) found that depressed patients prior to ECT had lowered levels of Glx (a composite measure of glutamate and its precursor and metabolite, glutamine) in anterior cingulate cortex, which was increased by ECT. Similarly, Njau *et al.* (2017) reported that ECT increased Glx levels in anterior cingulate cortex, and the increase correlated with clinical improvement. In hippocampus, however, ECT lowered Glx, though this again was associated with therapeutic response.

As noted above, there has been much interest in the role of the NMDA receptor antagonist, ketamine, as an antidepressant treatment, and ketamine has sometimes been used as an anaesthetic agent in patients receiving ECT, with reports that it might offset ECT-induced cognitive impairment (Anderson *et al.*, 2017). Anderson and colleagues (2017) carried out a randomised, placebo-controlled trial to study the effect of ketamine (0.5mg/kg) administered just prior to induction with propofol in 79 depressed patients receiving ECT. However, there was no evidence that, relative to saline infusion, ketamine resulted in benefits to cognitive function or improved recovery from depression. A systematic review also reported no benefit to either mood or cognitive performance when ketamine was employed as an adjunct to ECT (McGirr *et al.*, 2017).

ECT and Inflammation

There is some evidence that conventional antidepressants such as SSRIs possess anti-inflammatory effects in depressed patients and animal models (Hannestad *et al.*, 2011). A standard way of inducing inflammation and sickness behaviour in animals is to administer lipopolysaccharide (LPS). Pre-treatment with SSRIs diminishes some of the behavioural and biochemical responses to LPS, for example the increase in production of inflammatory cytokines such as IL-6 and Tumour Necrosis Factor-α (Tynan *et al.*, 2012; Dong *et al.*, 2016). However, repeated ECS does not prevent the behavioural effects of LPS or decrease microglial activation (van Buel *et al.*, 2015). Some studies have investigated peripheral cytokines in patients receiving ECT treatment. Acutely, seizures are associated with increases in blood levels of IL-6. Also, patients receiving ECT, as might be expected, have significantly raised levels of peripheral inflammatory markers such as IL-6 prior to treatment. However, there is disagreement as to whether, over the course of treatment, baseline levels of IL-6 are lowered, and whether or not this effect may correlate with therapeutic benefit (Rush *et al.*, 2016; Järventausta *et al.*, 2017).

Inflammation is also associated with alterations in the metabolism of the amino acid, tryptophan, leading to increased production of quinolinic acid, a proposed endogenous NMDA receptor agonist. Interestingly, in 19 depressed patients, treatment with ECT diminished plasma quinolinic acid which might be expected to lower the functional activity of NMDA receptors (Schwieler *et al.*, 2016). This intriguing result requires replication.

ECT and Monoamines

Monoaminergic mechanisms continue to play an important role in understanding the mode of action of antidepressant medications and in the development of new drug treatments (Harmer *et al.*, 2017). There is less research on the effects of ECT on mono-amine function; one difficulty in such work is that patients receiving ECT are often also taking antidepressant medication, making specific effects of ECT on monoamine mechanisms hard to discern.

Most antidepressant drugs are known to produce their therapeutic effects through acute facilitation of serotonin (5-HT) or noradrenaline activity. How this initial effect leads eventually to clinical improvement is still a matter of debate and may involve the increases in neuroplasticity and neurogenesis described above. Changes in neurogenesis could in turn be linked to implicit 'relearning' of aspects of emotional processing (Harmer *et al.*, 2017). Antidepressants tend to have little acute effect on dopaminergic mechanisms, though bupropion, which is licensed in the UK for smoking cessation, is a weak dopamine reuptake inhibitor (Cowen *et al.*, 2012).

Repeated ECS given to animals does produce reliable changes in monoamine mechanisms though these have similarities and differences to those seen with antidepressants. Perhaps the main contrast is that repeated ECS produces prominent enhancement of dopamine mediated locomotor behaviours, suggesting an increase in striatal dopamine function, though the precise mechanism involved has not been identified (Smith and Sharp, 1997). However, both repeated treatment of rats with antidepressants and ECS increases the expression of dopamine D_2 receptors in the nucleus accumbens, an important element in reward circuitry (Ainsworth *et al.*, 1998; Smith *et al.*, 1995). In non-human primates repeated ECS led to increases in dopamine D_1 receptor binding in the striatum and also elevated the expression of dopamine transporters in this brain region (Landau *et al.*, 2011). There is some agreement that ECT can benefit the movement disorder of Parkinson's disease (Narang *et al.*, 2014), supporting suggestions that it appears to facilitate dopamine function in the striatum in humans. However, the binding of dopamine D_2 receptors in the cingulate cortex is reportedly diminished following ECT treatment (Saijo *et al.*, 2010b).

ECT is known to produce antipsychotic effects in patients with depressive psychosis and those with refractory schizophrenia (Lally *et al.*, 2016) and see Chapter 10. From the current data, it does not appear as though the mechanism of this effect is due to the general decrease in dopamine neurotransmission which characterises the mechanism of action of conventional antipsychotic drugs (Cowen *et al.*, 2012).

Antidepressants and ECS both appear to decrease brain 5-HT_{1A} receptor sensitivity in rodents (Goodwin *et al.*, 1987), but while ECS increases cortical 5-HT_{2A} receptor binding, as well as associated 5-HT_{2A} receptor-mediated behaviours, the opposite effect is seen with tricyclic antidepressants (Goodwin *et al.*, 1984). There are few human imaging studies that have examined changes in 5-HT receptor binding during ECT. 5-HT_{1A} receptor binding may be decreased during ECT treatment, though there is a contrary report suggesting no change (Lanzenberger *et al.*, 2013; Saijo *et al.*, 2010a). In contrast to studies in rodents, ECT lowered 5-HT_{2A} receptor binding in the cortex in depressed patients (Yatham *et al.*, 2010).

Evidence that changes in monoamine function may not, in fact, be central to the action of ECT comes from studies of acute monoamine depletion using either the dietary manipulation of tryptophan depletion, which lowers central 5-HT levels, or alpha-methyl-para-tyrosine (AMPT) which blocks the synthesis of dopamine and noradrenaline.

Tryptophan depletion is known to reverse the antidepressant effect of serotonergic anti-depressants such as the SSRIs while AMPT blocks the antidepressant action of catecholaminergic agents such as the tricyclic antidepressant, desipramine (Ruhé *et al.*, 2007). In contrast, neither tryptophan depletion nor AMPT appear to reverse the antidepressant effect of ECT, suggesting that facilitation of 5-HT or catecholamine mechanisms is not critical to its antidepressant action (Cassidy *et al.*, 2010).

Conclusions

ECT remains a particularly effective treatment for patients with refractory mood disorders. However, its use is accompanied by public disquiet, and the problem of autobiographical memory loss is a significant drawback. For this reason, the search to understand the mechanism of action of ECT is as important as ever, because success in this respect might lead to ways of improving the acceptability of treatment, or even replacing it with equally effective but safer alternatives.

It seems unlikely that ECT is primarily effective in depressed patients through facilitation of monoamine neurotransmitters, though it is still possible that enhancement of dopaminergic mechanisms might be involved in its benefit in depressed patients with psychomotor changes and in the motor symptoms of Parkinson's disease. Depression is now viewed as a disorder involving abnormalities in distributed neural circuitry, and it seems likely that ECT might be best conceived as acting at this level. In this respect, changes in amino acid transmitters could play an important role in regulating the excitability of key cortical networks involved in the expression of emotion, affect and reward. Such changes in the balance of excitatory to inhibitory neurotransmission could underpin ECT-induced alterations in cortical resting state connectivity, including those observed in the default mode network. Multimodal imaging, combining MRS and resting state fMRI, are powerful tools to investigate this important possibility. An 'anticonvulsant' effect of ECT, particularly involving facilitation of brain GABA mechanisms, could underlie the beneficial effects of ECT in mania but seems less likely to explain its antidepressant activity. The antipsychotic effect of ECT apparently has a different mechanism to that of currently employed anti-psychotic medications.

The ability of ECT to increase hippocampal volume in depressed patients looks robust, which focuses attention on the role of neural plasticity in its therapeutic effects. It is also possible, however, that hippocampal changes could underpin the memory deficits associated with ECT; this could pose a challenge for the important aim of separating its therapeutic and cognitive adverse effects. Effects on inflammatory mechanisms are also worth exploring although current data from animal studies do not support this particular mode of action particularly strongly.

References

Abbott C C, Jones T, Lemke N T, *et al.* (2014) Hippocampal structural and functional changes associated with electroconvulsive therapy response. *Translational Psychiatry*, **4**, e483.

Ainsworth K, Smith S E, Zetterström T S, *et al.* (1998) Effect of antidepressant drugs on dopamine D1 and D2 receptor expression and dopamine release in the nucleus accumbens of the rat. *Psychopharmacology* **140**, 470–7.

Anderson I M, Fergusson G M (2013) Mechanism of action of ECT. In *The ECT Handbook* (eds J Waite and A Easton), pp. 1–7. Royal College of Psychiatrists.

Anderson I M, Blamire A, Branton T, *et al.* (2017) Ketamine augmentation of electroconvulsive therapy to improve neuropsychological and clinical outcomes in depression (Ketamine-ECT): a multicentre, double-blind, randomised, parallel group, superiority trial. *Lancet Psychiatry*, 4, 365–77.

Arnone D, McIntosh A M, Ebmeier K P, *et al.* (2012) Magnetic resonance imaging studies in unipolar depression: systematic review and meta-regression analyses. *European Neuropsychopharmacology*, 22, 1–6.

Arnone D, McKie S, Elliott R, *et al.* (2013) State-dependent changes in hippocampal grey matter in depression. *Molecular Psychiatry*, 18, 1265–72.

Arnone D, Mumuni A N, Jauhar S, *et al.* (2015) Indirect evidence of selective glial involvement in glutamate-based mechanisms of mood regulation in depression: meta-analysis of absolute prefrontal neuro-metabolic concentrations. *European Neuropsychopharmacology*, 25, 1109–17.

Bouckaert F, Sienaert P, Obbels J, *et al.* (2014) ECT: its brain enabling effects: a review of electroconvulsive therapy–induced structural brain plasticity. *Journal of ECT*, 30, 143–51.

Carvalho L A, Torre J P, Papadopoulos A S, *et al.* (2013) Lack of clinical therapeutic benefit of antidepressants is associated overall activation of the inflammatory system. *Journal of Affective Disorders* 148, 136–40.

Cassidy F, Weiner R D, Cooper T B, *et al.* (2010) Combined catecholamine and indoleamine depletion following response to ECT. *British Journal of Psychiatry*, 196, 493–4.

Cowen P J, Anderson I M (2015). New approaches to treating resistant depression. *BJPsych Advances*, 21, 315–23.

Cowen P J, Browning M (2015) What has serotonin to do with depression? *World Psychiatry*, 14, 158–60.

Cowen P, Harrison P, Burns T (2012) *Shorter Oxford Textbook of Psychiatry*. Oxford University Press, Oxford, UK.

Czuczwar S J, Patsalos P N (2001) The new generation of GABA enhancers. *CNS Drugs*, 15, 339–50.

Davachi L (2006) Item, context and relational episodic encoding in humans. *Current Opinion in Neurobiology*, 16, 693–700.

Dichter G S, Gibbs D, Smoski M J (2015) A systematic review of relations between resting-state functional-MRI and treatment response in major depressive disorder. *Journal Affective Disorders*, 172, 8–17.

Dong C, Zhang J C, Yao W, *et al.* (2016) Effects of escitalopram, R-citalopram, and reboxetine on serum levels of tumor necrosis factor-α, interleukin-10, and depression-like behavior in mice after lipopolysaccharide administration. *Pharmacology Biochemistry and Behavior*, 144, 7–12.

Duman R S, Voleti B (2012) Signaling pathways underlying the pathophysiology and treatment of depression: novel mechanisms for rapid-acting agents. *Trends in Neurosciences*, 35, 47–56.

Godlewska B R, Near J, Cowen P J (2015) Neurochemistry of major depression: a study using magnetic resonance spectroscopy. *Psychopharmacology*, 232, 501–7.

Goodwin G M, Green A R, Johnson P (1984) 5-HT2 receptor characteristics in frontal cortex and 5-HT2 receptor-mediated head-twitch behaviour following antidepressant treatment to mice. *British Journal of Pharmacology*, 83, 235–42.

Goodwin G M, Souza R J, Green A R (1987) Attenuation by electroconvulsive shock and antidepressant drugs of the 5-HT 1A receptor-mediated hypothermia and serotonin syndrome produced by 8-OH-DPAT in the rat. *Psychopharmacology*, 91, 500–5.

Hannestad J, DellaGioia N, Bloch M (2011) The effect of antidepressant medication treatment on serum levels of inflammatory cytokines: a meta-analysis. *Neuropsychopharmacology*, 36, 2452–9.

Harmer C, Duman R S, Cowen P (2017) How do antidepressants work? New perspectives for refining treatment approaches of the future. *Lancet Psychiatry* (in press).

Järventausta K, Sorri A, Kampman O, *et al.* (2017) Changes in interleukin-6 levels during electroconvulsive therapy may reflect the therapeutic response in major depression. *Acta Psychiatrica Scandinavica*, **135**, 87–92.

Joshi S H, Espinoza R T, Pirnia T, *et al.* (2016) Structural plasticity of the hippocampus and amygdala induced by electroconvulsive therapy in major depression. *Biological Psychiatry*, **15**, 282–92.

Kaiser R H, Whitfield-Gabrieli S, Dillon D G, *et al.* (2015) Dynamic resting-state functional connectivity in major depression. *Neuropsychopharmacology*, **41**, 1822–30.

Kolshus E, Jelovac A, McLoughlin D M (2017) Bitemporal v. high-dose right unilateral electroconvulsive therapy for depression: a systematic review and meta-analysis of randomized controlled trials. *Psychological Medicine*, **47**, 518–30.

Lally J, Tully J, Robertson D, *et al.* (2016) Augmentation of clozapine with electroconvulsive therapy in treatment resistant schizophrenia: a systematic review and meta-analysis. *Schizophrenia Research*, **171**, 215–24.

Landau A M, Chakravarty M M, Clark C M, *et al.* (2011) Electroconvulsive therapy alters dopamine signaling in the striatum of non-human primates. *Neuropsychopharmacology*, **36**, 511–18.

Lanzenberger R, Baldinger P, Hahn A, *et al.* (2013) Global decrease of serotonin-1A receptor binding after electroconvulsive therapy in major depression measured by PET. *Molecular Psychiatry*, **18**, 93–100.

Löscher W (2002) Basic pharmacology of valproate. *CNS Drugs*, **16**, 669–94.

McGirr A, Berlim M T, Bond D J, *et al.* (2015) A systematic review and meta-analysis of randomized, double-blind, placebo-controlled trials of ketamine in the rapid treatment of major depressive episodes. *Psychological Medicine*, **45**, 693–704.

McGirr A, Berlim M T, Bond D J, *et al.* (2017) Adjunctive ketamine in electroconvulsive therapy: updated systematic review and meta-analysis. *British Journal of Psychiatry*, **210**, 403–407.

Martinowich K, Manji H, Lu B (2007) New insights into BDNF function in depression and anxiety. *Nature Neuroscience*, **10**, 1089–93.

Narang P U, Glowacki A, Lippmann S T (2014) Electroconvulsive therapy intervention for Parkinson's disease. *Innovations in Clinical Neuroscience*, **12**, 25–8.

Newport D J, Carpenter L L, McDonald W M, *et al.* (2015) Ketamine and other NMDA antagonists: early clinical trials and possible mechanisms in depression. *American Journal of Psychiatry*, **172**, 950–66.

Njau S, Joshi S H, Espinoza R, *et al.* (2017) Neurochemical correlates of rapid treatment response to electroconvulsive therapy in patients with major depression. *Journal of Psychiatry & Neuroscience*, **42**, 6–16.

Oh D H, Son H, Hwang S, Kim S H (2012), Kim SH. Neuropathological abnormalities of astrocytes, GABAergic neurons, and pyramidal neurons in the dorsolateral prefrontal cortices of patients with major depressive disorder. *European Neuropsychopharmacology*, **22**, 330–8.

Perrin J S, Merz S, Bennett D M, *et al.* (2012) Electroconvulsive therapy reduces frontal cortical connectivity in severe depressive disorder. *Proceedings of the National Academy of Sciences*, **109**, 5464–8.

Pfleiderer B, Michael N, Erfurth A, *et al.* (2003) Effective electroconvulsive therapy reverses glutamate/glutamine deficit in the left anterior cingulum of unipolar depressed patients. *Psychiatry Research: Neuroimaging*, **122**, 185–92.

Price J L, Drevets W C (2012) Neural circuits underlying the pathophysiology of mood disorders, *Trends in Cognitive Sciences*, **16**, 61–71.

Raison C L, Miller A H (2011) Is depression an inflammatory disorder? *Current Psychiatry Reports*, **13**, 467–75.

Raison C L, Rutherford R E, Woolwine B J, *et al.* (2013) A randomized controlled trial of the tumor necrosis factor antagonist infliximab for treatment-resistant depression: the role of baseline inflammatory biomarkers. *JAMA Psychiatry*, **70**, 31–41.

Rocha R B, Dondossola E R, Grande A J, *et al.* (2016) Increased BDNF levels after electroconvulsive therapy in patients with major depressive disorder: a meta-analysis study. *Journal of Psychiatric Research*, **83**, 47–53.

Ruhé H G, Mason N S, Schene A H (2007) Mood is indirectly related to serotonin, norepinephrine and dopamine levels in humans: a meta-analysis of monoamine depletion studies. *Molecular Psychiatry*, **12**, 331–59.

Rush G, O'Donovan A, Nagle L, *et al.* (2016) Alteration of immune markers in a group of melancholic depressed patients and their response to electroconvulsive therapy. *Journal of Affective Disorders*, **205**, 60–8.

Sackeim H A, Prudic J, Devanand D P, *et al.* (2000) A prospective, randomized, double-blind comparison of bilateral and right unilateral electroconvulsive therapy at different stimulus intensities. *Archives of General Psychiatry*, **57**, 425–34.

Saijo T, Takano A, Suhara T, *et al.* (2010a) Effect of electroconvulsive therapy on 5-HT1A receptor binding in patients with depression: a PET study with [11C] WAY 100635. *International Journal of Neuropsychopharmacology*, **13**, 785–91.

Saijo T, Takano A, Suhara T, *et al.* (2010b) Electroconvulsive therapy decreases dopamine D2 receptor binding in the anterior cingulate in patients with depression: a controlled study using positron emission tomography with radioligand [11 C] FLB 457. *Journal of Clinical Psychiatry*, **71**, 793–9.

Sanacora G, Fenton L R, Fasula M K, *et al.* (2006) Cortical γ-aminobutyric acid concentrations in depressed patients receiving cognitive behavioral therapy. *Biological Psychiatry*, **59**, 284–6.

Sanacora G, Mason G F, Rothman D L, *et al.* (2002) Increased occipital cortex GABA concentrations in depressed patients after therapy with selective serotonin reuptake inhibitors. *American Journal of Psychiatry*, **159**, 663–5.

Sanacora G, Mason G F, Rothman D L, *et al.* (2003) Increased cortical GABA concentrations in depressed patients receiving ECT. *American Journal of Psychiatry*, **160**, 577–9.

Sanchez Gonzalez R, Alcoverro O, Pagerols J, *et al.* (2009) Electrophysiological mechanisms of action of electroconvulsive therapy. *Actas Españolas de Psiquiatría*, **37**, 343–51.

Schür R R, Draisma L W, Wijnen J P, *et al.* (2016) Brain GABA levels across psychiatric disorders: A systematic literature review and meta-analysis of 1H-MRS studies. *Human Brain Mapping*, **37**, 3337–52.

Schwieler L, Samuelsson M, Frye M A *et al.* (2016) Electroconvulsive therapy suppresses the neurotoxic branch of the kynurenine pathway in treatment resistant depressed patients. *Journal of Inflammation*, **13**, 51.

Setiawan E, Wilson A A, Mizrahi R, *et al.* (2015) Role of translocator protein density, a marker of neuroinflammation, in the brain during major depressive episodes. *JAMA Psychiatry* **72**, 268–75.

Sheline Y I, Barch D M, Price J L, *et al.* (2009) The default mode network and self-referential processes in depression. *Proceedings of the National Academy of Sciences*, **106**, 942–7.

Sheline Y I, Price J L, Yan Z, *et al.* (2010) Resting-state functional MRI in depression unmasks increased connectivity between networks via the dorsal nexus. *Proceedings of the National Academy of Sciences*, **107**, 11020–5.

Smith S E, Lindefors N, Hurd Y, *et al.* (1995) Electroconvulsive shock increases dopamine D1 and D2 receptor mRNA in the nucleus accumbens of the rat. *Psychopharmacology*, **28**, 333–40.

Smith S E, Sharp T (1997) Evidence that the enhancement of dopamine function by repeated electroconvulsive shock requires concomitant activation of D1-like and D2-like dopamine receptors. *Psychopharmacology*, **133**, 77–84.

Takamiya T, Chung J K, Liang K-C, *et al.* (2018) Effect of electroconvulsive therapy on hippocampal and amygdala volumes: systematic review and meta-analysis. *British Journal of Psychiatry*, **212**, 19–26.

Thomann P A, Wolf R C, Nolte H M, *et al.* (2017) Neuromodulation in response to electroconvulsive therapy in schizophrenia and major depression. *Brain Stimulation*, **10**, 637–44.

Tynan R J, Weidenhofer J, Hinwood M, *et al.* (2012) A comparative examination of the anti-inflammatory effects of SSRI and SNRI antidepressants on LPS stimulated microglia. *Brain, Behavior, and Immunity*, **26**, 469–79.

UK ECT Group (2003). Efficacy and safety of electroconvulsive therapy in depressive disorders: a systematic review and meta-analysis. *Lancet*, **361**, 799–808.

van Buel E M, Bosker F J, van Drunen J, *et al.* (2015) Electroconvulsive seizures (ECS) do not prevent LPS-induced behavioral alterations and microglial activation. *Journal of Neuroinflammation*, **12**, 232–41.

Wilkinson S T, Sanacora G, Bloch M H (2017) Hippocampal volume changes following electroconvulsive therapy: a systematic review and meta-analysis. *Biological Psychiatry: Cognitive Neuroscience and Neuroimaging*, **2**, 327–35.

Yatham L N, Liddle P F, Lam R W, *et al.* (2010) Effect of electroconvulsive therapy on brain 5-HT2 receptors in major depression. *British Journal of Psychiatry*, **196**, 474–9.

Yildiz A, Nikodem M, Vieta E, *et al.* (2015) A network meta-analysis on comparative efficacy and all-cause discontinuation of antimanic treatments in acute bipolar mania. *Psychological Medicine*, **45**, 299–317.

ECT in the Treatment of Depression

I Nicol Ferrier

Depression remains the most frequent disorder for which ECT is required. This chapter summarises the evidence for the efficacy of ECT in depression and discusses its use in the clinical management of unipolar depression. Current NICE Guidelines for the use of ECT in depression are to be found in Chapter 1.

Efficacy of ECT in Depression

Two large meta-analyses have concluded that ECT is the most effective short-term treatment for major depression (UK ECT Review Group, 2003; Pagnin *et al.*, 2004) and data supporting this statement are outlined below. Studies have also shown that ECT is associated with a good return to health-related quality of life and function (Rosenquist *et al.*, 2006) although there may be discontinuity between improvement in depression and improvement in function (Lin *et al.*, 2017). Reports from the Electroconvulsive Therapy Accreditation Service (ECTAS) and the Scottish ECT Accreditation Network (SEAN) (bodies that monitor ECT in England & Wales and Scotland under the auspices of the Royal College of Psychiatrists and the NHS National Services Scotland respectively) confirm these findings and indicate the effectiveness of ECT as currently administered in the UK (Fergusson *et al.*, 2004; Buley *et al.*, 2017).

Six randomised controlled trials comparing ECT with 'sham' ECT in the short-term treatment of depression were examined by the UK ECT Review Group (UK ECT Review Group, 2003). They included data on a total of 256 patients, mostly in-patients under the age of 70 with some form of depressive disorder. The depression ratings at the end of treatment showed the standardised effect size (SES) between real and simulated ECT to be −0.91 (95% CI −1.27 to −0.54), indicating a mean difference in the Hamilton Rating Scale for Depression (HRSD) of 9.7 (95% CI 5.7 to 13.5) in favour of ECT.

In 18 randomised controlled trials with a total of 1144 patients, ECT was compared with antidepressant medication in the short-term treatment of depression (UK ECT Review Group, 2003). Of these, 13 trials contained sufficient data to contribute to a pooled analysis. The SES of these trials was −0.80 (95% CI −1.29 to −0.29). This equates to a mean difference of 5.2 points (95% CI 1.37 − 8.87) on the HRSD in favour of ECT. It is noteworthy, however, that none of these trials compared ECT with newer antidepressant medications such as SSRIs, mirtazepine or venlafaxine although these antidepressants do not, as a group, show much greater efficacy than the older antidepressants against which ECT was superior.

Sackeim and colleagues showed that the addition of nortriptyline (but not venlafaxine) to ECT enhanced the latter's efficacy alone and reported that there were less cognitive side effects with the combination (Sackeim *et al.*, 2009). They concluded on the basis of this study and their review of the relevant literature that the efficacy of ECT is substantially increased by the addition of antidepressant medication. However, more recently, Song and colleagues have adduced evidence in an indirect comparison meta-analysis that in treatment-resistant depression, the addition of an antidepressant to ECT may come at the cost of increased incidence of memory deterioration (Song *et al.*, 2015).

Comparison of ECT and rTMS

There have been several well-controlled trials of ECT versus rTMS. These have been reviewed by the Cochrane Collaboration (Martín *et al.*, 2002) and more recently by Chen and colleagues (Chen *et al.*, 2017). Both reviews concluded that ECT showed significantly more efficacy than rTMS. Chen and colleagues showed a substantial difference in efficacy between ECT and rTMS but noted that the latter was better tolerated than the former. Further information on rTMS is given in Chapter 15.

Comparison of Bilateral and Unilateral ECT

NICE (National Collaborating Centre for Mental Health, 2010) concluded that there were few differences in efficacy between high-dose right unilateral ECT (i.e. treatment given at four (or more) times seizure threshold) and bi-temporal ECT. Recently, in a well powered non-inferiority trial, it was shown that high dose (6 times seizure threshold) right unilateral ECT was equally effective compared with ECT with bi-temporal placement (Semkovska *et al.*, 2016). This was also the conclusion of a systematic review and meta-analysis of RCTs comparing bi-temporal with high-dose unilateral ECT (Kolshus *et al.*, 2016). However, as Kellner and colleagues (2017a) point out, this equivalence may not apply to all patients. They illustrate this with the findings of Sackeim *et al.* (2000) who showed that some of those patients who did not respond to unilateral ECT subsequently responded to bilateral ECT although the effect of these patients just getting more treatment cannot be ruled out.

Kellner *et al.* (2010) demonstrated that bi-temporal ECT given at 1.5 times seizure threshold was more rapidly effective than right unilateral ECT at 6 times seizure threshold. In the same study, Kellner and colleagues also showed that bi-frontal ECT delivered at 1.5 times seizure threshold had no advantages in terms of either efficacy or side-effect profile and was associated with more impairment of executive function.

The cognitive effects of bilateral and unilateral ECT have been reviewed by Semkovska and colleagues (2011), who concluded that significant benefits for unilateral electrode placements are limited to the first three days after the end of treatment. It has been reported that left unilateral ECT may be preferred for patients with right cerebral language dominance (Kellner *et al.*, 2017b) but there has been insufficient research on the cognitive and clinical effects of this electrode placement. In a recent study, high dose right unilateral ECT was associated with better recall of autobiographical information (Semkovska *et al.*, 2016). The adverse cognitive effects of ECT are considered in more detail in Chapter 13.

Dose of Electrical Stimulus

For bilateral ECT, this remains an area of some contention. On the basis of available evidence from 12 studies, the NICE review group was not able to draw any firm conclusions

(National Collaborating Centre for Mental Health, 2010). They defined low-dose ECT as treatment up to 1.5 times seizure threshold; doses above this were reported as high dose. High-dose treatment was superior at achieving remission but this was not felt to be of clinically important magnitude and no differential benefit was suggested with the other outcome measures.

Pulse Width

Brief pulse (BP) ECT has long been recognised as a more efficient stimulus for inducing seizures than sine wave ECT with less cognitive side effects. More recently, interest has turned to the use of an ultrabrief pulse (UBP) ECT. Theoretically, UBP ECT (0.3 ms) should have less cognitive side effects than BP ECT (0.5–1.5ms) due to less direct stimulation of brain tissue. In the only RCT that compared BP ECT and UBP ECT stimulation for bi-temporal ECT, the combination of bi-temporal electrode placement and UBP ECT stimulation led to a reduction in efficacy (Sackeim et al., 2008). In the same study, high-dose unilateral UBP ECT was reported to produce less cognitive impairment, but another study showed it may be less effective (McCormick et al., 2009). Tor and colleagues (2015) conducted a systematic review and meta-analysis of all studies comparing right unilateral BP and UBP ECT. They concluded that BP ECT was slightly more efficacious in treating depression than UBP ECT and required fewer treatment sessions, but led to greater cognitive side effects. UBP ECT is therefore an option for selected patients at high risk of cognitive impairment but it is clear that further research is needed to fully evaluate right unilateral UBP ECT.

Frequency of ECT

In the USA, ECT is generally administered three times a week; in the UK, twice-weekly treatment is the norm. Gangadhar and Thirthalli (2010) reviewed the evidence on ECT frequency and concluded that twice-weekly ECT offers the best balance between therapeutic outcome and adverse effects.

Number of ECT Sessions

Guidance on the length of a course of ECT is given in Chapter 22. There is no evidence to indicate what number of sessions of ECT gains the best response. Neither is there any evidence to support the practice of giving two extra ECT sessions after the patient is considered to be well enough to discontinue ECT.

The Place of ECT in the Treatment of Depression

Although, as demonstrated above, ECT is a very, and probably the most, effective treatment for depression, there is little direct research evidence to make precise recommendations about the place of ECT within the sequence of treatments for depression. However, there is good research evidence on the types of depression that respond to it and robust data on predictors of response to ECT. This data is outlined below along with an account of the issue of relapse post-ECT and clinically important data about methods to reduce this risk. An account of ECT for depression occurring in the context of emergencies, treatment resistance and special populations is also given.

Types of Depression that Respond to ECT

ECT is effective for severe forms of depression including those with psychosis and/or psychomotor retardation. Remission (recovery to previous state of well-being) rates of around 60–80% have been reported when it is used as first line treatment in a severe depressive episode and remission rates are even higher in psychotic depression (Petrides *et al.*, 2001). Remission rates are high in the elderly who also show a more rapid response (Rhebergen *et al.*, 2015). Kellner and colleagues (2005) demonstrated the efficacy of ECT in depression with suicidal features with a substantial and rapid reduction in the expression of suicidal thoughts.

Predictors of Response and Non-Response

Positive predictors of response to ECT include delusions (Coryell and Zimmerman, 1984) and retardation (Buchan *et al.*, 1992) and these effects are more marked in the elderly and female patient. A recent review of this topic concluded that, in addition to the above factors, clinical features such as a high severity of suicidal behaviour and speed of response are shared by depressed patients who are good responders to ECT (Chen *et al.*, 2017). Lin and colleagues demonstrated that early improvement in depression (after six ECT sessions) strongly predicted high response and remission rates (Lin *et al.*, 2016). Conversely, in a meta-analysis of available studies, it was reported that treatment resistance and longer duration of depressive episode were less likely to have symptom reduction with ECT (Haq *et al.*, 2015). A recent study from Taiwan confirmed these findings and added that higher levels of pain were also associated with poor outcome (Chen *et al.*, 2017). Duthie and colleagues from Aberdeen showed that while ECT confers anticonvulsant effects, neither initial seizure threshold nor the magnitude of its increase is a predictor of clinical response to ECT. A rise in seizure threshold is not essential for ECT's therapeutic effect but may represent an important marker of underlying neuronal state (Duthie *et al.*, 2015).

Relapse Post-ECT

Despite its effectiveness in the acute episode, without prophylactic treatment the relapse rate is extremely high (over 80%) in the six months after successful ECT. Post-ECT relapse rates can be significantly reduced by pharmacotherapy. In a meta-analysis of randomised controlled trials, it was shown that antidepressant medication halved the risk of relapse compared with placebo in the first six months with a number needed to treat (NNT) of 3.3 (Jelovac *et al.*, 2013) and there is comparable, albeit less robust, data for lithium (Rasmussen, 2015).

There is also trial data showing a significant benefit for continuation ECT (designed to prevent relapse of an index episode of illness: c-ECT) in reducing post-ECT relapse rates. Combined pharmacotherapy and c-ECT was reported to reduce post-ECT relapse rates compared to pharmacotherapy alone (Nordenskjold *et al.*, 2013). This finding was confirmed in a large RCT in geriatric depression which showed that c-ECT after remission (in the study operationalised as four c-ECT treatments followed by further ECT only as needed) was beneficial in sustaining mood improvement for most patients and better than the venlafaxine plus lithium arm (Kellner *et al.*, 2016). Another RCT showed that c-ECT combined with antidepressant prolonged survival time in elderly patients with psychotic unipolar depression who had remitted with ECT compared to an antidepressant alone

(Navarro *et al.*, 2008). It has been shown that c-ECT is not associated with adverse memory outcomes (Brown *et al.*, 2014). However, despite continuation therapy, the risk of relapse within the first year following ECT remains substantial (between 30% and 50%) with the period of greatest risk being the first six months (Jelovac *et al.*, 2013). More effective strategies for relapse prevention following ECT are urgently needed.

Maintenance ECT (m-ECT) is ECT used as a strategy to prevent further episodes or a recurrence of illness. Uncontrolled studies have shown that m-ECT is effective in the longer term in reducing the frequency of relapse and recurrences of depression but further controlled studies are awaited (Brown *et al.*, 2014). Elias and colleagues have shown that in a naturalistic setting the efficacy of m-ECT may extend over several years while cognitive functions remain largely unaffected (Elias *et al.*, 2014). The latter finding was confirmed by Kirov *et al.* (2016) who reported that repeated courses of ECT did not lead to cumulative cognitive deficits.

ECT as an Emergency Treatment in Depression

Electroconvulsive therapy is still the treatment of choice for patients with a severe depressive episode, psychomotor retardation and associated problems of poor oral intake or physical deterioration. It is also used in patients with depression who are actively suicidal. The use of ECT in these circumstances is based on its efficacy and speed of action. Early improvement has been reported in all subtypes of depression (Sobin *et al.*, 1996) and it can be considered as a possible first-line treatment in all emergencies (Porter and Ferrier, 1999). In urgent situations, bilateral ECT should be administered, as it works faster than unilateral (Kellner *et al.*, 2010). Electroconvulsive therapy administered three times a week may produce a more rapid response (Shapira *et al.*, 1998).

The Use of ECT in Treatment-Resistant Depression

Treatment resistance does not rule out a favourable response to ECT (Kellner *et al.*, 2012). Patients who failed one or more adequate medication trials had a diminished but still substantial rate of response to ECT (Prudic *et al.*, 1996) compared with non-treatment-resistant patients with depression. Dombrovski reported that when ECT is used to treat unipolar major depression that has not responded despite vigorous antidepressant treatment, the remission rate was about 50% (Dombrovski *et al.*, 2005) and this was confirmed by Heijnen who reported a remission rate of 48% with ECT in resistant depression when multiple previous treatments had failed (Heijnen *et al.*, 2010).

The Use of ECT as Treatment for Depression in Different Populations

The use of ECT in depression in pregnancy and in the puerperium is discussed in Chapter 8. Its use in depression in children and adolescents is discussed in Chapter 9 and in the elderly in Chapter 6.

Summary: Clinical Implications

Electroconvulsive therapy is a proven effective treatment for depression. There are benefits in using it in emergencies, in suicidal and in severe and/or psychotic cases and treatment-resistant patients. It is safe even for those with medical illnesses (see Chapter 27 for further discussion) and should not be relegated to a treatment of last resort. ECT can, and probably should, be combined with antidepressant treatment. On the basis of the evidence reviewed above and described in more detail in Chapter 22, it is reasonable to use right unilateral ECT at 6 times seizure threshold with a 0.5–1.5ms pulse width as the default initial treatment, but that decision may need to be modified or changed later depending on the urgency of the situation and other specific clinical factors.

The Royal College of Psychiatrists ECT and Related Treatment Committee's 2017 position statement on those who should be offered ECT and when, is outlined below and can also be found at: www.rcpsych.ac.uk/docs/default-source/about-us/who-we-are/electrocon vulsive-therapy—ect-ctee-statement-feb17.pdf?sfvrsn=2f4a94f9_2

The Royal College of Psychiatrists ECT and Related Treatment Committee's 2017 Position Statement

ECT is a first-line treatment for patients:

- where a rapid definitive response for the emergency treatment of depression is needed
- with high suicidal risk
- with severe psychomotor retardation and associated problems of compromised eating and drinking and/or physical deterioration
- who suffer from treatment-resistant depression that has responded to ECT in a previous episode of illness
- who prefer this form of treatment.

ECT is a second-line treatment for patients:

- with treatment-resistant depression
- who experience severe side-effects from medication
- whose medical or psychiatric condition, in spite of other treatments, has deteriorated to an extent that raises concern.

References

Brown E D, Lee H, Scott D, Cummings G G. (2014). Efficacy of continuation/maintenance electroconvulsive therapy for the prevention of recurrence of a major depressive episode in adults with unipolar depression: a systematic review. *J ECT*, **30**, 195–202.

Buley N, Copland E, Hodge S, Chaplin R. (2017). A further decrease in the rates of administration of electroconvulsive therapy in England. *J ECT*, **33**, 198–202.

Chen C C, Lin C H, Yang W C, Chen M C. (2017). Clinical factors related to acute electroconvulsive therapy outcome for patients with major depressive disorder. *Int Clin Psychopharmacol*, **32**, 127–34.

Chen J J, Zhao L B, Liu Y Y, Fan S H, Xie P. (2017). Comparative efficacy and acceptability of electroconvulsive therapy versus repetitive transcranial magnetic stimulation for major depression: a systematic review and multiple-treatments meta-analysis. *Behav Brain Res*, **320**, 30–6.

Dombrovski A Y, Mulsant B H, Haskett R F, Prudic J, Begley A E, Sackheim H A. (2005). Predictors of remission after electroconvulsive therapy in unipolar major depression. *J Clin Psychiatry*, **66**, 1043–9.

Duthie A C, Perrin J S, Bennett D M, Currie J, Reid I C. (2015). Anticonvulsant mechanisms of electroconvulsive therapy and relation to therapeutic efficacy. *J ECT*, **31**, 173–8.

Elias A, Chathanchirayil S J, Bhat R, Prudic J. (2014). Maintenance electroconvulsive therapy up to 12 years. *J Affect Disord*, **156**, 228–31.

Fergusson G M, Cullen L A, Freeman C P, Hendry J D. (2004). Electroconvulsive therapy in Scottish clinical practice: a national audit of demographics, standards, and outcome. *J ECT*, **20**, 166–73.

Gangadhar, B N and Thirthalli, J. (2010). Frequency of electroconvulsive therapy sessions in a course. *J ECT*, **26**, 181–5.

Haq A U, Sitzmann A F, Goldman M L, Maixner D F, Mickey B J. (2015). Response of depression to electroconvulsive therapy: a meta-analysis of clinical predictors. *J Clin Psychiatry*, **76**, 1374–84.

Heijnen W T, Birkenhager T K, Wierdsma A I, van den Broek W W. (2010). Antidepressant pharmacotherapy failure and response to subsequent electroconvulsive therapy: a meta-analysis. *J Clin Psychopharmacol*, **30**, 616–19.

Jelovac A, Kolshus E, McLoughlin D M. (2013). Relapse following successful electroconvulsive therapy for major depression: a meta-analysis. *Neuropsychopharmacology*, **38**, 2467–74.

Kellner C H, Fink M, Knapp R, *et al.* (2005). Relief of expressed suicidal intent by ECT: a consortium for research in ECT study. *Am J Psychiatry*, **162**, 977–82.

Kellner C H, Knapp R, Husain M M, *et al.* (2010). Bifrontal, bitemporal and right unilateral electrode placement in ECT: randomized trial. *Br J Psychiatry*, **196**, 226–34.

Kellner C H, Greenberg R M, Murrough J W, Bryson E O, Briggs M C, Pasculli R M. (2012). ECT in treatment-resistant depression. *Am J Psychiatry*, **169**, 1238–44.

Kellner C H, Husain M M, Knapp RG, *et al.*; CORE/PRIDE Work Group. (2016). A novel strategy for continuation ECT in geriatric depression: Phase 2 of the PRIDE study. *Am J Psychiatry*, **173**, 1110–18.

Kellner C H, Cicek M, Ables J L. (2017a). Electrode placement in electroconvulsive therapy – bilateral is still the "gold standard" for some patients. *Psychol Med*, **47**, 1510–11.

Kellner C H, Farber K G, Chen X R, Mehrotra A, Zipursky GDN. (2017b). A systematic review of left unilateral electroconvulsive therapy. *Acta Psychiatrica Scand*, **136**, 166–76.

Kirov G G, Owen L, Ballard H, *et al.* (2016). Evaluation of cumulative cognitive deficits from electroconvulsive therapy. *Br J Psychiatry*, **208**, 266–70.

Kolshus E, Jelovac A, McLoughlin D M. (2016). Bitemporal v. high-dose right unilateral electroconvulsive therapy for depression: a systematic review and meta-analysis of randomized controlled trials. *Psychol Med*, **47**, 518–530.

Lin C H, Chen M C, Yang W C, Lane H Y. (2016). Early improvement predicts outcome of major depressive patients treated with electroconvulsive therapy. *Eur Neuropsychopharmacol*, **26**, 225–33.

Lin C H, Yang W. (2017). The relationship between symptom relief and psychosocial functional improvement during acute electroconvulsive therapy for patients with major depressive disorder. *Int J Neuropsychopharmacol*. [Epub ahead of print]

Martín J L, Barbanoj J M, Schlaepfer T E, *et al.* (2002). Transcranial magnetic stimulation for treating depression. *Cochrane Database of Systematic Reviews*, **2**, CD003493.

McCormick L M, Brumm M C, Benede A K, Lewis J L. (2009). Relative ineffectiveness of ultrabrief right unilateral versus bilateral electroconvulsive therapy in depression. *J ECT*, **25**, 238–42.

National Collaborating Centre for Mental Health, (2010). *National Institute for Health and Clinical Excellence: Guidance. Depression: The Treatment and Management of Depression in Adults (Updated Edition).* Leicester (UK), British Psychological Society.

Navarro V, Gastó C, Torres X, *et al.* (2008). Continuation/maintenance treatment with nortriptyline versus combined nortriptyline and ECT in late-life psychotic depression: a two-year randomized study. *Am J Geriatr Psychiatry*, **16**, 498–505.

Nordenskjöld A, von Knorring L, Ljung T, Carlborg A, Brus O, Engström I. (2013). Continuation electroconvulsive therapy with pharmacotherapy versus pharmacotherapy alone for prevention of relapse of depression: a randomized controlled trial. *J ECT*, **29**, 86–92.

Pagnin D, de Queiro V, Pini S, Cassano G B. (2004). Efficacy of ECT in depression: a meta-analytic review. *J ECT*, **20**, 13–20.

Petrides G, Fink M, Husain M M, *et al.* (2001). ECT remission rates in psychotic versus nonpsychotic depressed patients: a report from CORE. *J ECT*, **17**, 244–53.

Porter R, Ferrier I N. (1999) Emergency treatment of depression. *Advances in Psychiatric Treatment*, **5**, 3–10.

Prudic J, Haskett R F, Mulsant B, *et al.* (1996). Resistance to antidepressant medications and short-term clinical response to ECT. *Am J Psychiatry*, **153**, 985–92.

Rasmussen K G. (2015). Lithium for post-electroconvulsive therapy depressive relapse prevention: a consideration of the evidence. *J ECT*, **3**, 87–90.

Rhebergen D, Huisman A, Bouckaert F, *et al.* (2015). Older age is associated with rapid remission of depression after electroconvulsive therapy: a latent class growth analysis. *Am J Geriatr Psychiatry*, **23**, 274–82.

Rosenquist P B, Brenes G B, Arnold E M, Kimball J, McCall V. (2006). Health-related quality of life and the practice of electroconvulsive therapy. *J ECT*, **22**, 18–24.

Sackeim H A, Prudic J, Devanand D P, *et al.* (2000). A prospective, randomized, double-blind comparison of bilateral and right unilateral electroconvulsive therapy at different stimulus intensities. *Archives of General Psychiatry*, **57**, 425–34.

Sackeim H A, Prudic J, Nobler M S, *et al.* (2008). Effects of pulse width and electrode placement on the efficacy and cognitive effects of electroconvulsive therapy. *Brain Stimul*, **1**, 71–83.

Sackeim H A, Dillingham E M, Prudic J, *et al.* (2009). Effect of concomitant pharmacotherapy on electroconvulsive

therapy outcomes: short-term efficacy and adverse effects. *Arch Gen Psychiatry*, **66**, 729–37.

Semkovska M, Keane D, Babalola O, McLoughlin D M, (2011). Unilateral brief-pulse electroconvulsive therapy and cognition: effects of electrode placement, stimulus dosage and time. *J Psychiatric Res*, **45**, 770–80.

Semkovska M, Landau S, Dunne R, *et al.* (2016). Bitemporal versus high-dose unilateral twice-weekly electroconvulsive therapy for depression (EFFECT-Dep): a pragmatic, randomized, non-inferiority trial. *Am J Psychiatry* **173**, 408–17.

Shapira B, Tubi N, Drexler H, Lidsky D, Calev A, Lerer B. (1998) Cost and benefit in the choice of ECT schedule. Twice versus three times weekly ECT. *B J Psychiatry*, **172**, 44–8.

Sobin C, Prudic J, Devanand D P, Nobler M S, Sackeim H A. (1996) Who responds to electroconvulsive therapy? A comparison of effective and ineffective forms of treatment. *B J Psychiatry*, **169**, 322–8.

Song G M, Tian X, Shuai T, *et al.* (2015) Treatment of adults with treatment-resistant depression: electroconvulsive therapy plus antidepressant or electroconvulsive therapy alone? Evidence from an indirect comparison Meta-analysis. *Medicine (Baltimore)*, **94**, (26) e1052.

Tor P C, Bautovich A, Wang M J, Martin D, Harvey S B, Loo C. (2015) A systematic review and meta-analysis of brief versus ultrabrief right unilateral electroconvulsive therapy for depression. *J Clin Psychiatry*, **76**, 1092–8.

UK ECT Review Group (2003). Efficacy and safety of electro-convulsive therapy in depressive disorders: a systematic review and meta-analysis. *Lancet*, **361**, 799–808.

Chapter 4

ECT in Mania (and Mixed States)

R Hamish McAllister-Williams

While there is no mention of ECT in the current NICE guidelines on bipolar disorder (NICE Guidelines; CG185, 2014), ECT is included as a recommended treatment for both manic and mixed affective episodes in bipolar disorder in the American Psychiatric Association Clinical Practice Guidelines (2002), the World Federation of Biological Psychiatry guidelines (Grunze, *et al.*, 2010) and the British Association for Psychopharmacology bipolar guidelines (Goodwin, *et al.*, 2016). Since the previous edition of *The ECT Handbook*, two narrative and one systematic reviews have been published that describe the evidence base regarding the use of ECT in manic and mixed affective episodes (Loo, *et al.*, 2011; Versiani, *et al.*, 2011; Thirthalli, *et al.*, 2012).

Efficacy of ECT in Acute Mania

Randomised Trial Evidence

There is just one randomised, sham controlled, trial of ECT in mania published in the literature. This was a small study of 30 patients who fulfilled DSM–III–R criteria for a manic episode (Sikdar, *et al.*, 1994). The experimental group received bilateral ECT. All patients received concomitant chlorpromazine 600 mg/day. After eight treatments, 12/15 patients in the active treatment arm, versus 1/15 in the sham treatment arm, were described as recovered.

There are two randomised trials that compare the efficacy of ECT with lithium in the treatment of bipolar mania (Small, *et al.*, 1988; Mukherjee, 1989). In one of these studies, 34 patients were randomised to ECT or lithium, with both groups of patients also receiving antipsychotic medication (Small, *et al.*, 1988). Around half of the patients received unilateral ECT and the rest bilateral. There was no difference in outcomes between the two groups, though it is important to note that outcomes were not rated blind to treatment status. In the other study, patients who had failed to respond to lithium or an antipsychotic were randomised to either ECT (n=22, right unilateral, left unilateral or bitemporal) or the combination of lithium and haloperidol (n=5) (Mukherjee, 1989). While 13/22 of the ECT treated patients achieved remission, none of the pharmacotherapy group did.

Randomised trial data comparing differing ECT protocols for the treatment of mania (described below) have reported response rates of between 64.3% (Barekatain, *et al.*, 2008) and 92% (Mohan, *et al.*, 2009).

Non-Randomised Data

There are a number of non-randomised prospective and retrospective studies, without comparators, that have been systematically reviewed (Versiani, *et al.*, 2011). The largest of these studies (Black, *et al.*, 1987) is a retrospective non-comparator study. The majority of studies were conducted in the 1940s and hence were in patients who had not received any medication. However, three studies were in the 1980s in patients who had not responded to medication. Overall the response rates ranged from 48% to 100% across all 14 studies (Versiani, *et al.*, 2011). The most recent retrospective data comes from a report of 522 consecutive patients with bipolar disorder treated with ECT (Perugi, *et al.*, 2017). In this cohort, only eight patients were suffering from a manic episode and six (75%) of these were considered responders to the ECT.

In terms of prospective and retrospective data examining the efficacy of ECT for mania compared to a comparator, there are a number of studies reported in the literature. Black and colleagues reviewed the outcomes of 438 patients admitted with mania, comparing ECT with 'adequate' treatment with lithium, 'inadequate' treatment with lithium and neither ECT nor lithium (Black, *et al.*, 1987). A total of 78% of ECT treated patients had a marked improvement (defined clinically), compared to 62% and 56% on lithium (depending on adequacy of treatment) and 37% of patients receiving neither ECT nor lithium. Psychosis did not predict response. Similarly a cohort study of 28 patients treated with ECT, 28 with chlorpromazine and 28 with no treatment, found an advantage for ECT (McCabe, *et al.*, 1977). Unsurprisingly, both ECT and CPZ were better than no treatment. However, in addition 10 patients who did not respond to chlorpromazine responded to ECT (McCabe, *et al.*, 1977). It is important to note that the cohorts of patients were identified from hospital records in different eras, with the 'no treatment' group being identified prior to the advent of ECT or medication, creating a significant potential sampling bias and/or 'cohort effect'. However, the overall finding that ECT may be superior to medication in the treatment of mania is supported by a small prospective study following up 20 patients, who were in a manic episode, for six months (Ikeji, *et al.*, 1999). Compared with patients treated with pharmacotherapy, ECT treated patients had a shorter duration of hospitalisation. Seemingly at odds with this observation is a description of 425 admissions of 269 patients with mania or mixed episodes in Brazil which found that the average length of stay in hospital was longer for ECT treated patients compared with exclusively pharmacotherapy treated patients (18.8 versus 12.5 days) (Volpe and Tavares, 2003). However, this was explained mostly by delays in commencing ECT treatment.

Efficacy in Acute Mixed Affective Episodes

There is much less evidence regarding the efficacy of ECT in mixed affective episodes than for mania and certainly bipolar depression (Versiani, *et al.*, 2011). There is a prospective study which reports that response was seen in 23 out of 41 consecutive patients with a mixed episode after a mean of 7 ECT treatments, and that a more rapid and greater reduction in Montgomery-Åsberg Depression Rating Scale (MADRS) scores and suicidality was seen compared with 23 patients with bipolar depression also treated with ECT (Ciapparelli, *et al.*, 2001). Conversely, a retrospective study of 38 patients with bipolar depression, 5 with mania and 10 with a mixed episode (DSM-IV criteria) treated with ECT found that those with mixed episodes remained in hospital longest and needed more ECT treatments than the depressed patients (Devanand, *et al.*, 2000). However, overall the data appear to suggest that response rates are similar across all phases of bipolar disorder (Versiani, *et al.*, 2011; Perugi, *et al.*, 2017; Medda, *et al.*, 2010; Palma, *et al.*, 2016), with response rates of 65% (Stromgren, 1988) to 80% (Devanand, *et al.*, 2000) reported. The largest retrospective non-comparator study found a response rate of 73% in 207 patients with a DSM-IV defined mixed affective episode treated with twice weekly bilateral ECT (Perugi, *et al.*, 2017).

Incident Mania

Please see Chapter 5 for information about the frequency with which manic episodes ensue after a course of ECT for the treatment of depression.

Electrode Placement and Stimulation Parameters

There are no randomised trial data regarding the ECT stimulation parameters for mixed episodes, but there are a few small studies with regards to mania.

Bifrontal versus bitemporal electrode placement has been compared in two studies of patients with mania. In one of these, 28 patients with severe mania were randomised double blind to moderate dose bifrontal versus low dose bitemporal ECT (Barekatain, *et al.*, 2008). All patients had a minimum of six treatments. No difference was seen in Young Mania Rating Scale (YMRS) scores between the two groups, but bitemporal ECT was associated with fewer cognitive side effects. In the other, 36 patients were randomised to bifrontal or bitemporal ECT (Hiremani, *et al.*, 2008). No patients were on mood stabilisers. Faster improvement in YMRS was seen with bifrontal ECT with no difference in cognition post ECT between the groups.

In terms of stimulus intensity, one study compared patients randomly allocated to twice-weekly ECT just above seizure threshold to those given 2.5X seizure threshold. Totals of 24/26 patients in the threshold and 22/24 in the supra-threshold groups showed significant improvement. Across both groups 88% remitted, with no differences in any outcome between the two treatments (Mohan, *et al.*, 2009).

There is one small randomised trial of bilateral versus unilateral ECT for mania (Mukherjee, *et al.*, 1988). This found no difference between treatments, but its size (20 patients) meant that it lacks statistical power. However, this finding is supported by a larger retrospective data set (Black, *et al.*, 1987). These studies of the efficacy of unilateral ECT were conducted before it was clearly established that electrical dose is an important determinant of the efficacy of unilateral ECT in depressive illness. There have been no controlled comparisons of high-dose unilateral ECT with moderately supra-threshold bilateral ECT.

There has been a recent case series of three patients with mania successfully treated with right unilateral ultra-brief pulse ECT (Anand, 2016).

There are no published data specifically looking at the impact of duration of treatment, or number of ECT treatments, for the management of mania. While there are retrospective reviews of maintenance ECT in bipolar disorder (Minnai, *et al.*, 2011; Santos Pina, *et al.*, 2016), these are not able to look at the impact the treatment might have had specifically on manic relapses.

ECT for Mania and Concomitant Medication

There is a potential issue around concomitant medication with regards to the use of ECT for mania and mixed episodes given that two pharmacological options recommended by guidelines are valproate and lithium (NICE Guidelines; CG185, 2014; Goodwin, *et al.*, 2016).

The potential issue with valproate is with regard to its anticonvulsant properties potentially reducing the efficacy of ECT. This has been studied in a randomised controlled trial of ECT with or without sodium valproate (Jahangard, *et al.*, 2012). A total of 42 inpatients with DSM-IV diagnosed mania were included in the study. All patients underwent bifrontal ECT for at least six sessions. No difference was seen in response rates or time to response between the two groups. While this study is too small to rule out modest detrimental effects of valproate on response to ECT, it does suggest that any such effect, if it exists, is not large.

There have been concerns about the potential for ECT to increase lithium neurotoxicity (Schou, 1991) (see also Chapter 25). This issue has been specifically examined in patients with mania in a retrospective case series of 90 patients compared with 51 who had ECT but not lithium (Volpe, *et al.*, 2012). There was no difference in the length of hospitalisation or the number of ECT treatments that the two groups of patients received. No severe adverse effects were reported for any of the patients receiving both ECT and lithium, though subtle adverse effects could not be ruled out.

Recommendations

ECT has been shown to be an effective treatment in mania and mixed episodes. ECT should be considered for the treatment of persistent or life-threatening symptoms in severe or prolonged manic or mixed episodes where there is inadequate response to first-line treatments. What data there is suggests that it is possible to use ECT concomitantly with valproate and lithium (though see Chapter 25).

There is little data upon which to guide electrode placement or stimulus parameters for mania and mixed episodes. It is not possible to make a firm recommendation regarding bilateral versus unilateral, or bifrontal versus bitemporal electrode placement. It is parsimonious and probably sensible to use similar placements and similar parameters as for depression, and to use bitemporal ECT where the speed of response is critical. In terms of length of treatment, again it is parsimonious to at least treat to remission, as for depression.

References

American Psychiatric Association. 2002. Practice guideline for the treatment of patients with bipolar disorder (revision). *Am J Psychiatry*, Apr; 159:1–50.

Anand S. 2016. Ultrabrief electroconvulsive therapy for manic episodes of bipolar disorder. *J ECT*, Dec; 32:267–9.

Barekatain M, Jahangard L, Haghighi M, Ranjkesh F. 2008. Bifrontal versus bitemporal electroconvulsive therapy in severe manic patients. *J ECT*, Sep; 24:199–202.

Black D W, Winokur G, Nasrallah A. 1987. Treatment of mania: a naturalistic study of electroconvulsive therapy versus lithium in 438 patients. *J Clin Psychiatry*, Apr; 48:132–9.

Ciapparelli A, Dell'Osso L, Tundo A, Pini S, Chiavacci M C, Di S I, *et al.* 2001. Electroconvulsive therapy in medication-nonresponsive patients with mixed mania and bipolar depression. *J Clin Psychiatry*, Jul; 62:552–5.

Devanand D P, Polanco P, Cruz R, Shah S, Paykina N, Singh K, *et al.* 2000. The efficacy of ECT in mixed affective states. *J ECT*, Mar; 16:32–7.

Goodwin G M, Haddad P M, Ferrier I N, Aronson J K, Barnes T R H, Cipriani A, *et al.* 2016. Evidence-based guidelines for treating bipolar disorder: revised third edition. Recommendations from the British

Association for Psychopharmacology. J Psychopharm, Jun; 30:495–553.

Grunze H, Vieta E, Goodwin G M, Bowden C, Licht R W, Moller H J, et al. 2010. The World Federation of Societies of Biological Psychiatry (WFSBP) Guidelines for the Biological Treatment of Bipolar Disorders: Update 2010 on the treatment of acute bipolar depression. World J Biol Psychiatry, Mar; 11:81–109.

Hiremani R M, Thirthalli J, Tharayil B S, Gangadhar B N. 2008. Double-blind randomized controlled study comparing short-term efficacy of bifrontal and bitemporal electroconvulsive therapy in acute mania. Bipolar Disord, Sep; 10:701–7.

Ikeji O C, Ohaeri J U, Osahon R O, Agidee R O. 1999. Naturalistic comparative study of outcome and cognitive effects of unmodified electro-convulsive therapy in schizophrenia, mania and severe depression in Nigeria. East Afr Med J, Nov; 76:644–50.

Jahangard L, Haghighi M, Bigdelou G, Bajoghli H, Brand S. 2012. Comparing efficacy of ECT with and without concurrent sodium valproate therapy in manic patients. J ECT, Jun; 28:118–23.

Loo C, Katalinic N, Mitchell P B, Greenberg B. 2011. Physical treatments for bipolar disorder: a review of electroconvulsive therapy, stereotactic surgery and other brain stimulation techniques. J Affect Disord, Jul; 132:1–13.

McCabe M S, Norris B. 1977. ECT versus chlorpromazine in mania. Biol Psychiatry, Apr; 12:245–54.

Medda P, Perugi G, Zanello S, Ciuffa M, Rizzato S, Cassano G B. 2010. Comparative response to electroconvulsive therapy in medication-resistant bipolar I patients with depression and mixed state. J ECT, Jun; 26:82–6.

Minnai G P, Salis P G, Oppo R, Loche A P, Scano F, Tondo L. 2011. Effectiveness of maintenance electroconvulsive therapy in rapid-cycling bipolar disorder. J ECT, Jun; 27:123–6.

Mohan T S, Tharyan P, Alexander J, Raveendran N S. 2009. Effects of stimulus intensity on the efficacy and safety of twice-weekly, bilateral electroconvulsive therapy (ECT) combined

with antipsychotics in acute mania: a randomised controlled trial. Bipolar Disord, Mar; 11:126–34.

Mukherjee S, Sackeim H A, Lee C. 1988. Unilateral ECT in the treatment of manic episodes. Convuls Ther; 4:74–80.

Mukherjee S. 1989. Mechanisms of the antimanic effect of electroconvulsive therapy. Convuls Ther; 5:227–43.

National Institute for Health and Care Excellence. 2014. Bipolar disorder: assessment and management. NICE Guidelines; CG185.

Palma M, Ferreira B, Borja-Santos N, Trancas B, Monteiro C, Cardoso G. 2016. Efficacy of electroconvulsive therapy in bipolar disorder with mixed features. Depress Res Treat; 2016:8306071.

Perugi G, Medda P, Toni C, Mariani MG, Socci C, Mauri M. 2017. The role of electroconvulsive therapy (ECT) in bipolar disorder: effectiveness in 522 patients with bipolar depression, mixed-state, mania and catatonic features. Curr Neuropharmacol, Apr; 15:359–71.

Santos Pina L, Bouckaert F, Obbels J, Wampers M, Simons W, Wyckaert S, et al. 2016. Maintenance electroconvulsive therapy in severe bipolar disorder: a retrospective chart review. J ECT, Mar; 32:23–8.

Schou M. 1991. Lithium and electroconvulsive therapy: adversaries, competitors, allies? Acta Psychiatr Scand, Nov; 84:435–8.

Sikdar S, Kulhara P, Avasthi A, Singh H. 1994. Combined chlorpromazine and electroconvulsive therapy in mania. Br J Psychiatry, Jun; 164:806–10.

Small J G, Klapper M H, Kellams J J, Miller M J, Milstein V, Sharpley P H, et al. 1988. Electroconvulsive treatment compared with lithium in the management of manic states. Arch Gen Psychiatry, Aug; 45:727–32.

Stromgren L S. 1988. Electroconvulsive therapy in Aarhus, Denmark, in 1984: its application in nondepressive disorders. Convuls Ther; 4:306–13.

Thirthalli J, Prasad M K, Gangadhar B N. 2012. Electroconvulsive therapy (ECT) in bipolar disorder: a narrative review of literature. *Asian J Psychiatr*, Mar; 5:11–7.

Versiani M, Cheniaux E, Landeira-Fernandez J. 2011. Efficacy and safety of electroconvulsive therapy in the treatment of bipolar disorder: a systematic review. *J ECT*, Jun; 27:153–64.

Volpe F M, Tavares A. 2003. Impact of ECT on duration of hospitalizations for mania. *J ECT*, Mar; 19:17–21.

Volpe F M, Tavares A R. 2012. Lithium plus ECT for mania in 90 cases: safety issues. *J Neuropsychiatry Clin Neurosci*; 24:E33.

Electroconvulsive Therapy in Bipolar Disorder Depression

Ute Kessler

Depressive episodes dominate the longitudinal course of bipolar disorder (BD) (Judd, Schettler *et al.* 2003, Post, Denicoff *et al.* 2003, Kupka, Altshuler *et al.* 2007). Treating the depressive state of BD is a clinical challenge. Although pharmacotherapy is the mainstay treatment, the various pharmacological treatment options often have poor outcomes. The benefits of antidepressant agents remain controversial (Pacchiarotti, Bond *et al.* 2013). Electroconvulsive therapy (ECT) has been considered an effective treatment option in bipolar depression (Musetti, Del Grande *et al.* 2013), but the topic is still understudied (Sienaert, Lambrichts *et al.* 2013).

Efficacy of ECT in BD Depression

Earlier studies found ECT to be clearly more effective than pharmacological treatment in BD depression (Zornberg and Pope 1993). However, these studies were affected by methodological weaknesses, such as the use of antidepressants rather than mood stabilisers in pharmacological groups, outcomes measured in broad clinical terms rather than using formal rating instruments, imprecise diagnostic classifications and non-randomised designs (Loo, Katalinic *et al.* 2011). The recently reported first randomised controlled trial (RCT) of treatment-resistant BD depression included 73 patients randomised to either 6-week algorithm based pharmacological treatment (APT) or ECT. Patients randomised to ECT received three sessions per week for up to six weeks using right unilateral electrode placement and brief pulse stimulation. The results showed that ECT was significantly more effective than APT. After six weeks the mean score on the Montgomery-Åsberg Depression Rating Scale (MADRS) was 6.6 points lower in the ECT group than in the APT group. More than twice as many ECT patients responded (73.9% vs. 35.0%, p<0.01), but the remission rate did not differ between the groups and remained modest regardless of treatment choice (34.8% vs. 30.0%). This RCT was limited not only by the low sample size but also by a substantial drop-out rate (only 57% of patients completing). Data on long term efficacy and recurrence and relapse are still missing. The generalisability of the results is further limited by the exclusion of patients with a rapid cycling course (Schoeyen, Kessler *et al.* 2015) (see Table 5.1). A meta-analysis of trials investigating mixed samples of unipolar and bipolar major depression (UK ECT Review Group 2003) found ECT to be significantly more effective than pharmacotherapy. This finding, together with two meta-analyses indicating ECT to be equally effective in bipolar and unipolar depression (Dierckx, Heijnen *et al.* 2012, Haq, Sitzmann *et al.* 2015), thus support the results from the first RCT of ECT in BD depression that ECT is more effective than pharmacotherapy in the acute treatment of BD depression. The efficacy of ECT in BD depression is further supported by trials comparing

Table 5.1 Studies comparing electroconvulsive therapy (ECT) to pharmacological treatment in bipolar disorder (BD) depression

	n	Study design	Results
Greenblatt, Grosser et al. 1962, Greenblatt, Grosser et al. 1964	76 BD	Controlled trial	ECT more effective than AD (markedly improved: 78% vs. 37%)
Bratfos and Haug 1965	112 ECT, 133 AD	Open study	ECT more effective than AD (recovery rate: 61% vs. 25%)
Perris and d'Elia 1966	40 ECT, 23 AD	Chart review	ECT and AD equally effective (based on relapse rate)
Avery and Winokur 1977	14 ECT, 3 AD, 17 ECT+AD	Chart review	*Chart diagnosis manic depressed:* ECT, ECT+AD more effective than AD (marked improvement rate: 49% vs 57% vs. 25%) *Research diagnosis Bipolar I or II:* ECT, AD and ECT+AD equally effective (marked improvement rate: 43% vs. 33% vs. 39%, n.s.)
Avery and Lubrano 1979	8 ECT, 15 AD	Re-evaluation of a prospective study	Improvement rates: 100% and 47%
Homan, Lachenbruch et al. 1982	30 ECT, 16 AD, 7 ECT+AD	Chart review	ECT, AD and ECT+AD equally effective (marked improvement rate: 23% vs. 12.5% vs. 14%, n.s.)
Black, Winokur et al. 1986, Black, Winokur et al. 1987	55 ECT, 30 AD	Chart review	ECT and AD equally effective (improvement rate: 69% vs. 47%, n.s.)
Schoeyen, Kessler et al. 2015	36 ECT 30 APT	RCT	ECT more effective: response rate 73.9% vs. 35.0%, but the remission rate did not differ (34.8% vs. 30.0%)

AD, antidepressant agents; n.s. = not significant; APT, algorithm-based pharmacological treatment; RCT, randomised controlled trial

different ECT techniques and large cohort studies finding substantial response rates (Sienaert, Vansteelandt *et al.* 2009, Kellner, Knapp *et al.* 2010, Perugi, Medda *et al.* 2017).

When Should ECT Be Used in Bipolar Disorder Depression?

Due to the lack of evidence there is no consensus across international treatment guidelines for treatment-resistant BD (Parker, Graham and Tavella 2017). Individualised treatment decisions should therefore be made that account for family history, past and present symptoms, the course of illness including past treatment responses, side effects and patient preferences. This is especially true for the use of ECT in BD depression. The lack of studies that have used reliable methodologies to investigate the effects of ECT in BD depression has led to ECT being considered inferior when developing treatment guidelines. Thus, ECT is often reserved for the most-treatment-resistant or severe patients (Musetti, Del Grande *et al.* 2013), but this contrasts with the relatively high response and remission rates reported clinically (Versiani, Cheniaux *et al.* 2011, Dierckx, Heijnen *et al.* 2012, Perugi, Medda *et al.* 2016). In addition, ECT is also a treatment option in BD patients with catatonia, with psychotic symptoms, at a high risk of suicide or during pregnancy (Grunze 2005, Musetti, Del Grande *et al.* 2013, Perugi, Medda *et al.* 2016). A meta-analysis of studies, mainly including MDD but also BD patients, concluded that a longer duration of the current episode and a higher number of failed pharmacological trials predict a lower efficacy for ECT (Haq, Sitzmann *et al.* 2015, Perugi, Medda *et al.* 2016). This suggests that ECT should be applied early in the treatment course; that is, before a high degree of treatment resistance has appeared (Beale and Kellner 2000, Sienaert, Lambrichts *et al.* 2013). Although these findings also could be due to longer illness duration and more failed pharmacotherapy selecting for greater treatment resistance in the remaining non-responders, ECT should not be considered only as a last resort in the most-severe patients (Perugi, Medda *et al.* 2016). The paucity of RCTs is challenging, but should not necessarily stop clinicians from using an effective treatment.

General Treatment Principles

Within the limits of available evidence, it is clinically reasonable to administer ECT in the same manner for bipolar and non-bipolar depressed patients. Chapter 22 provides guidance on unilateral vs. bilateral electrode placement, frequency of ECT, stimulus dosing and number of sessions.

Psychotropic Drug Treatment during a Course of ECT

The concomitant use of psychotropic medicines during a course of ECT is common in BD, especially the use of lithium. Chapter 25 provides guidance on this topic.

Treatment-Induced Switch to Mania

When choosing a treatment for BD depression, data on efficacy in the acute phase have to be considered alongside tolerability and the likelihood of preventing switching, recurrence and relapse (Malhi, Adams *et al.* 2009). In this regard, ECT is in the unique position of being effective in all phases of the illness. Medda, Toni and Perugi (2014) emphasise the mood-stabilising effect of ECT, which is superior to pharmacological approaches. There is no evidence that ECT induces cycle acceleration. Nevertheless, treatment-emergent affective switching is a recognised problem that also occurs with ECT. Most authors consider such mood switches to be of less clinical importance, with mania often subsiding spontaneously within a few days (Lewis and Nasrallah 1986, Devanand, Prudic *et al.* 1992, Bailine, Fink *et al.* 2010, Perugi, Medda *et al.* 2016). Bost-Baxter, Reti and Payne (2012) found that a history of rapid cycling was not a predictor of mood switches with ECT. In the few studies addressing ECT-induced mood switches, the prevalence rates have ranged from less than 7% (Lewis and Nasrallah 1986) to more than 33% (Kukopulos, Reginaldi *et al.* 1980). These large differences in prevalence rates might be due to differences in defining treatment-induced mood switches, which vary from developing a manic episode to the emergence of mild hypomania. Angst and colleagues (1992) found high switch rates in psychotic BD patients receiving ECT (>30%), but these did not differ from those in patients who did not receive ECT. In the Norwegian RCT including 73 patients, two patients were excluded before starting treatment due to mood switches. A further two patients in the ECT group and two patients in the medication group scored >15 on the YMRS during the six-week treatment period (Kessler, Schoeyen et al. 2014).

The concomitant use of antimanic medications is a common strategy for preventing mood switches, but supporting evidence is lacking. There are no guidelines on how to treat ECT-induced mania. Clinicians should be aware of the relatively common occurrence of mood switches, but that this does not mean that ECT should be automatically discarded as a treatment option in BD. Close monitoring – especially in outpatients – is necessary in order to avoid adverse outcomes.

Recurrence and Relapse

The high relapse rate after successfully treating a depressive episode in BD remains a significant clinical problem, not only for ECT-treated patients. RCTs comparing the relapse rate after ECT vs. pharmacotherapy in BD depression are lacking. One-year relapse rates of 50–55% have typically been reported for ECT-treated BD patients (Medda, Mauri et al. 2013, Itagaki, Takebayashi et al. 2017, Popiolek et al. 2018). Such high rates are not surprising given that ECT is administered mainly to chronic and treatment-resistant patients. A recent study comparing the five-year periods before and after BD patients received ECT indicated that ECT lengthens the illness-free interval and reduces the number of affective episodes (Minnai, Salis et al. 2016). These authors also found a reduced risk of relapse in patients on mood stabilisers without the reinstatement of antidepressants.

Cognitive Side Effects of ECT in Bipolar Disorder Depression

The main concern with ECT treatment remains the risk of memory impairment. A few studies have addressed this issue specifically in BD patients. A recent RCT comparing ECT to APT found that neurocognitive functioning (measured mean three weeks after ECT with standardised neuropsychological instruments) was unaffected by right unilateral brief-pulse ECT (Kessler, Schoeyen et al. 2014). However, the ECT-treated patients remembered fewer recent autobiographical details than patients receiving pharmacological treatment. A follow up of the above mentioned RCT patients after six months showed that ECT did not reduce long-term general neurocognitive functions. The possibility of impaired autobiographical memory function acutely after ECT needs to be communicated to the patient before treatment, as part of a risk-benefit trade-off (Bjoerke-Bertheussen et al. 2017). Other cognitive side effects of ECT are discussed in Chapter 13.

Recommendations

Within the limits of available evidence, it is clinically reasonable to recommend ECT being used in the same way for bipolar as for unipolar depression (see recommendations for the use of ECT in unipolar depression in Chapter 3). The concomitant use of antimanic medications is a common strategy for preventing mood switches, but supporting evidence is lacking.

References

Angst, J., K. Angst, I. Baruffol and R. Meinherz-Surbeck (1992). ECT-induced and drug-induced hypomania. *Convuls Ther* **8**: 179–85.

Avery, D. and A. Lubrano (1979). Depression treated with imipramine and ECT: the DeCarolis study reconsidered. *Am J Psychiatry* **136**: 559–62.

Avery, D. and G. Winokur (1977). The efficacy of electroconvulsive therapy and antidepressants in depression. *Biol Psychiatry* **12**: 507–23.

Bailine, S., M. Fink, R. Knapp, *et al.* (2010). Electroconvulsive therapy is equally effective in unipolar and bipolar depression. *Acta Psychiatr Scand* **121**: 431–36.

Beale, M. D. and C. H. Kellner (2000). ECT in treatment algorithms: no need to save the best for last. *J ECT* **16**: 1–2.

Bjoerke-Bertheussen, J., H. Schoeyen, O. A. Andreassen, *et al.* (2017). Right unilateral electroconvulsive therapy does not cause more cognitive impairment than pharmacologic treatment in treatment-resistant bipolar depression: A 6-month randomized controlled trial follow-up study. *Bipolar Disord.* 2017 Dec 21. doi: 10.1111/bdi.12594 [Epub ahead of print].

Black, D. W., G. Winokur and A. Nasrallah (1986). ECT in unipolar and bipolar disorders: a naturalistic evaluation of 460 patients. *Convuls Ther* **2**: 231–37.

Black, D. W., G. Winokur and A. Nasrallah (1987). The treatment of depression: electroconvulsive therapy v antidepressants: a naturalistic evaluation of 1,495 patients. *Compr Psychiatry* **28**: 169–82.

Bost-Baxter, E., I. M. Reti and J. L. Payne (2012). ECT in Bipolar Disorder: Incidence of Switch from Depression to Hypomania or Mania. *J Depress Anxiety* **1**.

Bratfos, O. and J. O. Haug (1965). Electroconvulsive therapy and antidepressant drugs in manic-depressive disease. Treatment results at discharge and 3 months later. *Acta Psychiatr Scand* **41**: 588–96.

Devanand, D. P., J. Prudic and H. A. Sackeim (1992). Electroconvulsive therapy-induced hypomania is uncommon. *Convuls Ther* **8**: 296–98.

Dierckx, B., W. T. Heijnen, W. W. van den Broek and T. K. Birkenhager (2012). Efficacy of electroconvulsive therapy in bipolar versus unipolar major depression: a meta-analysis. *Bipolar Disord* **14**: 146–50.

Greenblatt, M., G. H. Grosser and H. Wechsler (1962). A comparative study of selected antidepressant medications and EST. *Am J Psychiatry* **119**: 144–53.

Greenblatt, M., G. H. Grosser and H. Wechsler (1964). Differential response of hospitalized depressed patients to somatic therapy. *Am J Psychiatry* **120**: 935–43.

Grunze, H. (2005). Reevaluating therapies for bipolar depression. *J Clin Psychiatry* **66**: 17–25.

Haq, A. U., A. F. Sitzmann, M. L. Goldman, D. F. Maixner and B. J. Mickey (2015). Response of depression to electroconvulsive therapy: a meta-analysis of clinical predictors. *J Clin Psychiatry* **76**: 1374–84.

Homan, S., P. A. Lachenbruch, G. Winokur and P. Clayton (1982). An efficacy study of electroconvulsive therapy and antidepressants in the treatment of primary depression. *Psychol Med* **12**: 615–24.

Itagaki, K., M. Takebayashi, C. Shibasaki, N. Kajitani, *et al.* (2017). Factors associated with relapse after a response to electroconvulsive therapy in unipolar versus bipolar depression. *J Affect Disord* **208**: 113–19.

Judd, L. L., P. J. Schettler, H. S. Akiskal, *et al.* (2003). Long-term symptomatic status of bipolar I vs. bipolar II disorders. *Int J Neuropsychopharmacol* **6**: 127–37.

Kellner, C. H., R. Knapp, M. M. Husain, *et al.* (2010). Bifrontal, bitemporal and right unilateral electrode placement in ECT: randomised trial. *Br J Psychiatry* **196**: 226–34.

Kessler, U., H. K. Schoeyen, O. A. Andreassen, *et al.* (2014). The effect of electroconvulsive therapy on neurocognitive function in treatment-resistant bipolar disorder depression. *J Clin Psychiatry* **75**: e1306–13.

Kessler, U. (2014). *Electroconvulsive therapy for bipolar disorder depression. Effects on depressive symptoms and cognitive function.* PhD Doctoral thesis, University of Bergen.

Kukopulos, A., D. Reginaldi, P. Laddomada, G. Floris, G. Serra and L. Tondo (1980). Course of the manic-depressive cycle and changes caused by treatment. *Pharmakopsychiatr Neuropsychopharmakol* **13**: 156–67.

Kupka, R. W., L. L. Altshuler, W. A. Nolen, *et al.* (2007). Three times more days depressed than manic or hypomanic in both bipolar I and bipolar II disorder. *Bipolar Disord* **9**: 531–35.

Lewis, D. A. and H. A. Nasrallah (1986). Mania associated with electroconvulsive therapy. *J Clin Psychiatry* **47**: 366–67.

Loo, C., N. Katalinic, P. B. Mitchell and B. Greenberg (2011). Physical treatments for bipolar disorder: a review of electroconvulsive therapy, stereotactic surgery and other brain stimulation techniques. *J Affect Disord* **132**: 1–13.

Malhi, G. S., D. Adams and M. Berk (2009). Medicating mood with maintenance in mind: bipolar depression pharmacotherapy. *Bipolar Disord* **11**: 55–76.

Medda, P., M. Mauri, S. Fratta, *et al.* (2013). Long-term naturalistic follow-up of patients with bipolar depression and mixed state treated with electroconvulsive therapy. *J ECT* **29**: 179–88.

Medda, P., C. Toni and G. Perugi (2014). The mood-stabilizing effects of electroconvulsive therapy. *J ECT* **30**: 275–82.

Minnai, G. P., P. Salis, M. Manchia, M. Pinna and L. Tondo (2016). What happens to the course of bipolar disorder after electroconvulsive therapy? *J Affect Disord* **195**: 180–84.

Musetti, L., C. Del Grande, D. Marazziti and L. Dell'Osso (2013). Treatment of bipolar depression. *CNS Spectr* **18**: 177–87.

Pacchiarotti, I., D. J. Bond, R. J. Baldessarini, *et al.* (2013). The International Society for Bipolar Disorders (ISBD) task force report on antidepressant use in bipolar disorders. *Am J Psychiatry* **170**: 1249–62.

Parker, G. B., R. K. Graham and G. Tavella (2017). Is there consensus across international evidence-based guidelines for the management of bipolar disorder? *Acta Psychiatr Scand.* **135**: 515–26.

Perris, C. and G. d'Elia (1966). A study of bipolar (manic-depressive) and unipolar recurrent depressive psychoses. IX. therapy and prognosis. *Acta Psychiatr Scand Suppl* **194**: 153–71.

Perugi, G., P. Medda, C. Toni, M. G. Mariani, C. Socci and M. Mauri (2017). The role of electroconvulsive therapy (ECT) in bipolar disorder: effectiveness in 522 patients with bipolar depression, mixed-state, mania and catatonic features. *Curr Neuropharmacol* **15**: 359–71.

Popiolek, K., O. Brus, T. Elvin, *et al.* (2018). Rehospitalization and suicide following electroconvulsive therapy for bipolar depression: a population-based register study. *J Affect Disord* **226**: 146–54.

Post, R. M., K. D. Denicoff, G. S. Leverich, *et al.* (2003). Morbidity in 258 bipolar outpatients followed for 1 year with daily prospective ratings on the NIMH life chart method. *J Clin Psychiatry* **64**: 680–90.

Schoeyen, H. K., U. Kessler, O. A. Andreassen, *et al.* (2015). Treatment-resistant bipolar depression: a randomized controlled trial of electroconvulsive therapy versus algorithm-based pharmacological treatment. *Am J Psychiatry* **172**: 41–1.

Sienaert, P., L. Lambrichts, A. Dols and J. De Fruyt (2013). Evidence-based treatment strategies for treatment-resistant bipolar depression: a systematic review. *Bipolar Disord* **15**: 61–9.

Sienaert, P., K. Vansteelandt, K. Demyttenaere and J. Peuskens (2009). Ultra-brief pulse ECT in bipolar and unipolar depressive disorder: differences in speed of response. *Bipolar Disord* **11**: 418–24.

UK ECT Review Group (2003). Efficacy and safety of electroconvulsive therapy in depressive disorders: a systematic review and meta-analysis. *Lancet* **361**: 799–808.

Versiani, M., E. Cheniaux and J. Landeira-Fernandez (2011). Efficacy and safety of electroconvulsive therapy in the treatment of bipolar disorder: a systematic review. *J ECT* **27**: 153–64.

Zornberg, G. L. and H. G. Pope, Jr. (1993). Treatment of depression in bipolar disorder: new directions for research. *J Clin Psychopharmacol* **13**: 397–408.

ECT in Older Adults

Stuart Watson, Jane Newby and Phil Laws

ECT is used more often in the elderly than in younger adults and most often for depression which, in the elderly, is common and is associated with significant morbidity and mortality (Whiteford, *et al.*, 2010). The high rates of treatment resistance (Whiteford, *et al.*, 2010), the relative absence of evidence based guidelines and the risks associated with biological treatments, particularly in view of the high rates of physical co-morbidity, suggest that the decision to use ECT should be considered often, but carefully, and that its application should be thoughtful.

Efficacy

A 90% remission in depressed over-65s treated with bitemporal ECT at 1.5 times seizure threshold has been demonstrated in The Consortium for Research in ECT (CORE) study (O'Connor, *et al.*, 2001). Case note reviews e.g. (Damm, *et al.*, 2010) and open label comparisons with antidepressants (Flint, *et al.*, 1988) support the efficacy of ECT in the elderly as do older prospective RCTs; a re-evaluation of the Nottingham ECT study data, for instance, showed a benefit of unilateral and bilateral ECT vs sham treatment in the over-60s (O'Leary, *et al.*, 1994). In these patients aged 60 or over, the rate of response positively correlated with age (O'Leary, *et al.*, 1994). This is in keeping with some (Wilkinson, *et al.*, 1993; Tew, *et al.*, 1999; Rhebergen, *et al.*, 2015) but not all (Hickie, *et al.*, 1996; Birkenhäger, *et al.*, 2010) previous studies. More recently, the Prolonging Remission in Depressed Elderly (PRIDE) study examined 240 unipolar depressed who were over 60. Existing medication was washed out and replaced by open label venlafaxine increasing, as tolerated, to a target dose of 225mg. ECT treatment was 3x/week right unilateral ultrabrief pulse, commenced at 6x seizure threshold and followed a clear protocol with dosage increases prompted by inadequate response. A total of 62% of patients met remission criteria, 10% were categorised as non-remitters and 28% dropped out. Average depression scores when plotted against treatment number showed a negative exponential pattern with over 85% of the improvement occurring by visit five, revealing a faster time to remission than the medication group (Kellner, *et al.*, 2015); this latter finding has also been shown by a Dutch group (Spaans, *et al.*, 2015; Rhebergen, *et al.*, 2015). Older age, absence of suicidal ideation and an improvement in mood after the first treatment were all good prognostic factors (Keller, *et al.*, 2016a). Of the remitters, 120 entered the six-month continuation and maintenance phase II of the PRIDE study. All patients entering this phase received lithium; patients were randomised to whether or not they additionally had open label continuation ECT. Here the regime was four fixed treatments over four weeks with an algorithm driven schedule with zero, one or two treatments per week dependent upon depression severity. There was a statistically significant and clinically relevant advantage to the ECT group (Kellner, et al., 2016b), this corroborated earlier demonstration of an advantage of continuation ECT in reducing risk of remission in the elderly (Navarro, et al., 2008).

Safety

Compared with younger adults, the elderly are at an increased risk of adverse events associated with antidepressant use (Coupland, et al., 2011) and ECT (Blumberger, et al., 2017) – including the risk of death (Blumberger, et al., 2017; Ryan, et al., 2008; Dennis, et al., 2017). Treatment should not be denied on the basis of age alone, rather there should be individualised care with emphasis on optimisation of chronic co-morbidities and collaboration between general practitioner, senior care of the elderly physicians, senior anaesthetist and psychiatrist (Callum, et al., 1999). Opportunities to deepen the inadequate knowledge base for anaesthesia in the elderly should be created (Griffiths, et al., 2014).

As patients age there is a reduced physiological reserve i.e. a reduced ability to increase cardiac output and ventilation. This is likely to be compounded by multiple chronic co-morbidities and associated risks of polypharmacy. As a result, elderly patients are at higher risk of death and morbidity after general anaesthesia for any procedure. The limited ability to increase cardiac output in the elderly is a result of reduced autonomic nervous system function, vascular compliance and baroreceptor dysfunction with reduced response to beta receptors and angiotensin II. These changes may be exaggerated further in patients with chronic co-morbidities including hypertension, ischaemic heart disease and the related cardiovascular polypharmacy. The ability of the lungs to transfer oxygen and match ventilation to perfusion declines with age (Corcoran, et al., 2011). These changes are exacerbated by smoking. This combination of cardiovascular and respiratory changes exposes the elderly patient to an increased risk of perioperative myocardial ischaemia and stroke, leading to increased morbidity and mortality. The elderly are also at greater risk of respiratory problems particularly if there are existing airway problems, obesity, unstable Chronic Obstructive Pulmonary Disease (COPD) or infection (Andrade, et al., 2016). This is notable, as pneumonia is one of the commoner ECT associated adverse events (Blumberger, et al., 2017). Smoking cessation will reduce the associated risk of anaesthesia (Møller, et al., 2002). The electrical stimulation induced parasympathetic surge seen in younger patients is often attenuated in the elderly; this combined with the likely multiple chronic co-morbidities (Divo, et al., 2014) engenders a greater risk of, and from, refractory tachycardia. A sympathetic surge follows during the clonic phase of a seizure – particularly if etomidate or ketamine are used as the induction agent. The sympathetic surge is associated with a noradrenergic and adrenergic response and hence tachycardia, hypertension, increased venous pressure and an increased cardiac oxygen demand; this latter can cause cardiac ischaemia or infarction if a corresponding increased oxygen supply doesn't follow and may reveal itself by ST depression or elevation (Burd and Kettl, 1998). If ST changes are seen during ECT then troponin (which, whilst it is a non-specific indicator of risk, typically is not elevated by the seizure itself (Duma, et al., 2017) unlike creatine phosphokinase) should be measured, a 12 lead ECG examined and the presence or absence of angina determined. However, chest pain may be absent in the elderly especially in the immediate post-anaesthetic phase. Temporary ST changes in the absence of other features of cardiac ischaemia should be interpreted as a risk factor for infarction and factored into the risk–benefit decision for ECT. There is also an increased likelihood in the elderly of transient, benign arrhythmias (Mirza, *et al.*, 2012). Tachycardia and hypertension can be reduced by pre-treatment with a relatively short acting beta blocker such as esmolol (Boere, *et al.*, 2014). The increased risk of cardiac problems in the elderly is further increased if there has been a recent cardiac event, left ventricular dysfunction or aortic stenosis but is still rare (Bryson, *et al.*, 2013). ECT associated cardiac death is extremely rare (Dennis, *et al.*, 2017; Raj, *et al.*, 2001; Østergaard, *et al.*, 2014) and recent myocardial infarction is not an absolute contraindication to ECT (Magid, *et al.*, 2005; Aloysi, *et al.*, 2011).

The cardiovascular response and the increased oxygen demand during the seizure are associated with an increase in cerebral blood flow and therefore an increased intracranial pressure. Hyperventilation, by reducing CO_2 concentrations, will reduce cerebral blood flow and attenuate this, as will brain autoregulation mechanisms, however, pre-existing increased intracranial pressure (for instance if there is a space occupying lesion) may impair the ability to autoregulate blood flow. Systolic pressure over 220 mmHg increases the risk of haemorrhagic cerebrovascular accidents; if this is anticipated it may be attenuated by pre-treatment with beta blockers. One would anticipate that cerebral aneurysm would be a major risk factor for haemorrhagic stroke, however ECT has been given in those with aneurysm and there are no reported cases to our knowledge of ruptured cerebral aneurysm during ECT (Wilkinson, *et al.*, 2014). Antiplatelet drugs may also increase the impact of any intracranial bleed (Suryanarayana, *et al.*, 2015). Alterations in cerebral blood flow and pressure may also be responsible, in combination with the anaesthetic medications, for the agitation and cognitive impairment of ECT, the risk of which is greater after bilateral treatment, with a high treatment dose–threshold ratio (Sackeim, *et al.*, 1987) and in the elderly (Tomac, *et al.*, 1997), particularly those with pre-existing dementia (Rao, *et al.*, 2000).

The making and communicating of good quality risk assessments, risk minimisation strategies and collaborative risk–benefit decisions are particularly important in the elderly and reveal the importance of the interactions between patient and family, referring teams and anaesthetic and mental health ECT team members.

Practical Considerations

Co-existing dementia creates additional ECT challenges. Alzheimer's and Lewy Body Dementia don't appear to negatively impact efficacy in acute or maintenance depression treatment (Rao, *et al.*, 2000; Rasmussen, *et al.*, 2003; Isserles, *et al.*, 2017) but the risk of post ECT cognitive impairment, unsurprisingly, appears elevated (Rao, *et al.*, 2000; Rasmussen, *et al.*, 2003) and there are potential difficulties with capacity decisions particularly if cognitive performance fluctuates. Case report and notes review evidence exists of the benefit for the treatment of agitation in non-depressed patients with dementia (Glass, *et al.*, 2017).

Seizure threshold can be higher in the elderly (Coffey, *et al.*, 1995). Hyperventilation and reduction of benzodiazepine drugs can be helpful in facilitating a seizure. In the case of failed seizures at 1 Coulomb or 100% of the capacity of the ECT machine there is value in switching to etomidate as the induction agent (Ayhan, *et al.*, 2015).

Cholinesterase inhibitors theoretically have the potential to augment the effect of suxamethonium, to increase the parasympathetic response with possible cardiac rhythm complications and to reduce the seizure threshold. These theoretical risks do not appear to be translating into real-world incidents. Of interest, preliminary studies suggest the potential for cholinesterase inhibitors to ameliorate ECT induced cognitive side effects but further trials are required before translation into practice (Henstra, *et al.*, 2017).

Recommendations

1. ECT is a rapidly effective treatment option, particularly for depression, in the elderly.
2. Medical assessment should be conducted to estimate and mitigate risk.
3. There are additional safety concerns, so careful monitoring is required.
4. Management of cardiac and cognitive side effects should be prioritised.
5. Co-morbid dementia should not prejudice the use of ECT for depression.
6. Practical considerations, including the tendency to higher seizure threshold, can be managed.
7. Co-morbid conditions should be managed prior to treatment.

Acknowledgements

The authors are grateful for the advice of the other members of the Northumberland Tyne and Wear NHS Foundation Trust ECT group.

References

Aloysi A S, Maloutas E, Gomes A, Kellner C H, 2011: Safe resumption of electroconvulsive therapy after non-ST segment elevation myocardial infarction. *J ECT*, 27:e39–41.

Andrade C, Arumugham S S, Thirthalli J, 2016: Adverse effects of electroconvulsive therapy. *Psychiatr Clin North Am*, 39:513–30.

Ayhan Y, Akbulut B B, Karahan S, Gecmez G, Oz G, Gurel S C, Basar K, 2015: Etomidate is associated with longer seizure duration, lower stimulus intensity, and lower number of failed trials in electroconvulsive therapy compared with thiopental. *J ECT*, 31:26–30.

Birkenhäger T K, Pluijms E M, Ju M R, Mulder P G, van den Broek W W, 2010: Influence of age on the efficacy of electroconvulsive therapy in major depression: a retrospective study. *J Affect Disord*, 126:257–61.

Blumberger D M, Seitz D P, Herrmann N, *et al.* 2017: Low medical morbidity and mortality after acute courses of electroconvulsive therapy in a population-based sample. *Acta Psychiatr Scand*, 136:583-93.

Boere E, Birkenhager T K, Groenland T H, van den Broek W W, 2014: Beta-blocking agents during electroconvulsive therapy: a review. *Br J Anaesth*, 113:43–51.

Bryson E O, Popeo D, Briggs M, Pasculli R M, Kellner C H, 2013: Electroconvulsive therapy (ECT) in patients with cardiac disease: hemodynamic changes. *J ECT*, 29:76-7.

Burd J, Kettl P, 1998: Incidence of asystole in electroconvulsive therapy in elderly patients. *The American Journal of Geriatric Psychiatry*.

Callum K G, Gray A J G, Hoile R W, *et al.*, 1999: 'Extremes of age'. In, The 1999 Report of the National Confidential Enquiry into Perioperative Deaths. London. https://www.ncepod.org.uk/1999ea.html

Coffey C E, Lucke J, Weiner R D, Krystal A D, Aque M, 1995: Seizure threshold in electroconvulsive therapy: I. Initial seizure threshold. *Biol Psychiatry*, 37:713–20.

Corcoran T B, Hillyard S, 2011: Cardiopulmonary aspects of anaesthesia for the elderly. *Best Pract Res Clin Anaesthesiol*, 25:329–54.

Coupland C, Dhiman P, Morriss R, Arthur A, Barton G, Hippisley-Cox J, 2011: Antidepressant use and risk of adverse outcomes in older people: population based cohort study. *BMJ*, 343:d4551.

Damm J, Eser D, Schule C, *et al.*, 2010: Influence of age on effectiveness and tolerability of electroconvulsive therapy. *J ECT*, 26:282–8.

Dennis N M, Dennis PA, Shafer A, Weiner RD, Husain MM, 2017: Electroconvulsive therapy and all-cause mortality in Texas, 1998–2013. *J ECT*, 33:22–5.

Divo M J, Martinez C H, Mannino D, 2014: Ageing and the epidemiology of multimorbidity. *Eur Respir J*, 44:1055–68.

Duma A, Pal S, Johnston J, et al., 2017: High-sensitivity cardiac troponin elevation after electroconvulsive therapy: a prospective, observational cohort study. Anesthesiology, 126:643–52.

Flint A J, Rifat S L, 1998: The treatment of psychotic depression in later life: a comparison of pharmacotherapy and ECT. Int J Geriatr Psychiatry, 13:23–8.

Glass O M, Forester B P, Hermida A P, 2017: Electroconvulsive therapy (ECT) for treating agitation in dementia (major neurocognitive disorder) – a promising option. International Psychogeriatrics, 29:717–26.

Griffiths R, Beech F, Brown A, et al., 2014: Perioperative care of the elderly 2014: Association of Anaesthetists of Great Britain and Ireland. Anaesthesia, 69:81–98.

Henstra M J, Jansma E P, van der Velde N, Swart E L, Stek M L, Rhebergen D, 2017: Acetylcholinesterase inhibitors for electroconvulsive therapy-induced cognitive side effects: a systematic review. Int J Geriatr Psychiatry, 32:522–31.

Hickie I, Mason C, Parker G, Brodaty H, 1996: Prediction of ECT response: validation of a refined sign-based (CORE) system for defining melancholia. Br J Psychiatry, 169:68–74.

Isserles M, Daskalakis Z J, Kumar S, Rajji T K, Blumberger D, 2017: Clinical effectiveness and tolerability of electroconvulsive therapy in patients with neuropsychiatric symptoms of dementia. Journal of Alzheimer's Disease: JAD, 57:45–51.

Kellner C H, Geduldig E T, Knapp R G, et al., 2015: More data on speed of remission with ECT in geriatric depression. The British Journal of Psychiatry, 206:167–67.

Kellner C H, Husain M M, Knapp R G, et al., 2016a: Right unilateral ultrabrief pulse ECT in geriatric depression: Phase 1 of the PRIDE Study. Am J Psychiatry, 173:1101–9.

Kellner C H, Husain M M, Knapp R G, et al., 2016b: A novel strategy for continuation ECT in geriatric depression: Phase 2 of the PRIDE Study. Am J Psychiatry, 173:1110–18.

Magid M, Lapid M I, Sampson S M, Mueller P S, 2005: Use of electroconvulsive therapy in a patient 10 days after myocardial infarction. J ECT, 21:182–5.

Mirza M, Strunets A, Shen W-K, Jahangir A, 2012: Mechanisms of arrhythmias and conduction disorders in older adults. Clinics in Geriatric Medicine, 28:555–73.

Møller A M, Villebro N, Pedersen T, Tønnesen H, 2002: Effect of preoperative smoking intervention on postoperative complications: a randomised clinical trial. The Lancet, 359:114–17.

Navarro V, Gasto C, Torres X, et al., 2008: Continuation/maintenance treatment with nortriptyline versus combined nortriptyline and ECT in late-life psychotic depression: a two-year randomized study. The American Journal of Geriatric Psychiatry, 16:498–505.

O'Connor M K, Knapp R, Husain M, et al., 2001: The influence of age on the response of major depression to electroconvulsive therapy: a C.O.R.E. Report. The American Journal of Geriatric Psychiatry, 9:382–90.

O'Leary D, Gill D, Gregory S, Shawcross C, 1994: The effectiveness of real versus simulated electroconvulsive therapy in depressed elderly patients. International Journal of Geriatric Psychiatry, 9:567–71.

Østergaard S D, Bolwig T G, Petrides G, 2014: No causal association between electroconvulsive therapy and death: a summary of a report from the Danish Health and Medicines Authority covering 99,728 treatments. J ECT, 30:263–4.

Raj S S, William H R, Thomas J C, 2001: An analysis of reported deaths following electroconvulsive therapy in Texas, 1993–1998. Psychiatric Services, 52:1095–7.

Rao V, Lyketsos C G, 2000: The benefits and risks of ECT for patients with primary dementia who also suffer from depression. Int J Geriatr Psychiatry, 15:729–35.

Rasmussen K G, Jr., Russell J C, Kung S, et al., 2003: Electroconvulsive therapy for patients with major depression and probable Lewy body dementia. J ECT, 19:103–9.

Rhebergen D, Huisman A, Bouckaert F, et al., 2015: Older age is associated with rapid remission of depression after electroconvulsive therapy: a latent class growth analysis. *The American Journal of Geriatric Psychiatry*, **23**:274–282.

Ryan J, Carriere I, Ritchie K, et al., 2008: Late-life depression and mortality: influence of gender and antidepressant use. *The British Journal of Psychiatry*, **192**:12–18.

Sackeim H A, Decina P, Portnoy S, Neeley P, Malitz S, 1987: Studies of dosage, seizure threshold, and seizure duration in ECT. *Biol Psychiatry*, **22**:249–68.

Spaans H-P, Sienaert P, Bouckaert F, et al., 2015: Speed of remission in elderly patients with depression: electroconvulsive therapy v. medication. *The British Journal of Psychiatry*, **206**:67–71.

Suryanarayana Sharma P M, Tekkatte Jagannatha A, Javali M, et al., 2015: Spontaneous subdural hematoma and antiplatelet therapy: does efficacy of Ticagrelor come with added risk? *Indian Heart Journal*, **67**:S30–5.

Tew J D, Mulsant B H, Haskett R F, et al., 1999: Acute efficacy of ECT in the treatment of major depression in the old-old. *Am J Psychiatry*, **156**:1865–70.

Tomac T A, Rummans T A, Pileggi T S, Li H, 1997: Safety and efficacy of electroconvulsive therapy in patients over age 85. *The American Journal of Geriatric Psychiatry*, **5**:126–30.

Whiteford H A, Degenhardt L, Rehm J, et al., 2010: Global burden of disease attributable to mental and substance use disorders: findings from the Global Burden of Disease Study. *The Lancet*, **382**:1575–86.

Wilkinson A M, Anderson D N, Peters S, 1993: Age and the effects of ECT. *International Journal of Geriatric Psychiatry*, **8**:401–6.

Wilkinson S T, Helgeson L, Ostroff R, 2014: Electroconvulsive therapy and cerebral aneurysms. *J ECT*, **30**:e47–9.

ECT in People with an Intellectual Disability

Peter Cutajar and Jo Jones

Introduction

The evidence base for the use of ECT in people with an intellectual disability is composed almost entirely of case reports or case series. An evidence search on the use of ECT for intellectual disabilities and learning disabilities, including those with autism or catatonia, was conducted on 19 May 2017. The limited nature of this evidence, compounded with specific issues around diagnosis and consent, partially explains why ECT seems to be used less frequently in people with an intellectual disability than in the general population. It is clear, however, that adults with an intellectual disability are susceptible to the whole range of psychiatric disorders seen in the general population and that ECT may be a suitable treatment for them in some clinical situations.

Diagnostic Issues

Mental illness can be reliably diagnosed using standard diagnostic classifications in those people with a mild intellectual disability (Meins, 1995; Hurley, 2006). However diagnosis is more difficult in those with a more severe level of intellectual disability. Diagnostic criteria are very much language-based, so they are less relevant to people with significant communication difficulties. It is then much more difficult, if not impossible, to assess cardinal features of mental illness such as low self-esteem, guilt (Hemmings, 2007), delusions or hallucinations. The presence of an intellectual disability will alter the way that signs of mental illness manifest themselves. Psychiatric diagnosis can be difficult because of the frequent assumption that symptoms could be part of the presentation of the intellectual disability, because of 'diagnostic overshadowing' (Santosh and Baird, 1999). However, Hayes *et al.* (2011) found that people with severe and profound intellectual disabilities show clear and measureable signs of low mood, and that there is a relationship between low mood and challenging behaviour, and that the Mood, Interest and Pleasure Questionnaire (MIPQ) was a strong predictor. Walton and Kerr (2016) commented that the Aberrant Behaviour Checklist proved useful as a tool to aid the diagnostic process. Their review, which focuses on depression, includes a summary table of instruments used in various studies (e.g. Diagnostic Assessment for the Severely Handicapped–II, Mood and Anxiety Semi-structured Interview). They conclude that depression is probably underdiagnosed in this population and that assessment by an experienced clinician is superior to the use of rating scales alone. The 'Diagnostic Criteria for Psychiatric Disorders for Use with Adults with Learning Disabilities/Mental Retardation' (DC–LD), (Royal College of Psychiatrists, 2001) can be useful in standardising the diagnosis of mental illness in those with a moderate to severe intellectual disability; it is based on a consensus of practice amongst psychiatrists working with people with intellectual disability. The NICE guideline 'Mental health problems in people with learning disabilities: prevention, assessment and management' (2016) provides an assessment process framework and suggests interventions to be considered.

Epidemiology of Psychiatric Disorders in People with an Intellectual Disability

There is an increased prevalence of psychiatric disorders (including depression) in people with an intellectual disability, compared to the general population (Cooper *et al.*, 2007; Cooper *et al.*, 2008; Smiley *et al.*, 2007). Deb *et al.* (2001) found an overall rate of psychiatric disorders of 14.4% in a sample of 90 adults with a mild intellectual disability. Bailey (2007) found a prevalence rate of psychiatric disorders in people with a moderate to profound intellectual disability of 57% (DC–LD diagnoses); this is more than three times the rate found in a similar study of the general population (Meltzer *et al.*, 1995). People with a more severe intellectual disability have a higher prevalence of psychiatric disorder (Cooper and Bailey, 2001). In people with intellectual disability affective disorders are associated with female gender, smoking, number of primary care physician appointments and preceding life events (Cooper *et al.*, 2008).

Robertson and colleagues (2011) described the benefits of targeted health checks in, and found evidence of, health gain due to mood stabilisation following medication review by psychiatrists.

Use of ECT in People with Intellectual Disability and Mood Disorders

People with a mild intellectual disability tend to have a similar presentation of depression to the general population. Those with a more severe intellectual disability, tend to present with somatic and behavioural changes, including energy level changes, sleep and appetite changes and social withdrawal (Vanstraelen *et al.*, 2003).

The paucity of evidence base pertaining to the use of ECT in people with intellectual disabilities was highlighted in the review of interventions for adults with mild intellectual disabilities and mental ill-health by Osago and Cooper (2016). There were no ECT studies that met their inclusion criteria. Thus, we often have to extrapolate from studies in the general population.

The literature in the area of intellectual disability comprises case series and case reports about the use of ECT in mood disorders in this population. These are summarised in Table 7.1.

However, some reports group all mood disorders in one study category making it difficult to distinguish response by diagnosis. There is also likely to be some publication bias in reporting mainly the positive effects of ECT in people with intellectual disability and mood disorders, although some case series do include some patients who have not responded to ECT. In most reports, ECT was the treatment of last resort. It was used most frequently in medication-resistant, psychotic depression associated with a serious risk to physical health.

Clinical consensus guidelines on the management of intellectual disability include ECT as part of the range of treatments available depending on clinical need (e.g. Bhaumik *et al.*, 2015). As described in the NICE guidance (2016), consideration must be given to the whole range of available treatment for the management of depression. ECT can be used in conjunction with other therapies.

Table 7.1 ECT in mood disorders in intellectual disability (ID)

Study	n	Patient	Treatment	Outcome	Comments
Siegel et al. (2012)	1	Boy aet 16, moderate ID, ASD, bipolar 1 Non-adherent with lithium	ECT x 10	Responded	Weekly maintenance ECT
Friedlander & Solomons (2002)	10	ID and psychiatric disorders of varying severity Mood disorders (6); Schizo-affective (4)	Bilateral ECT	Good outcome in 7/10	
Torr and d'Abrera (2014)	1	23-year-old woman Down syndrome (mosaic) Prolonged severe resistant depression Catatonic features	Bilateral ECT x 5	Responded	Maintenance ECT
Gensheimer et al. (2002)	1	Boy aet 15, Down syndrome Resistant major depressive disorder	Bilateral ECT x 4	Responded	
Chopra & Sinha (2002)	5	Mania (3) Recurrent depression (1) Unspecified psychosis (1)		All responded	Two patients had maintenance ECT No adverse effects
Reinblatt et al. (2004)	20	Mild (7) Moderate (5) Severe (1) Profound (7) ID Affective disorder (12) Psychosis (6) Intermittent explosive disorder (2) – both profound ID		All improved apart from those with intermittent explosive disorder (no response)	Irritability and hyperactivity may predict good response to ECT
Kessler (2004)	4	Mild ID, Depression (1), Rapid cycling bipolar (1), Mania (1), Schizoaffective (1)		Positive	Extensive follow-up information
Cutajar & Wilson (1999)	8	Depression (7) Autism, ID and catatonia (1) Mild ID (4) and Moderate ID (4)		Five responded (including one with post-natal depression) Best response in people with biological features and psychosis	One developed status epilepticus requiring iv anticonvulsants

Table 7.1 (cont.)

Study	n	Patient	Treatment	Outcome	Comments
Cutajar et al. (1998)	1	Mild ID post-natal depression	ECT x 6	Responded	
Ligas et al. (2009)	1	Bipolar disorder with catatonic features	Bilateral ECT	Full recovery	
Everman & Stoudemire (1994)	1	Acute mania, refractory	Unilateral ECT x 8	Responded	
Mackay & Wilson (2007)	1	Mild ID and major depression	ECT and CBT	Recovery	

ECT in People with an Intellectual Disability, Autism and Catatonia

Catatonia is a syndrome with evidence of motor dysregulation (see Chapters 10 and 11). Whilst most usually seen as motor slowing, it can also manifest as motor excitation. It was previously seen as a sub-type of schizophrenia, but Fink and Taylor (2003) argued the case for catatonia as a distinct syndrome, they also refer to 'catatonic spectrum' behaviours.

DSM-5 (American Psychiatric Association, 2013) recognises three types of catatonia:

Catatonia associated with a recognised mental disorder (including neurodevelopmental disorder), catatonia due to an underlying medical condition and catatonia not elsewhere classified (NEC).

In the last 20 years the presence of catatonic symptoms in those with autism spectrum disorder (ASD) has become increasingly recognised. Wing and Shah (2000) examined 506 patients with ASD for motor symptoms. Of their referrals aged 15 years or older, 17% had 'catatonia like deterioration'. They described psychological approaches to the management of catatonia-like deterioration in autism spectrum disorders (Shah and Wing, 2006).

Fink (2013) argues that catatonia can be operationally defined by treatment responsiveness: 'Patients who exhibit two or more motor signs of catatonia (recognized in Catatonia Rating Scales) for more than 24 h, and that quickly improve with test doses of lorazepam, are presumptively diagnosed as suffering from catatonia. Recovery of the illness with relief of the motor and vegetative signs after treatment with benzodiazepines and ECT validates the diagnosis.' Treatment responsiveness defining a diagnosis departs from the usually accepted practice of agreeing a classification based on common aetiology and/or description of symptoms and so the use of this approach is open to challenge.

Catatonia is a recognised indication for the use of ECT (NICE, 2003) but consideration of the diagnosis and treatment of catatonia in the intellectual disabilities/ASD context is complex. Motor phenomena within ASD are recognised but do not necessarily equate to the clinical condition of 'catatonia' (Shah and Wing, 2006). The evidence for use of ECT is case series based and the long term outcomes are contested (De Jong et al., 2014). We highlight in Table 7.2 some of the available literature; the case studies in the literature regarding catatonia in ASD and intellectual disabilities contain powerful narratives.

Dhossche, Shah and Wing (2006) produced treatment 'blueprints', which grade the acuteness and severity of the catatonic presentations. Before catatonia is diagnosed there should be a full work up of motor symptoms and a search for 'culprit medications.' Mild catatonia can be managed by psychological, supportive and environmental approaches (Shah and Wing, 2006),

Table 7.2 ECT in people with intellectual disability, autism and catatonia

Study	n	Patient(s)	Treatment	Outcome	Comments
Cutajar & Wilson (1999)	1	Autism, ID, catatonia	No response to antidepressants Bilateral ECT	No response	
Zaw et al. (1999)	1	Boy age 14, moderate ID, autism, catatonic stupor, affective components	No response to antidepressants Bilateral ECT	Response after 3x ECT-13 x total	Maintained on lithium / antipsychotic- history suggestive of bipolar disorder
Wachtel et al. (2010a)	1	Autism, Mild ID, Malignant catatonia,	Right UL ECT x10, then bilateral	No response to UL, slowly improved with BL	Maintenance ECT Lithium + olanzapine
Wachtel et al (2010b)	3	Autism, catatonia			Maintenance ECT
Wachtel et al. (2010c)	1	Autism, mild ID, 3 year history of severe depression with catatonic features and self-harm	Multiple antipsychotic trials and use of increasing lorazepam prior to ECT. Bi-temporal ECT	Dramatic response after first ECT	Maintained with ECT twice weekly, lithium, duloxetine, lorazepam & riluzole
Mazzone et al. (2014)	3	Autistic spectrum disorder, ID, catatonia	Medication	Responded without ECT	This is a review paper with a useful table of a number of case reports exploring catatonia in ASD, some treated by ECT.
Sajith et al. (2017)	2	Autism, ID, self-harm, poss 'agitated catatonia'	Medication includes Lorazepam max 4mg High dose rUL ECT	Reduction in symptoms - 1- temporary reduction	Maintenance ECT 1 - no long term F/U
Haq and Ghaziuddin (2014)	2	1. 16yr old with autism, catatonic feature and aggression (no ID?) 2. 15yr old with moderate ID, autism and 'agitated catatonia'	Bilateral ECT to both	Dramatic response in both 2. required intense treatment initially – mania like behaviour	1. Maintenance ECT 2 x per month total > 4yrs treatment and lorazepam 20–24mg; riluzole and valproate; 2. Maintenance ECT weekly for 5 months; relapsed at 11mths; restarted ECT with dramatic effect; at 20mths on ECT every 5 days, 16mgs lorazepam, lithium, trazodone and oxcarbazepine

in combination with lorazepam. In severe catatonia a trial of lorazepam 6-24 mg/ day, is recommended as initial treatment, prior to consideration of bilateral ECT (Fink *et al.*, 2006).

Dhossche *et al.* (2010) reviewed the literature on neurotransmitter function to develop a chemical theory for catatonic symptoms in ASD and hypothesised that central GABA dysfunction may be the cause. They summarise findings from genetic and immunological research and suggest a possible mechanism of action of ECT on neurotransmitter function (see Chapter 2).

De Jong *et al.* (2014) systematically reviewed the published literature on treatment interventions for catatonia in ASD. All the evidence consisted of case reports and case series. They considered 22 papers describing 28 cases. The majority of cases were teenage men given bilateral ECT and sometimes maintenance ECT and medication. Few studies of behavioural or sensory interventions have been published. They conclude that early intervention is helpful, and a range of treatments may be used. Most published cases are based on clinician impression; they describe a partial acute response to ECT and/or lorazepam. In many cases maintenance ECT was used. The literature on the prevalence and management of catatonia in ASD is also reviewed by Mazzone *et al.* (2014); this includes more case studies where ECT was used.

Use of ECT in People with an Intellectual Disability and Severe Challenging Behaviour

There are a number of case reports about the use of ECT in people with intellectual disability and self-injurious behaviour or aggression; some of these people also had ASD. Minshawi *et al.* (2015) reviewed use of ECT in people with intellectual disability and self-injurious behaviour or aggression. Additional case reports are summarised in Table 7.3.

In their review D'Agati *et al.* (2017) cite 16 published reports of children and adolescents with developmental disorders and self-injurious behaviour who were treated with ECT. These include eight who also had ASD. They invoke a possible mechanism of action of ECT via the GABA-ergic tone (see Chapter 2) to explain its action in self-injurious behaviour. They raise the possibility that other forms of neuromodulation, such as transcranial magnetic stimulation (Chapter 15), may have therapeutic potential. The interaction between psychiatric disorder, physical health, intellectual disability and challenging behaviour is a complex one. Not all challenging behaviour is an expression of psychiatric disorder; but untreated psychiatric disorder behaviours (Hemmings, 2007) and physical ill-health (Crocker *et al.*, 2014) in people with intellectual disability may be a factor in the manifestation of challenging behaviour. Challenging behaviour needs to be assessed, in order to implement appropriate treatment plans that can be audited (Deb *et al.*, 2006).

Self-injurious behaviour can be difficult to manage in this population and often persists for many years (Taylor *et al.*, 2010). Self-injury is more common in people with a more severe intellectual disability, autism or communication deficits (McClintock *et al.*, 2003).

Table 7.3 ECT in people with intellectual disability (ID) and severe challenging behaviour

Study	n	Patient	Treatment	Outcome
Consoli *et al.* (2013)	4	ID, aggression, self harm, resistant to psychological and drug treatment aet 12–14	ECT x 16 – 24	Significant reduction in aggression
Thuppal & Fink (1999)	1	Moderate ID, agitation, aggression	Bilateral ECT x 13	Marked improvement

Numerous psychopharmacological treatments have been suggested for the management of self-injury occurring in people with intellectual disability or autism, including antipsychotics, antidepressants, mood stabilisers, anxiolytics and opioid antagonists. The range indicates how difficult it can be to manage effectively and underlines the paucity of evidence.

There are difficulties in using ECT in these cases: self-injurious behaviour is not a diagnosis. The clinical heterogeneity of the reported cases illustrates the need to advise caution. Reported response to ECT raises the possibility that the underlying condition might have been a mood disorder or catatonia. However, in cases of severe persistent self-injury where other pharmacological or psychological interventions have failed, a trial of ECT could be considered.

This aspect of ECT use is becoming more prominent in recent literature which ascribes self-injurious behaviour and aggressive behaviour in ASD to catatonia. Whilst this might explain the efficacy of ECT, and justify its use, clinicians need to continue to study and understand these behaviours within their wider environmental context. As well as considering biological aspects, the role of sensory and psychological aspects needs to be considered, along with subsequent implications for treatment. Positive Behaviour Support (Hieneman, 2015) is increasingly being seen as part of the multidisciplinary approach to the management of challenging behaviour.

The NICE guidance on challenging behaviour and learning disabilities (2015) offers a structured framework to help the clinicians/clinical team assess the multiple factors likely to underlie behaviour that challenges (e.g. including a functional analysis of behaviour) and advises on how to formulate interventions. ECT is not mentioned in this guidance.

ECT Used in Other Situations

The use of ECT in people with syndromes associated with intellectual disabilities is summarised in Table 7.4, and in people with intellectual disabilities and schizophrenia in Table 7.5.

Observations on Use of ECT by Psychiatrists Working with People with an Intellectual Disability

Cutajar & Wilson (1999) studied the use of ECT during the years 1990–95 by consultant psychiatrists working with people with an intellectual disability in the East Midlands, UK (population 4.7 million). The use of ECT was low compared to general adult psychiatry; the suggested reasons for this included diagnostic difficulties, problems in obtaining consent and ECT being considered as a treatment of last resort.

Sayal & Bernard (1998) reported that trainee psychiatrists were less likely to suggest ECT for depressive illness in vignettes of cases of mild intellectual disability, even though they diagnosed psychotic depression more frequently in this group.

In their review of the use of ECT in people with intellectual disabilities, Collins *et al.* (2012) argued that ECT should not be seen as a treatment of last resort; given that, where indicated, ECT can produce dramatic improvement, it needs earlier consideration to minimise suffering, and could also reduce costs in terms of reduced levels of staffing and supervision required.

Similarly, in their review of the use of ECT in people with intellectual disability and concurrent psychiatric disorder, Little *et al.* (2002) concluded that there was a delay in the

Table 7.4 ECT in syndromes associated with intellectual disability (ID)

Study	n	Patients	Treatment	Outcome
Warren et al. (1989)	3	Five, aged 17–38 Down syndrome, of which three were given ECT	Laterality not specified	All three who were given ECT responded
Lazarus et al. (1990)	2	Down syndrome Severe depression	Bilateral ECT	Both responded
Gensheimer et al. 2002	1	Boy aged 15, Down syndrome Resistant major depressive disorder	Bilateral ECT	Responded
Poser & Trutia (2015)	1	25-year-old woman with Prader–Willi and features of catatonia and depression	Bilateral ECT	Some improvement in catatonic features and mood after some of the ECT treatments
Gothelf et al. (1999)	1	Velocardiofacial syndrome (22q11.2 deletion) and schizophrenia	Laterality not specified	No response
Renshaw et al. (1992)	1	Tay–Sachs disease and severe depression	Unilateral ECT	Responded

Table 7.5 ECT in intellectual disabiltity (ID) and schizophrenia

Study	n	Patient	Treatment	Outcome	Comments
Vowels et al. (2014)	1	18-year-old, moderate ID schizophrenia	Bilateral ECT	Responded	Continuation ECT
Chanpattana (1999)	3	Moderate ID (2) Severe ID (1) Schizophrenia	Bilateral ECT	All improved	All received maintenance ECT

use of ECT, yet, when there is a positive response to ECT, this is often reported as rapid. They discussed the possible ethical issues that could explain this reluctance in using ECT, which could be related to the paucity of the available evidence base; ECT is then used as a treatment of last resort. This situation raises the ethical issue of giving ECT to people who do not have the capacity to consent; carers can feel uneasy about the administration of ECT to this population.

The literature relevant to this topic indicates that ECT is used relatively less in people with an intellectual disability than in the general population; there are some reasons for this, including the fact that the literature is limited to case studies, as well as consent issues.

Conclusion

The evidence base for the use of ECT in this population is limited and there have been no randomised controlled trials. Case reports often lack information about concomitant medication, psychological intervention, or social changes happening during the course of ECT and are published when positive responses to treatment are described. The literature available is generally lacking in quantifiable outcome data.

As in the general population, ECT has not been restricted to the treatment of depressive disorders. Most case descriptions are of patients whose psychiatric disorder has failed to respond to medication or of patients who exhibit life-threatening behaviours.

There are case reports of ECT being used in people with an intellectual disability, autism and challenging behaviour not responding to other treatment. 'Challenging behaviour' is not a diagnosis; each case needs to be assessed on its own merits and the possibility kept in mind that the challenging behaviour could be a sign of mental illness.

The concept of catatonia in the literature seems to be broadening with respect to people with intellectual disabilities and/or autism, to include exacerbations of self-injurious behaviour (not a diagnosis), leading to the use of ECT, sometimes as maintenance treatment. It is clinically important to ensure that, in individual patients, the full range of potential contributory factors are assessed, including 'culprit' medication as described earlier (see Dhossche, Shah and Wing, 2006).

Whilst use of ECT seems to be less frequent in this population, intellectual disability per se is not a contra-indication to the use of ECT. Many of the case reports indicate that ECT is considered as a treatment of last resort; and can be effective when indicated. Collins *et al.* (2012) in their literature review make the case for prompt treatment with ECT where indicated.

Consideration of the use of ECT can be delayed due to the complexity of consent issues. These can be resolved through multidisciplinary decision-making; a second psychiatric opinion can be useful even if not obligatory. The Mental Capacity Act has clarified the decision-making process for people who do not have capacity to consent to ECT. This area is covered in detail in Chapter 28.

Recommendations

- It is good practice to consider the use of ECT in carefully selected cases where clinically indicated, usually where the psychiatric disorder has proved refractory, where there are unacceptable adverse effects of medication, or where the clinical condition of the patient has deteriorated severely.
- Intellectual disability of any severity is not a contra-indication to the use of ECT.
- In ASD with severe catatonia, ECT should be considered, subject to detailed assessment, formulation, after medication trial and other supportive treatment have been tried and where the risks are severe. The law on consent should not be an insurmountable barrier to the use of ECT where it is clinically indicated.
- Outcome measures relevant to the condition being treated should be used to assess the efficacy of ECT.
- It is good practice to ensure that the decision to prescribe ECT includes assessment and advice by a specialist in the psychiatry of intellectual disability as well as a psychiatrist with expertise in ECT.
- We need to keep in mind the possibility of positive reporting bias in an area where most of the evidence base consists of case reports. When a decision is made to prescribe ECT for people with an intellectual disability, care must be taken to prepare the person and carers for this treatment, regardless of their capacity to consent to treatment. There is help in the form of leaflets; information is available on the Royal College of Psychiatrists' website (https://www.rcpsych.ac.uk).

- Pre-treatment visits to the ECT suite, or the use of photos or videos of the ECT suite and social stories might also be helpful in the preparation process.
- The use of ECT in this population, and related issues, continue to be a fertile ground for further research.

Acknowledgement

The authors wish to thank Samantha Roberts, Nottinghamshire Healthcare NHS Foundation Trust, Library and Knowledge Services.

References

American Psychiatric Association (2013). *Diagnostic and Statistical Manual of Mental Disorders, Fifth Edition.* Washington, DC, American Psychiatric Association Publishing Inc.

Bailey, N. M. (2007). Prevalence of psychiatric disorders in adults with moderate to profound learning disabilities. *Advances in Mental Health and Learning Disabilities*, **1**, 36–44.

Bhaumik, S., Branford, D., Barrett, M. & Kumar Gangadharan, S. (2015). *The Frith prescribing guidelines for people with intellectual disability.* Wiley-Blackwell.

Chanpattana, W. (1999). Maintenance ECT in mentally retarded, treatment-resistant schizophrenic patients. *Journal of ECT*, **15**, 150–3.

Chopra, V. K. & Sinha, V. K. (2002). ECT in mentally retarded subjects with psychiatric illness. *Indian Journal of Psychiatry*, **44**, 57–64.

Collins, J., Halder, N. & Chaudry, N. (2012). Use of ECT in patients with an intellectual disability: review. *The Psychiatrist*, **36**, 55–60.

Consoli, A., Cohen, J., Bodeau, N., Guinchat, V., Wachtel, L. & Cohen, D. (2013). Electroconvulsive therapy in adolescents with intellectual disability and severe self-injurious behaviour and aggression: a retrospective study. *European Child Adolescent Psychiatry*, **22**, 55–62.

Cooper, S. A. & Bailey, N. M. (2001). Psychiatric disorders amongst adults with learning disabilities – prevalence and relationship to ability level. *Irish Journal of Psychological Medicine*, **18**, 45–53.

Cooper, S. A., Smiley, E., Morrison, J., *et al.* (2007). Mental ill-health in adults with intellectual disabilities: prevalence and associated factors. *British Journal of Psychiatry*, **190**, 27–35.

Cooper, S. A., Smiley, E., Allan, L., *et al.*, (2008). Prevalence and incidence of affective disorders and related factors: Observational study. *Journal of Intellectual Disability Research*, **52**, 725.

Crocker, A. G., Prokić, A., Morin, D. & Reyes, A. (2014). Intellectual disability and co-occurring mental health and physical disorders in aggressive behaviour. *Journal of Intellectual Disability Research*, **58**, 1032–44.

Cutajar, P., Wilson, D. N. & Mukherjee, T. (1998). ECT used in depression following childbirth, in a woman with learning disabilities. *British Journal of Learning Disabilities*, **26**, 115–17.

Cutajar, P. & Wilson, D. (1999). The use of ECT in intellectual disability. *Journal of Intellectual Disability Research*, **43**, 421–7.

D'Agati, D., Chang, A. D., Wachtel, L. E. & Reti, I. M. (2017). Treatment of severe self-injurious behaviour in autism spectrum disorder by neuromodulation. *Journal of ECT*, **33**, 7–11.

Deb, S., Thomas, M. & Bright, C. (2001). Mental disorder in adults with intellectual disability. 1: Prevalence of functional psychiatric illness among a community based sample population aged between 16 and 64 years. *Journal of Intellectual Disability Research*, **45**, 495–505.

Deb, S., Clarke, D., & Unwin, G. (2006). *Using medication to manage behaviour problems among adults with a learning disability.* University of Birmingham.

De Jong, H., Bunton, P. & Hare D.J. (2014). A systematic review of interventions used to treat catatonic symptoms in people with autistic spectrum disorder. *J Autism Dev Disorder*, **44**, 2127–36.

Dhossche, D. M., Shah, A. & Wing, L. (2006). Blue prints for the assessment, treatment and future study of Catatonia in Autistic Spectrum Disorders. *International Review of Neurobiology*, **72**, 267–84.

Dhossche, D. M., Stoppelbein, L., Rout, U. K. (2010). Etiopathogenesis of catatonia: generalizations and working hypotheses. *Journal of ECT*, **26**, 253–8.

Everman, D. B. & Stoudemire, A. (1994). Bipolar disorder associated with Klinefelter's syndrome and other chromosomal abnormalities. *Psychosomatics*, **35**, 35–40.

Fink, M. & Taylor, M. A. (2003) *Catatonia: A clinician's guide to diagnosis and treatment*. New York, Cambridge University Press.

Fink M., Taylor, M. A. and Ghaziuddin, N. (2006). Catatonia in autistic spectrum disorders: A medical treatment algorithm. *International Review of Neurobiology*, **72**, 233–44.

Fink M. (2013). Rediscovering catatonia: the biography of a treatable condition. *Acta Psychiatrica Scandinavica*, **127**, (Suppl. 441), 1–47.

Friedlander, R. I. & Solomons, K. (2002). ECT: use in individuals with mental retardation. *Journal of ECT*, **18**, 38–42.

Gensheimer, P. M., Meighen, K. G. & McDougle, C. J. (2002). ECT in an adolescent with Down syndrome and treatment-refractory major depressive disorder. *Journal of Developmental and Physical Disabilities*, **14**, 291–95.

Gothelf, D., Frisch, A., Munitz, H., *et al.* (1999). Clinical characteristics of schizophrenia associated with velo-cardio-facial syndrome. *Schizophrenia Research*, **35**, 105–12.

Haq, A. U. & Ghaziuddin, N. (2014). Maintenance electroconvulsive therapy for aggression and self-injurious behavior in two adolescents with autism and catatonia. *Journal of Neuropsychiatry and Clinical Neurosciences*, **26**, 64–72.

Hayes, S., McGuire, B., O'Neill, M., Oliver, C. & Morison, T. (2011). Low mood and challenging behaviour in people with severe and profound intellectual disabilities. *Journal of Intellectual Disability Research*, **55**, 182–9.

Hemmings, C. (2007) The relationships between challenging behaviours and psychiatric disorders in people with severe intellectual disabilities. In *Psychiatric and Behavioural Disorders in Intellectual and Developmental Disabilities* (ed: N. Bouras & G. Holt), pp 62–75. Cambridge: Cambridge University Press.

Hieneman, M. (2015). Positive behavior support for individuals with behavior challenges. *Behavior Analysis in Practice*, **8**, 101–8.

Hurley, A.D. (2006). Mood disorders in intellectual disabilities. *Current Opinion in Psychiatry*, **19**, 465–9.

Kessler, R. (2004). Electroconvulsive therapy for affective disorders in persons with mental retardation. *Psychiatric Quarterly*, **75**, 99–104.

Lazarus, A., Jaffe, R. L. & Dubin, W. R. (1990) Electroconvulsive therapy and major depression in Down's syndrome. *Journal of Clinical Psychiatry*, **51**, 422–5.

Ligas, A., Petrides, G., Istafanous, R. & Kellner, C. H. (2009). Successful electroconvulsive therapy in a patient with intellectual disability and bipolar disorder, and catatonic features misdiagnosed as encephalopathy. *Journal of ECT*, **25**, 202–4.

Little, J. D., McFarlane, J. & Ducharme, H. M. (2002). ECT use delayed in the presence of comorbid mental retardation: a review of clinical and ethical issues. *Journal of ECT*, **18**, 218–22.

Mackay, F. & Wilson, C. (2007). Successful multi-disciplinary and multi-treatment working for a person with learning disability who experienced major depressive disorder. *Learning Disability Review*, **12**, 39–47.

Mazzone, L., Postorino, V., Valeri, G. & Vicari, S. (2014). Catatonia in autism: prevalence and management. *CNS Drugs*, **28**, 205–15.

McClintock, K., Hall, S. & Oliver, C. (2003). Risk markers associated with challenging behaviours in people with intellectual disabilities: a meta-analytic study. *Journal of Intellectual Disability Research*, **47**, 405–16.

Meins, W. (1995). Symptoms of major depression in mentally retarded adults. *Journal of Intellectual Disability Research*, **39**, 41–5.

Meltzer, H., Gill, B., Peeticrew, M. & Hinds, K. (1995) *OPCS Survey of psychiatric morbidity in Great Britain. Report 1. The prevalence of psychiatric morbidity among adults living in private households*. London: HMSO.

Minshawi, N. F., Hurwitz, S., Morriss, D. & McDougle, C. J. (2015). Multidisciplinary assessment and treatment of self-injurious behaviour in autism spectrum disorder and intellectual disability: Integration of psychological and biological theory and approach. *J Autism Dev Disorder*, **45**, 1541–68.

NICE (2003). Guidance on the use of ECT, Technology Appraisal 59.

NICE (2015). Challenging behaviour and learning disabilities: prevention and interventions for people with learning disabilities whose behaviour challenges. NICE guideline. Published 29 May: nice.org.uk/guidance/ng11

NICE (2016). Mental health problems in people with learning disabilities: prevention, assessment and management. NICE guideline. Published 14 September: nice.org.uk/guidance/ng54

Osugo, M. & Cooper, S.-A. (2016). Interventions for adults with mild intellectual disabilities and mental ill-health: a systematic review. *Journal of Intellectual Disability Research*, **60**, 615–22.

Poser, H. M. & Trutia, A. E. Treatment of a Prader-Willi patient with recurrent catatonia (2015). *Case Reports in Psychiatry*, Volume 2015, 1–4.

Reinblatt, S. P., Rifkin, A. & Freeman, J. (2004). The efficacy of ECT in adults with mental retardation experiencing psychiatric disorders. *Journal of ECT*, **20**, 208–12.

Renshaw, P. R., Stern, T. A., Welch, C., *et al.* (1992). Electroconvulsive therapy treatment of depression in a patient with adult GM2 gangliosidosis. *Annals of Neurology*, **31**, 342–4.

Robertson, J., Roberts, H., Emerson, E., Turner, S. & Greig, R. (2011). The impact of health checks for people with intellectual disabilities: a systematic review of evidence. *Journal of Intellectual Disability Research*, **55**, 1009–19.

Royal College of Psychiatrists (2001). *Diagnostic Criteria for Psychiatric Disorders for Use with Adults with Learning Disabilities/ Mental Retardation (DC–LD)*. London: Gaskell.

Sajith, S. G., Liew, S. F. & Tor, P.C. (2017). Response to electroconvulsive therapy in patients with autism spectrum disorder and intractable challenging behaviors associated with symptoms of catatonia. *Journal of ECT*, **33**, 63–7.

Santosh, P. J. and Baird, G. (1999). Psychopharmacotherapy in children and adults with intellectual disability. *Lancet*, **354**, 233–42.

Sayal, K. & Bernard, S. (1998). Trainees' assessment and management of mental illness in adults with mild intellectual disability. *Psychiatric Bulletin*, **22**, 571–2.

Shah, A. & Wing, L. (2006). Psychological approaches to chronic catatonia-like deterioration in autistic spectrum disorders. *International Review of Neurobiology*, **72**, 245–64.

Siegel, M., Milligan, B., Robbins, D. & Prentice, G. (2012). Electroconvulsive therapy in an adolescent with autism and bipolar I disorder. *Journal of ECT*, **28**, 252–5.

Smiley, E., Cooper, S. A., Finlayson, J., Jackson, A., Allan, L., Mantry, D., McGrother, C., McConnachie, A. & Morrison, J. (2007). Incidence and predictors of mental ill-health in adults with intellectual disabilities: prospective study. *The British Journal of Psychiatry*, **191**, 313–19.

Taylor, L., Oliver, C. & Murphy, G. (2010). The chronicity of self-injurious behaviour: a long-term follow-up of a total population study. *Journal of Applied Research in Intellectual Disabilities*, **24**, 105–17.

Thuppal, M. & Fink, M. (1999). Electroconvulsive therapy and mental retardation. *Journal of ECT*, **15**, 140–9.

Torr, J. & D'Abrera, J. C. (2014). Maintenance electroconvulsive therapy for depression with catatonia in a young woman with

Down Syndrome. *Journal of ECT*, **30**, 332–6.

Vanstraelen, M., Holt, G., & Bouras, N. (2003). Adults with learning disabilities and psychiatric problems. In *seminars in the psychiatry of learning disabilities* (ed: W Fraser & M. Kerr), pp 155–69. London: Gaskell.

Vowels, E. C., Lingappa, H. L. & Bastiampillai, T. (2014). Combination clozapine and electroconvulsive therapy in a patient with schizophrenia and comorbid intellectual disability. *Australian & New Zealand Journal of Psychiatry*, **48**, 689–90.

Wachtel, L., Griffin, M., Dhossche, D. & Reti, I. (2010a). Brief report: Electroconvulsive therapy for malignant catatonia in an autistic adolescent. *Autism*, **14**, 349–58.

Wachtel, L., Hermida, A. & Dhossche, D. (2010b). Maintenance electroconvulsive therapy in autistic catatonia. *Progress in Neuro-Psychopharmacology and Biological Psychiatry*, **34**, 581–7.

Wachtel, L., Griffin, M. & Reti, I. (2010c). Electroconvulsive therapy in a man with autism experiencing severe depression, catatonia and self-injury. *Journal of ECT*, **26**, 70–3.

Walton, C. & Kerr, M. (2016). Severe intellectual disability: systematic review of the prevalence and nature of presentation of unipolar depression. *Journal of Applied Research in Intellectual Disabilities*, **29**, 395–408.

Warren, A. C., Holroyd, S. & Folstein, M. F. (1989). Major depression in Down's syndrome. *British Journal of Psychiatry*, **155**, 202–5.

Wing, L. & Shah, A. (2000). Catatonia in autistic spectrum disorders. *British Journal of Psychiatry*, **176**, 357–62.

Zaw, F. K. M., Bates, G. D. L., Murali, V., *et al.* (1999). Catatonia, autism and ECT. *Developmental Medicine and Child Neurology*, **41**, 843–5.

ECT in Pregnancy and Postnatally

Alain Gregoire and Joanne Spoors

Poor maternal mental health in pregnancy and postnatally has an obvious negative impact on the mother but may also adversely affect the child and the wider family. The treatment of severe mental illness during this period can be complicated by several factors: the potential for adverse effects of medication on the foetus or breastfed infant; the reduced acceptability of even low levels of risk; the reduced tolerability of adverse effects for women at this critical and demanding time in their lives; the potential for deterioration into extremely severe and high risk illness, particularly postnatally and its rapidity; and the urgency required for achieving recovery to reduce the risk of long term consequences for both mother and child. Electroconvulsive therapy (ECT), as an alternative or adjunctive treatment for severe perinatal mental illness, may offer some patients fewer such disadvantages than medication or psychological therapies, alone or in combination. The indications for ECT in the perinatal period are the same as those in a non-perinatal population. It has been suggested ECT is not considered often enough in the perinatal period (Focht & Kellner 2012). NICE guidelines state ECT should be considered for pregnant women with severe depression, severe mixed affective states or mania, or catatonia, whose physical health or that of the foetus is at serious risk (NICE 2015). There are no prospective randomised control trials assessing the risk and benefit of ECT in the perinatal population but retrospective data have been collected that can help us evaluate whether ECT is both an effective and safe treatment option.

ECT during Pregnancy

Two studies have provided retrospective data from uncontrolled cases of ECT use in pregnancy. Results from these must be interpreted with considerable caution due to the reporting and publication biases inherent in such data and the variability in intervention as well as outcome definitions and detection. Their findings are summarised for completeness rather than reliability, as they may provide a basis for precautions rather than quotable complication rates. Anderson and Reti (2009) reported on 339 cases of ECT use during pregnancy between 1941 and 2007. In the majority of cases, patients were recorded as having depression and where efficacy data was available, 78% of cases reported at least partial remission. There were thought to be 11 cases in which foetal or neonatal complications were related to ECT and 18 in which maternal complications were likely related to the ECT. Almost all the complications were transient and not life threatening to mother or foetus. They included foetal arrhythmias, vaginal bleeding and uterine contractions, but one foetal death occurred, secondary to status epilepticus. There was one miscarriage in the first trimester 24 hours after ECT and one case of multiple maternal cortical and deep white matter infarctions after multiple ECT courses, but it was not possible to establish causal link to the ECT.

A systematic review by Leiknes *et al.* (2015) examined published case reports and case series of women treated with ECT during pregnancy. This included 169 women, mainly with depression (including psychotic depression) or bipolar disorder, but cases of schizophrenia were also recorded. No maternal deaths were recorded, but the child mortality (foetuses and newborns) rate was 7.1% and the rates of adverse complications appear high: vaginal bleeding in 12%, premature labour in 28%, foetal cardiac arrhythmias or bradycardia in 43% and foetal malformations in 20% of cases. It should be noted that all adverse outcomes were included, including those extremely unlikely to be associated with the ECT or anaesthetic (e.g. anencephaly; transposition of great vessels).

Anaesthetic agents or ECT might be a cause of foetal bradycardia. A case study identified transient foetal bradycardia during a prolonged seizure induced by ECT. The anaesthetic agent methohexital was changed to propofol, reducing seizure duration and subsequently eliminating foetal bradycardia (De Asis *et al.* 2013).

A systematic review of cases and case series found 32 women who were given ECT in the first trimester. This showed similar transient adverse outcomes as those above, with one miscarriage in a patient who had vaginal bleeding before the administration of ECT. Vaginal bleeding, self-limiting abdominal pain and self-limiting foetal spasms were also observed (Calaway *et al.* 2016).

These studies, none of which were controlled for the adverse foetal/child outcomes associated with the underlying maternal illnesses, do not suggest any absolute contraindications to ECT in pregnancy but additional caution seems warranted in certain cases. An obstetric review should identify women with relevant high obstetric risks, particularly of vaginal bleeding or preterm labour. In close collaboration between psychiatric, obstetric, anaesthetic and, in the third trimester, paediatric teams, consider precautions such as foetal heart monitoring in later pregnancy and ECT administration in an obstetric hospital site. The anaesthetist will consider the risks of anaesthetic agents used; positioning of the patient to take pressure off the large vessels of the abdomen and the risk of aspiration, as pregnancy results in delayed gastric emptying.

Although ECT is not a medication free treatment the brief antenatal exposure to anaesthesia and neuromuscular blockade may be preferable to the high doses of medication and polypharmacy frequently required to treat severe mental illness. ECT's rapid action may reduce the risk that severe mental illness poses to the mother, and might also reduce the adverse impact on the foetus of continued exposure to antenatal stress (O'Donnell *et al.* 2014).

ECT in the Postnatal Period

Given ECT frequently has a rapid treatment effect it may be preferable when the urgency of treatment is paramount. This is particularly important when mother's illness is having a negative impact on the early mother–infant relationship and when mother and baby might be separated due to mother's poor mental health. The most acute risk follows the emergence of a puerperal psychotic episode, which constitutes one of the few true emergencies in psychiatry, due to the rapidity of onset of severe symptoms and high suicide risk. Two retrospective studies using non-postnatal controls both found that ECT appears to offer a more rapid therapeutic effect in women with depression postnatally, and greater improvement amongst women with postpartum psychosis (Reed *et al.* 1999; Haxton *et al.* 2016).

There are no robust data on the use of ECT in breastfeeding mothers. It is reasonable to assume that breastfeeding can be resumed once a mother feels recovered from the general anaesthetic agents. There is no credible evidence of negative outcomes on the breastfed infant.

There are no useful data on long term follow up of children born to mothers treated with ECT during pregnancy or in the postnatal period. It seems reasonable to assume that the value of achieving recovery, in some cases more rapidly than without ECT, outweighs any theoretical disadvantages. Research into short and long term outcomes would be valuable, whether to reinforce this assumption and reduce the reluctance to use ECT, or to reveal any hidden problems. It would also help clinicians and mothers if any additional predictors of outcome were identified in response to ECT treatment in the perinatal period.

In clinical practice, the stigma and negative misperceptions associated with ECT treatment are commonly seen amongst patients, friends, relatives and even staff who have not witnessed its remarkable effectiveness in some cases. It is not clear whether these important factors, which undoubtedly impact on clinical and patient decision-making, are different in the perinatal period. It seems plausible to suspect so, as women are admitted to hospital with some of the most severe and high risk conditions seen in psychiatry, at the most critical time in their lives and that of their families, and they are on average younger and less likely to have had similar previous psychiatric experiences. The effect of these factors may well lead to a reluctance to discuss this treatment option, and a lesser use of ECT than might be warranted by the indications and outcomes. If so, outcomes for women and babies may be worse than they need to be, and opportunities may exist for improving them.

Key Points

ECT should always be considered and discussed with women in the perinatal period as a relatively safe, effective and rapid treatment option for women with conditions for which it is indicated.

The risks and benefits of ECT to both mother and the infant should be considered.

If possible, discussion should involve the patient's family or close support network (with patient consent).

The alternatives to ECT should be discussed including the approximate time frame for treatment effect.

During pregnancy, close collaboration should be established between the psychiatrist and the woman's obstetrician, anaesthetist and paediatrician.

Plans for the procedure should consider additional risks and precautions, including foetal monitoring and conducting the ECT in an obstetric unit, particularly in the third trimester.

Additional information can be valuable, e.g. the Royal College of Psychiatrists' leaflet, and access to peer support from women who have had ECT.

References

Anderson E L, & Reti I M (2009) ECT in pregnancy: a review of literature from 1941 to 2007. *Psychosomatic Med*, 71: 235–42.

Calaway K, Coshal S, Jones K, Coverdale J, Livingston R (2016) A systematic review of the safety of electroconvulsive therapy use during the first trimester of pregnancy. *Journal of ECT*, 32: 230–5.

De Asis S J, Helgeson L, Ostroff R (2013) The use of propofol to prevent fetal deceleration during electroconvulsive therapy treatment. *Journal of ECT*, 29: e57–e58.

Focht A & Kellner C H (2012) ECT in the treatment of postpartum psychosis *Journal of ECT*, 28: 31–3.

Haxton C, Kelly S, Young D, *et al.* (2016) The efficacy of electroconvulsive therapy in a perinatal population. *Journal of ECT*, **32**: 113–15.

Leiknes K A, Cooke M J, Jarosch-von S L, Harboe I, Hoie B (2015) Electroconvulsive therapy during pregnancy: a systematic review of case studies. *Archive of Womens Mental Health*, **18**: 1–39.

National Institute for Health and Care Excellence (2015) Antenatal and postnatal mental health: clinical management and service guidance. NICE Guideline CG192.

O'Donnell K J, Glover V, Barker E D, O'Connor T G (2014) The persisting effect of maternal mood in pregnancy on childhood psychopathology. *Development and psychopathology*, **26**:393–403.

Reed P, Sermin N, Appleby L, Faragher B (1999) A comparison of clinical response to electroconvulsive therapy in puerperal and non-puerperal psychoses. *Journal of Affective Disorders*, **54**: 255–60.

Electroconvulsive Therapy in Children and Adolescents

Rosalind Y K Oliphant, Eleanor M Smith and
Aditya N Sharma

Introduction

The evidence base for the use of ECT in children and adolescents aged under 18 years (hereafter referred to as 'paediatric ECT') consists of individual case reports, case series and retrospective chart reviews, but no Randomised Controlled Trials (RCTs). This limited evidence base alongside concerns about the effects of ECT on the developing brain may help explain the infrequent use of ECT by child and adolescent psychiatrists. This chapter provides a summary of the issues and considerations pertaining to use of paediatric ECT within the British Isles (United Kingdom and Republic of Ireland). Although legal aspects relating to ECT are covered in Chapter 28, some reference specific to paediatric use is made here.

Epidemiology

According to the latest Electroconvulsive Therapy Accreditation Service (ECTAS) reports, paediatric ECT accounts for 0.1–0.2% of ECT use across the British Isles (excluding Scotland, which collects its own data but records those aged under 30 as one age category)(SEAN, 2016). This equates to one case in 2012–2013, three cases in 2014–2015, and two cases in 2016–2017 (Cresswell and Hodge, 2013; Cresswell *et al.*, 2014; Buley *et al.*, 2015; Buley *et al.*, 2017). This may, however, be an underestimate as not all ECT clinics are ECTAS registered, and some did not respond to the ECTAS questionnaires.

Indications for Use

As in adults, mood disorders (unipolar and bipolar), psychotic disorders, catatonia and neuroleptic malignant syndrome (NMS) are the main indications for use.

The American Academy of Child and Adolescent Psychiatry's 2004 'Practice Parameter for Use of Electroconvulsive Therapy with Adolescents' (AACAP, 2004) outlines three 'minimal standard' criteria that must be met before considering ECT, as outlined below:

1) Diagnosis: severe, persistent, major depression or mania +/- psychotic features, schizoaffective disorder, or, less often schizophrenia. May also be used to treat catatonia and NMS.
2) Severity of symptoms: must be severe, persistent and significantly disabling. May include life-threatening symptoms such as refusal to eat or drink, severe suicidality, uncontrollable mania, and florid psychosis.
3) Lack of treatment response: failure to respond to at least two adequate trials of appropriate psychopharmacological agents accompanied by other appropriate treatment modalities. Both duration and dose determine the adequacy of medication trials. ECT may be considered earlier when a) adequate medication trials are not possible because of intolerance of

psychopharmacological treatment, b) the adolescent is grossly incapacitated and thus cannot take medication, or c) waiting for a response to a psychopharmacological treatment may endanger life.

Reproduced from (AACAP, 2004) with permission from Elsevier.

This Practice Parameter recommends that cases with medical co-morbidities should be 'worked up' by a relevant specialist and that 'central nervous system tumours associated with elevated cerebrospinal fluid levels, active chest infection, and recent myocardial infarction be considered relative contraindications in adolescents' (AACAP, 2004).

The literature also includes case reports describing the use of paediatric ECT for severe self-injurious behaviour (SIB) occurring in the context of significant Intellectual Disability (ID) and/or Autism Spectrum Disorder (ASD), intractable seizures and pervasive refusal syndrome (Ghadziuddin and Walter, 2013; Griesemer et al., 1997; Shin et al., 2011; Carroll, 2012). It is noted that these indications are outwith current clinical guidelines.

Mood Disorders

Mood disorders are the most common indication for paediatric ECT. The majority of adolescents treated with ECT for a mood disorder suffer from severe depressive symptoms and have multiple areas of functional impairment (Ghadziuddin and Walter, 2013). There is more limited evidence of efficacy of ECT being used successfully to treat mania (Cohen et al., 1997). There is usually a history of treatment resistance, with several failed trials of medication, often in combination with psychotherapy. A Canadian study compared treatment outcomes of inpatient adolescents with bipolar disorder offered either ECT (16 patients accepted ECT) or standard care (6 patients refused ECT) (Kutcher and Robertson, 1995). The patients given ECT responded positively and their hospital admission was approximately half that of those receiving standard care (73.8 vs 176 days). A systematic review showed improvements in 63% of patients with depression and 80% of patients with mania (Rey and Walter, 1997). Remission may be improved by use of continuation ECT in combination with pharmacological and psychological treatment as appropriate. There is no consensus on preferred electrode placement for optimal response but there appears to be a preference for bilateral placement (Ghadziuddin and Walter, 2013).

Psychotic Disorders

There have been studies comparing adolescent patients with psychotic disorders to adult cohorts or a matched group of adolescents not receiving ECT (Bloch et al., 2001; Stein et al., 2004; Bloch et al., 2008; de la Serna et al., 2011). These found ECT effective in adolescents with psychotic disorders but less so than for affective disorders, in line with the aforementioned systematic review (Bloch et al., 2001; Stein et al., 2004; Rey and Walter, 1997). Paediatric ECT for psychotic disorders is reported to be generally safe in adolescents and there was no long-term cognitive impairment (de la Serna et al., 2011). ECT appears more effective for positive, affective and catatonic symptoms of psychosis and less effective (if at all) for negative symptoms (Ghadziuddin and Walter, 2013).

ECT is generally used as an adjunct to conventional psychopharmacological treatment rather than a standalone treatment for psychotic disorders. Resistance to antipsychotics, including clozapine, is the commonest reason for using paediatric ECT in adolescents with psychoses (Bloch et al., 2008; Baeza et al., 2010; de la Serna et al., 2011; Consoli et al., 2009).

ECT may also be indicated for intolerance to antipsychotic medication, florid psychosis with severe agitation causing risk to life, or in pregnancy, where it is deemed safer than the use of psychotropics (Ghadziuddin and Walter, 2013; Shiozawa *et al.*, 2015). Another study suggests early adjunctive ECT alongside pharmacotherapy may accelerate treatment response and reduce hospital stay (Zhang *et al.*, 2012).

Catatonia

Catatonia can be seen in affective or psychotic disorders or may exist as an independent diagnosis as reflected by the addition of 'Catatonia NOS' to the Diagnostic and Statistical Manual 5 (APA, 2013). As many as 12 to 17% of adolescents and young adults with ASD have features of catatonia (Billstedt *et al.*, 2005; Wing and Shah, 2000). For the treatment of catatonia seen in mood or psychotic disorders, paediatric ECT should be used as described in those sections in this chapter. With reference to ASD-associated catatonia, there are no RCTs, so management is based upon case reports and evidence regarding treatment of 'neurotypical' adults (Ghadziuddin and Walter, 2013). Case reports describe significant symptom relief after ECT, without altering the underlying ASD pathology. The frequency of ECT needed to improve catatonia symptoms may be more than for depression i.e. >2 sessions/week (Ghadziuddin and Walter, 2013). It should also be noted that in patients prescribed benzodiazepines for catatonia, the effect on seizure threshold should be acknowledged.

Neuroleptic Malignant Syndrome

There are case reports of paediatric NMS being treated successfully with ECT (Tanidir *et al.*, 2016; Araujo *et al.*, 2013; Steingard *et al.*, 1992, Ghaziuddin *et al.*, 2002) but there have also been contrasting reports of ECT being unsuccessful in reducing the course of NMS (Silva *et al.*, 1999). It has been suggested that variation in response may be related to the underlying cause of NMS, with those taking atypical antipsychotics appearing to respond more favourably than those taking typicals (Neuhut *et al.*, 2009).

Side Effects

The literature regarding side effects of paediatric ECT relates only to adolescents, not children. Some comparisons have been made with adults, e.g. adolescents are more likely to experience headaches and prolonged seizures than older people (Ghadziuddin and Walter, 2013). This may be related to a lower seizure threshold in younger people and, therefore, it may be advantageous to use propofol as the anaesthetic agent (see Chapter 23). There have been no reported deaths related to paediatric ECT (Ghadziuddin and Walter, 2013).

Studies describe a wide range of subjective memory impairments following ECT, from less than 5% to 50% of adolescent patients self-reporting (Kutcher and Robertson, 1995; Cohen *et al.*, 1997), but there have only been a handful of studies relating to adolescents' objective memory. Three studies reported no objective residual memory impairment several months following the final ECT session (Ghadziuddin *et al.*, 2000; de la Serna *et al.*, 2011; Cohen *et al.*, 2000). The sole study assessing long-term cognitive effects studied 10 adolescents an average of 3.5 years (+/-1.7 years) after ECT and did not demonstrate any measurable anterograde memory deficit (Cohen *et al.*, 2000). The AACAP guideline recommends 'every adolescent … must undergo age-appropriate memory assessment before treatment, at treatment termination and at appropriate time after treatment (usually between three and six months post-treatment)' (AACAP, 2004). They do not recommend specific tests but suggest 'cognitive testing should focus on short-term memory and new knowledge acquisition' (AACAP, 2004).

Other side effects such as nausea, vomiting, muscular pain and confusional states have often been reported but are transient (Cohen *et al.*, 1997; Walter and Rey, 1997; Ghadziuddin *et al.*, 1996). The AACAP guideline recommends side effects are 'systematically assessed with an appropriate side effect scale before the initiation of ECT and at treatment completion' and that 'side effect evaluation should occur after every treatment' but doesn't specify particular tools (AACAP, 2004).

ECT induced mania or hypomania may occur in adolescents and it is recommended that the course of ECT continues, but that appropriate precautions are taken to maintain safety and a mood stabiliser considered following ECT completion (Angst *et al.*, 1992).

Prognosis

Prognosis is thought to be influenced by multiple factors including: primary indication for ECT (discussed earlier in the chapter), comorbid diagnoses, pre-morbid functioning and presence of somatic symptoms. Children and adolescents with comorbid diagnoses, often anxiety disorders, may respond well to ECT but often require longer courses and ongoing additional therapeutic interventions (Ghadziuddin and Walter, 2013). Patients with better premorbid functioning are more likely to achieve complete remission of symptoms (Ghadziuddin and Walter, 2013). There is also some evidence suggesting that younger age at first presentation to psychiatric services may predict poorer outcomes (Ghadziuddin *et al.*, 2011). There is no evidence that a comorbid ID has any effect on response to paediatric ECT (Ghadziuddin, 2011).

Consent, Capacity and Legal Considerations

These are covered in more detail in Chapter 28. There are, however, certain considerations specific to paediatric ECT that are notable.

In England and Wales, paediatric ECT cannot be given without approval from a 'Second Opinion Appointed Doctor'. In cases where the child or adolescent is subject to the Mental Health Act the relevant treatment section would apply. If the child or adolescent is not subject to the Mental Health Act and is unable to provide consent (i.e. a 16- or 17-year-old lacking capacity or an under-16 found not to be competent) the legal authority to give ECT needs to be clarified. Whilst a person with parental responsibility is able to consent to treatments that fall within the zone of parental control, ECT is likely to fall outwith this (Department of Health, 2015). At present there is no case law relating to use of ECT in these circumstances.

In Scotland, paediatric ECT can only be given to informal patients who are deemed capable and give written consent, or, in those deemed incompetent to consent, written consent must be obtained from someone with parental responsibility and an independent 'Designated Medical Practitioner' (DMP) must approve this (Scottish Executive, 2005). Either the 'Registered Medical Officer' (RMO) recommending ECT or the DMP must be a child specialist. Paediatric ECT can be given to detained patients without the need for approval from a DMP if the patient is capable and provides written consent (Scottish Executive, 2005).

In Northern Ireland, there is currently a lack of specific guidance regarding legal authority to treat with paediatric ECT. When it comes into force, the Mental Capacity Act (Northern Ireland) 2016 will apply to all persons aged 16 and over. There will be no specific requirements about ECT for 16- to 18-year-olds. In the Republic of Ireland, it is not permissible to administer paediatric ECT to detained patients without approval of the

District Court (Mental Health Commission, 2006). There is no specific guidance regarding informal paediatric patients.

It is advised that specialist legal advice is sought before considering administering paediatric ECT.

Patients, Carers and Clinicians' Views

There have been several small studies assessing the views of children and adolescents of ECT, however these were carried out a number of years following ECT. An Australian team carried out a telephone survey of adolescents who had received ECT and later of their parents and found generally positive views (Walter *et al.*, 1999a and 1999b). A total of 50% of the adolescents thought ECT had been helpful and 69% would have it again. Only 8% felt ECT was worse than the illness itself. Of parents 86% would support using ECT again and 79% would have ECT themselves. Later French and Spanish studies had similar findings (Taieb *et al.*, 2001; Flamarique *et al.*, 2015).

A 1993 UK study surveyed child psychiatrists' views on the use of ECT in three different age groups; <12 years, 12–17 years and >17 years (Parmar, 1993). There were clear differences in the acceptability of ECT for the various age groups; e.g. for psychotic depression, it was felt to be 'unhelpful' in 42%, 19% and 5% of the respective age groups. A total of 79% of respondents had never used paediatric ECT and 22% of these stated it was because of lack of evidence. Other studies carried out in Australia, New Zealand and the USA report similar hesitance to use paediatric ECT amongst child psychiatrists (Walter *et al.*, 1997; Ghaziuddin *et al.*, 2001; Walter and Rey, 2003).

Gaps in the Evidence and Research Recommendations

The clear gap in the evidence base is that of a randomised controlled trial. However, there are consent and ethical concerns with this. A way forward could be to plan prospective cohort studies comparing children (under 12 years old) with adolescent and adult patients which could focus on follow up with regards to long-term symptom remission and cognitive side effects following ECT on the developing brain. Some of these gaps could be answered by active prospective surveillance epidemiology using established methodology such as that employed by the Royal College of Psychiatrists' Child and Adolescent Psychiatry Surveillance System (CAPSS) (Smith, 2016).

References

American Academy of Child and Adolescent Psychiatry (AACAP) (2004) Practice parameter for use of electroconvulsive therapy with adolescents. *Journal of the American Academy of Child & Adolescent Psychiatry*, **43**, 1521–39.

American Psychiatric Association (APA) (2013) *Diagnostic and statistical manual of mental disorders (Fifth Edition)*. Washington, DC.

Angst J, Angst K, Baruffol I, *et al.* (1992) ECT-induced and drug-induced hypomania. *Convulsive Therapy*, **8**, 179–85.

Araujo M, Queiros O, and Freitas D (2013) Electroconvulsive therapy in an adolescent with neuroleptic malignant syndrome: case report. *European Child and Adolescent Psychiatry*, **22**.

Baeza I, Flamarique I, Garrido J M, *et al.* (2010) Clinical experience using electroconvulsive therapy in adolescents with schizophrenia spectrum disorders. *Journal of Child and Adolescent Psychopharmacology*, **20**, 205–9.

Billstedt E, Gilberg I C and Gilberg C (2005) Autism after adolescence: population-based 13- to 22-year follow-up study of 120 individuals with autism diagnosed in childhood. *Journal of Autism and Developmental Disorders*, 35, 351–60.

Bloch Y, Levkovitz Y, Bloch A M, *et al.* (2001) Electroconvulsive therapy in adolescents: similarities to and differences from adults. *Journal of the American Academy of Child & Adolescent Psychiatry*, 40, 1332–6.

Bloch Y, Sobol D, Levkovitz Y, *et al.* (2008) Reasons for referral for electroconvulsive therapy: a comparison between adolescents and adults. *Australasian Psychiatry*, 16, 191–4.

Buley N, Hodge S and Hailey E (2015) ECT Minimum Dataset 2014–2015. Publication no: CCQI217. Royal College of Psychiatrists.

Buley N, Copland E and Hodge S (2017) ECT Minimum Dataset 2016–2017. Publication no: CCQI269. Royal College of Psychiatrists.

Carroll S (2012) Pervasive refusal syndrome and pediatric catatonia: is there a diagnostic overlap? A case report. *Journal of Neuropsychiatry and Clinical Neurosciences*, 24, 3.

Cohen D, Paillere-Martinot M L and Basquin M (1997) Use of electroconvulsive therapy in adolescents. *Convulsive Therapy*, 13, 25.

Cohen D, Taieb O, Flament M, *et al.* (2000) Absence of cognitive impairment at long-term follow-up in adolescents treated with ECT for severe mood disorder. *American Journal of Psychiatry*, 157, 460–2.

Consoli A, Boulicot V, Comic F, *et al.* (2009) Moderate clinical improvement with maintenance ECT in a 17-year-old boy with intractable catatonic schizophrenia. *European Child and Adolescent Psychiatry*, 18, 250–4.

Cresswell J and Hodge S (2013) ECT Minimum Dataset 2012–2013. Royal College of Psychiatrists. https://www.rcpsych.ac.uk/docs/default-source/improving-care/ccqi/quality-networks/electro-convulsive-therapy-clinics-(ectas)/dataset-reports/ectas-minimum-dataset-activity-report-2012-3.pdf?sfvrsn=1f847f3e_4

Cresswell J, Buley N and Hodge S (2014) ECT Minimum Dataset 2012–2013. Royal College of Psychiatrists. https://www.rcpsych.ac.uk/docs/default-source/improving-care/ccqi/quality-networks/electro-convulsive-therapy-

clinics-(ectas)/dataset-reports/ect-minimum-dataset-report-2014-15.pdf?sfvrsn=5ed22569_4

de la Serna E, Flamarique I, Castro-Fornieles J, *et al.* (2011) Two-year follow-up of cognitive functions in schizophrenia spectrum disorders of adolescent patients treated with electroconvulsive therapy. *Journal of Child and Adolescent Psychopharmacology*, 21, 611–19.

Department of Health (2015) Mental Health Act 1983: Code of Practice. https://assets.publishing.service.gov.uk/government/uploads/system/uploads/attachment_data/file/435512/MHA_Code_of_Practice.PDF

Flamarique I, Castro-Fornieles J, De La Serna E, *et al.* (2015) Patients' opinions about electroconvulsive therapy: what do adolescents with schizophrenia spectrum disorders think? *Journal of Child and Adolescent Psychopharmacology*, 25, 641–8.

Ghaziuddin N, King CA, Naylor MW, *et al.* (1996) Electroconvulsive treatment in adolescents with pharmacotherapy-refractory depression. *Journal of Child and Adolescent Psychopharmacology*, 6, 259–71.

Ghaziuddin N, Laughrin D and Giordani B (2000) Cognitive side effects of electroconvulsive therapy in adolescents. *Journal of Child and Adolescent Psychopharmacology*, 10, 269–76.

Ghadziuddin N, Kaza M, Ghazi N, *et al.* (2001) Electroconvulsive therapy for minors: experiences and attitudes of child psychiatrists and psychologists. *Journal of ECT*, 17, 109–17.

Ghadziuddin N, Alkhouri I, Champine D, *et al.* (2002) ECT treatment of malignant catatonia/NMS in an adolescent: a useful lesson in delayed diagnosis and treatment. *Journal of ECT*, 18, 95–8.

Ghadziuddin N, Dumas S and Hodges E (2011) Use of continuation or maintenance electroconvulsive therapy in adolescents with severe treatment-resistant depression. *Journal of ECT*, 27, 168–74.

Ghadziuddin N and Walter G (2013) *Electroconvulsive Therapy in Children and Adolescents.* Oxford University Press.

Griesemer D A, Kellner C H, Beale M D, *et al.* (1997) Electroconvulsive therapy for treatment of intractable seizures. Initial findings in two children. *Neurology*, **49**, 1389–92.

Kutcher S and Robertson H (1995) Electroconvulsive therapy in treatment resistant bipolar youth. *Journal of Child and Adolescent Psychopharmacology*, **5**, 167–75.

Mental Health Commission/Coimisiún Meabhair-Shláinte (2006) Reference Guide: Mental Health Act 2001. Part Two – Children. Mental Health Commission, Dublin. https://www.mhcirl.ie/File/refguidmha2001p2.pdf

Neuhut R, Lindenmayer J P and Silva R (2009) Neuroleptic malignant syndrome in children and adolescents on atypical antipsychotic medication: a review. *Journal of Child and Adolescent Psychopharmacology*, **19**, 415–22.

Parmar R (1993) Attitudes of child psychiatrists to electroconvulsive therapy. *Psychiatric Bulletin*, **17**, 12–13.

Rey J M and Walter G (1997) Half a century of ECT use in young people. *American Journal of Psychiatry*, **154**, 595–602.

Scottish Executive (2005) Mental Health (Care and Treatment) (Scotland) Act 2003. Code of Practice. Vol 1. Scottish Executive, St Andrew's House, Edinburgh.

SEAN (2016) *Scottish ECT Accreditation Network Annual Report 2016. A summary of ECT in Scotland for 2015*. NHS National Services Scotland.

Shin H W, O'Donovan C A, Boggs J G, *et al.* (2011) Successful ECT treatment for medically refractory nonconvulsive status epilepticus in pediatric patient. *Seizure*, **20**, 433–6.

Shiozawa P, Trevizol A, Bernardon R R, *et al.* (2015) Electroconvulsive therapy for a psychotic adolescent during the first trimester of pregnancy. *Trends in Psychiatry and Psychotherapy*, **37**, 166–7.

Silva R R, Munoz D, Alpert M, *et al.* (1999) Neuroleptic malignant syndrome in children and adolescents. *Journal of the American Academy of Child & Adolescent Psychiatry*, **38**, 187–94.

Smith E (ed) (2016) *The Child and Adolescent Psychiatry Surveillance System (CAPSS). The Seven Year Report: 2016*. Royal College of Psychiatrists Publications.

Stein D, Kurtsman L, Stier S, *et al.* (2004) Electroconvulsive therapy in adolescent and adult psychiatric inpatients: a retrospective chart design. *Journal of Affective Disorders*, **82**, 335–42.

Steingard R, Khan A, Gonzalez A, *et al.* (1992) Neuroleptic malignant syndrome: review of experience with children and adolescents. *Journal of Child and Adolescent Psychopharmacology*, **2**, 183–98.

Taieb O, Flament MF, Corcos M, *et al.* (2001) Electroconvulsive therapy in adolescents with mood disorder: patients' and parents' attitudes. *Psychiatry Research*, **104**, 183–90.

Tanidir C, Aksoy S, Canbek O, *et al.* (2016) Treatment of neuroleptic malignant syndrome with electroconvulsive therapy in an adolescent with psychosis. *Journal of Child and Adolescent Psychopharmacology*, **26**, 179–80.

Walter G and Rey J M (1997) An epidemiological study of the use of ECT in adolescents. *Journal of the American Academy of Child & Adolescent Psychiatry*, **36**, 809–15.

Walter G and Rey J M (2003) How fixed are child psychiatrists' views about ECT in the young. *Journal of ECT*, **19**, 88–92.

Walter G, Koster K and Rey J (1999a) Electroconvulsive therapy in adolescents: Experience, knowledge, and attitudes of recipients. *Journal of the American Academy of Child & Adolescent Psychiatry*, **38**, 594–9.

Walter G, Koster K and Rey J (1999b) Views about treatment among parents of adolescents who received electroconvulsive therapy. *Psychiatric Services*, **50**, 701–2.

Walter G, Rey J M and Starling J (1997) Experience, knowledge and attitudes of child psychiatrists about ECT in the young. *Australian and New Zealand Journal of Psychiatry*, **31**, 676–81.

Wing L and Shah A (2000) Catatonia in autistic spectrum disorders. *British Journal of Psychiatry*, **176**, 357–62.

Zhang Z J, Chen Y C, Wang H N, *et al.* (2012) Electroconvulsive therapy improves antipsychotic and somnographic responses in adolescents with first-episode psychosis: a case-control study. *Schizophrenia Research*, **137**, 97–103.

Chapter 10

The Use of ECT in the Treatment of Schizophrenia

Richard Braithwaite

Electroconvulsive therapy is widely used in the treatment of schizophrenia. Historically, in contrast to affective disorders, there has been relatively limited high-quality evidence to support its use for this indication. Consequently, the last edition of *The ECT Handbook* (Waite & Easton, 2013) sanctioned its use only as a short-term intervention, in clozapine-resistant illness. Since that time, there has been renewed interest in the topic amongst researchers and several recent publications have helped guide this updated chapter.

History

Chemically Induced Seizures

The convulsive therapies were developed in the 1930s specifically as a treatment for schizophrenia. László Meduna, a neuroanatomist from Budapest, had discovered an excess of glial cells at post-mortem examination of the brains of people with epilepsy (Meduna, 1932). Contrasting this with earlier findings of fewer glia in the brains of those with schizophrenia (Hechst, 1931), he formed the idea that schizophrenia and epilepsy might somehow antagonise one another. Drawing on previous research suggesting the two conditions very rarely co-existed (Gaupp, 1926), he hypothesised that inducing epilepsy in patients with schizophrenia might cure their condition (Shorter & Healy, 2007).

After preliminary animal trials to establish safety (Meduna, 1934), in early 1934, he gave intravenous camphor, a stimulant known to induce seizures, to a patient with schizophrenia who had been in a four-year catatonic stupor. He induced a 60-second tonic-clonic fit; after seven further treatments, spaced four days apart, the patient was cured (Fink, 1999). In a case series of 26 patients with schizophrenia subsequently treated with drug-induced seizures, remissions were seen in ten patients, including several non-catatonic patients (Meduna, 1935).

Switching to pentylenetetrazol, a more reliable convulsant than camphor, Meduna went on to report on a series of 110 patients with schizophrenia, whom he classified according to their stage of illness (Meduna, 1937). A total of 95% of patients in the acute, initial stages of the disease remitted with treatment, compared with 57% of chronic patients displaying mainly positive symptoms, and just 6% of those more chronic with predominant negative and cognitive symptoms. Overall, 54% of patients remitted. There were no deaths in this series of over 1,000 individual treatments, but four patients suffered dislocations of the arm or jaw (Pullar Strecker, 1937).

Electrically Induced Seizures

Meanwhile, Ugo Cerletti, an Italian professor of psychiatry, had been studying the effects of epilepsy by electrically inducing seizures in dogs. After he moved to Rome in 1935, he and his assistant, Lucio Bini, heard of Meduna's therapeutic success with drug-induced seizures (Shorter & Healy, 2007). Wondering whether electrically induced seizures might also be therapeutic in schizophrenia and act more instantly than camphor or pentylenetetrazol, they experimented on pigs to establish a safe dose (Fink, 1979).

Cerletti and Bini's team gave the first ever course of ECT to a patient with paranoid schizophrenia in the spring of 1938, bringing about full remission after 11 treatments (Cerletti & Bini, 1938). They went on to treat a further 20 patients that summer. Within two years, ECT had spread across the western hemisphere, with a gradual realisation of even greater efficacy in depressive illness (Shorter & Healy, 2007).

ECT remained the treatment of choice for schizophrenia until the introduction of chlorpromazine in 1953. By 1960 though, in the West, ECT had been replaced by antipsychotic drugs in the treatment of most patients with schizophrenia (Fink, 1979). As the twentieth century drew on, drugs, rather than ECT, featured heavily in clinical guidance, medical education and strategic policy (Fink, 1999).

Current Usage

Leiknes et al. (2012) carried out a systematic review of studies of ECT usage which documented diagnostic indications. The review included studies conducted worldwide and published between 1990 and 2011. Broadly, compared with depressive illness, the review showed very low usage of ECT for schizophrenia in Western Europe, Scandinavia, North America and Australasia, but high usage for this indication in Eastern Europe, Africa, South America and Asia. The division was not entirely along economic lines, though, with schizophrenia the leading indication for ECT in Japan and the United Arab Emirates, amongst others, but only a minor indication in Pakistan.

In England, Wales, Northern Ireland and the Republic of Ireland, data are drawn from biennial surveys conducted by the ECT Accreditation Service (ECTAS). For the twelve months ending in March 2017, extrapolation of data from approximately 60% of all ECT clinics across the regions (Buley et al., 2017) suggests that as few as 20 acute courses may be given for schizophrenia nationally each year. This compares with perhaps 2,700 courses for depressive illness, 100 for manic episode and 90 for catatonia. Two thirds of patients with schizophrenia receiving ECT were male. The mean age was around 40 years, compared with 60 years for other indications (Buley et al., 2017).

The National Institute for Health and Care Excellence (NICE) currently advises that 'the current state of the evidence does not allow the general use of ECT in the management of schizophrenia to be recommended' (NICE, 2009). The intended meaning of 'general' in this context is unclear, resulting in the guidance being difficult to interpret. The current NICE guideline for the management of schizophrenia (NICE, 2014) does not mention ECT once.

Efficacy and Effectiveness

A Cochrane review was last updated in 2005, including 26 randomised controlled trials (RCTs) of variable quality spanning five decades of research (Tharyan & Adams, 2005). A number of outcomes and comparisons were analysed across studies, which variously included acutely unwell patients as well as chronic or treatment-resistant cases. Several trials used 'sham' ECT as a control condition; this procedure entails general anaesthesia without an electrical charge.

The review confirmed that ECT is superior to placebo or sham ECT in the treatment of schizophrenia (number needed to treat (NNT) 6, 95% confidence interval (CI) 4–12). Data from three single-blind RCTs showed that ECT alone was less likely than antipsychotic drugs to bring about clinical improvement, but in two double-blind trials of antipsychotics, placebo medication, ECT and sham ECT, no difference between the two active treatments was observed.

Combined results from three trials suggest the addition of ECT to antipsychotics brings about no greater likelihood of improvement (Tharyan & Adams, 2005). It should be noted that two of these trials sampled relatively acute patients (Janakiramiah et al., 1982; Small et al., 1982), whilst the third (Naidoo, 1956), although its subjects were described as chronic, was undertaken at a time when drug treatment itself was the novel intervention. Thus, very few, if any, of the 151 patients across these three trials could be considered treatment-resistant. This is of note when considering the evidence set out below for the addition of ECT to antipsychotics in treatment-resistant populations.

The reviewers concluded that 'ECT, combined with treatment with antipsychotic drugs, may be considered an option for people with schizophrenia, particularly when rapid global improvement and reduction of symptoms is desired.' Whilst recognising that the clinical benefits may not last beyond the short term, the authors opined that 'there is no clear evidence to refute its use for people with schizophrenia' (Tharyan & Adams, 2005).

ECT in Treatment-Resistant Schizophrenia

Treatment resistance is defined as the failure of two antipsychotic medications and occurs in around thirty percent of patients with schizophrenia (Brenner et al., 1990). A recent systematic review and meta-analysis of 11 randomised controlled trials, comparing ECT augmentation of a non-clozapine antipsychotic with the same antipsychotic alone, incorporated data from over 800 patients across India, Thailand and, primarily, China (Zheng et al., 2016). Notably, this review included publications in Chinese as well as English, revealing RCTs overlooked by recent systematic reviews of ECT in schizophrenia such as Pompili et al. (2013). All but two of the included studies had been published since 2009.

This review showed a significant difference in favour of the combined treatment, in terms of immediate (one to two weeks) and medium term (8 to 24 weeks) symptomatic improvement. The pooled data showed that 51% of patients receiving ECT and antipsychotics responded to treatment, compared with 33% of those on the medication alone (NNT 6, 95% CI 4–10). For remission, the figures were 21% and 9% respectively (NNT 9, 95% CI 6–18) (Zheng et al., 2016).

Whilst such data are encouraging, it follows that around half of all treatment-resistant patients will not respond during a course of ECT given alongside pharmacotherapy. One must question therefore which patients are more or less likely to respond to such treatment. Chanpattana & Sackeim (2010) studied a single cohort of 253 treatment-resistant patients in Thailand, prospectively treated with thrice-weekly, bilateral ECT and flupentixol at a dose of 24 milligrams daily. There was a response to treatment in 55% of patients. Response was predicted by a shorter duration of the current episode of illness and by less severe negative symptoms, but not by shorter overall duration of disease.

ECT in Combination with Clozapine

Clozapine is considered the standard treatment for the third of all patients with schizophrenia whose illness is refractory to other treatments (Barnes, 2011), yet it remains largely underused (Nielsen, 2010). In those patients who initiate the drug, though, treatment fails in up to 70% (Petrides *et al.*, 2015) and a recent meta-analysis has questioned the superiority of clozapine over other second generation antipsychotics (Samara *et al.*, 2016). The common practice of subsequently augmenting clozapine with other antipsychotic medications is not well supported by meta-analysis (Sommer *et al.*, 2012), with sulpiride being the only such drug to show superiority over placebo, in one lone, small randomised trial (Shiloh *et al.*, 1997).

Within this bleak context, three controlled trials have compared ECT augmentation of clozapine with the drug alone. In Iran, Masoudzadeh and Khalilian (2007) non-randomly assigned 18 treatment-resistant, clozapine-naïve patients, in double-blind fashion, into three groups, receiving (a) 12 treatments of thrice-weekly, unilateral ECT with clozapine, (b) ECT with oral placebo, or (c) sham ECT with clozapine. Although there was significant symptomatic improvement in all three groups, the combination treatment (a) brought about significantly greater changes than either treatment alone.

Petrides *et al.* (2015) randomised 39 clozapine-resistant patients in Queens, New York, in a single-blind manner, to receive either 20 treatments of bilateral ECT alongside continued clozapine, or continued clozapine alone. Half the patients on combination treatment responded, compared to none of those continuing on clozapine alone (NNT 3, 95% CI 2–4). The latter group were then given ECT and half responded.

Lastly, Melzer-Ribeiro *et al.* (2017) randomised 23 clozapine-resistant patients in São Paulo, apparently in a single-blind manner, to receive either 12 treatments of thrice-weekly bilateral ECT alongside continued clozapine, or sham ECT with continued clozapine. Only one patient, in the combination group, responded in this pilot study; a full-powered study is underway.

Lally *et al.* (2016) published a systematic review of ECT augmentation of clozapine. They combined results from the first two controlled trials above, four prospective open-label trials, two retrospective chart reviews, six case series and 15 individual case reports. In total, the review encompassed data from 192 patients. Findings from this dataset are difficult to interpret in terms of effectiveness given the selection and publication biases inherent in case series and reports. More usefully, the reviewers were able to focus a meta-analysis on the single-blind RCT outlined above (Petrides *et al.*, 2015) and four prospective open-label trials, combining data from 71 patients. They found a response rate to clozapine and ECT of 54% (95% CI 22%–84%) (Lally *et al.*, 2016).

Focusing solely on RCTs, Wang *et al.* (2018) systematically reviewed 17 Chinese-language studies excluded by Lally *et al.* (2016). Their meta-analysis also included data from Petrides *et al.* (2015) and covered 1,769 patients. Sadly, not one of the Chinese RCTs was rater-blinded and their overall methodological quality was poor. Consequently, the observed association between ECT augmentation of clozapine and a markedly increased response rate (NNT 3, 95% CI 3–5) must be interpreted with caution.

Speed of Response

In a controlled study, 40 patients were randomised to receive either chlorpromazine alongside thrice-weekly, bilateral, unmodified ECT, or chlorpromazine alone (Wu *et al.*,

1989). The combination therapy group showed significantly lower symptom scores than the drug-only group at the end of treatment, but there was no significant difference between the groups at the mid-point of the treatment course. More recently, the meta-analysis by Zheng et al. (2016) showed a significant difference in symptom severity at one to two weeks between patients treated with antipsychotics alone and those whose medication was augmented with ECT, favouring the combination therapy.

Evidence of a faster response elicited by the use of a bifrontal electrode placement is presented in the section below.

Electrode Placement

The Cochrane review found three randomised trials comparing bilateral and unilateral electrode placements and found no difference in efficacy or side effects (Tharyan & Adams, 2005).

In India, Phutane et al. (2013) randomised 81 non-catatonic patients, in a double-blind fashion, to receive either bifrontal or bitemporal ECT. Bifrontal electrode placement was five centimetres superior to the outer angle of each orbit. Both treatments were given thrice-weekly, using stimulus titration at 1.5 times seizure threshold. At two weeks, response was 63% in the bifrontal group and 13% in the bitemporal group (NNT 3, 95% CI 2–4). At completion of treatment, 95% in the bifrontal and 79% in the bitemporal group had responded (NNT 7, 95% CI 4–51). Those having bifrontal treatment had longer seizures and required, on average, one treatment fewer than those receiving bitemporal ECT. Furthermore, following treatment they performed better on some cognitive tests than those in the bitemporal group (Phutane et al., 2013).

Frequency of Treatment

Most of the higher quality evidence on efficacy quoted in this chapter is based upon use of thrice- rather than twice-weekly treatments. All the controlled studies of clozapine augmentation have been conducted using thrice-weekly ECT.

There are no prospective studies comparing the two frequencies in non-resistant schizophrenia. One retrospective series has suggested a faster rate of response for thrice-weekly ECT (Chanpattana et al., 1999b).

Duration of Acute Treatment

In Meduna's case series (1937) of 110 patients undergoing medical convulsive therapy, most patients who successfully remitted had required 15 to 20 treatments (Pullar Strecker, 1937). Such findings set the tone for standard practice in the convulsive therapies in the years to come. By 1950, the length of an ECT course in schizophrenia had been established at between 12 and 20 treatments, compared with between 4 and 12 in depressive illness (Fink, 1979).

Subsequently, Baker et al. (1960) randomised 41 women with poor prognoses to receive fixed courses of either 12 or 20 treatments. Only 33% of those receiving 12 treatments showed clinical improvement, compared with 74% of those having 20, suggesting superiority of the longer course (Baker et al., 1960) (NNT 3, 95% CI 2–8). But patients did not receive concurrent antipsychotic medication in this study and consequently it is difficult to relate its findings to modern practice.

In the Thai cohort studied by Chanpattana & Sackeim (2010), those treatment-resistant patients who responded to the combination of ECT and antipsychotic medication had required a mean number of 13 treatments (standard deviation, SD, 4). In their systematic review, Lally *et al.* (2016) found a mean number of 11 treatments used in the attempted augmentation of clozapine, but this figure was drawn from all 192 patients studied, including those patients who did not respond and whose courses were terminated after as few as four treatments. In the two controlled trials and four prospective open label studies included in the review, means of 15 and 12 treatments respectively were administered (Lally *et al.*, 2016). The reviewers were unable to present any data on duration of treatment specifically in those who responded to treatment.

From these findings it may be reasonable to conclude that if ECT is given in the absence of antipsychotic medication, as many as 20 treatments may indeed be needed. But given in combination with medication, the necessary number of treatments is likely to be fewer than this, albeit probably more than might usually be needed to treat depressive illness.

In routine practice in the UK and the Republic of Ireland, the mean number of treatments given for schizophrenia, 10, is identical to the number given for all indications combined (Buley *et al.*, 2017). It is impossible to assess the extent to which this mean is reduced by an inability to exceed 12 treatments for clinically inappropriate legal reasons, by prematurely aborted courses in cases of perceived non-response, or, similarly, by a lack of awareness that longer courses than those used in depressive illness may be necessary for schizophrenia.

Continuation and Maintenance Treatment

Continuation ECT

Lack of a lasting treatment effect is a well recognised phenomenon associated with ECT in the treatment of depressive illness and it is logical to believe this holds for schizophrenia too. Long-term follow-up studies examining this phenomenon are lacking. But of the 62 patients with follow-up data reported in a systematic review of clozapine augmentation, 20 (32%) relapsed following cessation of ECT (Lally *et al.*, 2016). Given the likely short duration of follow-up in many of the included case series, this is probably a conservative estimate.

Consequently, it is natural for clinicians to look towards continuing in the longer term a treatment that has brought about an immediate positive response, especially when ECT has been well tolerated. Unsurprisingly, continuation ECT in schizophrenia has not been widely researched. In the only controlled trial to date, Chanpattana *et al.* (1999a) in Thailand studied 51 patients who had responded to an acute course of ECT with flupentixol. In a single-blind manner, subjects were randomised to then receive (a) six months of continuation ECT in combination with flupentixol, (b) continuation ECT alone, or (c) flupentixol alone. Those on combination treatment were significantly more likely to maintain global improvement and to avoid relapse than patients having either treatment alone. Specifically, the addition of continuation ECT to flupentixol reduced the proportion of relapses from 93% to 40% (NNT 2, 95% CI 2–4). Continuation ECT alone produced no benefits over antipsychotic medication alone. All those patients who had not relapsed during combination treatment then maintained remission over a further follow-up period ranging from 3 to 17 months.

There are numerous case reports and case series documenting the use of continuation ECT in schizophrenia. In the only other prospective trial published, Kho *et al.* (2004) studied three patients in the Netherlands who had relapsed following cessation of an acute course of twice-weekly unilateral ECT. After a second successful acute course, they received continuation ECT, once weekly, for between 6 and 12 weeks, alongside clozapine. All three patients are then reported to have remained well, although the duration of follow-up is unclear (Kho *et al.*, 2004).

Maintenance ECT

Maintenance ECT in schizophrenia, that is to say treatment extended beyond six months to prevent recurrence, has not been studied in any prospective trial. The literature is confined to single case reports and one small retrospective case series (Lévy-Rueff *et al.*, 2008). Findings are positive, but such reports are highly prone to selection and publication biases and must be interpreted with caution.

Adverse Effects and Risks

There is no reason to suppose the adverse effect profile of ECT administered to people with schizophrenia should differ from that given for other indications. Vuksan Ćusa *et al.* (2018) prospectively studied 31 patients with treatment-resistant schizophrenia in Croatia and found significantly improved functioning in several cognitive domains after a course of ECT, with no neurocognitive functions exhibiting deterioration following treatment. Many patients with depressive disorder undergoing ECT are co-prescribed antipsychotic medications and this practice is discussed in detail in Chapter 25. There is no reason to believe such a combination is inherently unsafe.

A theoretical exception to this logic is clozapine, rarely prescribed in affective disorder. It is known to lower seizure threshold, but thankfully any related concerns are not upheld in practice by the existing evidence. The recent systematic review of clozapine augmentation with ECT analysed data from 166 patients in original studies which reported adverse effects; only five patients experienced one or more prolonged seizures during their courses of treatment and none are reported to have had latent seizures (Lally *et al.*, 2016).

Legal Considerations

In the UK and the Republic of Ireland, the proportion of patients receiving ECT for schizophrenia who lack mental capacity to consent to the treatment, 77%, is almost double the 41% of patients receiving ECT for other indications who lack capacity (Buley *et al.*, 2017). This is perhaps unsurprising, given that poor insight is such a prominent feature of the illness.

UK legislation relating to the use of ECT is considered in Chapter 28. Focusing briefly on the law in England and Wales, however, the Mental Health Act 1983, as currently amended, stipulates that, if the patient lacks the requisite mental capacity, a centrally appointed independent psychiatrist must have agreed that the proposed treatment is appropriate to be given. This may be problematic, given that ECT for schizophrenia falls outside NICE guidance (NICE, 2009 & NICE, 2014). Anecdotally, this results in one set of second opinion doctors who, as a general rule, are content to authorise ECT in schizophrenia and another set of doctors who never do so. It is hoped that the recommendations in this chapter might help to unify practice in this regard.

Discussion

Schizophrenia is an unpleasant disease. For many, symptoms such as auditory hallucinations are so unbearable that more than one in ten die by suicide (Caldwell & Gottesman, 1992). For other patients, complex delusional systems may lead to hazardous behaviour. As a result, many patients require hospital admission, often compulsorily.

Given the plethora of first- and second-generation agents available, contraindication to all antipsychotic medication is extremely rare. Short- and long-acting intramuscular preparations and appropriate use of the legal framework may be helpful when poor insight and treatment concordance stand in the way of the practical administration of evidence-based pharmacotherapy in hospitalised patients with schizophrenia. Notwithstanding current concerns about dopamine receptor up-regulation and resultant antipsychotic resistance (Murray et al., 2016), such medication rightly remains the treatment of choice.

But treatment resistance is very frequent. Many such patients fail to respond to clozapine, have a contraindication to that drug, develop intolerable adverse effects on it, or simply refuse to initiate it or undergo the necessary blood monitoring. For those patients unable to reach or remain in remission using treatments based on robust, high quality evidence, it seems unreasonable to abandon all further efforts to relieve tormenting symptoms when treatments are available for which a lower level of evidence exists. Whilst the evidence base for ECT in treatment-resistant schizophrenia is far from comprehensive, it is much stronger than that for augmentation of clozapine with a second antipsychotic medication (Sommer et al., 2012).

From the onset of any given episode of schizophrenia, the likelihood of response to ECT steadily diminishes as time progresses. Standard antipsychotics, followed by clozapine if necessary, should be offered and titrated in a timely manner. In the event of clozapine failure, intolerance or refusal, ECT augmentation becomes the treatment of choice, yet the evidence we have suggests that its potential effectiveness may decrease steadily as the episode of illness draws on.

The evidence for continuation ECT in schizophrenia is relatively weak, as it derives from observational data and one small randomised controlled trial. However, this should not entirely preclude its use. For patients responding to an acute course of ECT but promptly relapsing following its cessation, a second acute course followed by continuation ECT should surely be considered. Certainly, the evidence for continuation ECT alongside antipsychotics in such a situation is not inferior to that for any other treatment strategy, including antipsychotic polypharmacy. In many cases, continuation ECT alongside licensed doses of drugs will be a safer option, in terms of adverse events, than off-label, excessive combined doses of chlorpromazine equivalents.

Recommendations

- ECT is an effective and safe augmentation strategy in schizophrenia.
- ECT augmentation is indicated in treatment resistance and should be considered early in all cases of clozapine failure, intolerance or refusal.
- Assuming it is tolerated, 10 to 12 treatments should be given before concluding ECT has been unsuccessful; it is reasonable to continue past 16 treatments if there has been gradual improvement in symptoms.
- Thrice-weekly treatment is recommended in schizophrenia.

- Unilateral, bitemporal and bifrontal electrode placements are all accepted modalities of treatment in schizophrenia.
- Continuation ECT, alongside antipsychotic medication, is indicated following a successful acute course, in patients who have previously relapsed after cessation of an acute course of ECT, despite prophylactic pharmacotherapy.
- Maintenance ECT, beyond six months, may be weighed up against other treatment options for which there is very limited evidence, in patients whose illness has previously recurred following cessation of a course of continuation ECT.

Acknowledgements

The author wishes to thank Vivek Phutane, Rafael Ribeiro and Wei Zheng for sharing data from their respective studies.

References

Baker, A., Bird, G., Lavin, N. & Thorpe, J. (1960) ECT in schizophrenia. *Journal of Mental Science*, **106**, 1506–11.

Barnes, T. R. (2011) Schizophrenia Consensus Group of British Association for Psychopharmacology: evidence-based guidelines for the pharmacological treatment of schizophrenia: recommendations from the British Association for Psychopharmacology. *Journal of Psychopharmacology*, **25**, 567–620.

Brenner, H. D., Dencker, S. J., Goldstein, M. J., et al. (1990) Defining treatment refractoriness in schizophrenia. *Schizophrenia Bulletin*, **16**, 551–61.

Buley, N., Copland, E. & Hodge, S. (2017) *ECT minimum dataset 2016–2017*. Electroconvulsive Therapy Accreditation Service, Royal College of Psychiatrists.

Caldwell, C. B. & Gottesman, I. I. (1992) Schizophrenia: a high-risk factor for suicide: clues to risk reduction. *Suicide & Life-Threatening Behavior*, **22**, 479–93.

Cerletti, U. & Bini, L. (1938) Un nuevo metodo di shocktherapie "L'elettro-shock". *Bollettino dell'Accademia medica di Roma*, **64**, 136–8.

Chanpattana, W., Chakrabhand, M. L., Sackeim, H. A., et al. (1999a) Continuation ECT in treatment resistant schizophrenia: a controlled study. *Journal of ECT*, **15**, 178–92.

Chanpattana, W., Chakrabhand, M. L., Kitaroonchai, W., Choovanichvong, S. & Prasertsuk, Y. (1999b) Effects of twice- versus thrice-weekly electroconvulsive therapy in schizophrenia. *Journal of the Medical Association of Thailand*, **82**, 477–83.

Chanpattana, W. & Sackeim, H. A. (2010) Electroconvulsive therapy in treatment-resistant schizophrenia: prediction of response and the nature of symptomatic improvement. *Journal of ECT*, **26**, 289–98.

Fink, M. (1979) *Convulsive therapy: theory and practice*. Raven Press.

Fink, M. (1999) *Electroshock: healing mental illness*. Oxford University Press.

Gaupp, R. (1926) Die Frage der kombinierten Psychosen. *Archiv für Psychiatrie und Nervenkrankheiten*, **76**, 73–80.

Hechst, B. (1931) Zur Histopathologie der Schizophrenie mit besonderer Berücksichtigung der Ausbreitung des Prozesses. *Zeitschrift für die gesamte Neurologie und Psychiatrie*, **134**, 163–7.

Janakiramiah, N., Channabasavanna, S. M. & Narasimha-Murthy N. S. (1982) ECT/chlorpromazine combination versus chlorpromazine alone in acutely ill schizophrenic patients. *Acta Psychiatrica Scandinavica*, **66**, 464–70.

Kho, K. H., Blansjaar, B. A., de Vries, S., Babuskova, D., Zwinderman, A. H. & Linszen, D. H. (2004) Electroconvulsive therapy for the treatment of clozapine non-responders suffering from schizophrenia: an open label study. *European Archives of Psychiatry & Clinical Neuroscience*, **254**, 372–9.

Lally, J., Tully, J., Robertson, D., Stubbs, B., Gaughran, F. & MacCabe, J. H. (2016) Augmentation of clozapine with electroconvulsive therapy in treatment resistant schizophrenia: a systematic review and meta-analysis. *Schizophrenia Research*, **171**, 215–24.

Leiknes, K. A., Jarosh-von-Schweder, L. & Høie, B. (2012) Contemporary use and practice of electroconvulsive therapy worldwide. *Brain & Behavior*, **2**, 283–302.

Lévy-Rueff, M., Jurgens, A., Lôo, H., Olié, J. P. & Amado, I. (2008) Maintenance electroconvulsive therapy and treatment of refractory schizophrenia. *Encephale*, **34**, 526–33.

Masoudzadeh, A. & Khalilian, A. R. (2007) Comparative study of clozapine, electroshock and the combination of ECT with clozapine in treatment-resistant schizophrenic patients. *Pakistan Journal of Biological Science*, **10**, 4287–90.

Meduna, L. J. (1932) Klinische und anatomische Beiträge zur Frage der genuinen Epilepsie. *Deutsche Zeitschrift für Nervenheilkunde*, **129**, 14–42.

Meduna, L. J. (1934) Über experimentelle Campherepilepsie. *Archiv für Psychiatrie*, **102**, 333–9.

Meduna, L. J. (1935) Versuche über die biologische Beeinflussung des Ablaufes der Schizophrenie: Campher und Cardiazol. *Zeitschrift für die gesamte Neurologie und Psychiatrie*, **152**, 235–62.

Meduna, L. J. (1937) *Die Konvulsionstherapie der Schizophrenie*. Carl Marhold.

Melzer-Ribeiro, D. L., Rigonatti, S. P., Kayo, M., et al. (2017) Efficacy of electroconvulsive therapy augmentation for partial response to clozapine: a pilot randomized ECT – sham controlled trial. *Archives of Clinical Psychiatry*, **44**, 45–50.

Murray, R. M., Quattrone, D., Natesan, S., et al. (2016) Should psychiatrists be more cautious about long-term prophylactic use of antipsychotics? *British Journal of Psychiatry*, **209**, 361–5.

Naidoo, N. (1956) The effects of reserpine (serpasil) on the chronic disturbed schizophrenic: a comparative study of rauwolfia alkaloids and electroconvulsive therapy. *Journal of Nervous and Mental Disease*, **123**, 1–13.

National Institute for Health and Care Excellence (2009) *Guidance on the use of electroconvulsive therapy* (Technology Appraisal TA59). NICE.

National Institute for Health and Care Excellence (2014) *Psychosis and schizophrenia in adults: prevention and management* (Clinical Guideline CG178). NICE.

Nielsen, J., Dahm, M., Lublin, H. & Taylor, D. (2010) Psychiatrists' attitude towards and knowledge of clozapine treatment. *Journal of Psychopharmacology*, **24**, 965–71.

Petrides, G., Malur, C., Braga, R. J., et al. (2015) Electroconvulsive therapy augmentation in clozapine-resistant schizophrenia: a prospective, randomised study. *American Journal of Psychiatry*, **172**, 52–8.

Phutane, V. H., Thirthalli, J., Muralidharan, K., Naveen Kumar, C., Keshav Kumar, J. & Gangadhar, B. N. (2013) Double-blind randomized controlled study showing symptomatic and cognitive superiority of bifrontal over bitemporal electrode placement during electroconvulsive therapy for schizophrenia. *Brain Stimulation*, **6**, 210–17.

Pompili, M., Lester, D., Dominici, G., et al. (2013) Indications for electroconvulsive treatment in schizophrenia: a systematic review. *Schizophrenia Research*, **142**, 1–9.

Pullar Strecker, H. (1937) Book review: Convulsion therapy in schizophrenia [Die Konvulsionstherapie der Schizophrenie] by Ladislaus von Meduna. *British Journal of Psychiatry*, **83**, 727–8.

Samara, M. T., Dold, M., Gianatsi, M., et al. (2016) Efficacy, acceptability and tolerability of antipsychotics in treatment-resistant schizophrenia: a network meta-analysis. *JAMA Psychiatry*, **73**, 199–210.

Shiloh, R., Zemishlany, Z., Aizenberg, D., et al. (1997) Sulpiride augmentation in people with schizophrenia partially responsive to clozapine: a double-blind, placebo-controlled study. *British Journal of Psychiatry*, **171**, 569–73.

Shorter, E. & Healy, D. (2007) *Shock therapy: a history of electroconvulsive treatment in mental illness.* University of Toronto Press.

Small, J. G., Milstein, V., Klapper, M., Kellams, J. J. & Small, I. F. (1982) ECT combined with neuroleptics in the treatment of schizophrenia. *Psychopharmacology Bulletin*, **18**, 34–5.

Sommer, I. E., Begemann, M. J. H., Temmerman, A. & Leucht, S. (2012) Pharmacological augmentation strategies for schizophrenia patients with insufficient response to clozapine: a quantitative literature review. *Schizophrenia Bulletin*, **38**, 1003–11.

Tharyan, P. & Adams, C. E. (2005) Electroconvulsive therapy for schizophrenia. *Cochrane Database of Systematic Reviews*.

Vuksan Ćusa, B., Klepac, N., Jakšić, N., *et al.* (2018) The effects of electroconvulsive therapy augmentation of antipsychotic treatment on cognitive functions in patients with treatment-resistant schizophrenia. *Journal of ECT*, **34**, 31–4.

Waite, J. & Easton, A. (eds.) (2013) *The ECT Handbook* (3rd edn) (Council Report CR128), pp140–57. Royal College of Psychiatrists.

Wang, G., Zheng, W., Li, X. B., *et al.* (2018) ECT augmentation of clozapine for clozapine-resistant schizophrenia: a meta-analysis of randomized controlled trials. *Journal of Psychiatric Research*, **105**, 23–32.

Wu, D., She, C. W., She C. W., *et al.* (1989) Using BPRS and serial numbers and picture recall to test the effectiveness of ECT and chlorpromazine versus chlorpromazine alone in the treatment of schizophrenia: 40 cases, single blind observations. *Chinese Journal of Nervous and Mental Disorders*, **15**, 26–8.

Zheng, W., Cao, X. L., Ungvari, G. S., *et al.* (2016) Electroconvulsive therapy added to non-clozapine antipsychotic medication for treatment resistant schizophrenia: meta-analysis of randomized controlled trials. *PLoS ONE*, **11**, e0156510.

The Use of ECT in the Treatment of Catatonia

Richard Braithwaite

In the previous edition of *The ECT Handbook* (Waite & Easton, 2013), treatment of catatonia was covered in the chapter on schizophrenia. This was partly in keeping with the diagnostic classifications at the time (American Psychiatric Association (APA), 2000; World Health Organisation, 1992), which listed the syndrome as a subtype of schizophrenia. Current classification confirms that the treatment of catatonia, a syndrome of multiple aetiologies, should be considered in its own right.

There have been several important original studies and reviews published since the last edition of the handbook. Several are worthy of mention in this chapter.

Classification and Diagnosis

According to the fifth edition of the *Diagnostic and Statistical Manual of Mental Disorders* (DSM-5; APA, 2013), the term catatonic schizophrenia should no longer be used. Instead, 'catatonia' may be used in three distinct ways:

- as a 'specifier' for neurodevelopmental disorders, mood disorders, schizophrenia and several other related psychotic disorders,
- as a diagnosis, secondary to a general medical condition, or
- as a diagnosis, due to an unspecified cause.

This follows the recognition that the syndrome of catatonia is less commonly seen in schizophrenia than across a plethora of other functional, organic, iatrogenic, toxic and neurodevelopmental states, including autism (Tandon *et al.*, 2013). In the West, around half of all catatonic patients have a diagnosis of affective disorder, whilst perhaps only a fifth have schizophrenia (Rosebush & Mazurek, 2010). Unsurprisingly, given so many underlying causes, the pathophysiology remains obscure, but there may be common themes relating to gamma-amino-butyric acid (GABA) deficiency (Northoff, 2002) or glutamate hyperactivity (Northoff *et al.*, 1997).

The syndrome may be significantly underdiagnosed (van der Heijden *et al.*, 2005). This may relate to a misconception that patients must present with a majority of the oft-quoted features, including some of the more bizarre motor symptoms that are extremely rare, at least in Western practice. *DSM-5* (APA, 2013) lists the following 12 signs, of which just three are required for a diagnosis:

- Stupor
- Catalepsy
- Waxy flexibility
- Mutism
- Negativism

- Posturing
- Mannerism
- Stereotypy
- Agitation
- Grimacing
- Echolalia
- Echopraxia.

A minority of cases present with a severe form complicated by autonomic dysfunction, in the form of tachycardia, hyperthermia, tachypnoea, high or labile blood pressure, excessive sweating, peripheral cyanosis, circulatory collapse and death (Wachtel *et al.*, 2010). This 'malignant catatonia' is often indistinguishable from neuroleptic malignant syndrome (Rasmussen *et al.*, 2016) and warrants emergency treatment (Fink, 2010) (see Chapter 12). A literature review by Singerman & Raheja (1994) found mortality had reduced from over 75% in the pre-benzodiazepine era to 31% by the late 1980s.

History

The first ever patient to be administered medical convulsive therapy in modern times, on 23 January 1934 by László Meduna in Budapest, had been in a mute, tube-fed, catatonic stupor for four years. He was cured of his symptoms after eight treatments (Fink, 1999). At that time, only barbiturates were available for the treatment of catatonia (Carroll, 2001), alongside supportive measures such as nasogastric feeding. Meduna's convulsive therapy became a widely used treatment for catatonic patients throughout the late 1930s (Shorter & Healy, 2007), before being steadily replaced by ECT after 1938 (Fink, 1979).

Benzodiazepines were introduced in 1960 (Sargant & Slater, 1963), but their utility in the treatment of catatonia was not established until the 1980s (Fricchione *et al.*, 1983). It is notable that a Cochrane review by Gibson & Walcott (2008) found no appropriately conducted randomised controlled trials of this intervention. But in view of the multitude of observational studies consistently supporting their efficacy, particularly that of lorazepam (Sienaert *et al.*, 2014), high-dose benzodiazepines remain the widely accepted first-line intervention in non-malignant forms of catatonia (Rosebush & Mazurek, 2010). The comprehensive review of malignant catatonia by Singerman & Raheja (1994) established ECT as the first-line treatment in that condition.

Current Usage

The National Institute for Health and Care Excellence (NICE) currently recommends that ECT is used in individuals with catatonia 'only to achieve rapid and short-term improvement of severe symptoms after an adequate trial of other treatment options has proven ineffective and/or when the condition is considered to be potentially life-threatening' (NICE, 2009). National data (Buley *et al.*, 2017), when extrapolated, suggest that around 90 patients receive an acute course of ECT for catatonia in the UK annually. This may be an underestimation, as many catatonic patients will have had an underlying affective episode documented as the indication for treatment.

Efficacy and Effectiveness

Research in populations with intellectual disability and neuropsychiatric conditions is presented in Chapters 7 and 12 respectively. The studies set out in this chapter have included patients with catatonia of various aetiologies, but predominantly functional mental illness.

Randomised Controlled Trials

There have only been three randomised controlled trials (RCTs) studying ECT specifically in the treatment of catatonia. The first was conducted by Miller *et al.* (1953) in Saskatchewan, Canada, on 30 patients with catatonic schizophrenia; outcome measurements were obscure (Tharyan & Adams, 2005) such that it is impossible to draw conclusions.

The other two RCTs were both conducted in Bangalore, India. One (Phutane *et al.*, 2013) is discussed in the section in this chapter on electrode placement. In the other, Girish & Gill (2003) selected 14 patients who had failed to respond to a trial of lorazepam at doses of up to 8 milligrams daily. They had been suffering with a non-affective catatonia for an average of 38 weeks. They were randomised, in a double-blind manner, to receive either thrice-weekly, bitemporal ECT and an oral placebo, or sham ECT and oral risperidone. Although both groups saw an overall mean improvement in symptoms, as measured by the Bush-Francis Catatonia Rating Scale (BFCRS), ECT brought about significantly greater gains than risperidone (p=0.035). Three patients who had not responded to risperidone then underwent ECT, two achieving complete remission (Girish & Gill, 2003).

Prospective Uncontrolled Studies

There have been several prospective, uncontrolled studies using objective outcome measures; four have included 10 or more patients and are worthy of specific mention.

Suzuki *et al.* (2003) treated 11 consecutive patients with catatonic schizophrenia using thrice-weekly, bilateral ECT, presumably using bitemporal electrode placement. They observed a pre-defined response using the Brief Psychiatric Rating Scale (BPRS) in all patients but did not specifically measure catatonic symptoms.

Also in Japan, Hatta *et al.* (2007) studied 50 consecutive patients whose relatives were sequentially given the options of thrice-weekly, bitemporal ECT, oral lorazepam (or parenteral diazepam for those refusing lorazepam), oral risperidone (or parenteral haloperidol if refusing risperidone), or oral chlorpromazine. There was complete remission of all catatonic symptoms in all 17 patients treated with ECT. Mean daily doses of benzodiazepines were remarkably low in this study (1.8 milligrams of lorazepam or 11.4 milligrams of diazepam) and this was reflected in an extremely poor remission rate in this group (1 of 41 patients, 2%). Doses of antipsychotic were somewhat more realistic (5.5 milligrams of risperidone or 9.4 milligrams of haloperidol; 158 milligrams of chlorpromazine) and remission rates variable (26%, 16% and 68% respectively). Although this study had a comparative element, it must be stressed that it was by no means randomised and patients served as their own comparators (Hatta *et al.*, 2007).

In Italy, Medda *et al.* (2015) studied 26 catatonic patients with bipolar disorder who showed resistance to benzodiazepines. Mean duration of catatonia was 17 weeks, with a standard deviation of 12 weeks and a range of 3 to 50 weeks. A total of 90% had a retarded clinical picture and 21 patients (81%) exhibited response to thrice-weekly, bitemporal ECT, as measured by Clinical Global Impression (CGI). Interestingly, the number of previous bipolar episodes was significantly higher in those who responded to ECT compared with those who did not (Medda *et al.*, 2015).

Unal *et al.* (2017), in Turkey, treated 42 consecutive patients who had failed to respond to three days' treatment with lorazepam and a further five whose condition had been considered life-threatening and in need of immediate ECT. All 47 patients were given thrice-weekly, bifrontal treatment; 44 (94%) fully recovered, including all five patients receiving ECT as a first-line treatment (Unal *et al.*, 2017).

Retrospective Studies

Retrospective studies are of variable size and quality. Nine studies included at least 10 patients receiving ECT and used objective outcome measures, mainly CGI or the BFCRS. It is impossible to draw conclusions from three of these (Rohland *et al.*, 1993; Dutt *et al.*, 2011; Ramdurg *et al.*, 2013). The remaining six are outlined below.

Maletzky (2004) reviewed the cases of 13 patients in Oregon with affective catatonia unresponsive to lorazepam, who were then given bitemporal ECT at least thrice-weekly; all showed marked improvement on CGI (Maletzky, 2004). A Dutch group (van Waarde *et al.*, 2010) reported on 27 patients, of whom 19 had had a failed trial of benzodiazepines. One was given unilateral ECT, while electrode placement for another was not specified; the remainder had bitemporal treatment. Only 16 patients (59%) improved on CGI. Patient characteristics associated with greater clinical improvements included younger age (p=0.05) and autonomic dysregulation at baseline (p=0.02), especially higher body temperature (p=0.02) (van Waarde *et al.*, 2010). The same cohort was reported on elsewhere alongside an additional four patients not given ECT (Tuerlings *et al.*, 2010).

In Massachusetts, England *et al.* (2011) observed 12 patients who had failed to respond to lorazepam; ECT was bilateral in all but two cases. Definite beneficial effects were seen in ten patients (83%), with likely beneficial effects in the remainder (England *et al.*, 2011). In Bangalore, 63 patients receiving thrice-weekly, bitemporal ECT were reported on by Raveendranathan *et al.* (2012). All but six had failed a trial of lorazepam. Complete response was noted in 56 patients (89%) with incomplete response in the remainder (Raveendranathan *et al.*, 2012).

Unal *et al.* (2013) in Turkey studied 57 patients treated with a combination of benzodiazepines and thrice-weekly, bifrontal ECT. Catatonic symptoms resolved in all 57 patients (Unal *et al.*, 2013). Lastly, in Texas, Kugler *et al.* (2015) studied 13 patients who received thrice-weekly, unilateral ECT. Complete resolution of catatonic symptoms was observed in ten patients (77%) (Kugler *et al.*, 2015).

Systematic Reviews

Hawkins *et al.* (1995) produced the first systematic review of case reports and series published to date. Covering 55 patients receiving ECT for catatonia of a variety of causes, they found an overall complete response rate of 85%, with all three patients suffering malignant catatonia responding (Hawkins *et al.*, 1995). Similarly, Consoli *et al.* (2010) collected data from 31 case reports and case series on 59 children treated with ECT for catatonia; the mean age was 15 years and mood disorder the most prevalent underlying cause. Response was 'favourable' in 45 patients (76%), partial in three patients and lacking in one; it is unclear what became of the remaining ten (Consoli *et al.*, 2010). It is likely that both these reviews are subject to selection and publication bias, as well as heterogeneity and lack of objective outcome measures.

The most recent systematic review of ECT in catatonia was conducted by Leroy *et al.* (2017). As well as critically analysing the RCTs and prospective and retrospective series published to date, the reviewers performed a meta-analysis on ten of the more methodologically sound studies from which appropriate data were available. On average, patients were less symptomatic following treatment than at baseline (standardised mean reduction 3.14, 95% confidence interval [CI] 2.34–3.95). Rates of response or remission were not presented in the meta-analysis, because of the heterogeneous definitions used across the included studies (Leroy *et al.*, 2017).

Electrode Placement

Almost all published research, including all three randomised controlled trials, all four larger uncontrolled prospective studies and eight of the nine larger retrospective series, has primarily used bilateral (either bitemporal or bifrontal) rather than unilateral electrode placements. Against this trend, Cristancho *et al.* (2014) and Kugler *et al.* (2015) have reported on a combined total of 18 patients in the United States given thrice-weekly, right unilateral treatment at five to six times seizure threshold; 78% reached complete symptom resolution. No studies have directly compared bilateral with unilateral treatment for catatonia in terms of overall efficacy or speed of response.

Two uncontrolled studies (Unal *et al.*, 2013; Unal *et al.*, 2017) have used bifrontal placement rather than bitemporal. Pooled results from these studies give a 97% response rate.

As part of a larger study in Bangalore of ECT in schizophrenia, Phutane *et al.* (2013) randomised 33 patients with benzodiazepine-resistant catatonia to receive either bifrontal or bitemporal thrice-weekly ECT in a double-blind fashion. Overall response to ECT in both groups was impressive, with the mean BFCRS score dropping from 17 to less than 1 and no significant difference between the groups at the end of treatment. However, response was significantly faster in the bifrontal group, with 8 of 11 patients having experienced complete resolution of all catatonic symptoms at two weeks compared with only 2 of 17 patients in the bitemporal group (Phutane *et al.*, 2013). When five early drop-outs are included in an intention-to-treat analysis, the number needed to treat (NNT) for bifrontal compared to bitemporal ECT at two weeks is 3 (95% CI 2–8).

Frequency of Treatment

Almost all published research has studied either thrice-weekly ECT or, for some patients, daily treatments. In the study by van Waarde *et al.* (2010), those 15 patients who underwent daily ECT during the first week were more likely to improve than the 12 having less frequent treatment (p=0.03), but it must be stressed that patients were not randomised into groups. Based on the published evidence to date, recommended practice is daily treatment, in the first instance at least, in malignant catatonia, or thrice-weekly sessions in less life-threatening forms of the syndrome (Fink *et al.*, 2016).

No studies have directly compared different frequencies of treatment with one another and research utilising twice-weekly treatment is confined to a handful of single case reports. A review of existing evidence confirming the superiority of twice-weekly ECT in routine practice relates only to its use in depressive illness and specifically excludes catatonia from its conclusions (Gangadhar & Thirthalli, 2010). Fink *et al.* (2016), in their recent editorial on ECT technique in catatonia, advise against twice-weekly treatments for treating this condition.

Duration of Acute Treatment

Prospective observational studies have variously reported the mean number of ECT sessions in a successful course as ten (Suzuki *et al.*, 2003; Medda *et al.*, 2015), nine (Hatta *et al.*, 2007), seven in patients who had failed to respond to benzodiazepines (Unal *et al.*, 2017) and four in patients receiving ECT as a first-line intervention for more severe illness (Unal *et al.*, 2017).

In their retrospective analysis, Dutt *et al.* (2011) found no statistically significant difference between the mean of 11 treatments given to their catatonic patients and the mean of 9 given to patients for other indications at that hospital during the same period. A larger retrospective series by Raveendranathan *et al.* (2012) found a mean number of seven treatments necessary. The researchers compared characteristics of patients who responded after four ECT with those who required five or more. The slower responders had been unwell for longer (p=0.02) but had had less severe initial symptoms (p=0.03) (Raveendranathan *et al.*, 2012). In their systematic review of all published studies, Leroy *et al.* (2017) found a range of sessions between 3 and 35, averaging 9, but this calculation includes unsuccessful courses; the unexpectedly wide range precisely matches that reported in the case series of Ramdurg *et al.* (2013).

Importantly, Fink *et al.* (2016) warn against the dangers of prescribing a set number of treatments at the outset, with its associated risks of poor response and early relapse.

Co-administration of Benzodiazepines

In non-malignant catatonia, patients will invariably be receiving high-dose benzodiazepines at the time of a subsequent decision to initiate ECT. In cases of malignant catatonia, it would be unreasonable to withhold medication that can be immediately administered whilst emergency ECT is organised. Although some researchers suggest stopping benzodiazepines for as long as three days prior to initiation of ECT (Suzuki *et al.*, 2005), others have routinely co-prescribed such medication during ECT to very good effect (Unal *et al.*, 2013). Pragmatically, it makes logical sense to continue benzodiazepines in cases of partial response to pharmacotherapy (Sienaert *et al.*, 2014).

In most patients, therefore, the ECT clinician must be prepared to induce a therapeutic seizure despite co-administration of an anticonvulsive agent, often at high dose. This inevitably requires a larger initial dose of electrical charge than would otherwise be necessary. Attention should also be given to the choice of induction agent, with propofol best avoided (see Chapter 23).

Consideration has been given to temporary antagonism of the action of benzodiazepines during ECT using flumazenil. Bailine *et al.* (1994) first reported on repeated, successful use of flumazenil at the time of anaesthetic induction in a non-catatonic patient who required benzodiazepine premedication for pronounced anxiety. Krystal *et al.* (1998) subsequently reported on 35 benzodiazepine-dependent patients in whom 0.4 to 1.0 milligrams of flumazenil, given immediately prior to anaesthetic induction, was safe and effective in ensuring therapeutic seizures during ECT. The technique has since been used in malignant

(Wachtel *et al.*, 2010) and autistic (Wachtel *et al.*, 2014) catatonia to good effect. Such use of flumazenil in catatonia is supported by Fink *et al.* (2016).

Continuation and Maintenance Treatment

Suzuki *et al.* (2005) prospectively studied seven patients with catatonic schizophrenia who had relapsed within six months of an acute course of ECT. Following a second successful acute course, continuation ECT was given at increasing intervals over six months. Four (57%) remained well at six months and there were no further relapses during the remainder of the first year (Suzuki *et al.*, 2005). The three who had relapsed had their continuation treatments increased in frequency to weekly, bringing about response in all three, followed by maintenance treatment for at least one year; two then remained well (Suzuki *et al.*, 2006).

In a recent presentation to the American Academy of Child & Adolescent Psychiatry, Wachtel (2017) reported on 22 children and young adults with autism and catatonia in Maryland. Twenty exhibited repetitive, dangerous self-injurious behaviour refractory to multiple pharmacological and non-pharmacological treatments. All 22 patients experienced a marked reduction in catatonic signs after an acute course of thrice-weekly, bilateral ECT, with a reduction in self-injurious behaviours in 18 of 20 (90%). Nineteen patients were then administered treatment in the longer term, at a frequency ranging between 5 and 21 days. Sixteen of these (84%) sustained their clinical improvement and 13 were still receiving maintenance ECT at the end of the 10-year study period, one patient having received 688 treatments (Wachtel, 2017).

Discussion

There is insufficient evidence from randomised controlled trials to confirm a statistically and clinically significant treatment effect of ECT in catatonia. On the other hand, data from observational studies are overwhelming; response rates are consistently in the majority even in cases of pharmacotherapeutic failure and, in most cases, above 80%. Naturally, such uncontrolled data must be interpreted with caution in the treatment of a syndrome which might be expected to spontaneously remit in many cases. As an illustration, 5 of the 28 patients selected by Bush *et al.* (1996) to receive a benzodiazepine protocol experienced a spontaneous remission of catatonic signs prior to starting treatment.

But untreated, catatonia is a dangerous syndrome. Even with supportive measures to prevent dehydration, those patients in excited states place themselves and others at risk of physical injury, whilst the stuporous can develop lethal pulmonary emboli, without progression to malignant catatonia. Prompt treatment is necessary in all cases and the withholding of a treatment that is most probably effective, purely for the purposes of medical research, would be unethical. For this reason, it is problematic for commentators such as Leroy *et al.* (2017) to call for double-blind randomised controlled trials to establish efficacy, beyond a comparison of lorazepam, ECT and both treatments combined.

Observationally, up to 80% of patients with catatonia respond to treatment with escalating doses of lorazepam (Sienaert *et al.*, 2014), although patients with underlying schizophrenia may fare less well than those with affective disorder (Rosebush & Mazurek, 2010). Almost all those who respond to lorazepam do so within three days (Bush *et al.*, 1996). Conversely, it is well established that antipsychotic medication is not only poorly effective (Hawkins *et al.*, 1995), but may exacerbate the condition and is best avoided (Fink *et al.*, 2016). ECT is, therefore, the most safe and effective second-line treatment in non-malignant catatonia unresponsive to a 72-hour trial of escalating doses of lorazepam.

Given its high lethality, treatment delay in malignant catatonia cannot be afforded. The conclusion of Singerman & Raheja (1994) that ECT should be the first-line treatment in malignant catatonia cannot be refuted by more recent evidence.

It has previously been suggested that the response to ECT in catatonia due to schizophrenia is less favourable than that due to affective disorder (Fear *et al.*, 2013) but there is no consistent evidence to uphold this view. On the contrary, much of the positive observational evidence for ECT quoted in this chapter derives from the study of patients with underlying schizophrenia. The RCT conducted by Phutane *et al.* (2013), for instance, sampled patients with schizophrenia and found a reduction in mean BFCRS score from 17 to less than 1. In their retrospective sample, Rohland *et al.* (1993) reported a non-significant difference between the proportions of patients with schizophrenia and affective disorder who responded to ECT, but no such difference appears to have been identified by more recent researchers in their samples.

Almost all published research on ECT in catatonia has used bilateral electrode placements. A recent meta-analysis of studies comparing bitemporal with unilateral treatment in depressive illness is highly supportive of high-dose unilateral ECT as the default treatment, unless speed of response is the key factor (Kolshus *et al.*, 2017). Indeed, it has been suggested that high-dose unilateral ECT may be associated with a slower initial response in depressive illness, not least because the dose given at a first session of unilateral treatment may be barely therapeutic (Kellner *et al.*, 2010). Given that catatonia, by its very nature, requires a rapid response, there can be no place for unilateral ECT in its initial treatment.

Similarly, save the odd single case report, all studies of ECT in catatonia relate to treatments given at least thrice-weekly. There is no evidence to support the use of twice-weekly ECT in the treatment of catatonia. Conversely, there is sufficient observational evidence for the safety and effectiveness of daily ECT in malignant catatonia to support its use for that condition.

Recommendations

- Benzodiazepine pharmacotherapy, preferably lorazepam, is the initial treatment of choice in non-malignant catatonia.
- ECT should be initiated following failure of a 72-hour trial of escalating doses of lorazepam; to this end, physical investigations necessary to establish fitness for anaesthesia should be completed during this period in anticipation of the possible need for ECT.
- ECT is the initial treatment of choice in malignant catatonia and should be started immediately.
- It may be appropriate to continue benzodiazepine treatment during a course of ECT for catatonia, in which case either a higher starting dose of electrical charge or intravenous flumazenil prior to anaesthetic induction will be required.
- Antipsychotic medication should be avoided as it may exacerbate catatonia.
- The frequency of treatment will depend on the clinical status. Patients with malignant catatonia may require daily treatment until life-threatening autonomic symptoms have subsided; the frequency of treatment can then be reduced. Treatment should usually be given thrice-weekly.

- Bilateral ECT should be used initially in the treatment of catatonia; both the bitemporal and bifrontal placements are accepted techniques.
- High-dose, right unilateral ECT may be considered in the event of severe cognitive side effects with bilateral treatment.
- Continuation ECT is indicated following a successful acute course, in patients who have previously relapsed after cessation of an acute course of ECT, despite prophylactic pharmacotherapy.
- Maintenance ECT, beyond six months, may be weighed up against other treatment options for which there is very limited evidence, in patients whose catatonia has recurred following cessation of continuation ECT.

Acknowledgements

The author wishes to thank Lee Wachtel, Neeraj Gill, Vivek Phutane and Arnaud Leroy for sharing data from their respective studies.

References

American Psychiatric Association (2000) *Diagnostic and statistical manual of mental disorders: DSM-IV-TR.* American Psychiatric Association.

American Psychiatric Association (2013) *Diagnostic and statistical manual of mental disorders* (5th edn). American Psychiatric Association.

Bailine, S. H., Safferman, A., Vital-Herne, J. & Bernstein, S. (1994) Flumazenil reversal of benzodiazepine-induced sedation for a patient with severe pre-ECT anxiety. *Convulsive Therapy,* 10, 65–8.

Buley, N., Copland, E. & Hodge, S. (2017) *ECT Minimum Dataset 2016-2017.* Electroconvulsive Therapy Accreditation Service, Royal College of Psychiatrists.

Bush, G., Fink, M., Petrides, G., Dowling, F. & Francis, A. (1996) Catatonia. II. Treatment with lorazepam and electroconvulsive therapy. *Acta Psychiatrica Scandinavica,* 93, 137–43.

Carroll, B. T. (2001) Kahlbaum's catatonia revisited. *Psychiatry and Clinical Neurosciences,* 55, 431–6.

Consoli, A., Benmiloud, M., Wachtel, L., Dhossche, D., Cohen, D. & Bonnot, O. (2010) Electroconvulsive therapy in adolescents with the catatonic syndrome: efficacy and ethics. *Journal of ECT,* 26, 259–65.

Cristancho, P., Jewkes, D., Mon, T. & Conway, C. (2014) Successful use of right unilateral ECT for catatonia. *Journal of ECT,* 30, 69–72.

Dutt, A., Grover, S., Chakrabarti, S., Avasthi, A. & Kumar, S. (2011) Phenomenology and treatment of catatonia: a descriptive study from north India. *Indian Journal of Psychiatry,* 53, 36–40.

England, M. L., Öngür, D., Konopaske, G. T. & Karmacharya, R. (2011) Catatonia in psychotic patients: clinical features and treatment response. *Journal of Neuropsychiatry and Clinical Neurosciences,* 23, 223–6.

Fear, C. F., Dunne, R. A. & McLoughlin, D. M. (2013) The use of ECT in the treatment of schizophrenia and catatonia. In, Waite, J. & Easton, A. (eds.) *The ECT Handbook* (3rd edn) (Council Report CR128), pp140–157. Royal College of Psychiatrists.

Fink, M. (1979) *Convulsive therapy: theory and practice.* Raven Press.

Fink, M. (1999) *Electroshock: healing mental illness.* Oxford University Press.

Fink, M. (2010) The intimate relationship between catatonia and convulsive therapy. *Journal of ECT,* 26, 243–5.

Fink, M., Kellner, C. H., & McCall, W. V. (2016) Optimizing ECT technique in treating catatonia. *Journal of ECT,* 32, 149–50.

Fricchione, G. L., Cassem, N. H., Hooberman, D. & Hobson, D. (1983) Intravenous lorazepam in neuroleptic-induced catatonia. *Journal of Clinical Psychopharmacology*, **3**, 338–42.

Gangadhar, B. N. & Thirthalli J. (2010) Frequency of electroconvulsive therapy sessions in a course. *Journal of ECT*, **26**, 181–5.

Gibson, R. C. & Walcott, G. (2008) Benzodiazepines for catatonia in people with schizophrenia and other serious mental illnesses. *Cochrane Database of Systematic Reviews*.

Girish, K. & Gill, N. S. (2003) Electroconvulsive therapy in lorazepam non-responsive catatonia. *Indian Journal of Psychiatry*, **45**, 21–5.

Hatta, K., Miyakawa, K., Ota, T., Usui, C., Nakamura, H. & Arai, H. (2007) Maximal response to electroconvulsive therapy for the treatment of catatonic symptoms. *Journal of ECT*, **23**, 233–5.

Hawkins, J. M., Archer, K. J., Strakowski, S. M. & Keck, P. E. (1995) Somatic treatment of catatonia. *The International Journal of Psychiatry in Medicine*, **25**, 345–69.

Kellner, C. H., Knapp, R., Husain, M. M., *et al.* (2010) Bifrontal, bitemporal and right unilateral electrode placement in ECT: randomised trial. *British Journal of Psychiatry*, **196**, 226–34.

Kolshus, E., Jelovac, A. & McLoughlin, D. M. (2017) Bitemporal v. high-dose right unilateral electroconvulsive therapy for depression: a systematic review and meta-analysis of randomized controlled trials. *Psychological Medicine*, **47**, 518–30.

Krystal, A. D., Watts, B. V., Weiner, R. D., *et al.* (1998) The use of flumazenil in the anxious and benzodiazepine-dependent ECT patient. *Journal of ECT*, **14**, 5–14.

Kugler, J. L., Hauptman, A. J., Collier, S. J., *et al.* (2015) Treatment of catatonia with ultrabrief right unilateral electroconvulsive therapy. *Journal of ECT*, **31**, 192–6.

Leroy, A., Naudet, F., Vaiva, G., Francis, A., Thomas, P. & Amad, A. (2017) Is electroconvulsive therapy an evidence-based treatment for catatonia? A systematic review and meta-analysis. *European Archives of Psychiatry and Clinical Neuroscience*. doi:

10.1007/s00406-017-0819-5. [Epub ahead of print]

Maletzky, B. M. (2004) The first-line use of electroconvulsive therapy in major affective disorders. *Journal of ECT*, **20**, 112–17.

Medda, P., Toni, C., Luchini, F., Giorgi Mariani, M., Mauri, M. & Perugi, G. (2015) Catatonia in 26 patients with bipolar disorder: clinical features and response to electroconvulsive therapy. *Bipolar Disorders*, **17**, 892–901.

Miller, D. H., Clancy, J. & Cumming, E. (1953) Reiter's machine, standard alternating current electro-shock (Cerletti method), and pentothal in chronic schizophrenia. *American Journal of Psychiatry*, **109**, 617–20.

National Institute for Health and Care Excellence (2009) *Guidance on the use of electroconvulsive therapy* (Technology Appraisal TA59). NICE.

Northoff, G. (2002) What catatonia can tell us about 'top-down modulation': a neuropsychiatric hypothesis. *Behavioural and Brain Sciences*, **25**, 555–77.

Northoff, G., Eckert, J. & Fritze, J. (1997) Glutaminergic dysfunction in catatonia? Successful treatment of three akinetic catatonic patients with the NMDA antagonist amantadine. *Journal of Neurology, Neurosurgery and Psychiatry*, **62**, 404–6.

Phutane, V. H., Thirthalli, J., Muralidharan, K., Naveen Kumar, C., Keshav Kumar, J. & Gangadhar, B. N. (2013) Double-blind randomized controlled study showing symptomatic and cognitive superiority of bifrontal over bitemporal electrode placement during electroconvulsive therapy for schizophrenia. *Brain Stimulation*, **6**, 210–17.

Ramdurg, S., Kumar, S., Kumar, M., Singh, V., Kumar, D. & Desai, N. G. (2013) Catatonia: etiopathological diagnoses and treatment response in a tertiary care setting: a clinical study. *Industrial Psychiatry Journal*, **22**, 32–6.

Rasmussen, S. A., Mazurek, M. F. & Rosebush, P. I. (2016) Catatonia: our current understanding of its diagnosis, treatment and pathophysiology. *World Journal of Psychiatry*, **6**, 391–8.

Raveendranathan, D., Narayanaswamy, J. C. & Reddi, S. V. (2012) Response rate of catatonia to electroconvulsive therapy and its clinical correlates. *European Archives of Psychiatry and Clinical Neuroscience*, **262**, 425–30.

Rohland, B. M., Carroll, B. T. & Jacoby, R. G. (1993) ECT in the treatment of the catatonic syndrome. *Journal of Affective Disorders*, **29**, 255–61.

Rosebush, P. I. & Mazurek, M. F. (2010) Catatonia and its treatment. *Schizophrenia Bulletin*, **36**, 579–81.

Sargant, W. & Slater, E. (1963) *An introduction to physical methods of treatment in psychiatry* (4th edn). E. & S. Livingstone Ltd.

Shorter, E. & Healy, D. (2007*) Shock therapy: a history of electroconvulsive treatment in mental illness*. University of Toronto Press.

Sienaert, P., Dhossche, D. M., Vancampfort, D., de Hert, M. & Gazdag, G. (2014) A clinical review of the treatment of catatonia. *Frontiers in Psychiatry*, **5**, 181.

Singerman, B. & Raheja, R. (1994) Malignant catatonia: a continuing reality. *Annals of Clinical Psychiatry*, **6**, 259–66.

Suzuki, K., Awata, S., Matsuoka, S. (2003) Short-term effect of ECT in middle-aged and elderly patients with intractable catatonic schizophrenia. *Journal of ECT*, **19**, 73–80.

Suzuki, K., Awata, S., Takano, T., Ebina, Y., Iwasaki, H. & Matsuoka, H. (2005) Continuation ECT for relapse-prevention in middle-aged and elderly patients with intractable catatonic schizophrenia. *Psychiatry and Clinical Neurosciences*, **59**, 481–9.

Suzuki, K., Awata, S., Takano, T., *et al.* (2006) Adjusting the frequency of continuation and maintenance electroconvulsive therapy to prevent relapse of catatonic schizophrenia in middle-aged and elderly patients who are relapse-prone. *Psychiatry and Clinical Neurosciences*, **60**, 486–92.

Tandon, R., Heckers, S., Bustillo, J., *et al.* (2013) Catatonia in DSM-5. *Schizophrenia Research*, **150**, 26–30.

Tharyan, P. & Adams, C. E. (2005) Electroconvulsive therapy for schizophrenia. *Cochrane Database of Systematic Reviews*.

Tuerlings, J. H. A. M., van Waarde, J. A. & Verwey, B. (2010) A retrospective study of 34 catatonic patients: analysis of clinical care and treatment. *General Hospital Psychiatry*, **32**, 631–5.

Unal, A., Bulbul, F., Alpak, G., Virit, O., Copoglu, U. S. & Savas, H. A. (2013) Effective treatment of catatonia by combination of benzodiazepine and electroconvulsive therapy. *Journal of ECT*, **29**, 206–9.

Unal, A., Altindag, A., Demir, B. & Aksoy, I. (2017) The use of lorazepam and electroconvulsive therapy in the treatment of catatonia: treatment characteristics and outcomes in 60 patients. *Journal of ECT*, **33**, 290–3.

van der Heijden, F. M. M. A., Tuinier, S., Arts, N. J. M., Hoogendoom, M. L. C., Kahn, R. S. & Verhoeven, W. M. A. (2005) Catatonia: disappeared or under-diagnosed? *Psychopathology*, **38**, 3–8.

van Waarde, J. A., Tuerlings, J. H. A. M., Verwey, B. & van der Mast, R. C. (2010) Electroconvulsive therapy for catatonia: treatment characteristics and outcomes in 27 patients. *Journal of ECT*, **26**, 248–52.

Wachtel, L. E., Griffin, M. M. Dhossche, D. M. & Reti, I. M. (2010) Brief report: electroconvulsive therapy for malignant catatonia in an autistic adolescent. *Autism*, **14**, 349–58.

Wachtel, L. E., Reti, I. M. & Ying, H. (2014) Stability of intraocular pressure after retinal reattachment surgery during electroconvulsive therapy for intractable self-injury in a 12-year-old autistic boy. *Journal of ECT*, **30**, 73–6.

Wachtel, L. (2017) Acute and maintenance electroconvulsive therapy for catatonia in autism spectrum disorders. *Journal of the American Academy of Child & Adolescent Psychiatry*, **56**, S104.

Waite, J. & Easton, A. (eds.) (2013) *The ECT Handbook* (3rd edn) (Council Report CR128), pp140–157. Royal College of Psychiatrists.

World Health Organisation (1992) *The ICD-10 classification of mental and behavioural disorders: clinical descriptions and diagnostic guidelines*. World Health Organisation.

ECT in Neuropsychiatric Disorders

Jasvinder Singh and David Andrew Cousins

Electroconvulsive therapy (ECT) has long been used in the treatment of patients with neuropsychiatric disorders and continues to be a valuable option for a variety of conditions. The range of conditions for which ECT has been used is broad, but in many instances there is a common indication such as the treatment of psychosis, depression or catatonia occurring in conjunction with the primary neuropsychiatric presentation. Substantial, systematically acquired data supports the use of ECT in the functional psychoses (as set out in Chapters 3–11) but the complexity of additional underlying pathology prevents simple inferences being made about the efficacy of ECT in neuropsychiatric conditions. Regrettably, the evidence for ECT as a treatment for neuropsychiatric disorders is generally low grade, mostly comprising case reports, case series and retrospective and observational studies rather than double-blind randomised controlled trials.

In this chapter we highlight the key points of evidence regarding the use of ECT in the major neuropsychiatric conditions for which it has been investigated. For each condition, where possible, we outline the nature of the disorder, the evidence for ECT in the treatment of that disorder, the evidence for treatment of associated conditions and review some practical considerations such as treatment duration and preferred modality. In some situations, for instance the use of ECT for the treatment of depression post-stroke, there might be legitimate concerns that ECT could aggravate the underlying neurological deficit – the available evidence is briefly reviewed to explore these tensions.

Parkinson's Disease

Parkinson's disease is an archetypal neuropsychiatric disorder characterised by the progressive degeneration of dopaminergic, serotonergic and cholinergic systems (Fenelon, 2008) and a multifaceted clinical presentation encompassing motor, behavioural, cognitive and autonomic dysfunction. Psychiatric presentations are common in Parkinson's disease and are a major determinant of quality of life, carer stress and the need for long-term care (Chang and Fox, 2016). Estimates of the prevalence of conditions such as depression vary widely, in part because presentations such as bradykinesia or bradyphrenia can mask or masquerade as depression. If motor and non-motor presentations were to share aetiology, effective treatment of depression might be expected to be associated with an improvement in the more neurological aspects of Parkinson's disease. However, tensions can exist between the management of the motor and psychiatric presentations – for instance the dopaminergic antagonists favoured in functional psychoses can aggravate bradykinesia, whilst dopamine agonists indicated for motor manifestations have been implicated in psychosis (Ecker et al., 2009). ECT has been used as a treatment for depression, psychosis and catatonia in Parkinson's disease but also in the management of movement disorder including the 'on and off' phenomenon (fluctuations in motor functioning associated with dopamine replacement therapy and illness progression) (Cumper *et al.*, 2014). It can prove a valuable option in patients not gaining benefit from conventional drugs and although the cognitive sequelae and long-term effects on Parkinson's disease progression are incompletely characterised, ECT is generally considered to be a safe and effective treatment (Nishioka *et al.*, 2014).

Movement Disorder

Variable success has been reported in the treatment of motor symptoms using ECT. Andersen *et al.* (1987) conducted a double-blind randomised controlled trial of ECT in patients with Parkinson's disease (n=11) without comorbid depression or dementia. Compared to the sham ECT group (n=5), those receiving active ECT (n=6) had significantly longer 'on phases' after treatment. Those randomised to sham treatment went on to have active ECT and in total, 9 of the 11 patients improved but transient confusion was reported in five patients. In a pilot study of nine patients, six of whom completed treatment, Pintor *et al.* (2012) reported the effects of ECT on axial symptoms partially unresponsive to levodopa, proposing that it may increase the sensitivity of dopaminergic receptors. Improvement was observed for gait and freezing episodes during the 'on' but not the 'off' phase after eight sessions of bilateral ECT, with all patients experiencing transient amnesia. Systematic assessment of the long-term impact of ECT on motor symptoms of Parkinson's disease is lacking, but a longitudinal observational study found highly variable effects, from minimal or transient improvement to marked efficacy lasting up to 35 months (Pridmore *et al.*, 1996).

Depression

A recent review (Borisovskaya *et al.*, 2016) of depression in Parkinson's disease identified numerous case reports and case series, appraising the results for a total of 116 patients. ECT was associated with an overall improvement in depression in 94% and a reduction in the severity of motor symptoms in 83% of patients. Transient confusion was common and sometimes necessitated cessation of treatment.

Psychosis

The extrapyramidal side effects of antipsychotics and the propsychotic potential of dopaminergic agonists make the management of psychosis in Parkinson's disease challenging (Ecker *et al.*, 2009). There is good evidence for low dose clozapine as a treatment for psychosis in Parkinson's disease (Pollak *et al.*, 1999) – although the idiosyncratic risk of agranulocytosis necessitates blood monitoring and vigilance is required for the development of potentially fatal cardiac complications such as myocarditis (Ronaldson *et al.*, 2015), the dose related metabolic effects are generally less problematic (Thomas and Friedman, 2010). Atypical antipsychotics that do not require such close monitoring are commonly prescribed for psychosis in Parkinson's disease, despite uncertain evidence of benefit (Divac *et al.*, 2016) and clear evidence of an increased hazard ratio of death (Weintraub *et al.*, 2016). In patients with Parkinson's disease and psychosis unresponsive to quetiapine (n=8), Usui *et al.* (2011) reported improvements in psychosis and motor features following ECT. In a retrospective analysis of a comparably treated group of patients (n=5), Ueda *et al.*

(2010) reported ECT related improvements in psychosis and motor rating scores lasting up to 30 weeks, with minimal adverse effects. To date, no studies have compared the efficacy of ECT and clozapine, and there is little to guide whether the two may be usefully combined in refractory cases. Practically, clozapine is associated with a reduction in seizure threshold but scarce data is available on how this might impact on ECT delivery. A single report described two patients with Parkinson's disease psychosis incompletely responding to clozapine, one improving swiftly with the addition of ECT and returning to maintenance treatment with low dose clozapine (Factor *et al.*, 1995).

Other Conditions

Obsessions are well recognised in Parkinson's disease patients and in severe cases can lead to marked functional impairment. A case report (Gadit, 2012) described the successful use of ECT for a severe obsessive-compulsive presentation in Parkinson's disease. There are also case reports supporting the use of ECT in catatonia associated with Parkinson's disease, the rationale and practical approach to which is considered later in this chapter.

Practical Considerations

Psychiatric manifestations in Parkinson's disease are often considered difficult to treat but in a retrospective study of 27 Parkinson's disease patients with a diagnosis of depression, psychotic depression or psychosis alone, Calderon-Fajardo *et al.* (2015) reported resolution of symptoms in all cases following a course of ECT. Brief Psychiatric Rating Scale and Hamilton Depression Rating Scale scores halved and motor symptoms improved without worsening of ratings on the Mini-Mental State Examination (MMSE). Treatment comprised an average number of 12 ± 2.8 sessions, and the required dose of levodopa was lower after ECT. Whilst the majority of case reports in Parkinson's disease describe bilateral ECT, the use of unilateral ultra-brief pulse ECT is growing, it is considered to be effective and advantageous because of its minimal interference with cognitive function (Williams *et al.*, 2017). Deep brain stimulation is also used in the treatment of Parkinson's disease but this does not prevent consideration of ECT – both bi-temporal and unilateral ECT have been used successfully in treatment refractory depression and psychosis in Parkinson's disease in patients with deep brain stimulators in situ (Nasr *et al.*, 2011).

Epilepsy

Broadly defined as the occurrence of two unprovoked seizures more than 24 hours apart, anticonvulsants are widely prescribed in epilepsy, often in combination. Treatment resistance is well-recognised and more invasive procedures such as vagal nerve stimulation or psychosurgery may be required. ECT has been considered as a treatment for seizures themselves, especially refractory status epilepticus, though more often it is used for associated presentations such as depression and psychosis.

Seizures

An increase in the seizure threshold may be observed over a course of ECT, arguably through the facilitation of GABA-ergic pathways (Williams *et al.*, 2017, Nasr *et al.*, 2011), and so it follows that ECT might reduce the likelihood of future seizures in those with epilepsy. There is scarce clinical data to support this proposition as a treatment option; a single report describes two children with treatment refractory epilepsy that responded to ECT (Sackeim, 1999).

Status Epilepticus

Prolonged convulsions carry a poor prognosis and if not responsive to conventional anticonvulsants, there is a risk of irreversible brain damage. The use of ECT in treatment refractory status epilepticus is supported by numerous case reports. A systematic review (Lambrecq et al., 2012) reporting eight case studies found seizure cessation in 80% and complete remission in 27% of cases. More recently, Zeiler et al. (2016) identified retrospective studies involving 19 patients (15 adults and four children) receiving ECT for refractory status epilepticus, finding that seizure control was established in 11 of the patients (duration range two weeks to three months). These reviews concluded that ECT could be considered as a viable therapeutic strategy for the most severe and resistant cases of status epilepticus, such as those failing to respond to two inductions of anaesthetic comas. In the case series reported, ECT parameters were variable but sustained improvements have been noted following intense but brief treatment regimes. Non-convulsive status epilepticus – continuous seizure activity on EEG but no objective, major motor manifestations – can also result in significant brain damage but is easily missed. Response to conventional anticonvulsants can vary and the use of ECT has limited evidence. Further, there are reports of post-ictal non-convulsive status epilepticus after ECT (Aftab et al., 2018), highlighting the merits of EEG monitoring.

Depression

There is a complex aetiological relationship between depression and epilepsy, but the presence of depression adversely affects treatment of seizures and has a major effect on quality of life measures. In practice, concern is often expressed that the use of antidepressant medications results in a reduction in seizure threshold and an increased risk of fits. However, a large meta-analysis of over 75,000 cases drawn from FDA trials demonstrated that antidepressants were associated with a lower incidence of seizures compared to placebo, with the exception of bupropion and clomipramine (Alper et al., 2007). Dopamine antagonists were associated with an increased incidence of seizures, a concern given their expanding role in the management of depression. These findings may have implications for the use of ECT in the treatment of depression in patients with epilepsy, but the effects of anticonvulsants on seizure threshold also require consideration. The evidence supporting ECT for depression in those with epilepsy is limited, largely based on case reports. In their report on 43 patients with epilepsy and associated psychiatric conditions including depression, Lunde et al. (2006) concluded that moderate to marked improvement in psychiatric symptoms could be achieved through the use of ECT without need to adjust antiepileptic medications in the majority of patients. Seven of the patients in the report had spontaneous seizures during the course of ECT (some of which were felt to be non-epileptic) and one showed improvement in seizure frequency. Adjustments to anticonvulsants were required in a small proportion of cases, when ECT seizures became more difficult to induce or of short duration. Overall, anticonvulsants seem to have less impact on the outcome of ECT than might be expected (Tang et al., 2017).

Stroke

Cerebrovascular accidents are a common cause of morbidity and mortality, often resulting in presentation with organic mood disorders. The use of ECT in the treatment of psychiatric disorders following a stroke is supported by low level evidence and the potential benefits should be carefully balanced against risks associated with treatment, such as anaesthetic procedures (see Chapter 23). The supporting evidence largely comprises case reports describing improvements in depressive symptoms following ECT in stroke patients (Harmandayan et al., 2012). In a retrospective study of 24 in-patients with post-stroke depression who received ECT, 20 showed a positive response to treatment (Romanowicz et al., 2012). ECT did not result in a worsening of neurological symptoms but three patients developed short-term memory problems. In a retrospective study of 14 patients who received ECT for depression post-stroke, 12 showed improvement in depression, 5 were observed to have improvement in cognition and deterioration was observed in none (Murray et al., 1986).

Huntington's Disease

This autosomal dominant trinucleotide repeat disorder, characterised by chorea arising from progressive basal ganglia degeneration, is often associated with depression, psychosis and anxiety. There are few specific treatment options for Huntington's disease but for the psychiatric presentations, conventional medications are typically prescribed. In refractory cases of depression or psychosis, ECT may be considered, with case level evidence supporting its effectiveness (Beale et al., 1997, Ranen et al., 1994). In the largest of the case series, Cusin et al. (2013) reported on seven patients with Huntington's disease, all of whom showed an improvement in depressive and psychotic symptoms with ECT. Treatment was well tolerated.

Catatonia

This psychomotor dysregulation syndrome, characterised by mutism, negativism, waxy flexibility, staring, posturing, rigidity, repetitive acts and verbalisations, can seriously compromise functioning and wellbeing. Catatonia is a well-recognised presentation of schizophrenia and the affective disorders (see Chapter 11; also autistic spectrum disorder Chapter 7) but the syndrome can arise from myriad aetiologies. Organic catatonia can result from almost any brain insult but some disorders, such as systemic lupus erythematosus (SLE), have well-established associations and specific supporting evidence regarding treatment.

Catatonia of various aetiologies is commonly treated with benzodiazepines, most often lorazepam, and a review of the literature showed that these are associated with a resolution of symptoms in 70% of treatment episodes (Hawkins et al., 1995). The same review recorded a complete response rate of 85% with ECT, albeit with fewer treatment episodes. Combined use of ECT and benzodiazepines has been examined in a relatively large (n=57) retrospective study (Unal et al., 2013), but the effect of benzodiazepines on seizure threshold may present challenges in practice.

In catatonia, the evidence for bilateral ECT is more robust than unilateral. However, Kugler et al. (2015) recently reported the effectiveness of ultra-brief right unilateral ECT in 13 cases of catatonia of various aetiologies, supported by the Cristancho et al. (2014)

description of a full response in four out of five catatonic patients. ECT is often considered as an acute treatment for catatonia, and the rapidity of response is greater in those with severe catatonia of brief duration (Raveendranathan et al., 2012). There is, however, case report evidence supporting its use in chronic catatonia (de Silva et al., 2013, Pigato et al., 2016).

Studies on the effects of ECT in organic catatonia often pool cases of different aetiologies, or report individually on a wide-ranging series of causes including space occupying lesions such as arachnoid cysts, developmental brain anomalies such as an enlarged septum pellucidum, cortical venous thrombosis, metabolic encephalopathy or in response to psychoactive agents. The rapid cessation of clozapine, for instance, can lead to a fluctuant catatonic state that can be very difficult to manage (Nasr and Ganapathy, 2015). Here, the mainstay treatment is to restart clozapine (Wadekar and Syed, 2010), though this may not always be effective or practicable. Whilst there are case reports supporting the combination of ECT and re-initiation of clozapine therapy, it is unclear whether ECT can be effective in isolation. The use of ECT for catatonia in SLE is slightly better defined, Bica et al. (2015) describing three cases gaining benefit without aggravation of the SLE.

Overall, ECT is considered an effective option for catatonia. Treatment is generally tolerated, with case reports highlighting relatively mild adverse effects such as transient cognitive impairment, mild elation or irritability, though mania induced by ECT (Lee et al., 2014) is also a recognised occurrence.

Neuroleptic Malignant Syndrome

Neuroleptic malignant syndrome (NMS) is a medical emergency that presents with altered sensorium and autonomic instability resulting either from rapid dopamine blockage or rapid withdrawal of dopamine antagonists or agonist drugs. If not corrected rapidly it carries high mortality and morbidity, so it is crucial to identify this condition and treat it effectively. In addition to supportive measures, use of dopamine agonists and calcium channel blockers is advocated but ECT can have a role in resistant or severe cases (Strawn et al., 2007). Trollor and Sachdev (1999) reviewed 45 reported cases and described nine new cases of NMS treated with ECT, concluding that ECT should be the preferred treatment in severe NMS. Malignant catatonia is conceptualised as a severe extension of NMS and in one case series of four patients in an intensive care setting (Dessens et al., 2016), significant improvement was observed following ECT, with a range of sessions from 6 to 23.

Multiple Sclerosis

This autoimmune inflammatory disorder, which primarily affects white matter tracts, has a varied presentation and course, but sensorimotor and neuropsychiatric disorders like depression, psychosis and anxiety are common. The role of ECT in this condition has focused on treatment of the most severe neuropsychiatric presentations rather than the disease process itself. Twenty-one case reports were identified and summarised by Palm et al. (2014), ECT reportedly effective in 19 cases. There is some evidence that patients with active white matter lesions may be at risk of neurological deterioration when ECT is given (Steen et al., 2015). Note that catatonia can arise in multiple sclerosis and, as with other causes, ECT can be an effective acute and maintenance treatment (Pontikes and Dinwiddie, 2010).

Encephalitis

Encephalitis may present with fluctuant cognitive impairment associated with various neuropsychiatric symptoms, and causes such as Herpes Simplex Virus (HSV) encephalitis and autoimmune disorders are increasingly well defined. Treatment should target the underlying pathology wherever possible but neuropsychiatric sequelae such as catatonia, psychosis, depression, seizures, movement disorder and behavioural disturbance may require management in their own right. The relatively recently described anti-N-methyl-D-aspartate receptor (NMDAR) encephalitis often presents first to psychiatry services, though the diagnosis may not be immediately obvious. The literature around the use of ECT in anti-NMDAR encephalitis is limited to case reports and largely with respect to the catatonic manifestations. Recently reviewed by Coffey and Cooper (2016), six case reports were identified of patients with anti-NMDAR encephalitis where ECT was used safely and effectively, irrespective of the timing of diagnosis, immunotherapy or removal of associated tumours.

Dementia

The use of ECT in various dementias has focused on its role in the treatment of associated depression, psychosis and behavioural disturbance, not as a potential modifier of disease course. Given the potential for ECT to adversely affect cognitive function, it is not surprising that a common side effect of treatment in dementia cases is post-ictal delirium (Rao and Lyketsos, 2000).

Behavioural Disturbance

Agitation and aggression commonly occur in dementia and as pharmacological treatment may prove ineffective or undesirable in the long term, ECT may prove a valuable alternative, particularly in severe cases (Bang et al., 2008). A recent systematic review of case reports, case series, retrospective chart reviews, retrospective case control studies and an open label prospective study examined the evidence for the use of ECT in agitation associated with dementia (Glass et al., 2017). In the patient outcomes reviewed (n=216), ECT was considered to improve agitation, maintenance treatment was found to be useful in patients who relapsed but the long-term effects of ECT in dementia were not elucidated. There were several notable studies within this review. In a prospective study of 23 patients with agitation and aggression in dementia, Acharya et al. (2015) reported a significant improvement in Clinical Global Impression (CGI) scores following ECT, as well as small increase in MMSE scores. Treatment was well tolerated, though two patients discontinued because of recurrence/adverse events. A retrospective case control study involving 23 patients with dementia also found ECT to be an effective and safe therapeutic intervention, reducing the risk of suicide and aggressive behaviour in dementia (Zhang et al., 2016). In a retrospective systematic chart review of 16 patients with agitation and aggression in the context of dementia, Ujkaj et al. (2012) found significant improvement after ECT, rated using the Pittsburgh Agitation Scale (PAS) and the CGI. The mean number of sessions was nine, mainly bilateral, and whilst eight patients showed transient post-ictal confusion, it was more severe in two patients. Tang et al. (2014) reported on a larger number of subjects (n=42) in a retrospective assessment of ECT in severe dementia, finding improvements in PAS scores. Whilst some patients had to be switched from right unilateral ECT to bilateral treatment due to poor response, side effects and post-treatment confusion rates were low, probably due to use of ultra-brief pulse durations.

Depression

In patients with dementia, depression can be common and often proves refractory to standard medication. ECT may be indicated but has the potential to worsen cognitive impairment in the short and medium term. Hausner *et al.* (2011) conducted a six-month prospective study of elderly inpatients (n=44) with major depressive disorder treated with ECT, grouped into 'no cognitive impairment', 'mild cognitive impairment' (MCI) and dementia. Six sessions of ECT proved to be an effective treatment for depression in all groups, improving MMSE scores in those with no cognitive impairment or MCI. In the dementia group, cognition in those taking drugs for dementia improved clinically but not statistically, whilst a deterioration was observed in those not on medication. Depression remained in remission at six months in all groups and the pre-ECT cognitive deficits were the best predictor of cognitive decline over the duration of the study. Takahashi *et al.* (2009) reported two cases of treatment-resistant depression in Dementia with Lewy Bodies (DLB) with a good response to ECT, but it remains unknown if there is a preferential response in subtypes of dementia.

Psychosis

The use of ECT as a treatment of psychosis in dementia has not been extensively studied. Katagai *et al.* (2007) reported its utility in a treatment-resistant case, the patient showing improvement after receiving only two sessions of ECT. Perceptual disturbances, especially visual hallucinations, commonly occur in DLB but the use of ECT for such presentations has not been systematically examined.

Delirium

Acute confusional states are very common in psychiatric and general medical settings, and often go undiagnosed. Management should focus on recognition, elucidation of the underlying cause and treatment thereof. Given that cognitive impairment and confusion can be a consequence of ECT, its use in delirium seems counterintuitive. Nevertheless, case reports have examined its use in certain settings. Nielsen *et al.* (2014) described a series of five patients with severe protracted delirium in an intensive care unit, refractory to standard treatment. Improvement in agitation, anxiety and discomfort following ECT was reported in four cases, the authors concluding the ECT may be considered when agitation cannot be controlled by medical therapy, when weaning becomes impossible because of agitation or prolonged sedation is the only alternative. More recently, van den Berg *et al.* (2016) described a case of severe delirium in which the fluctuating state improved with seven sessions of ECT.

Tardive Dyskinesia

Drug induced movement disorders are not uncommon in psychiatric practice. Some presentations, such as extrapyramidal side effects and the acute dystonias, may respond to dose reductions, drug cessation or supportive medications, but tardive dyskinesia can prove particularly intractable. Regrettably, the value of ECT in the treatment of tardive dyskinesia remains unclear, the most notable review of case level evidence reporting variously on improvement, little effect and worsening in the published series (Kennedy et al., 2003).

Other conditions

Traumatic brain injury (TBI) can result in challenging behaviour and ECT has been reported to improve agitation and aggression within six sessions of brief pulse bilateral administration (Kant et al., 1995). It is common for psychiatric illness to follow TBI and whilst challenging, such presentations can respond well to standard treatment. However, in the context of TBI, Martino et al. (2008) reported a case in which ECT proved to be an effective treatment of depression without worsening of cognitive functioning. The use of ECT in various degenerative and movement disorders has been reported, including multiple system atrophy, progressive supranuclear palsy, Wilson disease, Meige's syndrome and tic disorder (Kennedy et al., 2003). Improvement and worsening of presentations have been reported, such that no useful conclusions regarding efficacy can be made.

Summary

In the use of ECT in neuropsychiatric disorders, the strongest evidence relates to the treatment of Parkinson's disease, catatonia and refractory status epilepticus, but much of this evidence remains restricted to retrospective studies and case series. For these and the other conditions considered, case level evidence is generally positive with regard to the efficacy and tolerability of ECT, but such reports are typically prone to publication bias. Given the lack of high quality evidence for ECT in neuropsychiatric disorders, clinicians may wish to consider it only after treatments with a stronger evidence base have been tried without success or otherwise deemed unacceptable. In cases where a neuropsychiatric disorder is complicated by the presence of a psychiatric syndrome such as depression, it might be reasonable to expect both to benefit from ECT. However, comorbidity influences prognosis and so caution is advised when making such inferences. In general, a second psychiatric opinion should be considered before offering ECT for a non-standard indication. In conclusion, ECT is a potent intervention in terms of both efficacy and adverse effects, but the evidence supporting its use in neuropsychiatric disorders is low grade. There is a clear and pressing need for rigorous, systematic assessments of its merits in the treatment of major neuropsychiatric disorders in order to direct the best care in these challenging, complex and often refractory conditions.

References

Acharya, D., Harper, D. G., Achtyes, E. D., et al. 2015. Safety and utility of acute electroconvulsive therapy for agitation and aggression in dementia. International Journal of Geriatric Psychiatry, 30, 265–73.

Aftab, A., Vandercar, A., Alkhachroum, A., Lagrotta, C. & Gao, K. 2018. Nonconvulsive status epilepticus after electroconvulsive therapy: a review of literature. Psychosomatics, 59, 36–46.

Alper, K., Schwartz, K. A., Kolts, R. L. & Khan, A. 2007. Seizure incidence in psychopharmacological clinical trials: an analysis of food and drug administration (FDA) summary basis of approval reports. Biological Psychiatry, 62, 345–54.

Andersen, K., Balldin, J., Gottfries, C. G., et al. 1987. A double-blind evaluation of electroconvulsive-therapy in Parkinsons-disease with on-off phenomena. Acta Neurologica Scandinavica, 76, 191–9.

Bang, J., Price, D., Prentice, G. & Campbell, J. 2008. ECT treatment for two cases of dementia-related pathological yelling. *Journal of Neuropsychiatry and Clinical Neurosciences*, 20, 379–80.

Beale, M. D., Kellner, C. H., Gurecki, P. & Pritchett, J. T. 1997. ECT for the treatment of Huntington's disease: a case study. *Convulsive Therapy*, 13, 108–12.

Bica, B., Moro, A. L. D., Hax, V., et al. 2015. Electroconvulsive therapy as a treatment for refractory neuropsychiatric lupus with catatonia: three case studies and literature review. *Lupus*, 24, 1327–31.

Borisovskaya, A., Bryson, W. C., Buchholz, J., Samii, A. & Borson, S. 2016. Electroconvulsive therapy for depression in Parkinson's disease: systematic review of evidence and recommendations. *Neurodegenerative Disease Management*, 6, 161–76.

Calderon-Fajardo, H., Cervantes-Arriaga, A., Llorens-Arenas, R., Ramirez-Bermudez, J., Ruiz-Chow, A. & Rodriguez-Violante, M. 2015. Electroconvulsive therapy in Parkinson's disease. *Arquivos De Neuro-Psiquiatria*, 73, 856–60.

Chang, A. & Fox, S. H. 2016. Psychosis in Parkinson's disease: epidemiology, pathophysiology, and management. *Drugs*, 76, 1093–118.

Coffey, M. J. & Cooper, J. J. 2016. Electroconvulsive therapy in Anti-N-Methyl-D-Aspartate Receptor Encephalitis: a case report and review of the literature. *Journal of ECT*, 32, 225–9.

Cristancho, P., Jewkes, D., Mon, T. & Conway, C. 2014. Successful use of right unilateral ECT for catatonia: a case series. *Journal of ECT*, 30, 69–72.

Cumper, S. K., Ahle, G. M., Liebman, L. S. & Kellner, C. H. 2014. Electroconvulsive therapy (ECT) in Parkinson's disease: ECS and dopamine enhancement. *Journal of ECT*, 30, 122–24.

Cusin, C., Franco, F. B., Fernandez-Robles, C., Dubois, C. M. & Welch, C. A. 2013. Rapid improvement of depression and psychotic symptoms in Huntington's disease: a retrospective chart review of seven patients treated with electroconvulsive therapy. *General Hospital Psychiatry*, 35.

de Silva, V. A., Lakmini, W. D., Gunawardena, H. N. & Hanwella, R. 2013. Chronic catatonia treated with electroconvulsive therapy: a case report. *Journal of Medical Case Reports*, 7, 219–219.

Dessens, F. M., van Paassen, J., van Westerloo, D. J., van der Wee, N. J., van Vliet, I. M. & van Noorden, M. S. 2016. Electroconvulsive therapy in the intensive care unit for the treatment of catatonia: a case series and review of the literature. *General Hospital Psychiatry*, 38, 37–41.

Divac, N., Stojanovic, R., Vujovic, K. S., Medic, B., Damjanovic, A. & Prostran, M. 2016. The efficacy and safety of antipsychotic medications in the treatment of psychosis in patients with Parkinson's disease. *Behavioural Neurology*. doi: 10.1155/2016/4938154. Epub 2016 Jul 18.

Ecker, D., Unrath, A., Kassubek, J. & Sabolek, M. 2009. Dopamine agonists and their risk to induce psychotic episodes in Parkinson's disease: a case-control study. *BMC Neurology*, 9.

Factor, S. A., Molho, E. S. & Brown, D. L. 1995. Combined clozapine and electroconvulsive-therapy for the treatment of drug-induced psychosis in parkinsons-disease. *Journal of Neuropsychiatry and Clinical Neurosciences*, 7, 304–7.

Fenelon, G. 2008. Psychosis on Parkinson's disease: Phenomenology, frequency, risk factors, and current understanding of pathophysiologic mechanisms. *CNS Spectrums*, 13, 18–25.

Gadit, A. M. & Smigas, T. 2012. Efficacy of ECT in severe obsessive compulsive disorder with Parkinson's disease. *BMJ Case Reports*. https://casereports.bmj.com/content/2012/bcr.01.2012.5675

Glass, O. M., Forester, B. P. & Hermida, A. P. 2017. Electroconvulsive therapy (ECT) for treating agitation in dementia (major neurocognitive disorder) – a promising option. *International Psychogeriatrics*, 29, 717–26.

Harmandayan, M., Romanowicz, M. & Sola, C. 2012. Successful use of ECT in post-stroke depression. *General Hospital Psychiatry*, 34, 102.e5–6.

Hausner, L., Damian, M., Sartorius, A. & Frolich, L. 2011. Efficacy and cognitive side effects of electroconvulsive therapy (ECT) in depressed elderly inpatients with coexisting mild cognitive impairment or dementia. *Journal of Clinical Psychiatry*, 72, 91–7.

Hawkins, J. M., Archer, K. J., Strakowski, S. M. & Keck, P. E. 1995. Somatic treatment of catatonia. *International Journal of Psychiatry in Medicine*, 25, 345–69.

Kant, R., Bogyi, A. M., Carosella, N. W., Fishman, E., Kane, V. & Coffey, C. E. 1995. ECT as a therapeutic option in severe brain injury. *Convulsive Therapy*, 11, 45–50.

Katagai, H., Yasui-Furukori, N., Kikuchi, A. & Kaneko, S. 2007. Effective electroconvulsive therapy in a 92-year-old dementia patient with psychotic feature. *Psychiatry and Clinical Neurosciences*, 61, 568–70.

Kennedy, R., Mittal, D. & O' Jile, J. 2003. Electroconvulsive therapy in movement disorders: An update. *Journal of Neuropsychiatry and Clinical Neurosciences*, 15, 407–21.

Kugler, J. L., Hauptman, A. J., Collier, S. J., et al. 2015. Treatment of catatonia with ultrabrief right unilateral electroconvulsive therapy: a case series. *Journal of ECT*, 31, 192–6.

Lambrecq, V., Villega, F., Marchal, C., et al. 2012. Refractory status epilepticus: Electroconvulsive therapy as a possible therapeutic strategy. *Seizure-European Journal of Epilepsy*, 21, 661–4.

Lee, J., Arcand, L., Narang, P. & Lippmann, S. 2014. ECT-induced mania. *Innovations in Clinical Neuroscience*, 11, 27–9.

Lunde, M. E., Lee, E. K. & Rasmussen, K. G. 2006. Electroconvulsive therapy in patients with epilepsy. *Epilepsy & Behavior*, 9, 355–9.

Martino, C., Krysko, M., Petrides, G., Tobias, K. G. & Kellner, C. H. 2008. Cognitive tolerability of electroconvulsive therapy in a patient with a history of traumatic brain injury. *Journal of ECT*, 24, 92–5.

Murray, G. B., Shea, V. & Conn, D. K. 1986. Electroconvulsive-therapy for poststroke depression. *Journal of Clinical Psychiatry*, 47, 258–60.

Nasr, S., Murillo, A., Katariwala, N., Mothkur, V. & Wendt, B. 2011. Case report of electroconvulsive therapy in a patient with Parkinson's disease concomitant with deep brain stimulation. *Journal of ECT*, 27, 89–90.

Nasr, Y. & Ganapathy, R. 2015. Treatment resistant catatonia secondary to clozapine withdrawal. *Progress in Neurology and Psychiatry*, 19, 17–19.

Nielsen, R. M., Olsen, K. S., Lauritsen, A. O. & Boesen, H. C. 2014. Electroconvulsive therapy as a treatment for protracted refractory delirium in the intensive care unit-Five cases and a review. *Journal of Critical Care*, 29.

Nishioka, K., Tanaka, R., Shimura, H., et al. 2014. Quantitative evaluation of electroconvulsive therapy for Parkinson's disease with refractory psychiatric symptoms. *Journal of Neural Transmission*, 121, 1405–10.

Palm, U., Ayache, S. S., Padberg, F. & Lefaucheur, J. P. 2014. Non-invasive brain stimulation therapy in multiple sclerosis: a review of tDCS, rTMS and ECT results. *Brain Stimulation*, 7, 849–54.

Pigato, G., Roiter, B., Cecchin, D., et al. 2016. Electroconvulsive therapy in a patient with chronic catatonia clinical outcomes and cerebral (18)F fludeoxyglucose positron emission tomography findings. *Journal of ECT*, 32, 222–3.

Pintor, L. P., Valldeoriola, F., Fernandez-Egea, E., et al. 2012. Use of electroconvulsive therapy in Parkinson disease with residual axial symptoms partially unresponsive to L-Dopa: a pilot study. *Journal of ECT*, 28, 87–91.

Pollak, P., Destee, A., Lille, C. H. U., et al. Clozapine parkinson study, G. 1999. Clozapine in drug-induced psychosis in Parkinson's disease. *Lancet*, 353, 2041–2.

Pontikes, T. K. & Dinwiddie, S. H. 2010. Electroconvulsive therapy in a patient with multiple sclerosis and recurrent catatonia. *Journal of ECT*, 26, 270–1.

Pridmore, S., Lowrie, A., Holmes, G. & Pollard, C. 1996. ECT in Parkinson's disease:

neuropsychological response. *Convulsive Therapy*, 12, 257–9.

Ranen, N. G., Peyser, C. E. & Folstein, S. E. 1994. ECT as a treatment for depression in Huntingtons-disease. *Journal of Neuropsychiatry and Clinical Neurosciences*, 6, 154–9.

Rao, V. & Lyketsos, C. G. 2000. The benefits and risks of ECT for patients with primary dementia who also suffer from depression. *International Journal of Geriatric Psychiatry*, 15, 729–35.

Raveendranathan, D., Narayanaswamy, J. C. & Reddi, S. V. 2012. Response rate of catatonia to electroconvulsive therapy and its clinical correlates. *European Archives of Psychiatry and Clinical Neuroscience*, 262, 425–30.

Romanowicz, M., Sutor, B. & Sola, C. 2012. Safety and efficacy of electroconvulsive therapy for depression following cerebrovascular accident. *Acta Neuropsychiatrica*, 24, 226–9.

Ronaldson, K. J., Fitzgerald, P. B. & Mcneil, J. J. 2015. Clozapine-induced myocarditis, a widely overlooked adverse reaction. *Acta Psychiatrica Scandinavica*, 132, 231–40.

Sackeim, H. A. 1999. The anticonvulsant hypothesis of the mechanisms of action of ECT: Current status. *Journal of ECT*, 15, 5–26.

Steen, K., Narang, P. & Lippmann, S. 2015. Electroconvulsive therapy in Multiple Sclerosis. *Innovations in Clinical Neuroscience*, 12, 28–30.

Strawn, J. R., Keck, P. E. & Caroff, S. N. 2007. Neuroleptic malignant syndrome. *American Journal of Psychiatry*, 164, 870–6.

Takahashi, S., Mizukami, K., Yasuno, F. & Asada, T. 2009. Depression associated with dementia with Lewy bodies (DLB) and the effect of somatotherapy. *Psychogeriatrics*, 9, 56–61.

Tang, Y. L., Hermida, A. P., Ha, K., Laddha, S. R. & McDonald, W. M. 2014. Efficacy and safety of ECT for behavioral and psychological symptoms of Dementia (BPSD): a retrospective chart review. *American Journal of Geriatric Psychiatry*, 22, S114–S115.

Tang, V. M., Pasricha, A. N., Blumberger, D. M., et al. 2017. Should benzodiazepines and anticonvulsants be used during electroconvulsive therapy? A case study and literature review. *Journal of ECT*, 33, 237–42.

Thomas, A. A. & Friedman, J. H. 2010. Current use of clozapine in Parkinson disease and related disorders. *Clinical Neuropharmacology*, 33, 14–16.

Trollor, J. N. & Sachdev, P. S. 1999. Electroconvulsive treatment of neuroleptic malignant syndrome: a review and report of cases. *Australian and New Zealand Journal of Psychiatry*, 33, 650–9.

Ueda, S., Koyama, K. & Okubo, Y. 2010. Marked improvement of psychotic symptoms after electroconvulsive therapy in Parkinson disease. *Journal of ECT*, 26, 111–15.

Ujkaj, M., Davidoff, D. A., Seiner, S. J., Ellison, J. M., Harper, D. G. & Forester, B. P. 2012. Safety and efficacy of electroconvulsive therapy for the treatment of agitation and aggression in patients with Dementia. *American Journal of Geriatric Psychiatry*, 20, 61–72.

Unal, A., Bulbul, F., Alpak, G., Virit, O., Copoglu, U. S. & Savas, H. A. 2013. Effective treatment of catatonia by combination of benzodiazepine and electroconvulsive therapy. *Journal of ECT*, 29, 206–9.

Usui, C., Hatta, K., Doi, N., et al. 2011. Improvements in both psychosis and motor signs in Parkinson's disease, and changes in regional cerebral blood flow after electroconvulsive therapy. *Progress in Neuro-Psychopharmacology & Biological Psychiatry*, 35, 1704–8.

van den Berg, K. S., Marijnissen, R. M. & van Waarde, J. A. 2016. Electroconvulsive therapy as a powerful treatment for delirium: a case report. *Journal of ECT*, 32, 65–6.

Wadekar, M. & Syed, S. 2010. Clozapine-withdrawal catatonia. *Psychosomatics*, 51, 355–U126.

Weintraub, D., Chiang, C., Kim, H. M., et al. 2016. Association of antipsychotic use with mortality risk in patients with Parkinson disease. *Jama Neurology*, 73, 535–41.

Williams, N. R., Bentzley, B. S., Sahlem, G. L., *et al.* 2017. Unilateral ultra-brief pulse electroconvulsive therapy for depression in Parkinson's disease. *Acta Neurologica Scandinavica*, 135, 407–11.

Zeiler, F. A., Matuszczak, M., Teitelbaum, J., Gillman, L. M. & Kazina, C. J. 2016. Electroconvulsive therapy for refractory status epilepticus: a systematic review. *Seizure-European Journal of Epilepsy*, 35, 23–32.

Zhang, Q. E., Sha, S., Ungvari, G. S., *et al.* 2016. Demographic and clinical profile of patients with dementia receiving electroconvulsive therapy: a case-control study. *Journal of ECT*, 32, 183–6.

Cognitive Side-Effects of ECT

Martha Finnegan and Declan M McLoughlin

Importance of Cognitive Side-Effects

Cognitive side-effects of ECT are among the most important factors limiting prescription and uptake of ECT. Patients, families and clinicians alike share concerns about a variety of cognitive side-effects.

Factors affecting cognitive side-effects of ECT are many, and include pre-existing cognitive impairment and treatment factors such as laterality and pulsewidth (McClintock *et al.*, 2014). The effect of the combination of pre-existing depression, treatment with ECT and residual depressive symptoms, as well as individual patient factors, on cognitive performance during and after ECT has not been fully elucidated. There are few strong predictors of cognitive impairment during and after ECT and questions about the extent and persistence of some cognitive side-effects remain unanswered. There is an absence of standardised instruments designed specifically for cognitive assessment during ECT, while existing instruments may not detect subtle or patchy impairments that affect quality of life post-ECT.

Types of Adverse Cognitive Side-Effects

Cognitive side-effects can be divided into those occurring *immediately* after each treatment, those which are *subacute and longer-term* (apparent during, and at the completion of, a course of ECT), as well as *retrograde amnesia*.

Box 13.1 Cognitive Side-Effects of ECT (see also Lezak, 2012)

Anterograde amnesia: impaired ability to remember new information from the time of commencing ECT onwards

Retrograde amnesia: impaired ability to remember information learned before commencing ECT

Autobiographical amnesia: impaired ability to remember events personally experienced at a particular time and place (episodic autobiographical memories e.g. something that happened at a wedding one attended) and pieces of general information (semantic autobiographical memories, e.g. year of graduation) from one's own life

Subjective memory difficulty: the experience of feeling as though one has a problem with one's memory, regardless of performance on objective memory testing

Impaired executive function: impairment in higher brain functions such as judgement, planning and completing complex tasks

---

Immediate Cognitive Effects

Acute cognitive side-effects include disorientation, impaired attention and amnesia for the immediate time period of the ECT treatment and recovery. Disorientation is very common immediately following ECT and is transient, rarely persisting beyond 60 minutes (Sobin *et al.*, 1995). Time to reorientation can be measured as the time at which correct responses to 4/5 questions about orientation to person (name, date of birth, current age), place (name of hospital) and time (day of the week) are given, with 0 minutes corresponding to when the patient resumes spontaneous breathing (Semkovska *et al.*, 2016). In a trial of high-dose (6 times threshold) right unilateral ECT (RUL) vs bitemporal ECT at 1.5 times threshold, median time to recovery of orientation with RUL ECT was 19 minutes vs 26 minutes with bitemporal ECT (Semkovska *et al.*, 2016)), with no participant in either arm experiencing disorientation past 60 minutes. During a course of ECT, the number of ECT treatments is associated with longer periods of disorientation in older people (Martin *et al.*, 2015).

Longer time to reorientation has been reported to be associated with more persistent retrograde memory impairment following a course of ECT (Martin *et al.*, 2015, Sobin *et al.*, 1995) and has also been associated with better mood outcomes, though this requires further study (Bjølseth *et al.*, 2016). Routine assessment of time to reorientation therefore represents a low-burden, high-yield form of cognitive assessment during the ECT course that could help guide treatment strategies to minimise cognitive problems at the end of the course.

Persistent disorientation, for example disorientation beyond 90 minutes, is difficult to predict accurately but has been associated with older age (Martin *et al.*, 2015), poor cognitive function at baseline (Sobin *et al.*, 1995) and presence of psychotic symptoms (Calev *et al.*, 1991). Higher stimulus doses result in longer time to reorientation but may be necessary for treatment efficacy. Similarly, brief-pulse (0.5–1.0 msec) ECT is associated with longer time to reorientation but remains more effective than ultrabrief pulse (0.3 msec) ECT for depression (Tor *et al.*, 2015). Persistent disorientation is more likely with bitemporal ECT, occurring in 13% of those having high-dose bitemporal ECT (at 2.5 times threshold) vs 2% of those having high-dose RUL ECT (at 6 times threshold) (Sackeim *et al.*, 2000).

Another potential factor which may affect time to reorientation is choice of anaesthetic agent. However, there is little high-quality evidence to guide choice of agent based on effect on time to reorientation (see Chapter 23 for discussion of anaesthetic agents).

Lithium and ECT

There is ongoing debate about the potential for lithium to contribute to cognitive side-effects, specifically acute disorientation, possibly due to lithium's anticholinergic activity. There are also reports of prolonged seizure with concurrent use of lithium and ECT (Sartorius *et al.*, 2005). However, studies of lithium in combination with ECT are largely limited to retrospective or observational studies and case series (Volpe and Tavares Jr., 2012). Concerns about the combination of lithium and ECT may relate to those with higher serum lithium levels (Thirthalli *et al.*, 2011). Although there is no high-level evidence to guide practice, close monitoring of serum levels should take place. For those with serum lithium above 0.8mmol/L it may be prudent to reduce to a lower therapeutic range (0.4–0.5 mmol/L) during the course of ECT.

Post-ictal Delirium

There are varying estimates of the incidence of post-ictal delirium, an acute confusional state, from 12% to 65% of patients (Reti *et al.*, 2014). Severe disorientation and amnesia may present as restlessness and anxiety in the recovery period. Presence of catatonia and longer seizure duration have been found to be associated with risk of delirium (Kikuchi *et al.*, 2009, Reti *et al.*, 2014). Reorientation and supportive nursing care will often suffice to manage patients presenting with restlessness. Agitated patients who are at risk of accidental self-injury may require further doses of intravenous anaesthetic or a benzodiazepine and subsequent airway monitoring, resulting in a longer recovery period. Where delirium persists beyond four hours after treatment, medical assessment should be performed to rule out any contributory medical illness; see Chapter 23.

Subacute and Longer-term Cognitive Side-Effects

Cognitive side-effects occurring during the course of ECT and resolving soon after completion include anterograde amnesia and non-memory cognitive effects, such as impaired executive function.

Anterograde Amnesia

ECT does not cause impairment in the ability to learn new skills or movements (procedural memory), and other aspects of implicit memory such as perceptual priming (the ability to use cues and associations to remember multiple items) are seemingly unaffected, though not often studied (Squire *et al.*, 1984, Vakil *et al.*, 2000).

Anterograde amnesia during the course of ECT is common and is generally limited to a period of days to weeks after completion of the course, returning to pre-ECT baseline or improving beyond baseline two or more weeks after completion of a treatment course (Semkovska and McLoughlin, 2010). Verbal memory is more affected than visual memory, but impairment in either can result in practical difficulties for patients during the course of ECT, such as remembering medication dose changes, names of staff and aspects of the ECT treatment itself.

There is no evidence of cumulative cognitive impairment with repeated applications of ECT, including maintenance ECT (Brus *et al.*, 2017, Petrides *et al.*, 2011, Russell *et al.*, 2003, Smith *et al.*, 2010). The CORE studies from the USA of continuation ECT vs continuation pharmacotherapy after successful ECT for depression found no differences between the groups in cognitive outcomes at 24 weeks of treatment. Anterograde memory improved in both groups 12 weeks after completion of the acute ECT course, regardless of use of continuation ECT (Smith *et al.*, 2010).

Non-memory Cognitive Side-Effects

Though there are case reports of a variety of non-memory cognitive adverse effects following ECT, some reporting severe and permanent loss of function and reports of personality change, there is no objective evidence of lasting impairment following ECT.

Meta-analysis showed small to medium impairments in visual episodic memory (worse for delayed visual recall than for immediate visual recall) during the course of ECT, with recovery or improvement beyond baseline by 15 days post-ECT (Semvokska and McLoughlin, 2010). In one study, deficits were identified in visual and visuospatial memory in people having ECT, with some of these deficits persisting after one month, (Falconer *et al.*, 2010), however bilateral ECT was administered at twice the seizure threshold, likely to amplify cognitive problems. In another study, visual memory and learning improved during the course of ECT, a finding which correlated with improvement in depression (Maric *et al.*, 2016), but in this study ECT was administered three times per week and the finding may thus not be generalisable.

A meta-analysis concluded that deficits in executive functioning can be found soon after completing a course of ECT, suggesting these are also present during the treatment course (Semkovska and McLoughlin, 2010). However, all executive functioning measures included in the analysis showed improvement in performance at 4–15 days post ECT compared with pre-ECT baseline, and improvements continued beyond 15 days follow-up. Working memory, as measured by digit span backward, was not impaired at 0–3 days post-treatment and improved vs pre-ECT baseline at follow-up more than 15 days post-treatment (Semkovska and McLoughlin, 2010).

There is no evidence of cumulative cognitive impairment with repeated courses of ECT. In fact, in long-term follow-up, many cognitive functions improve compared to pre-ECT baseline. However, as cognitive function pre-ECT and pre-depression is not routinely measured, it is not clear whether the cognitive improvement following ECT is a return to a healthy level of normal cognitive function. Factors affecting long-term cognitive perform-ance include age (Sackeim *et al.*, 2007), severity of depression at the time of testing and the number of days since the last ECT session. One possibility is that subtle or patchy impairments in executive function following a course of ECT are not evident on routine cognitive testing but contribute to the experience of subjective memory difficulties expressed by patients.

Retrograde Amnesia

The ability to remember events from one's own life is strongly associated with identity. Thus autobiographical amnesia is distressing (Rose *et al.*, 2003) and consequently is the focus of research on ECT-related retrograde amnesia. More recent memories may be more vulnerable to loss during ECT than distant memories (Lisanby *et al.*, 2000).

Patient factors that confer increased risk of retrograde amnesia are estimated premorbid IQ, age (Sackeim *et al.*, 2007), global cognition at baseline (Sobin *et al.*, 1995), and longer time to reorientation (Martin *et al.*, 2015). As with anterograde amnesia, retrograde amnesia is more likely with more ECT treatments. High-dose RUL brief-pulse ECT is associated with higher percentage recall of autobiographical information than brief-pulse bitemporal ECT (Kolshus *et al.*, 2017). In turn, ultrabrief-pulse RUL ECT is associated with less retrograde amnesia than brief pulse RUL ECT, but is significantly less efficacious in treatment of depression (Tor *et al.*, 2015).

Though there is no high-level evidence of persisting retrograde amnesia after ECT, this does not preclude individuals having difficulty for a longer period than research findings suggest. Some individual studies have shown persistent impairment in autobiographical memory (up to three years) and there have been case reports of profound autobiographical memory loss after ECT (Fink, 2007). There is currently no standardised instrument for assessment of this major cognitive effect of ECT (Semkovska and McLoughlin, 2013). As a result, the precise nature and extent of autobiographical retrograde amnesia post-ECT is not clear, a major gap in our knowledge and the focus of much research.

Subjective Memory Difficulty

Up to one-third of patients report persistent subjective memory difficulty post-ECT (Rose et al., 2003), with some reports of persistence for years. Qualitative evidence reviewed by NICE suggested that the experience of cognitive impairment was variable among those who had received ECT, but that it often outweighed the person's perception of any benefit from ECT (NICE, 2009).

Subjective memory difficulty does not correlate with objective performance on cognitive assessment or any subset of memory functions, but correlates somewhat with depression severity. Assessment tools such as the Squire Subjective Memory Assessment (Squire et al., 1979) or the Subjective Assessment of Memory Impairment (Kumar et al., 2016) have been used in ECT research. Remission following ECT may be associated with lower risk of subjective memory difficulty, while younger, female patients may be more at risk (Brus et al., 2017).

It has been variously hypothesised that persistent subjective memory difficulty after ECT represents misattribution of the effects of age, mood or somatic complaints on memory (Fink, 2007). In addition, patients may become anxious about memory after ECT and misperceive a problem where their memory function is within the normal experience (Andrade et al., 2016).

Assessment

Remarkably, there are no specifically designed recommended instruments for cognitive testing in ECT practice. Although NICE, along with the American Psychiatric Association (APA, 2010), recommends a documented baseline assessment of potential risks and benefits of ECT for each individual, including anticipated cognitive effects, the guidelines do not suggest instruments for testing (NICE, 2009). This absence of specific recommendations may reflect the lack of suitable instruments for assessment.

What should we do? Unfortunately, there is no simple answer. Despite limitations in existing instruments, and in line with measurement-based care, there is enough evidence to recommend the practice of performing a global assessment of cognition at baseline, during the course of ECT (e.g. after six treatments), at a set time after ECT, e.g. within three days after the last ECT treatment, and after one to two months.

Ideally an assessment would include a measure of: immediate and delayed verbal recall, attention, working memory, autobiographical memory and at least one aspect of executive function.

Though use of the standardised Mini Mental State Exam (sMMSE) (Molloy et al., 1991) has become common, it is inadequate for monitoring adverse cognitive side-effects of ECT. The sMMSE is a screening tool for dementia that is insensitive to change, does not assess executive function, and can only detect substantial impairment (Tombaugh and McIntyre, 1992).

Although no purposely designed instrument for assessment of cognition before and after ECT exists, global cognitive assessments that incorporate measures of executive function are available, and screening batteries have been suggested (Martin et al., 2013). The Montreal Cognitive Assessment (MoCA) (Nasreddine et al., 2005) and the Addenbrooke's Cognitive Assessment Version III (ACE-III) (Hodges and Larner, 2017, Hseih et al., 2013) have the advantages of being sensitive to minor impairment as well as change. The ACE-III takes longer than the MoCA to administer but has high sensitivity to cognitive deficits, is freely available and does not require specialised training. Parallel, validated versions of both the MoCA and ACE-III are available for retesting during and after ECT. For more detailed cognitive assessment, a battery of assessments such as the CANTAB® (Cognitive assessment software, Cambridge Cognition 2017: http://www.cambridgecognition.com/cantab) can identify more subtle or discrete impairments in specific cognitive functions (Falconer *et al.*, 2010, Fray *et al.*, 1996, Tsaltas *et al.*, 2011).

Detailed repeat cognitive assessment is burdensome for patients and may not be practical in routine practice and is thus usually only performed as part of a research study. However, one could well argue that it should be part of regular ECT practice!

Based on meta-analytical evidence (Semkovska and McLoughlin, 2010), acute impairments in most cognitive domains should resolve within 15 days or more of completion of ECT, so we recommend that deficits persisting beyond one month after completing ECT require further assessment.

Retrograde Amnesia Assessment

The assessment of retrograde autobiographical amnesia is particularly difficult. Inability to retrieve information, whether on free or cued testing, indicates that memory decay has occurred over time (i.e. forgetting). Some memory decay is actually normal. It cannot be assumed that reduced consistency of recall is unique to depressed people treated with ECT, or to depressed people. Recall of autobiographical information normally declines over time in non-depressed people and consistency of recall in healthy controls declines even after an interval of two months (Semkovska *et al.*, 2012). Estimates of normal rate of loss of autobiographical memories range from 27% after six weeks (Talarico and Rubin, 2003) to 31–42% after two months (Anderson *et al.*, 2000).

It is difficult to separate the effect of ECT from the effect of change in depression severity on the normal rate of loss of previously reported memories. To do so would require robust normative information on the performance of:

• non-depressed persons
• depressed persons not treated with ECT

on the instruments used for retrograde memory assessment in ECT, before and after an interval of weeks. Unfortunately, this is not currently available.

Depression is associated with impaired ability to identify separate incidents from one's own life experience (reduced specificity of episodic autobiographical memory, or over-generalisation) and poor recollection of detail of the identified events. These are consistent findings across several types of assessment (Jelovac *et al.*, 2016). Reduced specificity in depressed patients prior to ECT (compared with non-depressed controls) was shown to persist at three months after ECT regardless of treatment response (Jelovac *et al.*, 2016). Thus depressed patients may score poorly on episodic autobiographical memory assessment even when their semantic autobiographical memory may seem unimpaired (Verwijk *et al.*, 2015). Testing retrograde memory is challenging for depressed patients experiencing reduced memory specificity and may result in patients providing information that is very limited or over-general.

The ideal instrument for assessment of retrograde autobiographical amnesia would be short and simple to administer and would provide scores for memory detail (semantic and episodic) as well as a consistency score on retesting after ECT. Results could be measured against the general population (and also depressed persons not treated with

ECT) at baseline and after several weeks of normal life. Unfortunately, currently used instruments for retrograde amnesia, e.g. the Columbia University Autobiographical Memory Interview (CUAMI, or the short form CUAMI-SF) (McElhiney et al., 2001, McElhiney et al., 1995) and the Kopelman Autobiographical Memory Interview (Kopelman et al., 1989), do not fulfil all these criteria. For a more detailed account of these issues see the following correspondence (Sackeim, 2014, Semkovska and McLoughlin, 2013, 2014).

The Columbia University Autobiographical Memory Interview is the most widely used instrument for assessment of autobiographical amnesia in ECT research (Sackeim et al., 2000). However, normative data for comparison of both healthy controls and depressed people not having ECT are not available (Semkovska and McLoughlin, 2013). Episodic recall is not measured separately to semantic recall, and the short form still takes 20–25 minutes to administer. Another disadvantage to the CUAMI-SF is that only information provided in the initial assessment is retested for consistency of recall. Therefore, scores cannot improve and the percentage recall score may be based on successful recall of very little information, i.e. a floor effect. Despite these drawbacks, the CUAMI has been useful in showing differences in retrograde amnesia associated with different ECT treatment modalities, such as laterality and pulse-width (Kolshus et al., 2017, Sackeim et al., 2000, Sackeim et al., 2008); see 'Prevention' in this chapter.

The Kopelman Autobiographical Memory Interview was originally designed for assessment of amnestic patients but has also been used in ECT research (Sienaert et al., 2010). It assesses both semantic and episodic autobiographical memory separately, with items scored on specificity and detail. It does not provide a measure of recall consistency and caution is required due to suggestions of a lack of sensitivity of the instrument to ECT-related retrograde amnesia (Jelovac et al., 2016). It is long (+25 minutes) and burdensome for depressed patients to complete. However, some normative data on the performance of healthy controls is available, and the instrument allows for improvement of scores on retesting should memory improve during or after a course of ECT.

Prevention

There is good evidence that modification of ECT treatment factors (laterality, pulsewidth, frequency) can help reduce the occurrence and severity of cognitive side-effects. Higher electrical stimulus (in relation to seizure threshold), though important for antidepressant effect, is associated with greater effect on cognition (Sackeim et al., 1993). More frequent ECT treatment (thrice-weekly vs twice-weekly) is associated with greater cognitive impairment (Lerer et al., 1995), and, though now unused, sine-wave stimulation resulted in more severe and persistent effects on cognition than contemporary brief-pulse stimuli (Sackeim et al., 2007).

RUL ECT is consistently associated with less severe and persistent cognitive effects (Sackeim et al., 1993, Sackeim et al., 2007). Antidepressant efficacy equal to bitemporal ECT can be preserved by administering RUL ECT at six times threshold dose (Kolshus et al., 2017).

Trials of ultrabrief pulse (UBP) ECT have shown a cognitive advantage over brief pulse (BP) ECT (Tor et al., 2015, Verwijk et al., 2012). Global cognition, anterograde memory (learning and recall) and retrograde memory were less affected by high-dose RUL UBP than

RUL BP ECT (Tor *et al.*, 2015). Although the cognitive benefit of UBP over BP ECT is consistent, UBP ECT is significantly less efficacious in treating depression than BP ECT and requires more treatments to achieve remission (Tor *et al.*, 2015).

Meta-analysis of bifrontal vs bitemporal ECT suggested bifrontal ECT may have slightly less impact on global cognitive function (as represented by decline in MMSE score) than bitemporal ECT (Dunne and McLoughlin, 2012), but there is currently not enough evidence to recommend routine use of bifrontal ECT with regards to its having substantial cognitive advantages over bitemporal or unilateral ECT.

Primary Prevention

Modification of treatment parameters associated with less cognitive impact should be considered for those identified as being at higher risk. Those who are older, have baseline cognitive impairment or a history of cognitive difficulties following ECT should be considered at risk.

If recovery from depression is an urgent concern and the person is at high risk of cognitive side-effects, high-dose unilateral BP ECT may be used. If rate of recovery is less urgent, unilateral UBP ECT may be considered. In addition, it would seem good practice to avoid unnecessary use of anticholinergic agents (e.g. atropine) during ECT administration. Further detail on anaesthetic agents is in Chapter 23.

Most of the patient-related risk factors for adverse cognitive effects are not malleable, e.g. age, cerebrovascular disease. However, clinical common sense indicates that physical condition should ideally be optimised pre-ECT, in particular with regards to cardiovascular, cerebrovascular and respiratory risk factors.

Preparation for the possibility of adverse cognitive side-effects and practical support during the treatment course may contribute to a positive experience that could help patients to avoid prematurely discontinuing a course of ECT due to distress. It is crucial that patients and their family, or advocates involved in the consent process, are adequately informed of the common occurrence of cognitive side-effects despite best treatment, and the effect this can be expected to have on their day-to-day activities during and for a limited time after ECT. In particular, patients should be informed that they should not drive during a course of ECT (www.gov.uk/government/publications/assessing-fitness-to-drive-a-guide-for-medical-professionals).

Secondary Prevention

There are no guidelines to inform clinicians about at what stage and under which conditions treatment should be changed. However, if cognitive effects become apparent during the course of ECT, treatment factors can be modified as above to utilise a form of treatment less likely to impair cognition.

Research focusing on reducing the frequency and severity of adverse cognitive effects of ECT has resulted in trials of ketamine anaesthesia for ECT (McGirr *et al.*, 2017) and augmentation of ECT with cognitive training (Choi *et al.*, 2017), although neither of these has led to clearly improved cognitive outcomes. Acetylcholinesterase inhibitors have been found to result in significantly better performance in cognitive testing after ECT although there is large heterogeneity between studies (Henstra *et al.*, 2017) and their use remains experimental. More research is likely to emerge on this topic.

Key Points

- Adverse cognitive side-effects are common and important to patients, families and clinicians and may contribute to premature discontinuation of treatment or lack of use of ECT where it is indicated.
- Cognitive side-effects include anterograde and retrograde amnesia, as well as impaired executive function.
- Most short-term effects will resolve within weeks of the last ECT treatment and there is no objective evidence of persisting anterograde memory impairment.
- The extent and duration of retrograde amnesia remains unclear and difficult to assess, with no ideal tool currently available for assessment.
- There is no evidence of cumulative cognitive impairment with repeated courses of ECT.
- Prevention of adverse cognitive side-effects is primarily through identifying patients at higher risk and modifying treatment factors such as laterality, pulsewidth, frequency of treatment, and stimulus dose.
- High-dose right unilateral BP ECT is equivalent to bitemporal BP ECT in antidepressant efficacy and is associated with better cognitive outcomes; unilateral UBP ECT is associated with less cognitive impact than unilateral BP ECT but is less effective.
- Assessment of cognition during ECT remains difficult due to a lack of validated instruments. However, cognitive function should be assessed prior to, during and post-ECT using available instruments. The sMMSE is inadequate, while the MoCA or ACE-III could be considered for routine practice where it may not be feasible to perform preferably more detailed cognitive testing.
- Time for recovery to orientation should be routinely assessed as it is relatively straightforward and may have predictive value for retrograde amnesia.

References

Anderson, S. J., Cohen, G. & Taylor, S. (2000). Rewriting the past: some factors affecting the variability of personal memories. *Applied Cognitive Psychology* 14, 435–54.

Andrade, C., Arumugham, S. & Thirthalli, J. (2016). Adverse effects of electroconvulsive Therapy. *Psychiatr Clin North Am* 39, 513–30.

APA (American Psychiatric Association, 2010). *Practice Guideline for the Treatment of Patients With Major Depressive Disorder* Third Edition. American Psychiatric Association, Virginia, USA.

Bjølseth, T. M., Engedal, K., Benth, J. Š., et al. (2016). Speed of recovery from disorientation may predict the treatment outcome of electroconvulsive therapy (ECT) in elderly patients with major depression. *Journal of Affective Disorders* 190, 178–86.

Brus, O., Nordanskog, P., Båve, U., et al. (2017). Subjective memory immediately following electroconvulsive therapy. *The Journal of ECT* 33, 96–103.

Calev, A., Cohen, R., Tubi, N., et al. (1991). Disorientation and bilateral moderately suprathreshold titrated ECT. *The Journal of ECT* 7, 99–110.

Choi, J., Wang, Y., Feng, T. & Prudic, J. (2017). Cognitive training to improve memory in individuals undergoing electroconvulsive therapy: negative findings. *Journal of Psychiatric Research* 92, 8–14.

Dunne, R. A. & McLoughlin, D. M. (2012). Systematic review and meta-analysis of bifrontal electroconvulsive therapy versus bilateral and unilateral electroconvulsive therapy in depression. *The World Journal of Biological Psychiatry* 13, 248–58.

Falconer, D., Cleland, J., Fielding, S. & Reid, I. C. (2010). Using the Cambridge

Neuropsychological Test Automated Battery (CANTAB) to assess the cognitive impact of electroconvulsive therapy on visual and visuospatial memory. *Psychological Medicine* 40, 1017–25.

Fink, M. (2007). Complaints of loss of personal memories after electroconvulsive therapy: evidence of a somatoform disorder? *Psychosomatics* 48, 290–3.

Henstra, M. J., Jansma, E. P., Velde, N., Swart, E. L., Stek, M. L. & Rhebergen, D. (2017). Acetylcholinesterase inhibitors for electroconvulsive therapy-induced cognitive side effects: a systematic review. *International Journal of Geriatric Psychiatry* 32, 522–31.

Hodges, J. R. & Larner, A. J. (2017). Addenbrooke's Cognitive Examinations: ACE, ACE-R, ACE-III, ACEapp, and M-ACE. In: Larner A. (ed) *Cognitive Screening Instruments*. Springer, Cham, Switzerland.

Hsieh, S., Schubert, S., Hoon, C., Mioshi, E. & Hodges, J. R. (2013). Validation of the Addenbrooke's Cognitive Examination III in frontotemporal dementia and Alzheimer's disease. *Dementia and Geriatric Cognitive Disorders* 36, 242–50.

Fray, P. J., Robbins, T. W. & Sahakian, B. J. (1996). Neuropsychiatric applications of CANTAB. *International Journal of Geriatric Psychiatry* 11, 329–36.

Jelovac, A., O'Connor, S., McCarron, S. & McLoughlin, D. M. (2016). Autobiographical memory specificity in major depression treated with electroconvulsive therapy. *The Journal of ECT* 32, 38–43.

Kikuchi, A., Yasui-Furukori, N., Fujii, A., Katagai, H. & Kaneko, S. (2009). Identification of predictors of post-ictal delirium after electroconvulsive therapy. *Psychiatry and Clinical Neurosciences* 63, 180–5.

Kolshus, E., Jelovac, A. & McLoughlin, D. (2017). Bitemporal v. high-dose right unilateral electroconvulsive therapy for depression: a systematic review and meta-analysis of randomized controlled trials. *Psychological Medicine* 47, 518–30.

Kopelman, M., Wilson, B. & Baddeley, A. (1989). The autobiographical memory interview: a new assessment of autobiographical and personal semantic memory in amnesic patients. *Journal of Clinical and Experimental Neuropsychology* 11, 724–44.

Kumar, D. R., Han, H. K., Tiller, J., Loo, C. K. & Martin, D. M. (2016). A brief measure for assessing patient perceptions of cognitive side effects after electroconvulsive therapy: the subjective assessment of memory impairment. *The Journal of ECT* 32, 256–61.

Lerer, B., Shapira, B., Calev, A., Tubi, N., Drexler, H. & Kindler, S. (1995). Antidepressant and cognitive effects of twice- versus three-times-weekly ECT. *Am J Psych* 1, 565.

Lezak, M. D. (2012). *Neuropsychological Assessment*, Fifth Edition. Oxford University Press.

Lisanby, S. H., Maddox, J. H., Prudic, J., Devanand, D. & Sackeim, H. A. (2000). The effects of electroconvulsive therapy on memory of autobiographical and public events. *Archives of General Psychiatry* 57, 581–90.

Maric, N. P., Stojanovic, Z., Andric, S., Soldatovic, I., Dolic, M., & Spiric, Z. (2016). The acute and medium-term effects of treatment with electroconvulsive therapy on memory in patients with major depressive disorder. *Psychological Medicine* 46, 797–806.

Martin, D. M., Katalinic, N., Ingram, A., et al. (2013). A new early cognitive screening measure to detect cognitive side-effects of electroconvulsive therapy? *Journal of Psychiatric Research* 47, 1967–74.

Martin, D. M., Gálvez, V. & Loo, C. K. (2015). Predicting retrograde autobiographical memory changes following electroconvulsive therapy: relationships between individual, treatment, and early clinical factors. *International Journal of Neuropsychopharmacology*. https://doi.org/10.1093/ijnp/pyv067

McClintock, S. M., Choi, J., Deng, Z.-D., et al. (2014). Multifactorial determinants of the neurocognitive effects of electroconvulsive therapy. *The Journal of ECT* 30, 165.

McElhiney, M. C., Moody, B. J., Steif, B. L., et al. (1995). Autobiographical memory and mood: effects of electroconvulsive therapy. *Neuropsychology* 9, 501.

McElhiney, M., Moody, B. & Sackeim, H. (2001). *Manual for Administration and Scoring the Columbia University Autobiographical Memory Interview—Short Form, Version 3*. In New York State Psychiatric Institute: New York.

McGirr, A., Berlim, M.T., Bond, P.Y. et al. (2017). Adjunctive ketamine in electroconvulsive therapy: updated systematic review and meta-analysis. *Br J Psychiat* 210, 403–47.

Molloy, D., Alemayehu, E. & Roberts, R. (1991). A standardized Mini-Mental State Examination (SMMSE): improved reliability compared to the traditional MMSE. *Am J Psych* 148, 102–5.

Nasreddine, Z. S., Phillips, N. A., Bédirian, V., et al. (2005). The Montreal Cognitive Assessment, MoCA: a brief screening tool for mild cognitive impairment. *Journal of the American Geriatrics Society* 53, 695–9.

NICE (National Institute for Health and Care Excellence) (2009). Guidance on the use of electroconvulsive therapy. In, NICE technology appraisal guidance [TA59]: www.nice.org.uk

Petrides, G., Tobias, K. G., Kellner, C. H. & Rudorfer, M. V. (2011). Continuation and maintenance electroconvulsive therapy for mood disorders: review of the literature. *Neuropsychobiology* 64, 129–40.

Reti, I. M., Krishnan, A., Podlisky, A., et al. (2014). Predictors of electroconvulsive therapy postictal delirium. *Psychosomatics* 55, 272–9.

Rose, D., Fleischmann, P., Wykes, T., Leese, M. & Bindman, J. (2003). Patients' perspectives on electroconvulsive therapy: systematic review. *British Medical Journal* 326, 1363.

Russell, J. C., Rasmussen, K. G., O'connor, M. K., Copeman, C. A., Ryan, D. A. & Rummans, T. A. (2003). Long-term maintenance ECT: a retrospective review of efficacy and cognitive outcome. *The Journal of ECT* 19, 4–9.

Sackeim, H. A., Prudic, J., Devanand, D., et al. (1993). Effects of stimulus intensity and electrode placement on the efficacy and cognitive effects of electroconvulsive therapy. *New England Journal of Medicine* 328, 839–846.

Sackeim, H. A., Prudic, J., Devanand, D., et al. (2000). A prospective, randomized, double-blind comparison of bilateral and right unilateral electroconvulsive therapy at different stimulus intensities. *Archives of General Psychiatry* 57, 425–34.

Sackeim, H. A., Prudic, J., Fuller, R., Keilp, J., Lavori, P. W. & Olfson, M. (2007). The cognitive effects of electroconvulsive therapy in community settings. *Neuropsychopharmacology* 32, 244–54.

Sackeim, H. A., Prudic, J., Nobler, M. S., et al. (2008). Effects of pulse width and electrode placement on the efficacy and cognitive effects of electroconvulsive therapy. *Brain Stimulation* 1, 71–83.

Sackeim, H. A. (2014). Autobiographical memory and ECT: don't throw out the baby. *The Journal of ECT* 30, 177.

Sartorius, A., Wolf, J. & Henn, F. A. (2005). Lithium and ECT–concurrent use still demands attention: three case reports. *The World Journal of Biological Psychiatry* 6, 121–4.

Semkovska, M. & McLoughlin, D. M. (2010). Objective cognitive performance associated with electroconvulsive therapy for depression: a systematic review and meta-analysis. *Biological Psychiatry* 68, 568–77.

Semkovska, M., Noone, M., Carton, M. & McLoughlin, D. M. (2012). Measuring consistency of autobiographical memory recall in depression. *Psychiatry Res* 197, 41–8.

Semkovska, M. & McLoughlin, D. M. (2013). Measuring retrograde autobiographical amnesia following electroconvulsive therapy: historical perspective and current issues. *The Journal of ECT* 29, 127–33.

Semkovska, M. & McLoughlin, D. M. (2014). Retrograde autobiographical amnesia after electroconvulsive therapy: on the difficulty of finding the baby and clearing murky bathwater. *The Journal of ECT* 30, 187–8.

Semkovska, M., Landau, S., Dunne, R., et al. (2016). Bitemporal versus high-dose unilateral twice-weekly electroconvulsive therapy for depression (EFFECT-Dep): a pragmatic, randomised, non-inferiority trial. *Am J Psychiatry* 173, 408–17.

Sienaert, P., Vansteelandt, K., Demyttenaere, K. & Peuskens, J. (2010). Randomized comparison of ultra-brief bifrontal and unilateral electroconvulsive therapy for major depression: cognitive side-effects. *Journal of Affective Disorders* 122, 60–7.

Smith, G. E., Rasmussen Jr, K. G., Cullum, C. M., *et al.* (2010). A randomized controlled trial comparing the memory effects of continuation electroconvulsive therapy versus continuation pharmacotherapy: results from the Consortium for Research in ECT (CORE) study. *The Journal of Clinical Psychiatry* 71, 185–93.

Sobin, C., Sackeim, H. A., Prudic, J. & Devanand, D. (1995). Predictors of retrograde amnesia following ECT. *Am J Psych* 152, 995.

Squire, L., Wetzel, C. & Slater, P. (1979). Memory complaint after electroconvulsive therapy: assessment with a new self-rating instrument. *Biological Psychiatry* 14, 791–801.

Squire, L. R., Cohen, N. J. & Zouzounis, J. A. (1984). Preserved memory in retrograde amnesia: Sparing of a recently acquired skill. *Neuropsychologia* 22, 145–52.

Talarico, J. M. & Rubin, D. C. (2003). Confidence, not consistency, characterizes flashbulb memories. *Psychological Science* 14, 455–61.

Thirthalli, J., Harish, T. & Gangadhar, B. N. (2011). A prospective comparative study of interaction between lithium and modified electroconvulsive therapy. *The World Journal of Biological Psychiatry* 12, 149–55.

Tombaugh, T. N. & McIntyre, N. J. (1992). The Mini-Mental State Examination: a comprehensive review. *Journal of the American Geriatrics Society* 40, 922–35.

Tor, P.-C., Bautovich, A., Wang, M.-J., Martin, D., Harvey, S. B. & Loo, C. (2015). A systematic review and meta-analysis of brief versus ultrabrief right unilateral electroconvulsive therapy for depression. *Journal of Clinical Psychiatry* 76, 1092–8.

Tsaltas, E., Kalogerakou, S., Papakosta, V.-M., *et al.* (2011). Contrasting patterns of deficits in visuospatial memory and executive function in patients with major depression with and without ECT referral. *Psychological Medicine* 41, 983–95.

Vakil, E., Grunhaus, L., Nagar, I., *et al.* (2000). The effect of electroconvulsive therapy (ECT) on implicit memory: skill learning and perceptual priming in patients with major depression. *Neuropsychologia* 38, 1405–14.

Verwijk, E., Comijs, H. C., Kok, R. M., Spaans, H.-P., Stek, M. L. & Scherder, E. J. (2012). Neurocognitive effects after brief pulse and ultrabrief pulse unilateral electroconvulsive therapy for major depression: a review. *Journal of Affective Disorders* 140, 233–43.

Verwijk, E., Spaans, H.-P., Comijs, H. C., *et al.* (2015). Relapse and long-term cognitive performance after brief pulse or ultrabrief pulse right unilateral electroconvulsive therapy: a multicenter naturalistic follow up. *Journal of Affective Disorders* 184, 137–44.

Volpe, F. M. & Tavares Jr, A. R. (2012). Lithium plus ECT for mania in 90 cases: safety issues. *The Journal of Neuropsychiatry and Clinical Neurosciences* 24, E33–E33.

Non-cognitive Adverse Effects of ECT

Jonathan Waite

Introduction

Before effective treatments for depression were available many people admitted to hospital died. After the introduction of ECT, the proportion of patients in psychiatric hospitals with depression who died in hospital fell from about 15% to 2% (Slater, 1951). Although ECT is a potentially hazardous treatment, the alternatives are not free from risk (Coupland *et al.*, 2011) and untreated depression carries a high morbidity and mortality.

Assessment Before ECT

The adverse effects of ECT are a major concern for people treated with ECT, their families and the public. The risk–benefit balance for a particular patient should be considered and discussed during the pre-ECT assessment process, before consent is sought. If there are reasons why this patient might be at greater risk of particular adverse effects, ways in which the risk might be minimised should be considered. Patients at high risk of physical complications should not be treated on a remote site (see Chapters 23 and 27).

Consent

Patients and their families should be involved in discussions about the treatment, its likely adverse effects and its anticipated benefits. The discussion should include consideration of alternative treatments and the risks of not having the treatment. The use of written as well as verbal information is good practice (see Chapter 28); information videos are also valuable (see https://www.leics-his.nhs.uk/ectapp/).

Mortality Rate

Electroconvulsive therapy is a low-risk procedure with a mortality rate similar to that of anaesthesia for minor surgical procedures, despite its frequent use in elderly people and those with major medical problems (Sackeim, 1998; Weiner *et al.*, 2000) (Table 14.1).

The studies cited in Table 14.1 are not directly comparable; they used varying methodologies and reported on deaths occurring in different intervals after treatment. The data from California (Kramer, 1999) and Texas (Shiwach *et al.*, 2001; Dennis *et al.*, 2017) are derived from statutory hospital returns; in the case of California, only deaths directly attributable to ECT were reported. Watts and colleagues based their study on reports of serious adverse reactions which were subject to root cause analysis. In this study there were no deaths directly attributable to ECT. Østergaard *et al.* (2014) used data from a national patient register, analysed by the Danish Health and Medicines Authority, and 'did not find a

Table 14.1 Deaths occurring in the period after patients have received ECT

Study	Period	Patients	Treatments	Early Deaths (period)	Later Deaths (period)
Kramer (1999)	1984–1994	28,437	160,847	3 0.0019% of treatments 0.011% of patients	
Nuttall et al. (2004)	1988–2001	2,279	17,394		18 (30 days) 0.01% of treatments 0.76% of patients
Schiwach et al. (2001)	1993–1998	8,148	49,048	7 (2 days) 0.0014% of treatments 0.084% of patients	30 (14 days) 0.061% of treatments 0.37% of patients
Watts et al. (2011)	1999–2010		73,440		
Østergaard et al. (2014)	2000–2007		99,728		78 (30 days) 0.078% of treatments
Dennis et al. (2017)	1998–2013	27,931	166,711	4 (1 day) 0.0024% of treatments 0.014% of patients	30 (14 days) 0.018% of treatments 0.11% of patients
Blumberger et al. (2017)	2003–2011	8,810	135,831	33 (7 days) 0.024% of treatments 0.37% of patients	65 (30 days) 0.048% of treatments 0.74% of patients

documentable association between ECT treatment and death'. Nuttall and colleagues (2004) performed a retrospective review of case records of patients treated at the Mayo Clinic in Minnesota; Blumberger and colleagues (2017) used data from health administration records to evaluate a population-based cohort. The patients in this series had high rates of medical co-morbidity, with a median of two physical diagnoses; they were taking on average 12 medications (median, IQR 8–16); 19% were classified as ASA Class 4 or above, (American Society of Anesthesiologists, 2014). In other studies of ECT the patients have typically had fewer co-morbidities and less concomitant medication (Nuttall et al., 2004).

Taken together these studies confirm that ECT carries a low risk compared with other treatments involving procedures such as day case endoscopy (Sarkar et al., 2012) or elective hernia repair (Bay-Nielsen et al., 2008). The American Psychiatric Association (2001) stated that a reasonable current estimate of the ECT-related adverse effects of ECT mortality rate was 1 per 10,000 patients or 1 per 80,000 treatments; Dennis *et al.* (2017) found a rate of 2.4 per 100,000 treatments.

There is an association between increasing age and mortality, but from the available data it is not possible to say whether there is a specific risk with ageing or simply that older people are more likely to have medical co-morbidities. In the Ontario series patients who died were more likely to have multiple medical co-morbidities (43% ASA Grade 3 (severe systemic disease), 39% ASA 4 (severe systemic disease that is a constant threat to life)). Overall 3.5% of the people receiving ECT were resident in a long-term care facility, but they accounted for 23% of those who died. Only 1% of patients had a diagnosis of dementia, but they had a mortality rate of 6%. Less than 1% of patients under 65 experienced serious adverse effects from ECT.

When considering the mortality associated with ECT it is important to bear in mind the high mortality of severely psychiatrically ill patients. A case-register study examined all deaths which occurred in patients who had received ECT at the Aarhus Hospital in Denmark between 1976 and 2000 (Munk-Olsen *et al.*, 2007). There was a lower mortality rate from natural causes for patients treated with ECT compared with other patients who had been admitted to the hospital. Rates of death for stroke and cancer were the same for both groups but ECT patients had lower rates of death from cardiac and respiratory disease.

Cardio-Pulmonary Adverse Effects

Cardiovascular and pulmonary complications are the most frequent physical causes of death and serious morbidity as a result of ECT (Shiwach *et al.*, 2001; Nuttall *et al.*, 2004; Munk-Olsen *et al.*, 2007). In the most recent audits (Dennis *et al.*, 2016; Blumberger *et al.*, 2017), cardiovascular deaths have formed a lower proportion of those who died, probably as a result of improved anaesthetic procedures.

Following the electrical stimulus, there is an initial parasympathetic discharge lasting 10–15s. Asystole (absence of electrical activity on ECG for >5 s) occurs in 5% of all stimulations, similar rates are found after sub-convulsive shocks applied during empirical dose titration and after convulsive shocks (Mizen *et al.*, 2015). The initial parasympathetic response is followed by increased sympathetic activity. Systolic arterial pressure may increase by 30–40% and heart rate may increase by 20% or more; the maximum effect is typically seen after 3–5 minutes. Myocardial oxygen consumption also increases (Uppal *et al.*, 2010).

Death from myocardial infarction following ECT does occur (Schiwach *et al.*, 2001), one case of ischaemic stroke after ECT has been reported (Bruce *et al.*, 2006) but Munk-Olsen *et al.* (2007) found that mortality rates from cardiovascular disease were lower amongst ECT treated patients than other psychiatric in-patients. Overall blood pressure does not change over a course of ECT (Albin *et al.*, 2007).

There are a number of reports of acute pulmonary oedema occurring after ECT (Mansoor *et al.*, 2016), possibly occurring as a result of the sympathetic catecholamine surge (Davison *et al.*, 2012). Takotsubo cardiomyopathy is a type of stress induced cardiac disorder, which is believed to be caused by high levels of catecholamines. It is most common in elderly women, believed to occur at a rate of 2–9/100,000 people in the general population and about 1 in 6,700 cases in the peri-anaesthetic period. It typically presents as acute pulmonary oedema, or an acute coronary syndrome, with reduced left ventricular ejection fraction, but without coronary artery obstruction. Amongst cases occurring as a result of anaesthesia, 82% resolve spontaneously within one week; mortality is 6%. In a review of seven reported cases where Takotsubo cardiomyopathy occurred during ECT, four of those affected went on to have further ECT without recurrence of cardiopulmonary problems (Sharp and Welch, 2011).

Electroconvulsive therapy clinic protocols and processes should identify individuals who present a high risk, including older patients (see Chapter 5) and those with co-morbid physical illnesses (see Chapter 26), and ensure that they are carefully assessed and treated to minimise the risks of ECT (Tess & Smetana, 2009). Such patients require close monitoring during and after the procedure in an environment that will allow rapid intervention should complications occur (see Chapters 21 and 22).

Suicide

Suicide accounted for a high proportion of the deaths occurring within one month of treatment in both Denmark (26%) (Østergaard et al., 2014), and Texas (30%) (Dennis et al., 2017). Neither study included a control group of patients with psychiatric disorder of a severity to warrant ECT. An earlier Danish study (Munk-Olsen et al., 2007) found that the rate of suicide following ECT was only marginally higher than the rate in all psychiatric in-patients (Rr=1.2). The US Veterans survey (Watts et al., 2011) reports two deaths by suicide, both of which occurred more than a week after the last ECT treatment: poor communication between the ECT team and the out-patient providers was cited as a contributory factor in both cases.

Prolonged Seizures

Prolonged seizures (lasting > 120s) are most likely to occur at the first treatment. Using an empirical dose titration protocol (see Chapter 22) the risk of prolonged seizures is of the order of 1–2% (Whittaker, Scott & Gardner, 2007). Prolonged seizures are more likely in patients taking medication that lowers their seizure threshold (see Chapter 25). Non-convulsive status epilepticus following ECT may be difficult to diagnose (Povlsen et al., 2003), most reported cases have signs of prolonged post-ictal confusion. EEG monitoring is recommended to indicate whether seizure activity has ceased (Chapter 26).

Mania

Up to 20% of patients with unipolar depression have been reported to develop elevated mood in follow-up studies (Bailine et al., 2010). The natural risk of a switch from depression to mania during recovery in a patient with bipolar disorder is from 4% to 8% (Grunze et al., 2010). Similar rates of treatment-emergent affective switches (Tohen et al., 2009) are reported among patients treated for depression with ECT (Medda et al., 2009; Bailine et al., 2010) and antidepressant medication (Grunze et al., 2010) (see Chapter 4).

Other Non-cognitive Adverse Effects

Only two large scale studies have looked at non-fatal adverse effects. Watts et al. (2011) reviewing adverse events recorded in a centralised database (National Center for Patient Safety) found that the most commonly reported more significant adverse effects were injuries to the mouth (see Chapter 23) and problems related to muscle relaxants (see Chapter 23). Blumberger *et al.* (2017) used linked mental health, hospital discharge and health insurance databases to seek adverse events up to 30 days after ECT. The prevalence of all adverse events was low: rates of falls and pneumonia were the most frequent. Increased rates of falls, suicide, seizures and strokes are also associated with antidepressant use in older people (Coupland *et al.*, 2011). ECT as a risk factor for falls has been previously reported (de Carle & Kohn, 2001).

Transient, minor adverse effects are common after treatment. Data on these symptoms are published regularly by SEAN (Scottish ECT Accreditation Network, 2016; Figure 14.1) and ECTAS (Hailey *et al.*, 2015). Patients may experience headaches (reported after 22% of treatments), muscular aches (9%) or nausea (6%). Anorexia, weakness and drowsiness are other frequent adverse effects. Although common, these are usually mild (Dinwiddie *et al.*, 2010) and respond to symptomatic treatments (e.g. ondansetron for nausea). People who commonly experience post-ECT headaches may benefit from prophylactic treatment before ECT with a non-steroidal anti-inflammatory drug (Leung *et al.*, 2003). Sumatriptan may also be helpful (Markowitz *et al.*, 2001). The Food and Drug Administration (FDA) warned of the possibility of serotonin syndrome when triptans were used in combination with SSRIs (Food and Drug Administration, 2006); recent research suggests that the risks of co-prescribing triptans and SSRIs may have been over-stated (Orlova *et al.*, 2018).

Studies of the prevalence of anxiety related to ECT have reported rates from 14% to 75% (Obbels *et al.*, 2017). This subject is discussed in more detail in Chapter 29.

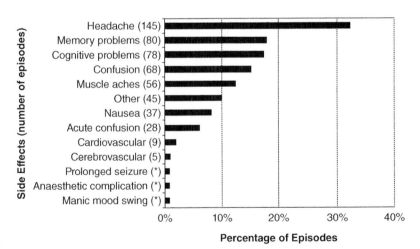

Figure 14.1 Prevalence of side effects in ECT (SEAN, 2016)
Notes:
* Percentages not calculated because of low numbers. Dummy values have been inserted in bar chart categories.
1. Figures total more than 100% because of the multiple response nature of the variables examined.
2. Cognitive side effects are recorded under four headings:
Acute confusion – defined as treatment emergent delirium, where the patient experiences confusion for a short period of time immediately on wakening after treatment – recorded by ECT staff.
Confusion – reported by the patients and occurring between treatments (e.g. on return to the ward).
Memory problems – short lived autobiographical memory impairment (e.g. names, events) reported by the patient.
Cognitive problems – problems with orientation, attention or concentration that were reported by the patients or noted by staff. (Reproduced with permission from the SEAN Annual Report 2016)

Regular Review

Regular review is necessary during the course of treatment to detect possible adverse effects (see also Chapter 22). If any are detected, this should prompt consideration of whether they could be avoided, minimised or treated. Staff in the ECT clinic, in conjunction with other ward or community staff caring for people being treated with ECT, may wish to develop and use standardised assessments of possible treatment-emergent adverse effects.

Recommendations

- During pre-ECT assessment, ways of minimising potential adverse effects should be considered, particularly for individuals who are deemed at high risk of adverse effects during treatment.
- During the consent process, patients should be informed of the likely adverse effects related to treatment within the context of considering the risks and benefits of treatment.
- Doctors prescribing or administering ECT should be aware of particular possible adverse effects of treatment.
- All ECT clinics should have a protocol for the management of prolonged seizures (see Chapter 6).
- People receiving ECT should be regularly monitored during the course of treatment for treatment-emergent objective and subjective adverse effects.
- Ways of preventing, minimising and treating adverse effects should be considered.

References

Albin, S. M., Stevens, S. R. & Rasmussen, K. G. (2007) Blood pressure before and after electroconvulsive therapy in hypertensive and nonhypertensive Patients. *Journal of ECT*, **23**, 9–10.

American Psychiatric Association (2001) Adverse effects. In, *The Practice of Electroconvulsive Therapy: Recommendations for Treatment, Training and Privileging* (2nd edn), pp. 59–76. APA.

American Society of Anesthesiologists (2014) ASA Physical Status Classification System http://www.asahq.org/quality-and-practice-management/practice-guidance-resource-documents/asa-physical-status-classification-system

Bailine, S., Fink, M., Knapp, R., *et al.* (2010) Electroconvulsive therapy is equally effective in unipolar and bipolar depression. *Acta Psychiatrica Scandinavica*, **121**, 431–6.

Bay-Nielsen, M. & Kehlet, H. (2008) Anaesthesia and post-operative morbidity after elective groin hernia repair: a nation-wide study. *Act Anaesthesilogia Scandinavica*, **52**, 169–74.

Blumberger, D. M., Seitz, D. P., Herrmann, N., *et al.* (2017) Low medical morbidity after acute courses of electroconvulsive therapy in a population based sample. *Acta Psychiatrica Scandinavica* DOI: 10.1111/acps.12815

Bruce, B., Henry, M. E. & Greer, D.H. (2006) Ischemic stroke after electroconvulsive therapy. *Journal of ECT*, **22**, 150–2.

Coupland, C., Dhiman, P., Morriss, R., *et al.* (2011) Antidepressant use and risk of adverse outcomes in older people: population based cohort study. *BMJ* **343** :d4551doi: 10.1136/bmj.d4551

Davison, D. L., Terek, M. & Chawla L. S. (2012) Neurogenic pulmonary edema. *Critical Care*, **16**, 212–19 doi:10.1186/cc11226

de Carle, A. J. & Kohn, R. (2001) Risk factors for falling in a psychogeriatric unit. *International Journal of Geriatric Psychiatry*, **16**, 762–7.

Dennis, N. M., Dennis, P. A., Shafer, A., *et al.* (2017) Electroconvulsive therapy and all-cause mortality in Texas, 1998–2013. *Journal of ECT*, **33**, 22–5.

Dinwiddie, S. H., Huo, D. & Gottlieb, O. (2010) The course of myalgia and headache after electroconvulsive therapy. *Journal of ECT*, **26**, 116–20.

Food and Drug Administration (2006) Information for healthcare professionals. Selective serotonin reuptake inhibitors (SSRIs), selective serotonin-norepinephrine reuptake inhibitors (SNRIs), 5-hydroxytryptamine receptor agonists (triptans) 19 July. https://wayback.archive-it.org/7993/20170406044818/https://www.fda.gov/Drugs/DrugSafety/PostmarketDrugSafetyInformation forPatientsandProviders/DrugSafety InformationforHeathcareProfessionals/ ucm085845.htm

Grunze, H., Vieta, E., Goodwin, G. M., *et al.* (2010) The World Federation of Societies of Biological Psychiatry (WFSBP) Guidelines for the Biological Treatment of Bipolar Disorders: Update 2010 on the Treatment of Acute Bipolar Depression. *World Journal of Biological Psychiatry*, **11**, 81–109.

Hailey, E., Hodge, S. & Buley, N. (2015) ECTAS interim report, patient perspectives: March 2013–April 2014. Royal College of Psychiatrists http://rcpsych.ac.uk/pdf/ ECTAS%20Interim%20Report.pdf

Kramer, B. A. (1999). Use of ECT in California, revisited: 1984–1994. *Journal of ECT*, **15**, 245–51.

Leung, M., Hollander, Y. & Brown, G. R. (2003) Pretreatment with ibuprofen to prevent electroconvulsive therapy-induced headache. *Journal of Clinical Psychiatry*, **64**, 551–3.

Mansoor, D., Trevino, S., Ganzini, L., *et al.* (2016) Negative pressure pulmonary edema after electroconvulsive therapy. *Journal of ECT*, **32**, e2–e3.

Markowitz, J. S., Kellner, C. H., de Vane, C. L., *et al.* (2001) Intranasal sumatriptan in post-ECT headache: results of an open-label trial. *Journal of ECT*, **17**, 280–3.

Medda, P., Perugi, G., Zanello, S., *et al.* (2009) Response to ECT in bipolar I, bipolar II and unipolar depression. *Journal of Affective Disorders*, **118**, 55–9.

Mizen, L., Morton, C. & Scott A. (2015) The cardiovascular safety of the empirical measurement of the seizure threshold in electroconvulsive therapy. *BJPsych Bulletin*, **39**, 14–18.

Munk-Olsen, T., Munk Laursen, T., Videbech, P., *et al.* (2007) All-cause mortality among recipients of electroconvulsive therapy. *Register-based cohort study. British Journal of Psychiatry*, **190**, 435–9.

Nuttall, G. A., Bowersox, M. R., Douglass, S. B., *et al.* (2004) Morbidity and mortality in the use of electroconvulsive therapy. *Journal of ECT*, **20**, 237–41.

Obbels, J., Verwijk, E., Bouckaert, F., *et al.* (2017) ECT-related anxiety: a systematic review. Journal of ECT, DOI: 10.1097/ YCT.0000000000000383

Orlova, Y., Rizzoli, P. & Loder, E. (2018) Association of coprescription of triptan antimigraine drugs and selective serotonin reuptake inhibitor or selective norepinephrine reuptake inhibitor antidepressants with serotonin syndrome. *JAMA Neurology*, **75**, 566–72.

Østergaard, S., Bolwig, T. & Petrides, G. (2014) No causal association between electroconvulsive therapy and death: a summary of a report from the Danish Health and Medicines Authority covering 99,728 treatments. *Journal of ECT*, **30**, 263–4.

Povlsen, U. J., Wildschiødtz, G., Høgenhaven, H., *et al.* (2003) Nonconvulsive status epilepticus after electroconvulsive therapy. *Journal of ECT* **19**, 164–9.

Sackeim, H. A. (1998) The use of electroconvulsive therapy in late-life depression. In *Geriatric Psychopharmacology* (3rd edn) (ed. C. Salzman), pp. 262–309. Williams & Wilkins.

Sarkar, S., Geraghty, J., Moore A. R., *et al.* (2012) A multicentre study to determine the incidence, demographics, aetiology and outcome of 6-day emergency re-admission following day-case endoscopy. *European Journal of Gastroenterology and Hepatology*, **24**, 1438–46.

Scottish ECT Accreditation Network (2016) *Annual Report 2016: A Summary of ECT in*

Scotland for 2015. NHS National Services Scotland.

Sharp, R. P. & Welch, E. B. (2011) Takotsubo cardiomyopathy as a complication of electroconvulsive therapy. *Annals of Pharmacotherapy,* **45,** 1559–65.

Shiwach, R. S., Reid, W. H. & Carmody, T. J. (2001) An analysis of reported deaths following electroconvulsive therapy in Texas, 1993–1998. *Psychiatric Services,* **52,** 1095–7.

Slater, E. (1951) Evaluation of electroconvulsive therapy as compared with conservative methods of treatment in depressive states. *Journal of Mental Science,* **97,** 567–9.

Tess, A. V. & Smetana, G. W. (2009) Medical evaluation of patients undergoing electroconvulsive therapy. *New England Journal of Medicine,* **360,** 1437–44.

Tohen, M., Frank, E., Bowden, C. L., *et al.* (2009) The International Society for Bipolar Disorders (ISBD) Task Force report on the nomenclature of course and outcome in bipolar disorders. *Bipolar Disorders,* **11,** 453–73.

Uppal, V., Dourish, J. & Macfarlane, A. (2010) Anaesthesia for electroconvulsive therapy. *Continuing Education in Anaesthesia, Critical Care & Pain,* **10,** 192–6.

Watts, B. V., Groft, A., Bagian, J. P., *et al.* (2011) An examination of mortality and other adverse events related to electroconvulsive therapy using a national adverse event report system. *Journal of ECT,* **27,** 105–8.

Weiner, R. D. & Krystal, A. D. (1993) EEG monitoring of ECT seizures. In, *The Clinical Science of Electroconvulsive Therapy* (ed. C. E. Coffey), pp. 93–109. American Psychiatric Press.

Weiner, R. D., Coffey, C. E. & Krystal, A. D. (2000) Electroconvulsive therapy in the medical and neurologic patient. In, *Psychiatric Care of the Medical Patient* (2nd edn) (eds Stoudemire, B. S. Fogel & D. Greenberg), pp. 419–28. Oxford University Press.

Whittaker, R., Scott, A. & Gardner M. (2007) The prevalence of prolonged cerebral seizures at the first treatment. *Journal of ECT,* **23,** 11–13.

Chapter 5

Transcranial Magnetic Stimulation

Alex O'Neill-Kerr and Sudheer Lankappa

Introduction

Transcranial magnetic stimulation (TMS) is a relatively new neuro stimulation technique, which has become available in a handful of centres in the UK over the past five years. The technique involves placing a high intensity magnetic coil on the scalp and delivering a rapidly changing magnetic field, which alters the electrical properties of the underlying cortical neurons. Repetitive transcranial magnetic stimulation (rTMS) involves repetitive trains of magnetic stimulations over a defined period of time.

Barker and his colleagues from University of Sheffield first demonstrated that rTMS could be applied to the scalp to stimulate the cerebral cortex (Barker *et al.*, 1985). The clinical use of rTMS involves repetitive magnetic pulses; response to the treatment is influenced by various factors including the frequency, intensity and duration of the stimulus. The treatment parameters can be adapted to inhibit or excite cortical areas. The strength of the magnetic field induced is similar to that of an MRI scanner (Rossi *et al.*, 2009).

Although initial clinical trials of rTMS showed only modest results, in recent trials a larger effect size has been found (Gross *et al.*, 2007). Early trials used low intensity stimulation at 80% of the resting motor threshold (RMT). Resting motor threshold is the minimal intensity of stimulation required to evoke a motor response in adductor muscles of hand (Rossini *et al.*, 1994). Current evidence suggests a higher intensity of up to 120% MT for the optimal antidepressant effect.

Putative Mechanism of Action

The exact mechanism by which rTMS produces improvement in depressive symptoms is not known. However some possible mechanisms have been suggested. These include changes in neurotransmitters, particularly GABA and glutamate, which mediate synaptic inhibitory/excitatory balance (see Chapter 2); there is evidence that rTMS results in elevated prefrontal cortex GABA function in major depressive disorder (Auer *et al.*, 2000; Bhagwagar *et al.*, 2008; Godlewska *et al.*, 2014; Hasler *et al.*, 2007; Levinson *et al.*, 2010).

The neurophysiological changes produced by rTMS depend on the intensity of the current generated, leading to depolarisation of cortical neurons. This can affect resting membrane potentials and thus alter brain activity (George, 2011). These effects are similar to long-term potentiation (LTP) or long-term depression (LTD) of stimulated neurons and lead to changes in synaptic plasticity – the ability of synapses to strengthen or weaken over time in response to increased or decreased activity (Fitzgerald *et al.*, 2006).

Functional MRI studies have shown changes in regional brain activity and metabolism following rTMS administration to the prefrontal cortex. Applying low frequency rTMS at the left dorsolateral prefrontal cortex (DLPFC) causes a reduction in blood flow to the prefrontal and orbitofrontal cortex as well as other regions which have a role in regulating emotional processing (Kito *et al.*, 2008).

Various brain networks are altered in patients with depression (see Chapter 2), the degree of change in their connectivity predicts the severity of depression. rTMS administered to the dorsomedial prefrontal cortex can result in reorganisation of connectivity patterns in the brain (Salomons *et al.*, 2014).

Clinical Guidance and Approvals

Internationally, rTMS is being used for the treatment of various neuropsychiatric conditions. rTMS as a treatment for depression has been thoroughly investigated; more recently rTMS has been proposed as a treatment strategy for other conditions such as autistic spectrum disorder (Enticott *et al.*, 2014), anxiety, PTSD, cocaine addiction and eating disorders (Guo *et al.*, 2017).

The US Food and Drug Administration (FDA) approved a TMS device for the treatment of patients in 2008. In the UK, NICE approved rTMS in the treatment of depression in IPG 542 (NICE, 2015). This review considered meta-analyses and systematic reviews for RCT, non-randomised comparative study, case series and case reports. They concluded that rTMS for depression may be used with normal arrangements for clinical governance and audit.

Indications

At present rTMS is indicated for the treatment of depression; it is usually only offered on the NHS for patients with treatment resistant depression. The treatment of anxiety, OCD, addiction etc., with rTMS, is not yet established within the NHS.

Efficacy in Depression

rTMS has been found to be effective in major depressive disorder (MDD) as an augmentation therapy or as a monotherapy, with a benign side effect profile (Berlim *et al.*, 2013a). A meta-analysis of 1164 patients in 30 randomised controlled trials (Schutter *et al.*, 2009) found that high frequency rTMS to the left dorsolateral prefrontal cortex is effective in treating MDD and the effect size compared to antidepressants. A systematic review and meta-analysis concluded that overall rTMS appears to be an effective treatment for MDD and for schizophrenia (Hovington *et al.*, 2013).

Table 15.1 shows overall efficacy data for rTMS in depression and NNT of 5 (Dell' Osso *et al.*, 2011).

A longitudinal study by Carpenter and colleagues on 257 patients found a relapse rate in patients followed for one year of 36% (Carpenter *et al.*, 2012). In another study where a rescue rTMS was used in patients who had responded to rTMS and were maintained on antidepressant monotherapy, the relapse rate was 13% after 24 weeks (Janicak *et al.*, 2010).

Similar results have been found in naturalistic studies with combined remission/response rates of 60% and overall remission rates of 37% (Carpenter *et al.*, 2012). Retrospective analysis of routine clinical data also showed a combined remission response rate of 51% and a remission rate 35% (Connelly *et al.*, 2012).

Table 15.1

Study	Number of trials	Comparison group	Effect Size
Shutter (2009)	30	Randomised double blind sham controlled studies	d = 0.39
Herrmann & Ebmeier (2006)	33	Randomised double blind parallel or crossover with sham trials	d = 0.65
Burt et al. (2002)	23	Comparing sham and active treatment and crossover studies	d = 0.67
Holtzheimer et al. (2001)	12	Randomised control trials with active and sham treatment groups	d = 0.81
Slotema et al. (2010)	40	rTMS vs sham studies	d = 0.55
Berlim et al. (2013b) (bilateral)	7	Randomised, double blind, bilateral rTMs and sham controlled trials	OR = 4.3 (response) OR = 6 (remission)
Berlim et al. (2014) (HF)	29	Randomised, double blind sham controlled trials	OR = 3.3 (response) OR = 3.3 (remission)
Berlim et al. (2013c) (LF)	8	Randomised controlled trial with active rTMS and sham rTMS	OR = 3.4 (response) OR = 4.7 (remission)

In addition to improvement in depressive symptoms, patients who received rTMS have shown improvement on some measures of cognitive function (Serafini et al., 2015).

Contraindications

There are a number of relative contraindications for rTMS treatment. These include:

- history of epilepsy or organic brain pathology
- acute alcohol withdrawal
- clinical conditions in which there is a significant reduction in seizure threshold
- recent heart disease
- presence of ferromagnetic material in or around the head or within 30 cm of the magnetic coil.

Any implanted cranial devices are likely to heat up under the magnetic field and this needs to be discussed with the relevant specialist.

Patient Selection

There is some evidence of rTMS being effective in Treatment Resistant Depression (TRD), defined as depression which has failed to respond to two adequate trials of antidepressant therapy for an adequate period of time as well as failure to respond to psychological therapy (Benadhira et al., 2017). NICE recommended rTMS for the treatment of depression if there are no contraindications.

Most randomised clinical trials of rTMS have included subjects who have depression of sufficient severity to interfere with daily functioning, but whose symptoms are not so severe as to prevent daily attendance on an outpatient basis to receive the treatment. Patients do not have to be in hospital to receive treatment; however those who are already in hospital can be considered for treatment if there are no contraindications. There are no studies relating to cost effectiveness of this approach.

It is hard to predict individual patient's treatment response, however:

- history of previous positive response to rTMS
- adjunctive antidepressant therapy
- stimulation intensity at greater than 100% MT
- greater than 1,000 pulses delivered per session
- treatment for more than 10 days

are positive predictors of response to treatment (Dumas *et al.*, 2012). Predictors of poor response include a high degree of treatment resistance, increased duration of current episode, advanced age and depression with psychotic symptoms.

The efficacy of TMS versus ECT has been addressed in a number of studies. ECT has been shown to be superior for short-term (less than 4 weeks) treatment and for psychotic depression. The remission rate with ECT was 53% vs. 34% with TMS (Ren, Li & Pala-niyappan, 2014; Berlim *et al.*, 2012). Magnezi and colleagues (2016) reported that ECT (P<0.0001) is more effective than rTMS (P<0.012) and TMS was better in terms of patient preference. The latest meta-analyses of studies comparing ECT and rTMS showed large effect in favour of ECT (CADTH, 2014; Chen *et al.*, 2017), However, reviews have reported a favourable side-effect profile and good tolerability compared to ECT (Baker *et al.*, 2012). Griffiths and colleagues (2019) have published data on 144 patients with treatment resistant depression treated with rTMS in a UK service from 2015 to 2018. Response and remission rates were 34.6% and 20.6% for the HAM-D and 31% and 31.8% for the CGI.

The cognitive effects of ECT and rTMS are influenced by many factors, including treatment parameters and the duration of the treatment. Studies have reported variable results on both acute and long-term cognitive functioning (Kedzior *et al.*, 2017); further research is needed.

Overview of rTMS Administration

Administration of rTMS is relatively straightforward. It requires a room of a suitable size to place an rTMS machine, which is approximately the size of a photocopier. The patient is seated in a comfortable chair; it is important that the chair is of a height that will allow easy access for the treatment administrator for placement of the coil. Most manufacturers supply a chair at an additional cost; these are usually electrically adjustable and allow the patient to adjust for their own comfort but also allow the rTMS operator flexibility placing the patient so that there is easy access for the rTMS coil.

Pillows can be used to ensure that the patient's hands and arms are comfortable, most purpose-designed rTMS chairs will have a suitable headrest which will prevent excessive movement of the patient's head and ensures that the coil does not move during the treatment session.

Prior to the administration of rTMS, the operator applies the coil to the motor cortex to establish the resting motor threshold (RMT). This is the minimum stimulus strength required to induce contractions of the adductor pollicis in the opposite hand. For treatment, the coil is positioned to stimulate the left dorsolateral prefrontal cortex. The typical excitatory treatment protocol used for depression is the application of a 10 Hz stimulus at 120% of RMT, in the position of F3 in the 10–20 EEG montage. The stimulus is applied for 4 seconds, with an inter-stimulus duration of 27 seconds, for 37½ minutes. This will deliver 3,000 pulses in the treatment session. There are other treatment protocols which use shorter intertrain intervals. To minimise the risk of seizure clinicians should refer to appropriate literature (Rossi et al., 2009), which is endorsed by the International Federation for Clinical Neurophysiology.

Inhibitory protocols employed for treatment of panic disorder with comorbid depression (Mantovani et al., 2013) use a continuous stimulus at 1 Hz for 20 minutes, at 120% of the motor threshold, on the right dorsolateral prefrontal cortex, in the position F4 in the 10–20 EEG montage.

Measuring bony landmarks is one of the standard techniques to ensure correct placement of the coil. There are a number of alternative methods including the 5 cm rule and the BEAM 3 method (Rusjan et al., 2010); these are time consuming, particularly in the case of BEAM 3 and reproducibility of the location is problematic. Rusjan and colleagues (2010) showed that using a pre-marked EEG cap is sufficient and is reproducible; in this model the dorsolateral prefrontal cortex is located between left F3 and F5.

Neuronavigation, based on individual patients' structural MRI scan is used in some centres, this helps in localisation of the region targeted for stimulation. It reduces variability (Rusjan et al., 2010) and improves efficacy (Fitzgerald et al., 2006; Fox et al., 2012).

Safety

rTMS is relatively a safe treatment (NICE, 2015). The potential side effects of rTMS include:

- seizure induction
- transient acute hypomania
- syncope
- transient headache
- neck pain and local discomfort.

An international consensus group has developed a protocol for the safe and ethical use of rTMS (Rossi et al., 2009); this provides useful safety information and protocols which can be incorporated into local TMS clinics' operating procedures.

Staff in the clinic should have appropriate training in the management of seizures which, if they occur are brief; status epilepticus has not been associated with TMS and therefore anticonvulsant medication such as buccal midazolam is not considered necessary. Staff should focus on making sure the patient is safe from accidental injury and ensure protection of the airway after the seizure has stopped. Although it is uncommon, staff should also be trained in the management of syncope.

Pain or discomfort at the treatment site may be related to the dose of magnetic strength; most patients find it difficult to tolerate doses above 110% of RMT particularly in the early stages of treatment (Borckardt et al., 2013). For those patients experiencing discomfort, staff can advise patients to take analgesics prior to attending treatment session. If discomfort remains problematic the dose of energy can be reduced and/or a topical anaesthetic agent applied to the area of stimulation. Most patients who experience discomfort in the first treatment session will find that this reduces as they continue to have rTMS.

Discontinuation rate is noted to be between 3% to 11% in various clinical studies.

rTMS in Pregnancy and in Older People

A review of published studies evaluating rTMS for treatment of depression in pregnancy between 1995 and 2014 reported significant response rate for acute depressive episodes and remission was achieved in many cases (Felipe & Ferrao, 2016). The procedure was well tolerated and there were no reports of complications to unborn children. More controlled trials with larger sample size are needed.

There are limited rTMS trials involving elderly patients. A systematic review by Sabesan and colleagues (2015) appraised the evidence regarding the safety and efficacy of rTMS in older adults. Although efficacy of the intervention varied between trials the procedure was safe and well tolerated by older individuals. There was no evidence that rTMS was ineffective in elderly people with depression. Factors other than age associated with reduced efficacy of rTMS include brain atrophy, intensity and number of pulses delivered and clinical profile of patients (Sabesan *et al.*, 2015). Delivery of a higher dose (larger number of pulses – 18,000 instead of 12,000) is more beneficial in the older than in the younger age group of patients with treatment resistant vascular depression (Jorge *et al.*, 2008).

Patients' Experience of TMS

Little has been published about patients' experience of rTMS. Rosedale *et al.* (2009) conducted a phenomenological study and found that 'a certain mindfulness' emerges during the treatment process.

At present very few rTMS clinics are run from NHS trusts, there are a few private providers. The capital cost of equipment is about £50,000 for the machine and chair; recurrent staffing costs are in the region of £60,000 annually, depending on the staffing. Finding suitable space may be challenging, although where a trust is running a dedicated ECT clinic it may be possible to add rTMS as a treatment option utilising existing space and staff for one or two treatments a day.

Training for rTMS Administration

Introduction

The use of rTMS is relatively new in the UK, although it has been widely used in the USA for several years and is part of an established practice in several countries around the world. The Royal College of Psychiatrists UK has a position statement on rTMS which can be accessed from the College website www.rcpsych.ac.uk/pdf/Repetative%20Transcranial%20Magnetic%20Stimulation%20-%20ECT%20ctee%20statement%20Feb17.pdf.

An article 'Transcranial magnetic stimulation in clinical practice' is a helpful resource for beginners (Hardy *et al.*, 2016). At present there are no nationally recognised rTMS training courses. Training is usually provided by the manufacturers of rTMS machines or can be gained by attending workshops at international scientific meetings.

Setting Up a Training Course

The principles of training clinicians in the use of rTMS and the practical aspects of delivering rTMS are similar to those involved in training clinicians in ECT. There should be some knowledge-based learning in small groups. Experience of practical administration of the procedure is best dealt with by participants observing the treatment being delivered by an experienced clinician and then having hands on training.

As with ECT, ongoing observation of application of rTMS by clinical staff including trainee doctors, nurses and healthcare assistants should form part of the training program at local clinics, in conjunction with the lead consultant for rTMS.

What Should Be Covered in a Training Course?

Training should include a brief history and basic physics of rTMS, neuroscience and mechanism of action. In addition, a knowledge of neuroanatomy is desirable to identify the motor cortex and target treatment sites.

The course should cover the basic recommendations of the NICE guidance on the use of rTMS in depressive illness. NICE does not comment on the use of rTMS in any other psychiatric condition although there is considerable research evidence of its use in anxiety disorders, PTSD and other neuropsychiatric conditions (CADTH, 2014).

In addition to indications, a section relating to the contraindications for rTMS such as history of epilepsy or organic brain pathology, or neuropsychiatric condition or treatment which may increase the risk of seizure, including alcohol misuse and alcohol withdrawal, should be considered. The interaction between the magnetic coil and ferro-magnetic material in and around the site of stimulation should be discussed.

Staff in the clinic should have appropriate training in the management of seizures; anticonvulsant medication such as buccal midazolam is not considered necessary. Staff should focus on making sure the patient is safe from accidental injury and ensure protection of the airway after the seizure has stopped. Staff should also be trained in the management of syncope as this can occur at any time during treatment.

The issue of patient selection should also be addressed and similarities and differences between the use of rTMS and ECT should be explored.

rTMS Administration

The training program should provide an overview of rTMS administration including the use of clinical rating scales, recording physical vital signs and safety check list and questionnaires to ensure adequate safety.

The localisation of target sites by various methods such as F3 placement using the 10–20 EEG, or '5 cm rule' methods should be explained and time for practical application of this knowledge during the training programme should be allowed. Staff should also be trained in acquiring RMT.

There are clinics in the UK which use a 10–20 EEG cap to measure the F3 position. Some centres use fixed dose protocols rather than establishing dose based on MT. Despite these clinical variations the basics of acquiring the RMT and determining the F3 position should always be taught as part of the course. Depending on the availability at the local centre, staff can be trained in neuronavigation or scalp-based navigation systems for identification of stimulus site on the scalp. Once the target site has been identified, placement and orientation of the magnetic coil and practical demonstration of its application should be covered.

Setting Up the Machine

Training on setting the parameters of the machine and inputting the number of pulses, trains and duration of treatment should be covered although this will vary for different machines. It may be demonstrated by the manufacturer on delivery of the machine; staff should also refer to the manufacturer's training manual.

The NICE guidance on transcranial magnetic stimulation does not provide any treatment paradigms and it is left to individual centres to decide which protocols would be most appropriate. One widely used protocol involves stimulating at the left DLPFC at an intensity of 80–120% RMT with 10 Hz trains (4 seconds on, 26 seconds off) for a total of 37½ minutes. Variations on this protocol which deliver more pulses by reducing the intertrain interval have been described in the literature. There are also protocols for right-sided inhibitory treatment.

Some machines are able to deliver theta burst stimulation. Evidence for the efficacy of theta burst stimulation (providing a shorter duration of treatment with high frequency 50 Hz stimulation) is beginning to emerge (Chung et al., 2015). Training in the use of theta burst protocols will be an area that trainers may wish to include in their training programme.

Efficacy and Safety

Training should include an explanation as to why monitoring during rTMS treatments is important, as well as ensuring that staff monitoring the treatment are trained in the management of seizures. These are potential but very uncommon side effects of rTMS. The overall risk of seizure is estimated to be less than 1 in 50,000 treatment sessions (<0.002%). Other side effects include discomfort at the site of stimulation, headache and facial twitching. TMS practitioners should be given advice as to how the side effects might be managed. Management and identification of vasovagal syncope should also be included in the training. It is the consensus of the Clinical TMS Society that IV access, cardiac defibrillators, suction and oxygen are NOT necessary for the safe administration of TMS in an outpatient TMS office.

Applied Aspects

It would be useful to review the practical aspects of the delivery of rTMS with participants. Issues such as coil overheating, the need to have noise levels assessed in the clinic and for staff and patients to use earplugs should be covered. Consideration of an annual hearing test for staff should be discussed. The necessity for clinical guidelines policies and consent procedures which need to follow the clinics' usual governance processes should be highlighted.

Summary

rTMS is a safe treatment, which is effective in the management of depression.

It is not as effective as ECT in the management of severe depression with suicidality where clinicians may choose ECT over rTMS on the basis of more rapid onset of improvement with ECT.

References

Auer, D. P., Pütz, B., Kraft, E., Lipinski, B., Schill, J. and Holsboer, F. (2000). Reduced glutamate in the anterior cingulate cortex in depression: an in vivo proton magnetic resonance spectroscopy study. *Bio/Psychiatry,* **47** 305–13.

Baker, P. L., Trevino, K., McClintock, S. M., Wani, A. and Husain, M. M. (2012). Clinical applications of electroconvulsive therapy and transcranial magnetic stimulation for the treatment of major depressive disorder: a critical review. *Neuropsychiatry*, 2 443–51.

Barker, A., Jalinous, R. and Freeson, I. (1985). Non-invasive magnetic stimulation of the human motor cortex. *Lancet*, 1 1106–7.

Benadhira, R., Thomas, F., Bouaziz, N. *et al.* (2017). A randomized sham controlled study of maintenance rTMS for treatment resistant depression. *Psychiatry Research*. https:// doi.org/10.1016/jpsychres.2017.08.029.

Berlim, M., Van den Eynde, F. and Daskalakis, Z. (2013a). A systematic review and meta-analysis on the efficacy and acceptability of bilateral repetitive transcranial magnetic stimulation (rTMS) for treating major depression. *Psychol Med*, 43 2245–54.

Berlim, M., Van den Eynde, F. and Daskalakis, Z. (2013b). Efficacy and acceptability of high frequency repetitive transcranial magnetic stimulation (rTMS) versus electroconvulsive therapy (ECT) for major depression: a systematic review and meta-analysis of randomized trials. *Depress Anxiety*, 30 614–23.

Berlim, M., Van den Eynde, F. and Daskalakis, Z. (2013c). Clinically meaningful efficacy and acceptability of low-frequency repetitive transcranial magnetic stimulation (rTMS) for treating primary major depression: a meta-analysis of randomized, double-blind and shamcontrolled trials. *Neuropsychopharmacology*, 38 543–51.

Berlim, M. T., Van den Eynde, F., Tovar-Perdomo, S. and Daskalakis, Z. J. (2014). Response, remission and drop-out rates following high-frequency repetitive transcranial magnetic stimulation (rTMS) for treating major depression: a systematic review and meta-analysis of randomized, double-blind and sham-controlled trials. *Psychological Medicine*, 44 225–39.

Bhagwagar, Z., Wylezinska, M., Jezzard, P. *et al.* (2008). Low GABA concentrations in occipital cortex and anterior cingulate cortex in medication-free, recovered depressed patients. *Int J Neuropsychopharmacol*, 11 255–60.

Borckardt, J. J., Nahas, Z. H., Teal, J., *et al.* (2013). The painfulness of active, but not sham, transcranial magnetic stimulation decreases rapidly over time: results from the double-blind phase of the OPT-TMS trial. *Brain Stimulation*, 6 925–8.

Burt, T., Lisanby, S. H. and Sackeim, H. A. (2002). Neuropsychiatric applications of transcranial magnetic stimulation: a meta analysis. *Int J Neuropsychopharmacol*, 5 73–103.

Canadian Agency for Drugs and Technology in Health (CADTH) (2014). Transcranial magnetic stimulation for the treatment of adults with PTSD, GAD, or depression: a review of clinical effectiveness and guidelines. Canadian Agency for Drugs and Technology in Health.

Carpenter, L. L., Janicak, P. G., Aaronson, S. T. *et al.* (2012). Transcranial magnetic stimulation (TMS) for major depression: a multisite, naturalistic, observational study of acute treatment outcomes in clinical practice. *Depress Anxiety*, 29 587–96.

Chen, J. J., Zhao, L. B., Liu, Y. Y., Fan, S. H. and Xie, P. (2017). Comparative efficacy and acceptability of electroconvulsive therapy versus repetitive transcranial magnetic stimulation for major depression: a systematic review and multiple-treatments meta-analysis. *Behav Brain Res*, 320 30–6.

Chung, S. W., Hoy, K. E. and Fitzgerald, P. B. (2015). Theta-burst stimulation: a new form of TMS stimulation for depression? *Depression and Anxiety*, 32 182–92.

Connolly, K., Helmer, A., Cristancho, M. *et al.* (2012). Effectiveness of transcranial magnetic stimulation in clinical practice post-FDA approval in the United States: results observed with the first 100 consecutive cases of depression at an academic medical center. *J Clin Psychiatry*, 73 567–73.

Dell'Osso, B., Camuri, G., Castellano, F. *et al.* (2011). Meta-review of metanalytic studies with repetitive transcranial magnetic stimulation (rTMS) for the treatment of major depression. *Clinical Practice and Epidemiology in Mental Health*, 7 167–77.

Dumas, R., Padovani, R., Richieri, R. and Lançon, C. (2012). Repetitive transcranial magnetic stimulation in major depression: response factor. *L'Encephale*, 38 360–8.

Enticott, P. G., Fitzgibbon, B. M., Kennedy, H. H. *et al.* (2014). A double blind randomized trial of deep repetitive transcranial magnetic stimulation (rTMS) for autistic spectrum disorder. *Brain Stimulation*, 7 206–11.

Felipe, R. D. M. and Ferrão, Y. A. (2016). Transcranial magnetic stimulation for treatment of major depression during pregnancy: a review. *Trends in Psychiatry and Psychotherapy*, 38 190–7.

Fitzgerald, P., Fountain, S. and Daskalakis, Z. (2006). A comprehensive review of the effects of rTMS on motor cortical excitability and inhibition. *Clinical Neurophysiology*, 117 2584–96.

Fox, M. D., Liu, H. and Pascual-Leone, A. (2012). Identification of reproducible individualized targets for treatment of depression with TMS based on intrinsic connectivity. *NeuroImage*, 66 151–60.

George, M. S. and Post, R. M. (2011). Daily left prefrontal repetitive transcranial magnetic stimulation for acute treatment of medication-resistant depression. *American Journal of Psychiatry*, 168 356–64.

Godlewska, B. R., Near, J. and Cowen, P. J. (2014). Neurochemistry of major depression: a study using magnetic resonance spectroscopy. *Psychopharmacology (Berl.)*, 232 501–7.

Gross, M., Nakamura, L., Pascual-Leone, A. et al. (2007). Has repetitive transcranial magnetic stimulation (rTMS) treatment for depression improved? A systematic review and meta-analysis comparing the recent vs. the earlier rTMS studies. *Acta Psychiatrica Scandinavica*, 116 165–73.

Guo, Q., Li, C. and Wang, J. (2017). Updated review on the clinical use of repetitive transcranial magnetic stimulation in psychiatric disorders. *Neuroscience Bulletin* https://doi.org/10.1007/s12264-017-0185-3

Hardy, S., Bastick, L., O'Neill-Kerr, A., Sabesan, P., Lankappa, S. and Palaniyappan, L. (2016). Transcranial magnetic stimulation in clinical practice. *BJPsych Advances*, 22 373–9.

Hasler, G., van der Veen, J.W., Tumonis, T., Meyers, N., Shen, J. and Drevets, W.C. (2007). Reduced prefrontal glutamate/glutamine and gamma-aminobutyric acid levels in major depression determined using proton magnetic resonance spectroscopy. *Arch Gen Psychiatry*, 64 193–200.

Herrmann, L. and Ebmeier, K. (2006). Factors modifying the efficacy of transcranial magnetic stimulation in the treatment of depression: a review. *J Clin Psychiatry*, 67 1870–6.

Holtzheimer, P. E. 3rd, Russo, J. and Avery, D. H. (2001). A meta-analysis of repetitive transcranial magnetic stimulation in the treatment of depression. *Psychopharmacol Bull*, 35 149–69.

Hovington, C. L., McGirr, A., Lepage, M. and Berlim, M. T. (2013). Repetitive transcranial magnetic stimulation (rTMS) for treating major depression and schizophrenia: a systematic review of recent metaanalyses. *Ann Med*, 45 308–21.

Janicak, P., Nahas, Z., Lisanby, S. et al. (2010). Durability of clinical benefit with transcranial magnetic stimulation (TMS) in the treatment of pharmacoresistant major depression: assessment of relapse during a 6-month, multisite, open-label study. *Brain Stimul*, 3 187–99.

Janicak, P. G., Dunner, D. L., Aaronson, S. T. et al. (2013). Transcranial magnetic stimulation (TMS) for major depression: a multisite, naturalistic, observational study of quality of life outcome measures in clinical practice. *CNS Spectrums*, 18 322–32.

Jorge, R. E., Moser, D. J., Acion, L. and Robinson, R. G. (2008). Treatment of vascular depression using repetitive transcranial magnetic stimulation. *Arch Gen Psychiatry*, 65 268–76.

Kedzior, K. K., Schuchinsky, M., Gerkensmeier, I. et al. (2017). Challenges in comparing the acute outcomes of high frequency rTMS vs ECT in major depression: a systematic review. *J Psychiat Res*, 91 14–17.

Kito, S., Fujita, K. and Koga, Y. (2008). Regional cerebral blood flow changes after low-frequency transcranial magnetic stimulation of the right dorsolateral prefrontal cortex in treatment-resistant depression. *Neuropsychobiology*, 58 29–36.

Levinson, A. J., Fitzgerald, P. B., Favalli, G., Blumberger, D. M., Daigle, M. and

Daskalakis, Z. J. (2010). Evidence of cortical inhibitory deficits in major depressive disorder. *Biol Psychiatry*, **67** 458–64.

Magnezi, R., Aminov, E., Shmuel, D., Dreifuss, M. and Dannon, P. (2016). Comparison between neurostimulation techniques repetitive transcranial magnetic stimulation vs electroconvulsive therapy for the treatment of resistant depression: patient preference and cost-effectiveness. *Patient Preference and Adherence*, **10** 1481.

Mantovani, A., Aly, M., Dagan, Y. *et al.* (2013). Randomized sham controlled trial of rTMS to the dorsolateral prefrontal cortex for the treatment of panic disorder with comorbid major depression. *Journal of Affective Disorders*, **144** 153–9.

National Institute for Health and Care Excellence. (2015). Interventional procedure consultation document: Repetitive transcranial magnetic stimulation for depression. https://www.nice.org.uk/guidance/ipg542/chapter/1-recommendations

Ren, J., Li, H., Palaniyappan, L. *et al.* (2014). Repetitive transcranial magnetic stimulation versus electroconvulsive therapy for major depression: A systematic review and meta-analysis. *Progress in Neuro-Psychopharmacology and Biological Psychiatry*, **51** 181–9.

Rosedale, M., Lisanby, S. and Malaspina, D. (2009). The structure of the lived experience for persons having undergone rTMS for depression treatment. *J Am Psychiatr Nurses Assoc*, **15** 333.

Rossi, S., Hallett, M., Rossini, P. *et al.* (2009). Safety, ethical considerations, and application guidelines for the use of transcranial magnetic stimulation in clinical practice and research. *Clinical Neurophysiology*, **120** 2008–39.

Rossini, P. M., Barker, T., Berardelli, A. *et al.* (1994). Noninvasive electrical and magnetic stimulation of the brain, spinal cord and roots: basic principles and procedures for routine clinical application. Report of an IFCN committee. *Electroenceph Clin Neurophysiol*, **91** 79–92.

Rusjan, P., Barr, M., Farzan, F. *et al.* (2010). Optimal transcranial magnetic stimulation coil placement for targeting the dorsolateral prefrontal cortex using novel magnetic resonance image-guided neuronavigation. *Hum Brain Mapp*, **31** 1643–52.

Sabesan, P., Lankappa, S., Khalifa, N., Krishnan, V., Gandhi, R. and Palaniyappan, L. (2015). Transcranial magnetic stimulation for geriatric depression: Promises promises and pitfalls. *World Journal of Psychiatry*, **5** 170.

Salomons, T., Dunlop, K., Kennedy, S. *et al.* (2014). Resting-state cortico-thalamic-striatal connectivity predicts response to dorsomedial prefrontal rTMS in major depressive disorder. *Neuropsychopharmacology*, **39** 488–98.

Serafini, G., Pompili, M., Murri, M. B. *et al.* (2015). The effects of rTMS on cognitive performance in treatment-resistant depression: a systematic review. *Neuropsychobiology*, **71** 125–39.

Shutter, D. (2009). Antidepressant efficacy of high-frequency transcranial magnetic stimulation over the left dorsolateral prefrontal cortex in double-blind sham-controlled designs: a meta-analysis. *Psychol Med*, **39** 65–75.

Slotema, C., Blom, J., Hoek, H. *et al.* (2010). Should we expand the toolbox of psychiatric treatment methods to include Repetitive Transcranial Magnetic Stimulation (rTMS)? A meta-analysis of the efficacy of rTMS in psychiatric disorders. *J Clin Psychiatry*, **71** 873–84.

Chapter 6

Neurosurgery for Mental Disorder

Keith Matthews and Christine A Matthews

There is a general recognition that, notwithstanding recent advances and improvements in the targeting and delivery of ECT, within routine clinical practice there continue to be a significant minority of patients who are either not helped by, or are unable to tolerate, ECT (Scottish Electroconvulsive Therapy Accreditation Network, 2016). Failure to sustain a useful antidepressant effect, even with diligent attention to all available maintenance measures, remains a particular clinical challenge. In the previous edition of *The ECT Handbook* (Waite & Easton, 2013), emerging evidence to support the use of different brain stimulation therapies was reviewed. With repetitive Transcranial Magnetic Stimulation (rTMS) now addressed within a separate chapter (Chapter 15), here we consider the present status of three distinct forms of neurosurgical intervention: vagus nerve stimulation (VNS), deep brain stimulation (DBS) and stereotactic ablative (lesion generation) surgery. Each of these therapeutic approaches are also addressed within the 2017 Royal College of Psychiatrists' Position Statements on Neurosurgery for Mental Disorders (NMD) (RCPsych CERT 05/17, 2017).

It is worth noting that the evaluation of published evidence with respect to neurosurgical treatments – in this case as intended therapies for depression – sits at the heart of contemporary debates about the relative merits and limitations of randomised and non-randomised research evidence (Howick & Medbius, 2015). To summarise briefly a complex, unresolved and nuanced debate, it is suggested that critical emphasis be placed primarily upon the *quality* of research rather than simple acknowledgement of global study design characteristics. There are, for sure, many low-quality, unreliable randomised controlled trials (RCT). Equally, there have been numerous high quality, informative observational studies that have closely approximated the eventual outcome revealed from subsequent high-quality RCT evaluation (Benson & Hartz, 2000). Observational studies remain essential within clinical domains where RCT designs are either impossible, or considered unethical. However, for two of the interventions considered here, relevant, randomised, blinded, sham-controlled evidence is available.

'Neuromodulation'

Both vagus nerve stimulation (VNS) and deep brain stimulation (DBS) are considered as forms of 'neuromodulation' whereby the activity within key brain circuitry is modified by the application of intermittent electrical stimuli. In the case of VNS, this represents an 'indirect' stimulation technique achieved by electrical stimulation of the cervical portion of the left vagus nerve by an implanted and programmable pulse generator (IPG), which makes contact through a surgically implanted helical electrode wrapped around the vagus nerve. While VNS is a neurosurgical intervention, there is no intracranial component to the implantation surgery. DBS, on the other hand, involves the stereotactic implantation of intracranial electrodes, usually bilaterally, deep within the substance of the brain. These electrodes are connected to one or more IPGs that deliver adjustable electrical stimuli. These independent parameter adjustments are possible because each IPG has modifiable programming and can utilise the full spread of potential electrode contacts at the tip of the implanted electrodes to determine the size and shape of the electrical stimulation field. Both VNS and DBS IPGs are typically surgically implanted within the superficial tissues of the anterior chest or abdominal wall (bilaterally in the case of DBS) and they communicate with the respective stimulating electrodes via connecting cables tunnelled under the skin.

Vagus Nerve Stimulation

VNS was first explored as a treatment for medication-refractory epilepsy. Although considered a relatively 'established' therapy in this neurological context, the breadth and quality of evidence supporting its use remains modest and the optimum deployment and mechanisms of action of VNS in epilepsy remain speculative (Morris et al., 2013).

Over the past 15 years, there have been several open-label case series reporting apparently encouraging results for the use of VNS in patients with chronic and otherwise relatively 'treatment refractory' depression. However, the literature is generally observational in nature, of low to moderate quality, with high risk of bias, and the single pivotal blinded controlled comparison of active VNS with sham stimulation failed to demonstrate efficacy (Rush et al., 2005). Accordingly, there is considerable uncertainty as to whether either the preceding or subsequent observational data suggesting beneficial effects of VNS are sufficiently robust to support a clear clinical recommendation. This uncertainty is reflected within relevant UK guidance (NICE IPG 330, 2009).

Technical Aspects

Surgical implantation of the electrode and IPG is usually performed by a neurosurgeon, under general anaesthetic, although subsequent replacement of the IPG when battery depletion occurs (approximately 2–5 years depending upon stimulation parameters) can be performed under local anaesthetic. Two weeks after implantation, the IPG is programmed using a handheld computer that is connected to a programming wand. In the clinic, the patient holds the wand over the IPG, which allows the clinician to program the device and to tailor stimulation according to acute tolerability, clinical response and longer-term adverse effects.

In most clinical studies, and in clinical practice, stimulation is active for 30 seconds every five minutes (30/300 seconds) and this 'duty cycle' repeats continuously over a 24-hour period. The frequency of the pulse is typically 20Hz with the pulse width ranging from 130 microseconds to 500 microseconds. Often, the shorter pulse widths are associated with improved tolerability of stimulation (e.g. reduced jaw discomfort). The stimulating current is usually commenced at a low setting (e.g. 0.25mA) and is gradually increased, according to tolerability, over multiple clinic visits over a period of weeks. Target current settings range from 0.75mA to 2.0mA, although a clear relationship between stimulating current and beneficial clinical effect has not been determined. Achieving the 'target' stimulating current usually requires multiple clinic visits over a period of weeks.

Putative mechanisms of action for VNS both as an anticonvulsant and antidepressant therapy remain highly speculative. Approximately 80% of the fibres within the left cervical vagus nerve are afferent fibres that terminate in the nucleus tractus solitarius of the brain stem. From there, they project onwards to central noradrenergic systems via the locus coeruleus and to serotonergic systems via the raphe nuclei. Therefore, in theory, VNS has the potential to modify at least two major neurotransmitter systems that have been posited as relevant to the pathophysiology of depression. Additionally, vagal afferent projections reach to the amygdala, the thalamus and the hypothalamus via the nucleus tractus solitarius, potentially exerting more direct effects within these structures. Hence, it has been hypothesised that by modulating neuronal activity in the cervical portion of the left vagus nerve, the functioning of 'upstream', central neural systems can be modified. Many of these systems are implicated in emotional processing and autonomic–sensory integration.

Outcome Studies

The majority of the clinical outcome data relating to VNS are derived from manufacturer-sponsored studies with an associated elevated risk of bias. As mentioned earlier, the key comparison of active 'v' sham VNS failed to show efficacy, possibly because the primary endpoint was too early (10 weeks). There was, however, weak evidence of modestly improved outcomes after 12 months of VNS compared with an opportunistic, non-randomised, 'treatment as usual' (TAU) comparator group (George *et al.*, 2005). The most recent substantive VNS report is a long-term registry based study comparing the observational outcomes at up to five years for 494 patients with VNS and 301 patients managed as TAU (Aaronson *et al.*, 2017). These authors reported improved response and remission rates in the VNS treated group (68% 'v' 43% and 41% 'v' 26% respectively). However, this observational study design does not permit strong inferences about potential efficacy. On a more positive note, these data do suggest, along with previous reports, that VNS is a relatively safe intervention with the most common adverse effects consistent across studies. Most adverse effects are stimulation-related and modifiable through altered programming. The most common stimulation-related adverse effect is voice alteration, occurring in around 60% of patients. This is experienced as hoarseness and is present only during periods of active stimulation. The risk of post-implantation infection is generally small (3–5%) and can usually be managed with antibiotics. A temporary vocal cord paralysis can occur in approximately 1 in 100 patients.

There are a few clinical circumstances when VNS is contraindicated. These include: presence of a cardiac pacemaker; previous history of neck surgery that would make implantation difficult; significant cardiac dysrhythmia; and previous left or bilateral cervical vagotomy.

Notably, however, whilst VNS is often described as a 'reversible' therapy, once the VNS system is implanted, shortwave, microwave and ultrasound diathermy is contraindicated because of the risk of induction of current in the VNS electrodes and consequent damage to the vagus nerve. Additionally, the same possibility of nerve damage exists with exposure to MRI and although it is possible to perform MRI with a VNS system in situ, this can only be done safely with a separate head coil and where there is relevant expertise in the imaging department. This risk of nerve damage reduces after the device is explanted, but since the helical electrode wrapped around the nerve remains in perpetuity, high intensity MRI scanning (> 1.5 Tesla) is cautioned against.

The presence of a VNS device is not considered to represent a contraindication to ECT (Burke & Husain, 2006). It is, however, recommended that the VNS device be stopped and restarted before and after each ECT treatment.

Place for VNS in the Management of Refractory Depression

Whilst there are some data to support the contention that VNS may have a useful anti-depressant effect, the majority of these data are derived from manufacturer sponsored, observational study designs and are of low to moderate quality. There is, on the basis of the single blinded RCT, evidence of no effect of VNS, although the duration of the stimulation period may have been too brief to allow active treatment to demonstrate an effect on the primary outcome. VNS appears to present few hazards to treated patients. Undoubtedly, there will be a significant non-specific/placebo response to any treatment trial with an IPG, particularly where patients are consistently aware of device activity.

NICE (2009) recommended '. . . this procedure (VNS) should be used only with special arrangements for clinical governance, consent, audit or research. It should be used only in patients with severe depression who have not responded to medical therapy'. (NICE IPG330, 2009).

Because of the continuing unresolved uncertainty over efficacy; the uncertainty over optimal patient selection procedures and programming parameters; the *irreversible* nature of the electrode implantation with an associated permanent need to avoid diathermy and high resolution MRI scanning; the requirement for VNS to be delivered within an experienced multidisciplinary team with close working between neurosurgical teams and psychiatric teams, it is presently recommended that VNS remain considered as *an investigational procedure* and that it should ideally only be offered to patients within the context of an ethically approved research protocol.

Deep Brain Stimulation

DBS represents an established neurosurgical treatment for a range of neurological disorders; for example the bilateral implantation of electrodes in the motor component of the subthalamic nucleus is offered as a treatment for medication non-responsive Parkinson's disease (Limousin *et al.*, 1995). In the wake of this success, small trials followed in patients with obsessive-compulsive disorder (OCD), with initial surgical targets mirroring established ablative surgical targets such as the anterior limb of the internal capsule (Nuttin *et al.*, 1999). The first open case series of DBS for patients with depression was published in 2005 (Mayberg *et al.*, 2005), in this case targeting subgenual cingulate white matter tracts. Whilst several targets have been explored, most depression DBS experience has been with the anterior limb of the internal capsule (also known as VC/VS stimulation) (Dougherty *et al.*, 2015) and subgenual cingulate white matter tracts (Holtzheimer *et al.*, 2017).

Technical Aspects

The mechanisms of action of DBS are uncertain and the subject of considerable debate. DBS has been proposed to be excitatory, inhibitory and 'modulatory'. It is not clear whether a common mode of action explains all the effects of DBS irrespective of site and indication.

Outcome Studies

Although there is a wealth of data from observational studies targeting different neural structures and circuitry, here, for brevity, we confine our review to the two, key, blinded sham-stimulation controlled studies. The RECLAIM study (Dougherty *et al.*, 2015) randomised 30 patients to receive 16 weeks of either active DBS or sham DBS, with the target site being the ventral capsule/ventral striatum. This was followed by a 24-month open-label continuation phase. At 16 weeks, there was no difference in response rate between active (20%) and sham (14%) stimulation groups. It is possible that – as with the key VNS RCT – the duration of the active 'v' sham stimulation phase was insufficient to demonstrate significant differences between groups. However, it is at least as likely that both groups benefited equally from the non-specific/placebo effects of treatment and that there was no additional benefit from active stimulation.

Similarly, in the BROADEN study of subcallosal cingulate white matter DBS for refractory depression, 90 participants were randomised to either active (n=60) or sham (n=30) stimulation for six months, followed by six months of open-label DBS (Holtzheimer *et al.*, 2017). Both groups showed clinical improvement, but there was no statistically significant difference in response rate during the double-blinded, sham-controlled phase. Participants also continued to improve uniformly during the six months open-label phase. The response and remission rates for participants receiving active open-label DBS were, respectively, 40% and 19% at 12 months, 51% and 17% at 18 months, and 48% and 25% at 24 months.

Place for DBS in the Management of Refractory Depression

There is no relevant NICE guidance relating to DBS for refractory depression.

There is considerable ongoing debate about why DBS for depression failed to demonstrate benefit, after so much promise was attributed to open-label, uncontrolled trials. There has been much speculation about the potential for more precise targeting of specific fibre tracts and possibly improved patient selection. However, it is entirely possible that non-specific (i.e. placebo) effects are not only more significant in these patient populations than previously thought, but also that such effects are substantial and long-lasting. Although it is possible that improved patient selection and surgical targeting could lead to more compelling efficacy data, DBS for depression remains *an investigational procedure* and should not be performed unless within the context of an ethically approved research protocol.

Ablative (Lesion) Neurosurgery for Mental Disorder

The overwhelming majority of patients affected by psychiatric disorders can experience significant benefit from the broad range of available pharmacological, psychological and other interventions. However, a considerable number of patients fail to experience significant, or sustained benefit despite the optimised delivery of such therapies – often over a period of many years. The evidence base to support the use of almost all interventions in such clinical circumstances is effectively non-existent, with the notable exception of some neurosurgical therapies. As articulated within the 2017 Royal College of Psychiatrists' Position Statement, it is considered that:

> For carefully selected patients, with difficulties in specific symptom domains – specifically those with Depressive Disorders and Obsessive Compulsive Disorders – neurosurgical therapies may reasonably be considered. In each individual case, consideration of the appropriateness of offering any form of NMD must balance the risks and benefits of surgery with the risks and benefits of continuing with 'treatment as usual' and should also acknowledge patient preference.
>
> (Royal College of Psychiatrists, CERT 05/17, 2017)

The College position on the clinical place for NMD and the requirement for strong clinical governance and safeguarding is consistent with that recently articulated by the

Psychiatric Neurosurgery Committee of the World Society for Stereotactic and Functional Neurosurgery (Nuttin *et al.*, 2014).

Technical Aspects

Ablative neurosurgery (the creation of small targeted lesions by focal applications of radiofrequency induced heat, by radiation or by focused ultrasound), is the form of NMD with the strongest evidence base and longest reported follow-up. In particular, although there is a broad literature considering multiple procedures and multiple proposed clinical indications, this literature relates to the two procedures most commonly offered as treatments for patients with otherwise refractory and disabling depression and/or OCD – anterior cingulotomy and anterior capsulotomy. Both procedures have been considered as representing established acceptable, safe and effective clinical practice in the UK for many years, including following review by independent, multidisciplinary expert groups (CRAG working group on mental illness, 1996; RCPsych working group, 2000).

The delivery of safe and effective ablative NMD – subject to the general caveats above – represents an important element of the ethical and optimised management of patients with chronic, otherwise treatment refractory depression and OCD. There is, however, currently no compelling evidence to support ablative NMD for any other psychiatric indication, although this position may change with ongoing studies across the world.

Outcome Studies

There are no RCT data relating to lesion surgery for depression, although there are positive contemporary data from a blinded RCT of gamma capsulotomy for OCD (Miguel *et al.*, 2019). The accrued evidence for NMD for depression is, therefore, observational, but does encompass detailed clinical evaluation of entire cohorts from baseline to long-term follow up and the published outcomes originate from multiple centres internationally. We are unaware of ongoing blinded RCTs to supplement the observational evidence, although the possibility to conduct these will present soon with the advent of two 'non-invasive' methods for lesion generation – focused irradiation (gamma knife surgery) and focused ultrasound (Jung *et al.*, 2015). These methods will likely overcome the consistently expressed ethical barrier to RCT evaluation with 'sham lesioning' by conventional methods.

In the absence of formal RCT evidence, recent long-term observational reports of outcome include those for anterior capsulotomy (Christmas *et al.*, 2011, Subramanian *et al.*, 2017) and for anterior cingulotomy (Steele *et al.*, 2008, Shields *et al.*, 2008, Volpini *et al.*, 2017).

Place for Ablative Neurosurgery in the Management of Refractory Depression

The College Position has recently been summarised (RCPsych CERT 05/17, 2017):

1. NMD procedures must only ever be performed with a specific therapeutic intention, i.e., for symptom relief and restoration of function.
2. NMD provision (lesion procedures AND all invasive stimulation methods) should be subject to ethical and clinical governance oversight by an independent body. Special attention must be paid to the processes of patient advocacy, the assessment of capacity and the nature of informed consent.

3. NMD should only be provided by neurosurgeons familiar with functional stereotactic surgery and it should be conducted within specialist centres. Further, the clinical programme should be led by experienced psychiatrists with relevant expertise in the target disorders.

4. All patients who are considered as candidates for NMD must be informed that neurosurgery is only one component of a more comprehensive psychiatric management plan that will also include attention to wider aspects of psychological, social and occupational functioning.

5. Relevant Mental Health legislation (there are regional variations within the UK) must be adhered to.

6. Candidates for all forms of NMD (including lesion procedures and invasive stimulation methods) must be robustly evaluated by clinicians with specific expertise in the management of the target disorder and confirmed to meet consensus criteria with respect to the severity and refractoriness of the presenting condition.

5. Patient selection procedures and any discussions about possible NMD should be conducted by experienced multidisciplinary teams with close working between – as a minimum – stereotactic and functional neurosurgeons, psychiatrists, mental health nurses and expert psychological therapists.

8. Comprehensive pre- and post-operative evaluation – with specific attention to disorder-specific symptom outcomes, cognition, social and interpersonal functioning and health-related quality of life measures – must take place, with an identified mechanism for reporting the immediate and longer-term outcomes within a robust clinical governance structure.

9. Post-operative care plans should be developed collaboratively; should cover a period of at least 12-months; and should include the full participation of locality mental health services. Surgery should not take place unless a detailed, collaborative, patient-centred post-operative care plan has been agreed.

Summary

For patients who do not respond to ECT, or who fail to sustain satisfactory response, there are presently three neurosurgical approaches that may be considered. Of these, VNS represents the least 'invasive' procedure, but evidence for efficacy largely rests with low to moderate quality observational data and a single negative blinded RCT. Hazards associated with VNS are, however, low. In the wake of two convincingly negative blinded RCTs, DBS remains investigational, with no clear recommendation possible with respect to either optimal target, nor indeed, whether an efficacy 'signal' can be discerned.

In terms of intracranial surgeries, ablative neurosurgery with lesions generated by thermal stimuli remains the most clearly established neurosurgical approach, with consistent observational data from several centres over several decades supporting reasonable safety and benefit at long-term follow up. Such data exist for both thermal anterior capsulotomy and thermal anterior cingulotomy.

References

Aaronson S T, Sears P, Ruvuna F et al. (2017) A 5-year observational study of patients with treatment resistant depression treated with vagus nerve stimulation or treatment as usual: comparison of response, remission and suicidality. American Journal of Psychiatry, **174**, 640–8.

Benson K and Hartz A J (2000) A comparison of observational studies and randomized controlled trials. *New England Journal of Medicine*, 342, 1878–86.

Burke M J and Husain M M (2006) Concomitant use of vagus nerve stimulation and electroconvulsive therapy for treatment resistant depression. *Journal of Electroconvulsive Therapy*, 22, 218–22.

Christmas D, Eljamel M S, Butler S et al. (2011) Long term outcome of thermal anterior capsulotomy for chronic, treatment refractory depression. *Journal of Neurology, Neurosurgery and Psychiatry*, 82, 594–600.

CRAG Working Group on Mental Illness (1996) *Neurosurgery for Mental Disorder. A Report by a Good Practice Group of the CRAG Working Group on Mental Illness*. Scottish Office J2318, 7/96. Edinburgh: HMSO.

Dougherty D D, Rezai A R, Carpenter L L et al. (2015) A randomized sham-controlled trial of deep brain stimulation of the Ventral Capsule / Ventral Striatum for chronic treatment resistant depression. *Biological Psychiatry*, 78, 240–8.

George M S, Rush A J, Marangell L B et al. (2005) A one year comparison of Vagus Nerve Stimulation with treatment as usual for treatment resistant depression. *Biological Psychiatry*, 58, 364–73.

Holtzheimer P, Husain M M, Lisanby S H et al. (manuscript in press) Subcallosal cingulate deep brain stimulation for treatment-resistant depression: a multi site, randomized, sham controlled trial. *Lancet Psychiatry*.

Howick J and Mebius A (2015) Randomised trials and observational studies: the current philosophical controversy. In *Handbook of the philosophy of medicine* (eds Schramme T and Edwards S), https://link.springer.com/referenceworkentry/10.1007/978-94-017-8706-2_45-1.

Jung H H, Kim S J, Roh D et al. (2014) Bilateral thermal capsulotomy with MR-guided focused ultrasound for patients with treatment-refractory obsessive-compulsive disorder: a proof-of-concept study. *Molecular Psychiatry*, 20, 1205–11.

Limousin P, Pollak P, Benazzouz A et al. (1995) Bilateral subthalamic nucleus stimulation for severe Parkinson's disease. *Movement Disorders*, 10, 672–4.

Mayberg H S, Lozano A M, Voon V et al. (2005) Deep Brain Stimulation for Treatment-Resistant Depression. *Neuron*, 45, 651–60.

Miguel E C, Lopes A C, McLaughlin N C R et al. (2019) Evolution of gamma knife capsulotomy for intractable obsessive-compulsive disorder. *Mol Psychiatry*, 24, 218–40. doi: 10.1038/s41380-018-0054-0. Epub 2018 May 9.

Morris G L 3rd, Gloss D, Buchhalter J et al. (2013) Evidence based guideline update: vagus nerve stimulation for the treatment of epilepsy. *Neurology*, 81, 1453–9.

National Institute for Clinical Excellence (2009) *Vagus nerve stimulation for treatment-resistant depression* (Interventional procedures guidance IPG330). National Institute for Clinical Excellence. (https://www.nice.org.uk/guidance/ipg330). Accessed 25 September 2017.

National Institute for Clinical Excellence (2009) *Vagus nerve stimulation for severe depression* (interventional procedures consultation), Interventional Procedures Guidance [IPG330]. National Institute for Clinical Excellence. (https://www.nice.org.uk/guidance/ipg330/documents/vagus-nerve-stimulation-for-severe-depression-interventional-procedures-consultation-). Accessed Sept 25th 2017.

Nuttin B, Cosyns P, Demeulemeester H et al. (1999) Electrical stimulation in anterior limbs of internal capsules in patients with obsessive-compulsive disorder. *Lancet*, 354, 1526.

Nuttin B, Wu H, Mayberg H et al. (2014) Consensus on guidelines for stereotactic neurosurgery for psychiatric disorders. *Journal of Neurology, Neurosurgery and Psychiatry*, 0, 1–6. (doi:10.1136/jnnp-2013-306580).

Royal College of Psychiatrists Committee on ECT and related treatments (2017) *Statement on Neurosurgery for Mental Disorder (NMD), also known as Psychiatric Neurosurgery* (Position statement CERT 05/17). Royal College of Psychiatrists.

Royal College of Psychiatrists (2000) *Neurosurgery for Mental Disorder. Report from the Neurosurgery Working Group of the Royal College of Psychiatrists.* Royal College of Psychiatrists.

Rush A J, Marangell L, Sackheim H A *et al.* (2005) Vagus Nerve Stimulation for treatment resistant depression: a randomized controlled acute phase trial, *Biological Psychiatry*, **58**, 347–54.

Scottish electroconvulsive therapy accreditation network (2016) *Annual report*, NHS National Services Crown Copyright.

Shields D C, Asaad W, Eskandar E *et al.* (2008) Prospective assessment of stereotactic ablative surgery for intractable major depression. *Biological Psychiatry*, **64**, 449–54.

Steele J D, Christmas D, Eljamel M S *et al.* (2008) Anterior cingulotomy for major depression: clinical outcome and relationship to lesion characteristics. *Biological Psychiatry*, **63**, 670–7.

Subramanian L, Bracht T, Jenkins P *et al.* (2017) Clinical improvements following bilateral anterior capsulotomy in treatment resistant depression. *Psychological Medicine*, **47**, 1097–106.

Volpini M, Giacobbe G R, Levitt A *et al.* (2017) The history and future of ablative neurosurgery for major depressive disorder. *Stereotactic and Functional Neurosurgery*, **95**, 216–28.

Waite J and Easton A (2013) *The ECT Handbook (3rd edition)*, Royal College of Psychiatrists.

Ketamine for Psychiatric Disorders

Rupert McShane

Introduction

Ketamine and related compounds, such as esketamine, are of relevance to ECT practice for several reasons. First, as a drug with marked rapid antidepressant activity in people with treatment resistant depression (TRD), it may become an alternative to ECT in some cases. Second, ECT suites are a suitable setting for intravenous or other routes of directly observed therapy and ECT staff have experience with this patient group. Third, there may be synergy between ketamine and neuromodulatory therapies such as TMS.

Clinical Effect

The first formal observation that ketamine might improve mood in patients with depression was made at Yale in 2000 in a small cross-over study (Berman *et al.*, 2000). Whereas initial feelings of 'high' returned to baseline within a few hours of a 40-minute intravenous infusion of 0.5mg/kg ketamine, patients continued to show a 13 point difference in the Hamilton Rating Scale score three days later. The study was undertaken because preclinical data had suggested that NMDA receptor expression might be different in successful versus unsuccessful antidepressant use (Paul *et al.*, 1994; Boyer *et al.*, 1998). The dose of ketamine was chosen on the basis that it was the maximum that did not make patients so obtunded that they could not answer questions.

The acute benefit of ketamine in TRD was confirmed in controlled trials using saline placebo at the National Institute of Mental Health (NIMH) (and other centres) (Zarate *et al.*, 2006). The magnitude of the effect size – 0.81 at 24 hours in the largest midazolam-controlled trial to date (Murrough *et al.*, 2013) – is substantial and compares favourably with the effect size of 0.3–0.35 of conventional antidepressants at eight weeks. The duration of benefit from a single dose is also strikingly longer than expected given the short half-life (2.5–3 hours) of ketamine or its metabolites. Given that these effects were being seen in patients who had had highly resistant depression, the effects were dramatic.

Meta-analyses show that the effect of a single intravenous infusion lasts, on average, a week (Caddy *et al.*, 2015) but the duration of benefit following a single intravenous infusion is variable and strategies are needed to extend the benefit. These may take the form of dose adjustments, addition of other drugs, repeated ketamine, adjunctive psychotherapy, or all four. All these are the subject of active investigation.

Higher and longer doses may lead to slightly longer effect. A pilot study comparing 40-minute infusions with much longer infusions (96-hour accompanied by clonidine) suggests a sustained benefit at eight weeks of the longer treatment (Lenze *et al.*, 2016). There is preliminary evidence that if the patient has not responded to the first three infusions of 0.5mg/kg, a strategy of increasing the dose to 0.75mg/kg for a further three infusions may be worthwhile (Cusin *et al.*, 2017). There is also open label evidence that the second and subsequent infusions may result in greater effect on mood than the first (Diamond *et al.*, 2014).

Patients describe the benefit of ketamine in depression in variable ways. In a qualitative analysis, researchers from Yale recently reported that a sense of peace and serenity was common and was associated with an improved ability to steer thoughts away from worries. Dissociative symptoms such as altered time and sensory perception and unusual bodily sensations were also found but it was noted that the clinical effects of ketamine in depression were not fully captured by an instrument designed to measure dissociation (van Schalkwyk *et al.*, 2018).

The effect on suicidal ideation is particularly interesting. Most antidepressants take at least two weeks to build efficacy and this is a period during which the risks of suicide can be high. Almost all studies have found ketamine has an abrupt effect, within a day and lasting up to a week, on reducing suicidal ideation (Grunebaum *et al.*, 2017; Wilkinson *et al.*, 2018). Effect sizes are moderate to large (0.5–0.9) and there is some evidence that the effect is independent of the effect on depression.

Other Compounds and Routes

Intravenous ketamine has the advantage that bioavailability is assured and controlled, but the disadvantage of cost and inconvenience. Since ketamine is readily absorbed by other routes, these are of interest.

In patients who had previously been admitted as in-patients, the use of twice weekly oral ketamine was associated with a 38% reduction in admissions – from 171 to 65 – over an equivalent period (Hartberg *et al.*, 2018). This large effect clearly warrants further prospective examination. A small RCT of 40 TRD out-patients receiving 1mg/kg orally showed a 13-point MADRS reduction at 21 days compared with 3 points in the placebo group (6 versus 0 remissions) (Domany *et al.*, 2019).

Esketamine

Intranasal esketamine was awarded breakthrough status in the USA for treatment resistant depression and for acute suicidality in major depressive disorder by the Food and Drug Administration, facilitating fast track development. Like racemic ketamine, esketamine is available as a generic compound.

A phase 2 study of esketamine showed rapid onset, dose related response in patients with treatment resistant depression which persisted for more two months. Participants had been resistant to at least one antidepressant trial in the current episode. Dosing was initially twice weekly at a dose of up to 84mg and could be reduced, based on clinician judgement, to every two weeks (Daly *et al.*, 2018). The size of the effect at one week was greater than that seen at six to eight weeks with other antidepressants (Khan *et al.*, 2017). The plasma esketamine levels achieved by 56–84mg intranasal esketamine were comparable to those achieved by 0.2mg/kg intravenous esketamine, which produced a similar outcome to that for 0.5mg/kg racemic ketamine. Dissociative symptoms resolved within two hours of administration and attenuated with repeated administration. A phase 2 study of intranasal ketamine in patients with major depressive disorder at imminent risk of suicide showed more rapid reduction in suicidal ideation than placebo but this difference was not apparent 24 hours later (Canuso *et al.*, 2018).

Janssen has undertaken a series of studies of intranasal esketamine in patients with treatment resistant depression (defined as patients who had not responded to two or more currently available antidepressants at adequate dose and duration in the current episode of depression). At the time of going to press, preliminary reports are available from four of these studies (Janssen, 2018). A long term, open label, safety study was conducted in 802 patients who took intranasal esketamine 26, 56 or 84mg twice weekly for a month and then weekly or fortnightly for 11 months (Wajs et al., 2018). Acute side effects were common: dizziness (33%), dissociation (27%), nausea (25%) and drowsiness (17%). Four subjects (0.5%) had a serious adverse event thought to be related to the esketamine spray. Patients in this study had a 16-point reduction in the MADRS at four weeks, with only a 0.3-point change over the subsequent 11 months. The sample was enriched for responders, which perhaps parallels real practice. Nevertheless, the long term remission rate at 52 weeks of ~46% was substantially greater than that seen in the STAR*D study (4% a year in those who had failed at least two antidepressants) (Sackeim, 2016).

A double blind, placebo controlled, randomised controlled trial (DBPCRCT) of weekly 56 or 84mg flexible dosing, in 227 patients with depression resistant to at least two antidepressants (one of which was assessed prospectively), found a 4-point difference from placebo in the MADRS, and improved remission (53% versus 31%) at 28 days (Popova et al., 2018).

In a relapse prevention DBPCRCT, 705 patients who had responded to 16 weeks of esketamine and a new oral antidepressant were re-randomised to a further 16 weeks of either placebo or intranasal esketamine. Amongst those who had been in stable remission at the point of randomisation, 27% of those taking esketamine and 45% of those taking placebo relapsed at the four month endpoint (Daly et al., 2018).

In a DBPCRCT of flexibly titrated esketamine, with 138 patients over 65 years old, there was a 3.6-point MADRS change at 28 days with those patients under 75 years old doing better than those over 75 years old. The study did not reach significance on its primary outcome (Ochs-Ross et al., 2018).

Mechanism of Antidepressant Action

Glutamate is the principle excitatory neurotransmitter in the brain. Ketamine is a potent antagonist of the glutamate (N-methyl-D-aspartate) NMDA receptor (see Chapter 2). This action is responsible for its activity as a dissociative anaesthetic and analgesic. Whether NMDA antagonism is also directly responsible for the antidepressant effect is contentious. Although there has been a suggestion from animal work that the antidepressant action may not be dependent on NMDA antagonism and may be due to the action of the metabolite 2R, 26R hydroxynorketamine (Zanos et al., 2016), this does not fit with the observed clinical effect of esketamine and may have been related to doses used in rodent experiments (Kavalali & Monteggia, 2018).

Ketamine probably disinhibits pyramidal cell function, thereby increasing outflow of glutamate. A likely mechanism for this is the inhibition of glutamate excitation of GABAergic inhibitory interneurons (Wohleb et al., 2017). Speculatively, interneurons with terminals which are well placed to act as a brake on cortical pyramidal cell outflow – for example, on the initial axonal segment – may be involved. This increased glutamate outflow then stimulates a second class of glutamate receptor, the α-amino-3-hydroxy-5-methyl-4-isoxazolepropionic acid (AMPA) receptor, which leads to release of brain derived neurotrophic factor (BDNF). A subsequent cascade of molecular events, including activation of the molecular target of rapamycin (mTOR), stimulates rapid increases in synaptic plasticity – in particular dendritic spine outgrowth (Duman & Li, 2012). Animal models suggest a separate mechanism, whereby ketamine blocks NMDAR-dependent bursting activity of lateral habenula neurons, which has the effect of disinhibiting downstream monoaminergic reward centres (Yang et al., 2018).

There is still much to be resolved. For example, it is not known whether ketamine affects the different symptoms of depression (e.g. suicidality, anhedonia, concentration and anergia) by the same, or distinct, mechanisms of action.

At a psychological level, it does not seem that the 'ego dissolution' which sometimes accompanies dissociative levels of ketamine is a necessary part of the antidepressant effect. On the one hand, oral, non-dissociative doses appear to be antidepressant (Hartberg, 2018). On the other, dissociation does seem to be associated with more marked antidepressant effect, which lasts longer than non-dissociative doses. This may simply be because dissociation is associated with higher peak concentrations of ketamine. Alternatively, the ego-dissolution may, of itself, help provide new perspectives of oneness and humility, a sense of connectedness, and reductions in depressive ruminations which help to maintain the effect.

A small pilot suggests that CBT might prolong the benefit produced by ketamine (Wilkinson, 2017).

Ketamine and ECT

Two UK-based RCTs have explored the use of ketamine administration at the same time as ECT. In the multicentre Ketamine-ECT trial (Anderson et al., 2017), a slow bolus of 0.5mg/kg intravenous of ketamine (or placebo) was given directly before induction at each ECT treatment. In the KANECT trial (Fernie et al., 2017), ketamine 2mg/kg was compared with propofol as the anaesthetic for ECT. Ketamine did not improve the outcome in either trial, either in terms of mood or cognitive function. A similar lack of benefit of ketamine when administered at the same time as ECT has been confirmed in other studies, summarised in McGirr et al. (2017).

Given the large effect size of both ECT and ketamine, the fact that ketamine does not enhance the effect of ECT suggests that the two may act through a final common pathway. Arguably, then, this would indicate a possible role for ketamine in relapse prevention post ECT. However, the duration of action is important here. Relapse is very high – perhaps even 80–100% – a few months after a course of ketamine, but 'only' about 38% at six months with ECT (Jelovac et al., 2013). It is therefore important that people seeking ketamine treatment are appraised of the stronger evidence base and longer effect of ECT. Patients are often more concerned about the known effect on memory of ECT than the unknown effects of repeated ketamine.

In contrast to these RCT findings in which there is neither mood nor cognitive benefit from concomitant ECT and ketamine, a case series raises the possibility of more prolonged benefit when an intravenous infusion of ketamine and rTMS treatment are given at the same time (Best & Griffin, 2015).

Adverse Effects

The possibility that ketamine could give rise to unacceptable side-effects – particularly dependence – and the associated mechanisms, is debated in informative detail by Sanacora and Schazberg (2015).

In a comprehensive review Loo and colleagues (Short, 2018), found the most common acute side effects to range from headache (35%), through dizziness, dissociation, increased blood pressure, blurred vision and nausea, to sedation (17%) and anxiety (15%). Several authors have commented on the unpredictable occurrence of intense anxiety in patients who have previously had multiple repeated infusions without incident. This remains unexplained. The frequency of side-effects with repeated use is under-reported. The most important currently identified potential effects are bladder effects, dependence, and cognitive impairment.

Abuse Potential

Like benzodiazepines, opiates, amphetamines, cannabis, cocaine and nitrous oxide, ketamine is a medically useful agent that has abuse potential. The Advisory Council on the Misuse of Drugs (ACMD, 2013) estimate that 57,000 people use it illegally each month. In 2016, of 288,000 people seeking treatment for drug misuse in England and Wales, 415 (0.1%) were for ketamine only, compared with 7% (21,000) for benzodiazepine (NDTMS, 2018). Ketamine is usually used with other illegal drugs. Deaths attributable to ketamine alone are rare: it was mentioned on death certificates of 12 people in 2012, compared with 284 benzodiazepine-related deaths. Ketamine use, which is closely linked to cost and availability, peaked in 2012 but declined after being rescheduled from class C to class B in 2014 and as authorities cracked down on illegal factories in South China and diversion from legitimate medical factories in Maharastra in western India. The most common harms arising with illegal ketamine use are related to the acute impairments of psychomotor functioning of intoxication: accidents, falls and assaults (ACMD, 2013).

Those who are addicted to ketamine typically use grams daily. A daily use of approximately 500mg intranasally is required for physical dependence (ACMD, 2013). Withdrawal symptoms are mainly psychological (craving, depression, suicidal ideas, psychosis, cognitive impairment, sleep disturbance), but irregular heart beat, rapid breathing and loss of coordination also occur. The extent and predictors of tolerance and tachyphylaxis with repeated medical use is poorly described. Case reports describe instances of medical ketamine use for depression leading to psychological dependence and demands for increased doses. In one such report, the patient committed suicide some time after the ketamine was withdrawn (Schak et al., 2016). This is complicated by the wide variation in bioavailability of ketamine when administered by routes other than intravenous. As with other drugs with a wide dose range, this raises the question of whether a previously remitted patient who relapses, perhaps in the face of persisting psychosocial adversity, is becoming tolerant, or now simply has more severe disease which requires more aggressive treatment.

Cognitive Impairment

Preclinical literature suggests that ketamine can produce cognitive dysfunction and excitotoxic neurodegeneration (Featherstone et al., 2012; Schobel et al., 2013; Sun et al., 2014). In Chinese ketamine addicts, there is evidence of a diffuse structural effect with scattered white matter lesions and atrophy (Wang et al., 2013) and cognitive impairment is widespread, but related to dose and duration. There is no good evidence either way about the long term effect of ketamine when used repeatedly in a medical setting. When used to treat depression, ketamine does not appear to have the same acute cognitive effects as ECT. However, it does not reduce the cognitive impairment produced by ECT (Anderson *et al.*, 2017).

Cardiovascular Effects

Ketamine infusions cause a transient increase in systolic (mean 20mmHg) and diastolic (mean 13mmHg) blood pressure. BP or heart rate exceeded 180/100mmHg or 110 beats per minute in 30% (Wan *et al.*, 2015). Although the rise in BP with ketamine has not been associated with adverse events, and patients with depression are prone to white coat hypertension, the balance of risk and benefit should be considered for those with BP above 150/95mmHg. Blood pressure may also drop and vasovagal episodes have been reported (Diamond *et al.*, 2014; Riva-Posse *et al.*, 2018). BP should be routinely assessed before starting ketamine and monitored during initial treatments.

Bladder

When the concentration of ketamine or metabolites in the bladder reaches a certain level, it is toxic to the urothelium (Baker *et al.*, 2016). If this persists so that the urothelial regenerative capacity is exceeded, permanent damage occurs. The initial symptoms of interstitial cystitis are of low abdominal pain, frequency and dysuria. Bladder symptoms are strongly related to dose and duration of ketamine use. It is rare for medically controlled use to cause bladder symptoms. A potential confounding factor is that depression and bladder symptoms tend to co-occur, irrespective of drug treatment. Routine assessment of urinary symptoms and pelvic pain using, for example, the O'Leary-Sant interstitial cystitis symptom index (Lubeck *et al.*, 2001) is therefore recommended before starting ketamine to facilitate interpretation of any new urological symptoms.

Formulations and Licensing

Ketamine is available in licensed form for IV and IM administration for analgesia and anaesthesia. In these forms, it can be used as an 'off-label' licensed medicine. It is however, also available in a variety of other, unlicensed, formulations. The term 'Specials' is used in the UK ('Compounded' in the US) to denote these unlicensed reformulations. Specials are produced by pharmacies with the appropriate licence and can be distributed by pharmaceutical wholesalers, but no claims can be made publicly about their effect. Responsibility for adverse events lies with the prescribing doctor rather than the 'Marketing Authorisation Holder' – i.e. the drug company which holds the licence for the original formulation.

Why is this important? Oral tablets and liquid, intranasal powder and sprays, sublingual tabs, lozenges and subcutaneous formulations – all of which are entirely legal but unlicensed – have all been used and have at least case reports of efficacy in treating depression (Wilkinson *et al.*, 2017). They are all simpler and cheaper to administer than intravenous ketamine. This is important if repeated ketamine is shown to be safe and efficacious, with an effect that can be sustained.

However, because ketamine is a 'schedule 2' controlled drug, this also requires specific precautions. The 'scheduling' results in specific requirements in pharmacies for tracking what happens to stocks of the drug: detailed logs need to be kept of ketamine which is dispensed, administered and destroyed.

Ketamine in Other Disorders

Obsessive Compulsive Disorder

In addition to its rapid anti-depressant effects, ketamine has been shown to have rapid anti-obsessional effects for the treatment of Obsessive Compulsive Disorder (OCD) (Rodriguez *et al.*, 2013): 8/15 were still treatment responders a week after a single infusion compared to none taking placebo.

Post-Traumatic Stress Disorder

A pilot study in 41 patients with chronic Post-Traumatic Stress Disorder (PTSD) (Feder *et al.*, 2014) showed significant reduction in symptoms 24 hours after a single iv infusion of ketamine (0.5mg/kg).

Eating Disorders

In a case series, Mills *et al.* (1998) treated 15 patients with refractory anorexia nervosa who were taking amitriptyline with between two and nine infusions of 20mg per hour ketamine for 10 hours and 20mg twice daily. Measures of compulsion and depression were reduced in nine patients. More recently, short term improvements in 6 of 9 patients treated with a combination of repeated iv and oral ketamine over 3–19 months were reported.

Anxiety Disorders

Glue *et al.* (2018) treated 20 patients with generalised and social anxiety disorders with weekly or fortnightly individualised doses (e.g. 1mg/kg) of subcutaneous ketamine. After three months, 18 were still in remission, but most reported partial or complete recurrence within two weeks of stopping the maintenance treatment. Taylor *et al.* (2018) report benefit from ketamine in a study of 18 adults with DSM-5 Social Anxiety disorder.

This signal of efficacy in other psychiatric disorders has important implications. The history of all antidepressant, anxiolytic (and indeed antipsychotic) drugs is that they have been very widely used for diagnoses outside the core indication. It seems likely that the ketamine can be of benefit across the same wide range of disorders as monoaminergic drugs. This perhaps reflects 'comorbidity', 'overlapping pathophysiology', 'spurious diagnostic specificity' or 'a lack of biomarkers' depending on one's position. It may also mean that, before long, we may need to be asking the question: 'from whom should ketamine be withheld'?

Ketamine Clinics and Guidance

Ketamine clinics have proliferated rapidly since 2016 in the United States but not yet in other countries. This reflects entrepreneurial spirit and the culture and structure of the health services, rather than any fundamental transnational difference in regulations. These US clinics vary widely in their operating model; the website ketaminecost.com gives a sense of the range of private clinics. At one end of the spectrum, some clinics are run by anaesthetists who do not require psychiatric referral or evaluation: patients simply self-refer. At the other, the dissociation induced by ketamine is used to facilitate psychotherapy conducted during the infusion.

However, there is much that is not known. Because it has not been comprehensively evaluated as an antidepressant, ketamine may not be a simple drug to use repeatedly. The wide therapeutic range, possible bell-shaped response curve, and variability in bioavailability of ketamine when administered by routes other than intravenous, all mean that research and guidance are needed on how to deal with lack of, or loss of, response. What happens to the suicidal patient between the infusion and the benefit – which sometimes only occurs after several infusions? How is follow-up organised? What are the risks of repeated ketamine? And of withdrawing ketamine?

These known unknowns are important practical problems which require careful exploration. How should this exploration be conducted? There is a consensus that 'the genie is out of the bottle' and that, because ketamine is a comparatively safe drug, excessive restrictions on practice may be counterproductive, and drive patients to seek illegal ketamine. Conversely, clinical experience, if well collated, could enable rapid optimisation of protocols.

Registries and Monitoring

There is a consensus that large registries are needed to collate information about the long term safety of ketamine and related compounds (Sanacora et al., 2017; Singh et al., 2017; Loo, 2018). The Royal College of Psychiatrists, UK (2017) has issued a statement, which is closely aligned with that of the Royal Australian and New Zealand College of Psychiatrists (2017), and which includes the following recommendations:

> Ketamine should be used under research trial conditions that include oversight by an institutional research or ethics committee and careful monitoring and reporting of outcomes. For persons with treatment resistant depression who are not participating in a research trial but are able and willing to consent to treatment with ketamine, the treating psychiatrist should consider such treatment as a novel or innovative treatment, which should include discussion with peers (preferably including a second opinion) and institutional review by the [relevant NHS Trust Drugs and Therapeutic Committee or its equivalent].
>
> (The Royal College of Psychiatrists, UK, 2017)

The UK statement also specifies that 'Treatment for depression occurring outside formal research studies should be collated across centres using a regular mood monitoring framework'.

The American Psychiatric Association Position Statement (Sanacora et al., 2017) provides detailed supplementary recommendations. These include:

- Patient selection
- Clinician training
- Treatment setting (including monitoring)
- Medication delivery (including dosage)
- Follow up.

The Future

This is a rapidly moving field. If the preliminary promise is realised, ketamine-like drugs could both transform and disrupt psychiatric practice. Having been something of a backwater in psychiatric practice, ECT clinics may find themselves at the sharp end of a disruptive new and exciting improvement in psychopharmacology. There will be much work to be done in establishing new service models and to establish long term safety. We will also need basic scientists to develop models in which to test different candidate drugs for prolonging the beneficial effect and reducing the abuse potential of ketamine.

Summary

Ketamine has been used for many years in anaesthesia and in the treatment of chronic pain, it may cause hallucinations and has also been a drug of abuse. There are robust data from clinical studies that ketamine has a rapid but short lived effect on depressive symptoms.

The evidence that the long term beneficial effects of ketamine outweigh its potential to cause harm is limited. Its use should be restricted along the lines of the Royal College of Psychiatrists' consensus statement.

Although some limited data on the use of ketamine in treating other psychiatric conditions have been published, these are insufficient to justify the use of ketamine in those conditions outside formal monitoring structures and/or research.

References

ACMD (Advisory Council on Misuse of Drugs) (2013) *Ketamine: a review of use and harms.* https://www.gov.uk/government/publications/ketamine-report

Anderson I. M., Blamire A., Branton T. *et al.* (2017) Ketamine augmentation of electroconvulsive therapy to improve neuropsychological and clinical outcomes in depression (Ketamine-ECT): a multicentre, double-blind, randomised, parallel group, superiority trial. *Lancet Psychiatry*, 4, 365–77.

Baker S. C., Shabir S., Georgopoulos N. T. *et al.* (2016) Ketamine-induced apoptosis in normal human urothelial cells: a direct, N-Methyl-d-Aspartate receptor-independent pathway characterized by mitochondrial stress. *American Journal of Pathology*, 186, 1267–77.

Berman R. M., Cappiello A., Anand A. *et al.* (2000) Antidepressant effects of Ketamine. *Biological Psychiatry*, 47, 351–4.

Best S. R. & Griffin B. (2015) Combination therapy utilizing ketamine and TMS for treatment-resistant depression: a case-report. *International Journal of Neuroscience*, 125, 232–4.

Boyer P. A., Skolnick P. & Fossom L. H. (1998) Chronic administration of imipramine and citalopram alters the expression of NMDA receptor subunit mRNAs in mouse brain. A quantitative *in situ* hybridization study. *J Mol Neurosci*, 10, 219–33.

Caddy C., Amit B. H., McCloud T. L., Rendell J. M., Furukawa T. A., McShane R. *et al.* (2015) Ketamine and other glutamate receptor modulators for depression in adults. Cochrane Database Syst. Rev.; CD011612.

Canuso C. M., Singh J. B., Fedgchin M. *et al.* (2018) Efficacy and safety of intranasal esketamine for the rapid reduction of symptoms of depression and suicidality in patients at imminent risk for suicide: results of a double-blind, randomized, placebo-controlled study. *AJP in Advance* (doi: 10.1176/appi.ajp.2018.17060720).

Cusin C., Ionescu D. F., Pavone K. J. *et al.* (2017) Ketamine augmentation for outpatients with treatment resistant depression: Preliminary evidence for two-step intravenous dose escalation. *Australia and New Zealand Journal of Psychiatry*, 51, 51–64.

Daly E. J., Singh J. B., Fedgchin M. *et al.* (2018) Efficacy and safety of intranasal esketamine adjunctive to oral antidepressant therapy in treatment-resistant depression: a randomized clinical trial. *JAMA Psychiatry*, 75, 139–48. doi: 10.1001/jamapsychiatry.

Daly E., Singh J., Trivedi M. *et al.* (2018) A randomized withdrawal, double-blind, multicenter study of esketamine nasal spray plus an oral antidepressant for relapse prevention in treatment-resistant depression. Abstract WP 68, American Society of Clinical Psychopharmacology, Miami Beach, FL.

Diamond P. R., Farmery A. D., Atkinson S. *et al.* (2014) Ketamine infusions for treatment resistant depression: a series of 28 patients treated weekly or twice weekly in an ECT clinic. *J Psychopharmacol*, 28, 536–44.

Domany Y., Bleich-Cohen M., Tarrasch R. *et al.* (2019) Repeated oral ketamine for outpatient treatment of resistant depression: randomised, double-blind, placebo-controlled, proof-of-concept study. *Br J Psychiat*, 214, 20–6.

Duman R. S. & Li N. (2012) A neurotrophic hypothesis of depression: role of synaptogenesis in the actions of NMDA receptor antagonists. *Philosophical Transactions of the Royal Society of London B*, 367, 2475–84.

Featherstone R. E., Liang Y., Saunders J. A. *et al.* (2012) Subchronic ketamine treatment leads to permanent changes in EEG, cognition and the astrocytic glutamate transporter EAAT2 in mice. *Neurobiology of Disease*, 47, 338–46.

Feder A., Parides M. K., Murrough J. W., Perez A. M., Morgan J. E., Saxena S. *et al.* (2014) Efficacy of intravenous ketamine for treatment of chronic posttraumatic stress disorder: a randomized clinical trial. *JAMA Psychiatry*, 71, 681–8.

Fernie G., Currie J., Perrin J. S. *et al.* (2017) Ketamine as the anaesthetic for ECT: the KANECT randomised controlled trial. *British Journal of Psychiatry*, 210, 422–8.

Glue P., Neehoff S. M., Medlicott N. J., Gray A., Kibby G. & McNaughton N. (2018) Safety and efficacy of maintenance ketamine treatment in patients with treatment-refractory generalised anxiety and social anxiety disorders. *J Psychopharmacol*, Mar 1:269881118762073. doi: 10.1177/0269881118762073.

Grunebaum M. F., Galfalvy H. C., Choo T. H. *et al.* (2017) Ketamine for rapid reduction of suicidal thoughts in major depression: a midazolam-controlled randomized clinical trial. *American Journal of Psychiatry*, appiajp201717060647. doi: 10.1176/appi.ajp.2017.17060647. [Epub ahead of print].

Hartberg J., Garrett-Walcott S. & De Gioannis A. (2018) Impact of oral ketamine augmentation on hospital admissions in treatment-resistant depression and PTSD: a retrospective study. *Psychopharmacology (Berl)*, 235, 393–8.

Janssen (2018) www.janssen.com/long-term-phase-3-study-shows-esketamine-nasal-spray-plus-oral-antidepressant-delayed-time-relapse accessed 5 June 2018.

Jelovac A., Kolshus E. & McLoughlin D. M. (2013) Relapse following successful ECT for Major Depression: a meta-analysis. *Neuropsychopharmacology*, 38, 2467–74.

Kavalali E. T. & Monteggia L. M. (2018) The ketamine metabolite 2R,6R-hydroxynorketamine blocks NMDA receptors and impacts downstream signalling linked to antidepressant effects. *Neuropsychopharmacology*, 43, 221–2. doi:10.1038/npp.2017.210 ia.

Khan A., Fahl Mar K., Faucett J, Khan Schilling S., Brown W. A. (2017) Has the rising placebo response impacted antidepressant clinical trial outcome? data from the US Food and Drug Administration 1987–2013. *World Psychiatry*, 16, 181–92.

Lenze E. J., Farber N. B., Kharasch E. *et al.* (2016) Ninety-six hour ketamine infusion with co-administered clonidine for treatment-resistant depression: A pilot randomised controlled trial. *World Journal of Biological Psychiatry*, 17, 230–8.

Loo C. K., Katalinic N., Garfield J. B. B., Sainsbury K., Hadzi-Pavlovic D., MacPherson R. (2012) Neuropsychological and mood effects of ketamine in electroconvulsive therapy: A randomised controlled trial. *Journal of Affective Disorders*, 142, 233–40.

Loo C. (2018) Can we confidently use ketamine as a clinical treatment for depression? *Lancet Psychiatry*, 5, 11–12. doi: 10.1016/S2215-0366(17)30480-7.

Lubeck D. P., Whitmore K., Sant G. R., Alvarez-Horine S. & Lai C. (2001) Psychometric validation of the O'Leary-Sant interstitial cystitis symptom index in a clinical trial of pentosan polysulfate sodium. *Urology*, 57(6 Suppl 1), 62–6.

McGirr A., Berlim M. T., Bond D. J. *et al.* (2017) Adjunctive ketamine in electroconvulsive therapy: updated systematic review and meta-analysis. *British Journal of Psychiatry*, **210**, 403–7.

Mills I. H., Park G. R., Manara A. R. & Merriman R. J. (1998) Treatment of compulsive behaviour in eating disorders with intermittent ketamine infusions. *QJM*, **91**, 493–503.

Murrough J. W., Iosifescu D. V., Chang L. C. *et al.* (2013) Antidepressant efficacy of ketamine in treatment-resistant major depression: a two-site randomized controlled trial. *American Journal of Psychiatry*, **170**, 1134–42.

NDTMS (National Drug Treatment Monitoring System) (2018) *Adult substance misuse statistics –1 April 2015 to 31 March 2016* https://assets.publishing.service.gov.uk/government/uploads/system/uploads/attachment_data/file/733323/NDTMS_Reference_Data_document_CDSO_14.02.pdf

Ochs-Ross R., Daly E., Zhang Y. *et al.* (2018) Effiacy and safety of esketamine nasal spray plus an oral antidepressant in elderly patients with treatment-resistant depression. Abstract W27 American Society of Clinical Pharmacology, Florida.

Okamoto N., Tetsuji N. & Sakamoto K. (2010) Rapid antidepressant effect of ketamine anesthesia during ECT of treatment resistant depression: Comparing ketamine and propofol anesthesia. *Journal of ECT*, **26**, 223–7.

Paul I. A., Nowak G., Layer R. T., Popik P. & Skolnick P. (1994) Adaptation of the N-methyl-D-aspartate receptor complex. *J Pharmacol Exp Ther*, **269**, 95–102.

Popova V., Daly E., Trivedi M. *et al.* (2018) Randomized, double-blind, study of flexibly-dosed esketamine nasal spray plus oral antidepressant vs. active control in treatment-resistant depression. Abstract W30. American Society of Clinical Pharmacology, Florida.

Riva-Posse P., Reiff C. R., Edwards J. A. *et al.* (2018) Blood pressure safety of subanesthetic ketamine for depression: a report on 684 infusions. *Journal of Affective Disorders* DOI: https://doi.org/10.1016/j.jad.2018.02.025

Rodriguez C. I., Kegeles L. S., Levinson A., Feng T., Marcus S. M., Vermes D. *et al.* (2013) Randomized controlled crossover trial of ketamine in obsessive-compulsive disorder: proof-of-concept. *Neuropsychopharmacology*, **38**, 2475–83.

Royal Australian and New Zealand College of Psychiatrists (2017) *Clinical memorandum: Use of ketamine for treating depression.* https://www.ranzcp.org/Files/Resources/College_Statements/Clinical_Memoranda/CLM-PPP-Ketamine-to-treat-depression-(November-201.aspx

Royal College of Psychiatrists (2017) *Statement on ketamine to treat depression.* www.rcpsych.ac.uk/pdf/Ketamine%20to%20treat%20Depression%20-%20ECT%20ctee%20statement%20Feb17.pdf

Sackeim H. A. (2016) Acute continuation and maintenance treatment of major depressive episodes with transcranial magnetic stimulation. *Brain Stimulation*, **9**, 313–19.

Sanacora G. & Schatzberg A. F. (2015) Ketamine: promising path or false prophecy in the development of novel therapeutics for mood disorders? *Neuropsychopharmacology*, **40**, 259–67.

Sanacora G., Frye M. A., McDonald W. *et al.* (2017) A consensus statement on the use of ketamine in the treatment of mood disorders. *JAMA Psychiatry*, **74**, 399–405. doi: 10.1001/jamapsychiatry

Schak K. M., Vande Voort J. L., Johnson E. K. *et al.* (2016) Potential risks of poorly monitored ketamine use in depression treatment *Am J Psychiatry*, **173**, 215–18; doi: 10.1176/appi.ajp.2015.15081082.

Schobel S. A., Chaudhury N. H., Khan U. A. *et al.* (2013) Imaging patients with psychosis and a mouse model establishes a spreading pattern of hippocampal dysfunction and implicates glutamate as a driver. *Neuron*, **78**, 81–93.

Short B., Fong J., Galvez V., Shelker W. & Loo C. K. (2018) Side-effects associated with ketamine use in depression: a systematic review. *Lancet Psychiatry*, **5**, 65–78. doi: 10.1016/S2215-0366(17)30272-9.

Singh I., Morgan C., Curran V., Nutt D., Schlag A. & McShane R. (2017) Ketamine treatment for depression: opportunities for clinical innovation and ethical foresight. *Lancet Psychiatry*, **4**, 419–26. doi: 10.1016/S2215-0366(17)30102-5.

Sun L., Li Q., Li Q. *et al.* (2014) Chronic ketamine exposure induces permanent impairment of brain functions in adolescent cynomolgus monkeys. *Addiction Biology*, **19**,185–94. doi: 10.1111/adb.12004. Epub 2012 Nov 12.

Taylor J. H., Landeros-Weisenberger A., Coughlin C. *et al.* (2018) Ketamine for social anxiety disorder: a randomized, placebo-controlled crossover trial. *Neuropsychopharmacology*, **43**, 325–33.

van Schalkwyk G. I., Wilkinson S. T., Davidson L. *et al.* (2018) Acute psychoactive effects of intravenous ketamine during treatment of mood disorders: Analysis of the Clinician Administered Dissociative State Scale. *Journal of Affective Disorders*, **227**, 11–16.

Wajs E., Aluisio L., Morrison R. *et al.* (2018) Long term safety of intranasal esketamine plus oral antidepressant in patients with treatment-resistant depression: phase 3, open-label, safety and efficacy study (Sustain-2). Abstract T67 American Society of Clinical Psychopharmacology, Miami Beach FL.

Wan L. B., Levitch C. F., Perez A. M. *et al.* (2015) Ketamine safety and tolerability in clinical trials for treatment-resistant depression. *J Clin Psychiatry*, **76**, 247–52.

Wang C., Zheng D., Xu J., Lam W. & Yew D. T. (2013) Brain damages in ketamine addicts as revealed by magnetic resonance imaging. *Frontiers in Neuroanatomy*, **7**, 23. doi: 10.3389/fnana.2013.00023. eCollection 2013.

Wilkinson S. T., Toprak M., Turner M. S., Levine S. P., Katz R. B. & Sanacora G. (2017) A survey of the clinical, off-label use of ketamine as a treatment for psychiatric disorders. *American Journal of Psychiatry*, **174**, 695–6. doi: 10.1176/appi.ajp.2017.17020239.

Wilkinson S. T., Wright D., Fasula M. K. *et al.* (2017) Cognitive behavior therapy may sustain antidepressant effects of intravenous ketamine in treatment-resistant depression. *Psychotherapy & Psychosomatics*, **86**, 162–7. doi: 10.1159/000457960.

Wilkinson S. T., Ballard E. D., Bloch M. H. *et al.* (2018) The effect of a single dose of intravenous ketamine on suicidal ideation: a systematic review and individual participant data meta-analysis. *American Journal of Psychiatry*, **175**, 150–8. doi: 10.1176/appi.ajp.2017.17040472. Epub 2017 Oct 3.

Wohleb E. S., Gerhard D., Thomas A. & Duman R. S. (2017) Molecular and cellular mechanisms of rapid-acting antidepressants ketamine and Scopolamine. *Current Neuropharmacology*, **15**, 11–20.

Yang Y., Cui Y., Sang K. *et al.* (2018) Ketamine blocks bursting in the lateral habenula to rapidly relieve depression. *Nature*, **554**, 317–22.

Zanos P., Moaddel R., Morris P. J. *et al.* (2016) NMDAR inhibition-independent antidepressant actions of ketamine metabolites. *Nature*, **533**, 481–6.

Zarate A. A., Singh J. B., Carlson P. J. *et al.* (2006) A randomised trial of an NMDA antagonist in treatment-resistant major depression. *Archives of General Psychiatry*, **63**, 856–64.

The ECT Accreditation Service (ECTAS)

Jill Emerson

ECTAS was launched in May 2003 coinciding with the publication of the NICE (National Institute for Clinical Excellence) guidance on the use of ECT (NICE, 2003). Its aim was to improve the standard of practice in ECT units in the United Kingdom and Republic of Ireland using a model of continuous quality improvement.

The NICE technology appraisal highlighted concerns about the current state of ECT practice. Despite efforts to improve standards (including the publication of the first *ECT Handbook* in 1995) clinics were still underperforming in terms of policy, practice and staff training (Mental Health Act Commission, 2001). NICE recommended that:

> ECT should be administered only in a suitably equipped unit by professionals who have been trained in its delivery and in the anaesthetic techniques required for the administration of ECT. These professionals should maintain an appropriate level of skill, both through the regular clinical practice of ECT and through undertaking appropriate continuing professional development.
> Urgent consideration should be given to the establishment of units dedicated to ECT, and of audit networks, which have been shown to be successful in Scotland.

SEAN (Scottish ECT Accreditation Network) had been established in 1997 (see Chapter 19). A similar body for the remainder of the UK, which could monitor and accredit clinics as satisfying guidelines for best practice and safety had been previously suggested (Eranti and McLoughlin, 2003).

ECTAS is a collaboration between the Royal College of Psychiatrists, the Royal College of Anaesthetists and the Royal College of Nursing. It is managed by the Royal College of Psychiatrists Centre for Quality Improvement (CCQI).

In October 2003, the first ECTAS standards were published. They were based on the *ECT Handbook* (1st edition), the NICE technology appraisal (2003), the work of SEAN and in consultation with the College Special Committee and service users and groups (ECTAS, 2005).

The Standards, currently in their 13th edition, cover all aspects of the ECT process from clinic facilities, staffing, through assessment and consent, to administration and follow up. They are reviewed every 18 months by a multidisciplinary reference group. New standards have been introduced over time, as a result of developments in clinical practice, others have been made more stringent in order to continuously drive up quality.

There are three categories of standard:

TYPE 1 Essential standards. Failure to meet these would mean risk to patient safety, rights or dignity and/or would breach the law.

TYPE 2 Expected standards that all clinics should meet.

TYPE 3 Desirable standards that a high functioning clinic should meet.

To achieve accreditation a clinic must meet all type 1 standards, 80% of type 2 and 60% of type 3. Provided there are no safety concerns, clinics can have accreditation deferred to allow them to make the necessary changes to achieve any unmet standards.

Prior to January 2016, clinics could be accredited as excellent if they fulfilled all type 1 standards, 95% of type 2 and the majority of type 3. Subsequently the term 'excellence' has been dropped in line with the other programmes run by the CCQI (ECTAS, 2015). It has, however, recently been agreed that ECTAS can acknowledge excellence in particular standard domains.

The accreditation process has a three year cycle. After initial registration the clinic performs a self-review. This includes a review of policies, procedures and protocols and of the clinic environment, together with an audit of 10–20 patient case notes, collecting information pertaining to the standards. There are questionnaires for the lead nurse and for referring psychiatrists. In a further move to drive up quality, ECTAS has made the patient experience more central to the accreditation process. The patient questionnaire is part of the self-review and now carries greater weight; rather than just being narrative data, it contributes towards meeting or not meeting a standard. There is also a friends, carers and family questionnaire.

After completion of the self-review there will be a peer review visit. The review team comprises an anaesthetist, a psychiatrist and a nurse who work in other ECT units. A service user is now also present on approximately half of the visits. The data from the self and peer reviews are then collated by the ECTAS team. A summary of the data is reviewed by the Accreditation Committee, who recommend accreditation status. There is an appeals procedure.

Accreditation is generally for three years, subject to completion of an interim self-review. After the three years the cycle begins again (ECTAS, 2016).

Currently ECTAS has a total of 96 member clinics. There are 78 in England (94% of the total number of clinics), 3 in Northern Ireland (33% of total), 9 in the Republic of Ireland (53% of total) and 6 in Wales (86% of total) (ECTAS website: https://www.rcpsych.ac.uk/improving-care/ccqi/quality-networks-accreditation/ectas/ectas-members).

In addition to its role of accreditation and monitoring of clinics, ECTAS also supports quality networks. It publishes a twice yearly newsletter with contributions from member clinics and service users. It also hosts a national forum, providing staff from member clinics and service users a chance to meet face to face and to share examples of best practice and recent research. The ECTAS website has a resource library with generic protocols, check lists and useful links. For staff of member clinics and service user representatives there is an active web discussion forum. ECTAS holds a library of these discussion threads going back for ten years.

The service provides training and support for its peer reviewers with a one day interactive course. An online course for anaesthetists and operating department practitioners (ODPs) has recently been launched. Working in partnership with the National Association of Lead Nurses in ECT (NALNECT) ECTAS has developed an ECT nurses training course. A more advanced course for lead nurses is planned for 2018.

In 2012, ECTAS began collecting a minimum data set. This includes information on every patient beginning a new course of ECT. This provides valuable nationwide demographics on numbers, sex, age and Mental Health Act status of patients. There are also data on the use of maintenance ECT (Buley et al., 2017). Outcome (measured using the Clinical Global Impression score) shows that 72% of patients are much or very much improved at the end of treatment.

ECTAS, its accreditation process and standards have had a profound positive impact on the practice of ECT (Murphy *et al.*, 2013). Although some smaller units have closed and their services have been centralised, remaining clinics report more investment, concentration of resources and expertise, with subsequent improvement in standards (Bickerton *et al.*, 2009; Buley *et al.*, 2017). The majority of clinics perform better as they move through the accreditation cycle (ECTAS, 2016). Clients and their carers report that they feel reassured by the dedicated and knowledgeable staff whom they encounter. They also state that they have confidence in the safety of the equipment and procedures (Kershaw *et al.*, 2007; Rayner *et al.*, 2009; ECTAS, 2015).

NHS trusts can also be reassured when their ECT units have been accredited, as ECTAS has been approved as an official source of robust and reliable information to support the Care Quality Commission (CQC) in its inspections.

The ECTAS process has enhanced the role of the ECT lead nurse, making it central to delivery of the service. The involvement of ECTAS and its specialist training course for lead nurses has put the ECT clinic nurse on a par with other specialist nurse roles. The Nurse Administered ECT project (see Chapters 21 and 22) offers the opportunity for further developments.

Prior to the inception of ECTAS, rates of ECT were declining. In 2005, it was suggested that if the rate of decline did not slow, then by 2012 use of ECT could cease (Freeman, in ECTAS, 2005). Since the inception of ECTAS the decline in ECT usage has continued, but at a much slower rate (Buley *et al.*, 2017). ECT remains a viable, NICE-approved treatment option.

ECT is still a controversial and feared treatment but through the work of bodies such as ECTAS there is the assurance that ECT is being delivered to appropriate people, by well-trained, dedicated staff, using the optimal techniques, in the safest possible environment.

References

Bickerton, D., Worrall, A. & Chaplin, R. (2009). Survey to establish trends in the administration of ECT in England. *Psychiatric Bulletin*, 33, 61–3.

Buley, N., Copland, E., Hodge, S. *et al.* (2017). A further decrease in the rates of administration of ECT in England. *Journal of ECT*, 33, 198–202.

ECT Accreditation Service (2005). *First National Report October 2003 – October 2005*. ECTAS.

ECT Accreditation Service (2015). Interim report: patient perspectives March 2013 – April 2014.

ECT Accreditation Service (2016). *Sixth National Report October 2013 – October 2015*. ECTAS.

Eranti, S. V. & McLoughlin, D. M. (2002). Electroconvulsive therapy: state of the art. *British Journal of Psychiatry*, 182, 8–9.

Freeman, C. P. L. (2005). Foreword to ECT Accreditation Service *First National Report October 2003 – October 2005*. ECTAS.

Kershaw, K., Rayner, L. & Chaplin, R. (2007). Patients' views on the quality of care when receiving ECT. *The Psychiatrist*, 31, 414–17.

Mental Health Act Commission (2001). *Ninth Biennial Report 1999–2001*. London: Stationery Office.

Murphy, G., Doncaster, E., Chaplin, R. *et al.* (2013). Three decades of quality of improvement on electroconvulsive therapy: exploring the role of accreditation. *Journal of ECT*, 29, 312–17.

National Institute for Health and Clinical Excellence (2003). *Guidance on the Use of Electroconvulsive Therapy* (Technology Appraisal TA59). NICE.

Rayner, L., Kershaw, K., Hanna, D. *et al.* (2009). The patient perspective of the consent process and side effects of electroconvulsive therapy. *Journal of Mental Health*, 18, 379–88.

The Scottish ECT Accreditation Network (SEAN)

Linda Cullen and Alistair Hay

SEAN continues to have a profound influence on the practice of ECT in Scotland since its inception in 1997. From 2005, in addition to its audit role, it has been involved in the systematic formal accreditation of all 18 clinics in Scotland where ECT is administered.

The main aims of SEAN remain:

- To monitor ECT practice throughout Scotland and ensure equitable high standards of care and treatment across all 18 clinics and produce an annual report on this work (SEAN, 2017).
- To provide a clinical network of multidisciplinary peer support for professionals of all grades and disciplines involved in the clinical practice of ECT.
- To maintain informal close communication and sharing of good practice, amongst the ECT clinics in Scotland.

SEAN currently sits within the Scottish Healthcare Audit Team in the Information Services Division (ISD), National Services Scotland (NSS). There is no financial charge to ECT clinics for being affiliated to SEAN. There is a National Clinical Co-ordinator to oversee the smooth running of the project. SEAN itself is overseen by a 20-member steering group. Membership of this group comprises representation from:

- All Health Boards in Scotland where ECT is given
- Chairman of patient and carers reference group
- Scottish Government
- Mental Welfare Commission Scotland
- Analysts from ISD
- Quality Assurance Manager from ISD.

The group is chaired by Dr Alistair Hay (Consultant Psychiatrist) with Dr Nasim Rasul as vice chair. All relevant professions involved in the clinical administration of ECT are represented specifically: consultant psychiatrists, psychiatric trainees, consultant anaesthetists, ECT nurses and anaesthetic/recovery nurses.

Of crucial importance is service user input provided through the Service User and Carer's Reference Group that meet independently of the steering group as well as having representation on the steering group.

The standards of care and treatment in each clinic are measured against evidence based, measurable and achievable quality standards. In doing so, SEAN adheres to the principles outlined in the Healthcare Quality Strategy in its ambitions for healthcare delivery in NHS Scotland as outlined in the following sections.

Patient-Centred

There continues to be proactive input from service users and carers through an independent reference group. Issues highlighted from this group are fed into the SEAN steering group and actioned together as appropriate. SEAN actively encourages service users and carers to work alongside clinical staff in identifying areas for improvement and finding solutions. The views of service users and carers are vitally important and the Service User and Carer Reference Group organise and present at the afternoon program of the annual SEAN conference. A section of the SEAN annual report is written by the reference group.

Safe

SEAN remains committed to onsite accreditations. In addition to formal accreditation visits, SEAN is undertaking unannounced visits to all centres further to monitor and ensure the ongoing quality of practice. Data are collected on every critical incident recorded annually during ECT. These are evaluated and clinics encouraged to review the incident with a view to lessons learned.

Effective

SEAN uses validated outcome measures i.e. the Montgomery-Asberg Depression Rating Scale (MADRS) (Montgomery-Asberg, 1979) and the 'severity of illness' question from the Clinical Global Improvement scale (CGI) (Guy, 1976). Data on outcomes appear in the final paragraph of this chapter.

In order for treatment to be delivered in the most effective way, continuing personal development and education is an integral part of ensuring the delivery of optimal care and treatment. The Committee of Nurses at ECT in Scotland (CONECTS) in conjunction with the Service Users and Carers Reference Group have developed and launched an online LearnPro module for ward/escort nurses. Currently, online modules for consultants prescribing ECT and lead ECT consultants are being developed and will be launched in 2018. In September 2015, SEAN ran the first training courses for psychiatrists who prescribe ECT. The course received excellent feedback and it is planned to run these courses biennially.

Equitable

All clinics are accredited against a set of national evidence-based standards to ensure that care is delivered to an equally high standard in all geographical areas across Scotland. There are eleven standards covering the following areas:

STANDARD 1 Information, consent and prescription
STANDARD 2 Preparation for ECT
STANDARD 3 Environment
STANDARD 4 Equipment
STANDARD 5 Drugs
STANDARD 6 Psychiatry
STANDARD 7 Anaesthesia

STANDARD 8 Nursing
STANDARD 9 Recovery
STANDARD 10 Team Aspects
STANDARD 11 Protocols and Documentation.

Within each standard there are a number of criteria graded at 3 levels:

Level 1 – Mandatory
Level 2 – Standard good practice
Level 3 – Additional desirable practice.

In addition to actively monitoring and improving standards through our accreditation visits, SEAN encourages and facilitates both formal and informal multidisciplinary interaction amongst professionals clinically involved with ECT.

One of the main aims of SEAN continues to be to monitor the practice of ECT throughout the 18 centres in Scotland where the treatment is currently administered. In doing so we aim to maintain, monitor and, where appropriate, improve the already high quality ECT treatment that is currently provided throughout Scotland. This is achieved through a series of accreditation visits to all the centres where ECT is administered.

All centres are visited on a three-yearly basis by a trained accreditation team comprising a consultant psychiatrist with clinical responsibility for ECT, a consultant anaesthetist working in an ECT clinic, an ECT specialist nurse and the SEAN clinical coordinator. The members of the accreditation team are circulated with details collated by the local service, in relation to the standards, in advance of the visit date to allow the team to review all the documentation. During the visit ECT is observed (if appropriate and with consent of the patient). On the day of the visit, the inspection is followed up by an informal meeting involving the visiting team, members of the ECT team, senior management and clinical governance from the hospital. At this meeting findings will be fed back prior to the draft report being drawn up and circulated. If necessary, shortly after the draft report has been circulated, the national clinical coordinator will return to the hospital to review whether any changes which were recommended have been implemented and all improvements made will be referenced in the final report.

One of the strengths of SEAN lies, not just in its accreditation role, but rather in its informal networking role. This facilitates formal and, possibly more important, informal meetings and interactions amongst professionals of all grades and disciplines allowing them to share ideas and good practice leading to quality improvements being disseminated across the country. This is facilitated through several mechanisms. Of particular relevance is the SEAN annual meeting, a training event attended by both service providers and service users. This meeting provides an opportunity to meet, hear about and discuss recent advances in ECT and to share good clinical practice. This has led to more informal multidisciplinary contacts through which examples of good practice can be disseminated, often through the NHS email system.

The first half of the meeting is attended only by clinicians as this allows them to meet in a forum where relevant clinical presentations can be made without breeching patient confidentiality. Such meetings and the ensuing debate have enabled professionals from centres throughout Scotland to get to know one another and, through this, germinate and share ideas and experiences all leading to improvement in practice. The second half of the meeting is attended by service users and carers who play a very active and vital role in giving presentations about the patient and carer experience leading to subsequent discussions on how improvements can be made.

As SEAN has expanded there has been the development of professional subgroups allowing individuals to meet and network with those of the same discipline working in the speciality of ECT from across Scotland. Of critical importance is the Service Users and Carers Reference Group that meets regularly and feeds directly into the Steering Group. In 2007, the CONECTS group formed with a view to enhancing the quality of care that is given to patients receiving ECT through improved structured education and informal sharing of good ideas and practice. This group is funded by SEAN and is open to all nursing disciplines involved with ECT i.e. ECT nurses, anaesthetic and recovery nurses. Similarly, a Medics group was set up in 2012 for psychiatrists and anaesthetists to discuss local and national issues, difficult cases etc. Through the network, an unmet need for training for prescribing consultants was identified and therefore a SEAN prescribers' day was held in 2015. This has taken place biennially and has consistently attracted very positive feedback from attendees.

Although not the primary purpose of SEAN, the organisation has collected naturalistic data of all ECT treatments given in Scotland over many years of data collection. This provides a fertile ground for potential research opportunities that are currently being undertaken. The review process involves collection of MADRS data on all patients before treatment and at the end of their treatment episode. Of great significance is the fact that this data has produced powerful, incontrovertible outcome data as to the effectiveness of ECT as a treatment in a purely clinical setting. This data is collected from all 14 NHS Health Boards in Scotland (population 5.5 million) and, in 2016, included 344 patients receiving ECT who experienced an average 61.5% reduction in MADRS score following a course of treatment.

References

Montgomery S A, Asberg M. (1979) A new depression scale designed to be sensitive to change. *British Journal Psychiatry*, **134**, 382–9.

Guy W, editor. (1976) *ECDEU Assessment Manual for Psychopharmacology*. Rockville, MD: US Department of Heath, Education, and Welfare Public Health Service Alcohol, Drug Abuse, and Mental Health Administration.

SEAN Annual Report 2017. Scottish ECT Accreditation Network. www.sean.org.uk/AuditReport/_docs/SEAN-Report-2017-171113.pdf?2

Medical Training for Psychiatrists in ECT

Vimal Sivasanker and Ian O Nnatu

The Royal College of Psychiatrists' Good Practice Guide to ECT Training document (2018) sets out training requirements for psychiatrists of all grades and the level to which these competencies should be met. It is recommended that this document be used as the basis for devising ECT training at local level. All psychiatrists should be familiar with the basic principles of ECT which can be found in the College Position statement on ECT (2017).

In addition to mentioning training, the ECTAS Standards 2019 from the Royal College of Psychiatrists set out the requirements for psychiatrists working in ECT services. The recommendation is that there is a named lead consultant for ECT who has dedicated sessional time for the role in their job plan and who is covered by a suitably competent psychiatrist in their absence. It is also recommended that ECT is delivered by a small cohort of experienced psychiatrists who regularly attend the ECT clinic.

Junior doctors are required to attend ECT regularly and to receive appropriate training, including a comprehensive introduction and direct assessment of competence, for example, by using the Royal College of Psychiatrists' Good Practice Guide to ECT Training document (2018).

The duties of the lead consultant can be summarised as follows:

1) Developing and maintaining service delivery
2) Training and supervision
3) Achieving and maintaining appropriate service standards.

This chapter discusses these roles. The duties and training requirements for anaesthetists are discussed in Chapter 23.

Developing and Maintaining Service Delivery

The lead consultant should ensure that policies and protocols are in place to enable safe and effective provision of ECT, including at sites away from the ECT suite (e.g. the local general hospital) if necessary. They should update themselves regularly as to evidence regarding the mechanism of action of ECT, technical aspects of treatment and factors affecting outcome, which all inform the development of optimum treatment protocols.

Such protocols should cover all aspects of referral, assessment, monitoring and follow-up, including:

- Pre-ECT work up, including required investigations
- Consent to treatment and assessment of capacity to give this consent
- Prescription of ECT
- ECT for special populations (e.g. day patients, patients deemed to be at higher risk)
- Process of administration of ECT

- Bilateral *v.* unilateral electrode placement
- Stimulus dosing
- Termination of prolonged seizures
- Procedure for dealing with missed seizures
- Documentation of individual treatment sessions
- Observations in the recovery period, including the recording of any immediate post-ECT confusion or other side effects
- Assessments by staff and patients of outcome, including side effects, between treatments and at the end of the course.

The responsibilities of the patient's clinical team and the ECT team need to be defined with clarity. Historically, the patient's psychiatrist (i.e. from their clinical team) has prescribed ECT and the ECT consultant has determined the dose of electricity to be delivered, and, in some services, this system continues to work effectively. However, there are increasing numbers of patients being offered ECT as day patients and it is not always feasible for their community psychiatrists to review them and prescribe ECT between each treatment, twice a week. There has also been a national trend for ECT clinics to amalgamate and it is well documented that, in the areas where ECT clinics have closed, subsequent referral rates drop; for example, one study (McAllister *et al.*, 2011) looked at ECT use in Glasgow, Scotland, where two ECT services were closed in the north of the city in 2000 and 2005, and found that ECT use declined in the north, but remained unchanged in the south of the city, where there had been no ECT service closures. The inference is that ECT is no longer being offered to patients who require it, rather than believing that the need for ECT in these areas has suddenly decreased. The lead consultant for ECT has a role in developing a solution to this lack of access to ECT for those who should be appropriately referred to the service.

One model which is being widely used is the 'one-stop shop' clinic (Chapter 21), in which all referral, investigative, assessment, monitoring and follow-up procedures and paperwork are undertaken by the ECT team. Anecdotally, this seems to produce a more coherent experience for the patient (e.g. a day patient no longer has to attend ECT twice weekly and see their community psychiatrist also twice weekly), higher quality decision making about ECT treatment and improved access for day patients and those who are located at some distance from the ECT clinic. Some clinics take responsibility for all ECT patients while others only take responsibility for community patients (i.e. under crisis teams or community mental health teams), as the barriers to effective treatment mostly seem to affect this group. The lead consultant should decide on the precise model to be used as appropriate for local circumstances.

In all situations and with any model of service delivery, there is a need for a clear two-way communication between referring and treating teams if the treatment is to be as effective as possible.

Training and Supervision

Lead ECT consultants need to be able to demonstrate that they are competent to undertake all the duties described above. The Good Practice Guide to ECT Training sets out the knowledge and skills which lead consultants are expected to achieve and maintain. These cover:

- Theory and background
- Practical aspects of treatment

- Other aspects including:
  - involvement in audit
  - undertaking one day of continuing professional development in ECT practice annually
  - advising consultant colleagues regarding ECT referrals and practice
  - regular review of policies and procedures
  - training and supervision of junior doctors.

Lead consultants will need to include ECT in their personal development plan, to attend formal update training and to keep up to date with research developments. The College runs training days for ECT consultants annually and ECTAS runs a multidisciplinary meeting every two years. Consultants of services that use ECT infrequently should arrange to attend a neighbouring clinic for practical updates. Assessment by the lead consultant from a neighbouring clinic may also be the only sensible way to demonstrate that ECT consultant competencies are being met.

The Good Practice Guide to ECT Training also sets out the knowledge and skills which consultants who prescribe ECT should be able to demonstrate. A learning module on the prescription of ECT can be found on the College's CPD Online website (www.psychiatrycpd.co.uk/learningmodules/theprescriptionofelectrocon.aspx). ECT lead consultants should be involved in updating their colleagues on the latest evidence and practice in ECT, for example through local academic or regional College meetings.

The Good Practice Guide to ECT Training was initially developed for consultants running ECT services or prescribing ECT and trainees delivering ECT. However, it can also be used as a training framework for specialty doctors, who are increasingly involved in delivering and prescribing ECT. They should aim to achieve the level of competence commensurate with their involvement with ECT.

Finally, the Good Practice Guide to ECT Training also sets out the required competencies for junior doctors. The training and supervision of junior doctors is probably the most time-consuming duty of the ECT consultant. Diminishing numbers of psychiatric trainees, along with increasing demands on their time and the impact of full-shift on-call rotas mean that it is not a simple matter for them to achieve the required knowledge, skills and attitudes, which will enable them to fulfil their role in an ECT session unsupervised by the end of core training.

Trainees administering ECT should not be left unsupervised until they have achieved the required level of competence; the time taken for this will vary from trainee to trainee and will also depend on how busy the clinic is. The Good Practice Guide to ECT Training can be used as a monitoring tool for achievement of individual skills, but additional recording of ECT training can be done via workplace-based assessments, which can be completed online. The most common type of workplace-based assessment used is a direct observation of procedural skills (DOPS), but other assessments (e.g. case-based discussed, mini-assessed clinical encounter) should also be used to demonstrate a broad understanding of ECT in clinical practice and appropriate non-technical skills and knowledge (e.g. explaining the procedure to patients or carers and assessing capacity to consent to treatment). In Scotland, SEAN have developed LearnPro, an e-learning module which can be used to meet the theoretical training requirements for ECT; this resource may become available more widely in future.

Some centres have used simulation for the training of psychiatrists and anecdotally this has been well received by trainees who benefit from being able to practise their skills on a mannequin and develop their confidence before treating a live patient. One study found that the acquisition of clinical skills was superior when high fidelity patient simulation was compared to didactic teaching (Rabheru *et al.*, 2013).

In May 2017, the General Medical Council of the UK published its Generic Professional Capabilities document (GMC, 2017), which outlines capabilities required of all doctors in all specialties and indicates that these should be emphasised in all curricula and robustly assessed throughout training. This has triggered a review into core and specialty psychiatric training curricula and it is envisaged that training in ECT will be integrated into these revised curricula, along with clearly-defined outcomes. It is hoped that this will lead to more robust ECT training and increased support for it from healthcare organisations who host trainee psychiatrists.

Where other trainees, such as foundation or general practice trainees, are accessing ECT training, this should be broadly similar to that provided to core trainees. It is also important to remember that these trainees also have workplace-based assessments to complete and the systems are slightly different from those described above.

Achieving and Maintaining Appropriate Service Standards

Two systems of audit and accreditation operate in the UK and Ireland:

- the ECT Accreditation Service (ECTAS) for England, Wales and Ireland https://www.rcpsych.ac.uk/improving-care/ccqi/quality-networks-accreditation/ectas (see Chapter 18)
- the Scottish ECT Accreditation Network (SEAN) for Scotland (www.sean.org.uk) (see Chapter 19).

Lead ECT consultants are expected to take a leading role in discussions with management to make sure that all aspects of the service reach the standards expected for safe and effective delivery of treatment.

Key Points

- Lead ECT consultants should be competent to undertake their role.
- ECT consultants should take a leadership role in service development and delivering training.
- All psychiatrists prescribing or administering ECT should achieve the training goals set out in the Good Practice Guide to ECT Training.
- Supervision of treating doctors should continue until they are deemed competent to work in the ECT clinic unsupervised.
- All ECT staff should undertake continuing professional development related to ECT.

References

ECT Accreditation Service (ECTAS) 2019. Standards for the Administration of ECT (14th edition: January 2019). Royal College of Psychiatrists.

General Medical Council (2017). Generic professional capabilities framework https://www.gmc-uk.org/education/standards-guidance-and-curricula/standards-and-outcomes/generic-professional-capabilities-framework

McAllister M *et al.* (2011). Effect of closing facilities on electroconvulsive therapy use in Glasgow. *J ECT*, 27, 131–3.

Rabheru K *et al.* (2013). Comparison of traditional didactic seminar to high-fidelity simulation for teaching electroconvulsive therapy technique to psychiatry trainees. Journal of ECT, 29, 291–6.

Royal College of Psychiatrists 2018. Good Practice Guide to ECT Training. Royal College of Psychiatrists. https://www.rcpsych.ac.uk/about-us/our-people-and-how-we-make-decisions/committees-of-council/committee-on-ect-and-related-treatments

Royal College of Psychiatrists (2017). Statement on Electroconvulsive Therapy (ECT). Position statement CERT01/17 https://www.rcpsych.ac.uk/docs/default-source/about-us/who-we-are/electroconvulsive-therapy—ect-ctee-statement-feb17.pdf?sfvrsn=2f4a94f9_2

Nursing Care of the Patient Receiving ECT and the Roles of the ECT Nurse

Kara Hannigan

Introduction

The role and responsibilities of the nurse caring for the patient having ECT have grown and developed over recent years. This chapter outlines some of the main themes of nursing care in ECT and discusses the expanding role of the nurse in this context.

Providing Education to Patients, Carers and Other Health Care Workers

ECT still has a public stigma attached to it. ECT is often misunderstood, with perceptions of the public (and sometimes health care practitioners too) relying on outdated representations. This creates an important role for nurses in improving the knowledge and understanding of patients, the public and fellow professionals. It has been shown that knowledge about ECT among health professionals is associated with developing more positive attitudes (Lutchman et al., 2001). Patients who have had ECT are often favourably disposed towards it but also report having limited knowledge of it (Chakrabarti et al., 2010). One element of the role of the ECT nurse (working in partnership with other members of the ECT team) is therefore to act as a local resource for up to date information on all aspects of treatment.

Acting as a resource in this way has a number of elements. The ECT nurse is well-placed to provide both verbal and written information to all patients and their carers prior to the commencement of a course of ECT treatment. The nurse is also in a good position to provide accurate information to patients whose consultants are considering ECT as a treatment option. There is important information to be given to the patient and/or their family members on procedures, processes, benefits and risks. The nurse should also make space for any questions to be answered and signpost the patient to other appropriate information sources such as those provided by the Royal College of Psychiatrists (see https://www.rcpsych.ac.uk/mental-health/treatments-and-wellbeing) and the Scottish ECT Accreditation Network (SEAN) ECT guide (2017). For many patients, meeting with the ECT nurse and visiting the clinic before starting treatment can help alleviate anxiety, with the nurse then being a familiar face on the first day of therapy.

Providing information in different formats to meet individual needs is important. Examples include providing information in languages other than English, which in Wales (in line with Welsh language legislation) means also including information in Welsh. Information being provided in other community languages is also important, reflecting the characteristics of the populations served in each clinic's locality. Written information can also be provided in large print, using simple and accessible language for the benefit of patients with a learning disability or who are very unwell at the time of their referral and who might struggle with concentration. In these situations, using a visual medium in the form of a video can be particularly helpful.

Provision of education and information does not stop with patients and their families. As a key member of the ECT team the nurse should take part in regular ECT updates for referring psychiatrists and junior doctors. Nurses should also provide regular, up to date education to student nurses, qualified mental health nurses and other allied professionals within the mental health team. More generally, the nurse has a role as an ambassador representing ECT appropriately and accurately in the public domain and signposting the public to organisations which can provide comment on ECT issues.

Inpatient and Day Patient ECT

In the past, most patients receiving ECT were inpatients, and would be transferred from wards to the ECT clinic and then be helped to return following treatment and recovery. Although national figures are no longer published, anecdotal evidence suggests that in recent years the number of patients receiving day patient ECT has increased. Data from ECTAS show that just under 80% of people having maintenance ECT treatments were day patients in 2016–17 (ECT Accreditation Service, 2017). Day patients are people who attend the ECT clinic on the day of treatment and are discharged home to the care of a responsible adult following recovery from the anaesthetic.

Suitability for day patient ECT should be considered at the point of referral by the referring and ECT teams, in line with local ECT clinic policies and ECTAS (ECT Accreditation Service, 2018) and SEAN (Scottish ECT Accreditation Network, 2018) standards. Key considerations include the patient having a responsible adult able to be with them for 24 hours post-ECT treatment and assessment of their suicide risk. The patient's ability to remember and manage their pre-ECT preparation (including fasting) needs to be considered. Patients having day patient ECT should have adequate social support and help from their local community mental health team (CMHT). Attention should also be paid to patients' physical health, and how this may affect their recovery from a general anaesthetic (Verma et al., 2011; see also Chapter 23). The patient's distance from the clinic and travelling time should be assessed.

Once a decision has been made to offer ECT on a day patient basis, patients should be invited to attend the clinic with a carer or relative prior to the course of treatment. This provides an opportunity for the patient and those around them to meet with members of the ECT team, who can explain ECT and the procedures on treatment days. The nurse should be prepared to answer questions, providing accurate information both verbally and in writing. Pre-treatment assessments of mood and cognition (see Chapters 13 and 22) can be completed along with the Clinical Global Impression (CGI) (Guy, 1976) if this has not already been recorded by the referring team. There is the opportunity to check all paperwork recording the patient's consent and to confirm their understanding of the nature and purpose of ECT. An additional benefit of a pre-treatment visit is the chance for patients and carers to look around the clinic, which should reduce their anxiety on the first day of treatment.

All patients should have a cognitive assessment prior to ECT commencing. Preparation ahead of treatment commencing includes working through a pre-anaesthetic check list and coordinating an assessment by an anaesthetist. The nurse has a role in organising any pre-ECT physical work-up such as the taking of bloods, the recording of an ECG and the conduct of a physical examination.

Box 20.1   Patient Discharge Form

If you are receiving ECT as an outpatient your doctor will have explained the procedure to you to ensure that you meet the requirements needed so that you have safe and effective ECT treatments.

You and your carer will both need to sign the form below each time you attend for a treatment to confirm that you have read and understood the following information.

During ECT you will receive a general anaesthetic and therefore the following standard precautions apply.

You must:

- Be in the company of a responsible adult for 24 hours following the treatment.
- Be accompanied home.
- Not leave the hospital if you are feeling unsteady or confused.
- Not operate machinery or appliances for 24 hours.
- Take DVLA advice on driving following an episode of mental illness. (Your psychiatrist should inform you of this.)
- Not be left in sole charge of young children until the following morning.
- Not sign any legal document or make important decisions for 24 hours.
- Not consume alcohol for 24 hours.

Once you have returned home, if you begin to feel unwell, please contact:

....

If you are unable to attend for an ECT treatment, please contact:

....

I confirm that I have read and understood the following guidelines.

Signed:

Patient..

Carer...

On the day when ECT takes place, the day patient should be accompanied both to and from the ECT clinic by a responsible adult; patients having maintenance treatment may bring themselves to the clinic if it is clinically appropriate, but they must be accompanied from the clinic by an adult able and willing to take responsibility for their immediate post-recovery care. Patients are accompanied from the waiting room through the ECT suite to recovery by a member of the ECT team or accompanying staff. Policies for escorting patients within the ECT department will vary between clinics and regions but should be in line with national standards such as ECTAS for England, Wales and Northern Ireland and the Republic of Ireland or SEAN for Scotland.

Both the patient and the responsible adult accompanying them must be given written guidance relating to driving, drinking alcohol and being accompanied home after each treatment, for which they should both sign (see Box 20.1).

Each clinic should have clear criteria for the discharge of patients following an individual treatment. These should include assessment of suitability for discharge from the clinic agreed with the local anaesthetic department, and which reflect national standards for ECT and anaesthesia. In Scotland, where possible, all day patients should be reviewed by a doctor prior to discharge. Elsewhere, one option is the adoption of an anaesthetic discharge scoring system like the Post Anaesthetic Discharge Scoring System (PADSS) (Chung et al., 1995) that could be adopted for ECT patients, and in all cases the nurse should ensure that after each treatment there is a pre-discharge assessment of orientation, possible confusion and mood.

For day patients the ECT clinic should plan treatment dates ahead of time in consultation with the patient and his or her carers, allowing for adjustments reflecting personal commitments and work. If day patients have a problem securing the help of their usual responsible adult on a particular day then alternatives must be investigated. Options which the patient and the nurse can explore include approaching another friend or relative, securing the assistance of a local community care service, making use of a crisis house or negotiating inpatient admission for one night post-treatment, in order to avoid disruption to the course of treatment and to ensure continuity of therapy. Ensuring close liaison between the clinic, the referring team and CMHT is important, so that information is exchanged on progress and any concerns about patients (including relating to their responsible adult) can be shared throughout the course of treatment. Transport for patients should be arranged in advance when they or their carers cannot provide this themselves. Consideration needs to be given to travel and treatment time.

Inpatients receiving ECT should experience the same level of care, with particular attention being paid to communication between the inpatient unit and the ECT department. Ward teams need to be aware of the guidance for day patients, so that this is taken into consideration when leave from the unit is planned during periods of ECT treatment.

Accompanying and Providing Emotional Support to Patients and Carers

Supporting patients and carers through the ECT journey is a vitally important part of the nursing and care team's work. Patients' and carers' anxiety about treatment is likely to be heightened on each treatment day. Nurses and support workers should use all their skills to build relationships that allow patients and carers to express their anxieties and ask any questions. Providing reassurance and support will enhance the patient experience particularly if it comes from someone known to the patient as a regular part of their journey through ECT.

In the United Kingdom and Ireland there are different standards for staff accompanying patients to and from the clinic and during the ECT process. Current standards for Scotland are found in the SEAN standards (2018), whilst ECTAS standards are in place for England, Wales, Northern Ireland and the Republic of Ireland (ECT Accreditation Service, 2018). It is important for ward nurses, ECT nurses and the multidisciplinary team to communicate and consider clinical risk, staff training and good practice when making decisions around the selection of accompanying staff. The nurse determining which member of staff accompanies each patient remains accountable for this decision. In all cases adequate staffing levels should be agreed in advance with local management and all relevant teams, and provision made to meet staffing needs on ECT treatment days. This may require treatments to be staggered. Accompanying staff should be known to the patient and should be aware of the patient's legal and consent status and the ECT process.

Staff should ensure the safekeeping of patients' valuables and any prostheses, in line with local guidelines. In the case of prostheses like false teeth these should only be removed immediately before treatment, in the treatment room. The ECT nurse should be familiar with each patient's medication and liaise with the accompanying staff, patient or carer about this. As the role of the accompanying nurse in the recovery room varies, it is important that local protocols on this are developed and communicated to all members of staff.

Preparing the Patient for ECT Treatment

The ECT lead nurse will receive referrals, liaise with the referring and treating teams and ensure that each patient has been fully assessed and prepared prior to their first ECT treatment. Physical assessments, ECG, bloods, memory tests and anaesthetic assessments will need to be completed. The patient's consent and legal status will need to be confirmed, and all appropriate documentation completed.

On arrival at the clinic on the day of treatment, the patient should be greeted and shown to the waiting room where distractions (such as a television, magazines and radio) should be available. The nurse should introduce themselves and others to the patient, carers or accompanying staff in line with guidance from the #hellomynameis campaign (see: http://hellomynameis.org.uk/). The ECT nurse should check all documentation, paying particular attention to documents relevant to consent and to mental health and/or mental capacity legislation. The nurse should review the patient privately before treatment to complete all the pre-treatment assessments and confirm consent and capacity ensuring that the patient is happy to proceed with treatment. In some clinics, ECT teams are providing 'one stop shops' where nurses conduct formal assessments of mood, cognition and mental health using recognised tools (see Chapter 22). If the patient does not wish to accept treatment and there is no legal authority to treat them, the procedure outlined in Chapter 28 should be followed.

Care needs to be taken to review that morning's cardiovascular observations, or to record them if these have not already been taken. Assessment should incorporate using a recognised scoring system such as the National Early Warning Score (NEWS) 2 (Royal College of Physicians, 2017). Blood glucose should be recorded where appropriate (see Chapter 22). The nurse must correctly identify the patient in accordance with Association of Anaesthetists of Great Britain and Ireland guidelines (AAGBI, 2016). They should also check for allergies, fasting status, medications taken or omitted and dental health status (particularly the presence of crowns or dentures) (see Chapter 24). The possibility of pregnancy should be established where relevant, which may include carrying out a pregnancy test. Secure storage must be offered for the safekeeping of valuables, and patients should be reminded to pass urine prior to treatment. These final checks also offer the opportunity for the nurse to ask the patient for any further questions and provide further reassurance.

Nursing Care in the ECT Treatment Room

The role of the nurse in the treatment room includes acting as an advocate for the patient, and ensuring safety, dignity and respect are maintained throughout. Prior to each treatment session the ECT nurse is responsible for ensuring the clinic is ready. This includes checking that equipment has been maintained and prepared. Anaesthetic staff will have responsibility for checking anaesthetic equipment, and ECT clinic nurses will have responsibility for checking the safety of ECT and emergency equipment (see Chapter 22). Planning each clinic, and knowing which patients are attending on each treatment day, should be done in advance. Handover of information between inpatient staff, CMHT staff and referring teams is imperative. The ECT nurse should check patients' notes prior to treatment.

Before the patient enters the treatment room the ECT team should follow guidance from the National Patient Safety Agency *Five Steps to Safer Surgery* (National Patient Safety Agency, 2010). This includes a 'briefing' with the core ECT team members present, so that the sharing of vital information about patients, safety, equipment and staffing is made. In Scotland, a Scottish Patient Safety Programme (SPSP) brief must be carried out prior to the treatment session beginning, which must include details on all the patients for the day, any issues or concerns and a plan to deal with any potential critical incidents. This brief is usually led by the ECT nurse, and all members of the ECT team must be present. A record of the brief then has to be documented and kept on file.

The treating clinician should determine the ECT dose to be used. The ECT machine should be prepared and checked, jointly by the ECT nurse and the treating clinician. The treatment room nurse should be aware of each patient's legal status, and ahead of the patient entering the room a handover should take place to ensure that the team is ready for treatment to progress. The nurse providing ECT care in the treatment room should confirm that written consent has been obtained and/or that any legal documents (such as those relating to relevant Mental Health or Mental Capacity Act status) are complete and present.

On entry to the treatment room the patient should be introduced to the professionals present, making sure that each practitioner is identified by name and role. The patient should also be asked if any students attending can observe. The patient is assisted onto the trolley or bed, and the electroencephalogram (EEG) monitoring is applied. The nurse should ensure at this point that any prostheses, like false teeth, are removed where appropriate and safely stored. Many clinics in their pre-treatment checks now incorporate the use of an adapted WHO safety checklist (Chapter 22). Studies have shown improvement in team communication, information sharing, planning and decision making through the use of structured briefings and checklists of this type (Russ *et al.*, 2013). In Scotland a Scottish Patient Safety Programme Surgical (Treatment) Pause must be carried out just prior to each treatment. This includes checking all details relating to that individual, including his or her name, electrode placement and dose. Once the patient has been checked and anaesthetised, and the treating clinician is ready to administer the dose, the nurse and the treating clinician should confirm the impedance and the charge. Once confirmed, the administration button is pressed as per local protocols. The treatment room nurse may assist in the accurate timing of the seizure, both visually and using EEG monitoring. The treatment room nurse should ensure all documentation is completed by the appropriate treating professionals, handing over verbally and electronically any relevant information from the ECT treatment or anaesthesia to professionals involved in the patient's ongoing care. The debriefing part of the *Five Steps to Safer Surgery* should then take place at the end of the ECT list. The nurse should also follow up on, and hand over as necessary, any requests for reviews or investigations prior to the next ECT treatment.

Recovery Care and Discharge from the ECT Clinic

Recovering patients from anaesthesia is highly skilled, and is addressed in appropriate guidance from SEAN, ECTAS and other professional bodies including the Association of Anaesthetists of Great Britain and Ireland (2016), and the British Anaesthetic and Recovery Nurses Association (2012). The ECTAS standards (2018) state that the recovery practitioner must be competent in caring for the unconscious patient and be fully conversant with aspiration/suction techniques and resuscitation procedures including basic life support.

In the recovery room the minimum number of staff should exceed the number of unconscious patients by one, with the nurse remaining present as the patient recovers consciousness (ECT Accreditation Service, 2018). The recovery practitioner should inform the anaesthetist of any concerns. Their role includes the recording of pulse rate, blood pressure, oxygen saturation and time to reorientation whilst providing gentle reassurance as the patient recovers. The recovery staff give personal care as required, and enquire about side-effects (such as headaches and/or nausea). These are documented and treated as necessary. The decision to move the patient from the recovery room to the step-down post-recovery waiting room is made by the recovery practitioner when the patient is physiologically stable and awake. The recovery practitioner and/or the ECT nurse will manage the patient's discharge from the clinic, in accordance with local protocols using the appropriate nursing and/or medical assessments. Plans should be in place for monitoring, documenting and handing over any post-ECT changes in mental state such as confusion or agitation (see Chapter 22). Arrangements will also be made with the patient, accompanying nurse or carer for the next appointment for ECT.

ECT in Theatres and the Role of the ECT Nurse in the Theatre Environment

Many ECT clinics operate on remote sites. Patients who are at high anaesthetic risk should be treated on a general hospital site, usually in the main theatre suite where enhanced post-anaesthesia care can be provided. Some ECT clinics treat all their patients in a theatre setting whilst others located on acute hospital sites will have local protocols to distinguish which patients will need to be treated in a theatre setting.

Making and maintaining effective working relationships with theatre and recovery staff is a prerequisite for the provision of high-quality care for patients having ECT in theatre. Local protocols are needed covering the transition of patients from mental health or home settings, ensuring national standards and guidelines are maintained within the theatre environment.

The ECT Nurse Specialist and Managing the ECT Clinic

The ECT nurse specialist role continues to develop, particularly in the context of the development of nurse-administered ECT (see further in this chapter). The nurse responsible for the running of the ECT clinic should be a registered nurse who is a minimum (in the UK) of a Band 6, or a Band 7 if they are a budget holder (equivalent to CNM2 in Ireland). They should be primarily employed as an ECT nurse specialist or seconded to this role. The lead nurse should also have a fully trained deputy who regularly attends ECT sessions and who should be available to provide cover for the clinic during the absence of the nurse in charge.

The nurse should have specialist ECT knowledge and protected time to carry out all the duties required of them. They should not be expected to cover a ward or carry other responsibilities on the days of treatment. The protected time allocated should be sufficient to allow the ECT nurse specialist to carry out the responsibilities associated with managing a specialist service and all that this entails. This includes training and education, and staff management along with outreach to other departments and to ECT patients. The role also demands maintenance of a safe environment, audit, governance, work to ensure continued accreditation with SEAN or ECTAS and the provision of continually updated evidence-based patient care. As a specialist, the ECT nurse requires a comprehensive knowledge of up to date ECT care and practice, as well as experience and knowledge of mental health nursing and the care of patients undergoing (and recovering from) anaesthesia. General experience, and knowledge, of managing a department and being part of a multidisciplinary team are also necessary.

Nurses specialising in ECT and leading clinics have responsibilities to promote ECT nursing as a career choice, and to create opportunities for others. Lead nurses in ECT can play a part in challenging the stigma associated with working in this area, sometimes experienced even within the mental health nursing profession. For change to take place it is important for lead nurses to participate in the wider ECT community, including (for example) by becoming part of ECTAS accreditation peer review teams or applying to assume formal roles and/or join national or local committees. Key organisations specialist nurses should work with, are the National Association of Lead Nurses in ECT (NALNECT), the Royal College of Psychiatrists (which runs ECT accreditation and standards committees), and SEAN. Becoming involved not only helps provide a voice for ECT nurses but ensures the nursing profession takes a lead role in improving care and standards in ECT clinics as they are developed.

Clinics Practising Nurse-Administered ECT

Traditionally ECT treatment has been administered by specialist or trainee psychiatrists, with support provided by nurses. Two ECT departments in England conducted a pilot study into nurse-administered ECT; it was found that senior specialist nurses with the appropriate training and support could safely administer ECT. This could increase the capacity and capability of the ECT team and improve services for patients (Hardy *et al.*, 2015).

The fourteenth edition of the ECTAS standards (2018) includes specific standards for nurses and clinics wanting to practice nurse-administered ECT. Nurse-administered ECT is not included in the current SEAN standards, and is not used in clinics in Scotland. Where it is permitted with appropriate national standards in support, the plan to introduce nurse-administered ECT and the treatment setting for this is decided by the medical team, the individual nurse, clinic staff and the host trust or health board subject to local clinical governance arrangements.

Nurse Training and Development

ECT nurse specialists have responsibility to ensure that all qualified nurses and health care support workers within the clinic fulfil annual mandatory training. They also have a personal responsibility to develop and maintain their own knowledge and competency within the ECT context. This involves taking opportunities at both local and national levels, including participating in ECTAS forum conferences and attending ECTAS and NALNECT nurse competency training and study days. Opportunities are also available to take part in conferences such as those organised by NALNECT, Royal College of Psychiatrists team days, or, in Scotland, the SEAN LearnPro e-learning modules and the annual SEAN conference. Attending regional groups to participate in the sharing of knowledge contributes to achieving national standards. Scottish ECT nurses must attend at least two of the three annual Committee of Nurses at ECT in Scotland (CONECTS) meetings; in Wales nurses should be attending and hosting multidisciplinary All Wales ECT Network (AWEN) meetings. In Ireland nurses have All Ireland ECT Group (AIECT) meetings and in England nurses have Special Interest Group (SIG) meetings within their local regions two to three times a year. Nurses should also train for, and maintain, their annual certificates in in-hospital resuscitation, and consider gaining competencies in those for 12 lead ECG, intravenous therapy, venepuncture and cannulation. Developing skills and knowledge in pre-assessment screening and the administration of ECT enhances the care given in ECT clinics, improves patient experiences and further develops specialist nurses' roles.

Clinical Governance in ECT

The ECT nurse has an important role in clinical governance within the ECT clinic. Clinical governance is a framework which enables organisations to continually improve the quality of their services, safeguard high standards of patient care and create an atmosphere where excellence in clinical care succeeds. It requires a commitment to education, training and clinical audit. The accreditation of a clinic by ECTAS or SEAN after a process of peer review will fulfil many requirements of clinical governance. Clinical governance also involves maintaining clinical effectiveness, participating in research and development, and leading and taking part in safety and quality initiatives. It involves using evidence to inform the development of local policies and protocols, and being involved in the wider clinical ECT community by sharing good practice.

Clinical governance requires lead nurses to report and act on adverse incidents and they should involve others within host health boards or trusts in investigations and collaborate to change practice as a result of lessons which are learned. Commitment to clinical governance means ensuring that risk assessments for the care and treatment of patients are in place and implemented, and that care plans are formulated for the different phases of ECT nursing. Lead nurses should ensure that these include manual handling issues and the possibility of violence and aggression. At clinic level the lead ECT nurses have responsibilities for managing and acting on safety risk alerts. They must ensure that environmental risk assessments and audits in infection control, hand hygiene, fire and ligature points are in place. They should actively seek feedback from patients, carers and other professionals using and visiting the clinic to improve practice and inform change. Nurses should manage concerns and compliments appropriately, following local policy and protocols. They should meet with other members of the multidisciplinary team to explore these along with other clinical and policy issues.

Conclusion

The nurse has a key role to play in promoting safety and quality, and in educating the public, other professionals and students in an area of mental health care about which outdated ideas and misconceptions still persist. This chapter has provided an up to date, comprehensive account of the varied role of the nurse in the ECT clinic setting.

Acknowledgements

Thanks go to John Leyden, Linda Cullen and members of the National Association of Lead Nurses in ECT.

References

Association of Anaesthetists of Great Britain And Ireland [AAGBI] 2016. Recommendations for standards of monitoring during anaesthesia and recovery 2015. *Anaesthesia*, 71, 85–93.

British Anaesthetic and Recovery Nurses Association [BARNA] 2012. *Standards of Practice*. www.barna.co.uk/media/uploads/downloads/barna-standards-of-practice-2012.pdf

Chakrabarti, S., Grover, S. & Rajagopal, R. 2010. Electroconvulsive therapy: a review of knowledge, experience and attitudes of patients concerning the treatment. *World Journal of Biological Psychiatry*, 11, 525–37.

Chung, F., Chan, V. W. S. & Ong, D. 1995. A post-anesthetic discharge scoring system for home readiness after ambulatory surgery. *Journal of Clinical Anesthesia*, 7, 500–6.

ECT Accreditation Service 2017. *ECT Minimum Dataset 2016–17. Activity data report: England, Wales, Northern Ireland and Republic of Ireland*, London, Royal College of Psychiatrists.

ECT Accreditation Service 2018. *Standards for the Administration of ECT*, London, Royal College of Psychiatrists.

Guy, W. (ed.) 1976. *ECDEU Assessment Manual for Psychopharmacology*, Rockville, US Department of Health, Education, and Welfare.

Hardy, S., Cornish, J., Leyden, J., Vaughan, J. J. & O'Neill-Kerr, A. 2015. Should nurses administer electroconvulsive therapy? *The Journal of ECT*, 31, 207–8.

Lutchman, R. D., Stevens, T., Bashir, A. & Orrell, M. 2001. Mental health professionals' attitudes towards and knowledge of electroconvulsive therapy. *Journal of Mental Health*, 10, 141–50.

National Patient Safety Agency 2010. *Five Steps to Safer Surgery*, London, National Patient Safety Agency.

Royal College of Physicians 2017. *National Early Warning Score (NEWS) 2: standardising the assessment of acute-illness severity in the NHS*, London, Royal College of Physicians.

Royal College of Psychiatrists 2015. *Information on ECT*. https://www.rcpsych.ac.uk/healthinformation/treatmentsandwellbeing/ect.aspx

Russ, S., Rout, S., Sevdalis, N., Moorthy, K., Darzi, A. & Charles, C. 2013. Do safety checklists improve teamwork and communication in the operating room? A systematic review. *Annals of Surgery*, 258, 856–71.

Scottish ECT Accreditation Network 2017. *ECT in Scotland: A guide to Electroconvulsive Therapy*. www.sean.org.uk/docs/ECTGuide 2017-Final-Version.pdf

Scottish ECT Accreditation Network 2018. *SEAN Standards*, Edinburgh, NHS National Services Scotland.

Verma, R., Alladi, R., Jackson, I., *et al.* 2011. Day case and short stay surgery: 2. *Anaesthesia*, 66, 417–34.

Practical Aspects of ECT

Ross A Dunne, Alex O'Neill-Kerr,
Declan M McLoughlin and Jonathan Waite

Introduction

The Royal College of Psychiatrists recommends that a specially designated space for ECT treatment should be available (ECTAS, 2018). As the number of patients being referred for ECT continues to decline (Buley *et al.*, 2017) the availability of ECT for patients who require it may be compromised. The College ECT Committee is supportive in helping clinics to find alternative treatments for depression which may be delivered in the ECT centre. A number of centres already provide additional services to ECT, for example clozapine and depot clinics. ECT clinics are also used for the delivery of rTMS (Chapter 15) and ketamine infusions (Chapter 17).

Treatment Room

The clinic should have a designated waiting area; this should be comfortable, preferably with an outside window, as well as reading material and the availability of TV and radio. Patients should not be able to hear treatments being administered from the waiting room. The treatment room should be of sufficient size to allow room for the patient trolley, treatment machine and anaesthetic equipment, as well as permitting clinicians involved in delivering ECT sufficient space to move around unhindered.

Equipment

Any environment in which patients receive anaesthesia or sedation must have full facilities for resuscitation available, including a defibrillator, suction, oxygen, airway devices and a means of providing ventilation. All patient trolleys should be capable of being tipped into the head-down position and be easily transferrable to the rest of the hospital. Access to lifts for easy trolley transfer must be available. Continuous waveform capnography must be used in all patients undergoing general anaesthesia (AAGBI, 2015; Royal College of Anaesthetists, 2016).

There should be hand washing facilities available, a clock with a second hand, a refrigerator for medication and sufficient space for the completion of paperwork. Equipment for blood glucose monitoring is required. If the trust uses such a system there should be a computer terminal linked to the electronic patient record (ECTAS, 2018).

There should be easy access from the treatment room through to the recovery area, which should contain sufficient bays to accommodate patients until they have recovered. Each bay should have curtains to ensure privacy and dignity, and be equipped with monitors for pulse rate, blood pressure and blood oxygen levels (AAGBI, 2015).

The recovery area should lead to a post recovery room with facilities for drinks and food.

A designated room for the clinical team and ECT nurses should be available and contain sufficient desk space and computer terminals to access the electronic patient system. A separate clinic room where patients can be reviewed by the nursing staff or doctors should be available on treatment days.

Trolley

A suitable surgical theatre trolley or equivalent with braked wheels and cot sides is required. It must comfortably accommodate a reclining adult and should be capable of rapid tilting to the head down position. One trolley per patient is required. Usually the transfer of patients from the treatment room to recovery area is via the trolley.

There should be moving and handling equipment, including a sheet to help turn the patient. The clinic should have facilities for the management of obese patients (Royal College of Physicians, 2015). All clinics should have basic equipment such as a large blood pressure cuff. More specialised equipment may need to be loaned from the multi-disciplinary team for obesity services.

Disposal

Appropriate disposal facilities are required for sharps and clinical waste.

ECT Equipment

An ECT machine providing brief pulse square wave output together with a printable EEG should be standard for any treatment centre. The machine should be capable of providing a range of stimuli (see 'Stimulus Dosing' in this chapter). It should be possible to alter stimulus settings easily and quickly.

It is important that there is a backup arrangement in case the ECT machine develops a fault. Appropriate electrodes and conducting gel are also required.

Rationalisation and Closure of ECT Suites Nationally

There has been a steady reduction in ECT treatments in the UK since 1999 (Bickerton *et al.*, 2009; Buley *et al.*, 2017). Key reasons put forward for the decline are more restrictive guidelines, availability of safe alternative antidepressants, patient resistance and reduction in inpatient numbers. A balance needs to be struck between providing ECT services close to patients' homes and the need to perform sufficient numbers of treatments to maintain staff expertise. McAllister *et al.* (2011) suggested that the closure of ECT centres reduces the use of ECT. They compared ECT treatments in Glasgow following the closure of two suites in north Glasgow in 2000 and 2005. The number of ECT treatments reduced from 100 in 1996 to 60 in 2000 at the time of the first closure. There was a further decline with the closure of the second suite. There was no change in ECT use in south Glasgow during this period.

With the closure of ECT suites linked to the reduction in the numbers of patients treated, some ECT is now delivered on a regional basis. ECT suites that are 'stand alone' and have dedicated staff are particularly vulnerable to cost cutting programs. The ECTAS National Report (2016) found that three ECT clinics have closed since October 2013. A full list of ECT clinics in England, Wales, Northern Ireland and the Republic of Ireland, together with their participation and accreditation status, can be found at www.ectas.org.uk. The SEAN Annual Report (2016) confirms that there were 19 active centres in Scotland.

Advantages

- Reduction in staffing costs
- Rationalisation of resources and potentially better utilisation of hospital floor space
- May lead to better patient quality, consistency of approach and experience if the ECT suite is moved to a single centre
- Equipment from the closed suite could serve as a backup in the remaining suite.

Disadvantages

- The time taken to access ECT facilities if these are at a distance from the patient. Most patients will tolerate a three quarters of an hour journey.
- Patients who are acutely unwell may need to be transferred to the hospital operating the ECT suite. A process for determining patients' suitability to travel should be produced locally.
- Reduction in the use of ECT and reduced prescribing in the areas which have closed an ECT suite.

Staffing: General

There should be one person trained in cardiopulmonary resuscitation with each unconscious patient. The number of staff in the recovery area should exceed the number of unconscious patients by one. Additional nurses and all specially trained Health Care Assistants (HCAs) should be available to help in the recovery area of a busy clinic or if required for backup (ECTAS, 2018).

All clinical staff present during a treatment session should be trained in basic life support. Qualified staff should be competent in immediate life support.

Nursing Staff

The number of nursing staff required at each ECT session will depend on the number of patients undergoing treatment. If there are patients receiving ketamine infusion (Chapter 17) in the clinic when ECT is taking place, then suitable nursing staff to monitor these patients must be available. Nursing numbers also vary depending on whether nurses are administering ECT.

There should be one member of nursing staff designated for each treatment list and who carries the responsibility for coordinating the team and ensuring adequate cover in the treatment room and recovery area. One trained nurse should be in charge at each stage of the treatment process. There should be one trained nurse, known to the patient, accompanying them throughout the treatment session. Nursing staff accompanying patients to the ECT suite should have specific training in roles, duties and responsibilities required of the escorting nurse (see Chapter 21).

Nurse administered ECT has been found to be safe and effective (Hardy et al., 2015). The ECTAS standards have been changed to accommodate nurses administering ECT.

Medical Staff

There should be a designated consultant psychiatrist who is the lead consultant for ECT and the consultant should be in the ECT suite on at least one of the treatment days per week and available by phone on the other day.

A suitably trained clinician should be allocated to administer the ECT treatment. This may be a junior doctor, consultant psychiatrist or nurse suitably trained in the administration of ECT. With nurse administered ECT becoming available for some treatment centres, the nurse administering the ECT treatment should be in addition to the nursing staff supporting treatment and recovery.

Prescription and Monitoring

ECT should be prescribed by a consultant psychiatrist. It is expected that the consultant in charge of the patient's treatment and management should assess whether the patient has capacity to consent to the procedure (see Chapter 28) and arrange for appropriate formalities to be carried out to comply with the law. The prescribing consultant should discuss with the lead consultant for ECT the technical details of the treatment, e.g. unilateral or bilateral ECT.

The lead consultant for ECT in conjunction with the anaesthetist will decide whether the patient should have ECT and assess the risks and benefits. The experience of most ECT centres in the UK is that patients being referred for ECT have multiple co-morbidities and physical problems that may increase the risk of anaesthesia. The anaesthetist may need further investigations and/or consultation with other specialists when determining the risk (see Chapter 23).

NICE guidance (2016) stipulates that staff should:

- 1.10.4.8 Assess cognitive function before the first ECT treatment and monitor at least every three to four treatments, and at the end of a course of treatment.
- 1.10.4.9 Assessment of cognitive function should include:
  - orientation and time to reorientation after each treatment
  - measures of new learning, retrograde amnesia and subjective memory impairment carried out at least 24 hours after a treatment.

NICE do not offer any suggestions about how this cognitive function should be assessed; guidance on instruments suitable for assessment of cognitive function and subjective memory impairment can be found in Chapter 13; there are no established instruments that are satisfactory for the routine assessment of retrograde amnesia.

Before the beginning of the course and after each treatment, the patient's clinical status should be assessed using a formal valid outcome measure (NICE, 2016). ECTAS (2018) recommend that the Clinical Global Impression (CGI) (Guy & Bonato, 1976) is administered after each treatment together with weekly assessment by the Hamilton (1960) or Montgomery & Åsberg (1979) depression rating scale. The consultant psychiatrist in charge of the patient's treatment should review the patient after every two ECTs have been delivered and make a determination as to whether to continue with further ECT treatments, or to discontinue.

How Often Should ECT Be Prescribed?

Electroconvulsive therapy is usually given twice-weekly in the UK, Ireland and other European countries, whereas in the USA, treatment thrice-weekly is common practice. The UK ECT Review Group (2003) did not find significant differences in efficacy between twice- and thrice-weekly bitemporal ECT with a fixed number of treatments. There was a trend for thrice-weekly ECT to have more cognitive side-effects.

Reducing the frequency of ECT may help to reduce the cognitive adverse effects of ECT that are most common in elderly patients. However, this risks decreasing the efficacy of ECT. There is more evidence that reducing stimulus intensity or changing to unilateral electrode placement will reduce cognitive side-effects than there is for reducing the frequency of treatment (Semkovska *et al.*, 2011). For patients who experience cognitive side-effects with twice-weekly ECT, it is worth considering changing to ultra-brief pulse width rather than reducing the frequency of treatment. ECT given once a week is less therapeutically effective and unless there are very marked cognitive side-effects it is probably best avoided (Janakiramaiah *et al.*, 1998). Weekly or less frequent treatment may be considered for continuation or maintenance ECT (Kellner *et al.*, 2016b).

WHO Checklist

Treatment centres should have a modified WHO checklist suitable for ECT (Woodcock *et al.*, 2015). The WHO checklist is divided into four main areas: sign in, surgical issues, anaesthetic issues and sign out, but these have been modified by ECTAS to a simple sign in and sign out (Figure 22.1).

Sign In

The team introduce themselves by name, designation and function to the patient.
The senior nurse and anaesthetist check the patient's name and date of birth.
The patient's continuing consent and legal status are confirmed (see Chapter 28).
The pulse oximeter is attached and checked.
Any difficulties with the patient's airway and risk of aspiration are checked.
A check is made for any allergies.

Psychiatric Issues

The planned procedure is confirmed:

- Dosage
- Laterality, and
- Arrangements for re-stimulation (if necessary).

Anaesthetic Issues

The ASA grade (see Chapter 23) and any relevant medical or dental conditions (Chapter 24) are checked.

Pre-ECT blood glucose should be measured, especially in situations where patients are not eating or drinking because of their depression. Hypoglycaemia may result in prolonged seizures. Concomitant medication should also be checked, as this may cause cardiac arrhythmias or prolonged seizures (see Chapter 25).

Sign Out

Any complications or concerns are recorded.

A post session debriefing is held at the end of the treatment session with all of the clinicians involved during the ECT session. Any issues that have arisen during the treatment session are discussed, e.g. timings, equipment issues, staffing issues or concerns.

WHO Surgical Safety Checklist   Date
(Modified for ECT including NPSA advice)

                              Hosp No   D.O.B.
                              Surname
                              First Name

                              Address

☐ Have all the team members been introduced by name and role ?
☐ Has there been a team brief before the start of the session ?

Sign In (To be read out loud)

☐ Has the patient's identity been confirmed ?

    Has the procedure been confirmed ?
☐   Laterality
☐   Dosing

    Has consent been confirmed ?
☐   Consent form
☐   Assessment of capacity
☐   M.H.A. Documentation

☐   Does the patient have any known allergies ?
☐   Is there any airway/aspiration risk ?
☐   Are there any other patient specific concerns ?

Name	Signature of registered practitioner

Sign Out (To be read out loud)

☐ Are there any specific concerns for recovery and management of this patient ?

Name	Signature of registered practitioner

Figure 22.1 WHO checklist modified for ECT

Electrode Placement

Bilateral Electrode Placement

Commonly used electrode placements are shown in Figure 22.2. Bitemporal placement is the standard form of bilateral ECT (Figure 22.2(a)). The electrodes are placed on each temple 4 cm perpendicularly above the midpoint of a line joining the lateral canthus of the eye and the tragus of the ear. This placement has been used in all major research studies on bitemporal ECT.

(a)

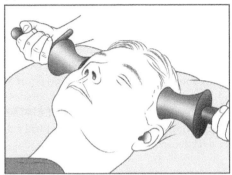

Figure 22.2 Electrode placements during ECT: (a) bitemporal, (b) bifrontal and (c) unilateral electrode placements.

(a) Bitemporal placement was the original electrode placement in ECT. It involves placing the electrodes 4 cm above the midpoint of a line joining the outer canthus and the tragus of the ear. Good contact between skin and electrode is important.

(b) Bifrontal electrodes are placed 5 cm above the lateral angle of each orbit on a line parallel to the sagittal plane (Letemendia *et al.*, 1993).

(c) d'Elia placement for right unilateral ECT was developed in 1970 and maximises the inter-electrode distance to prevent shunting. Application of a little electrode gel to the hair and scalp provides contact for the posterior electrode. It is placed 3 cm lateral to the vertex on the right hand side. The anterior electrode is placed 4 cm above the midpoint of a line joining the outer canthus and the tragus of the ear.

(b)

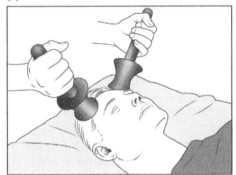

(c)

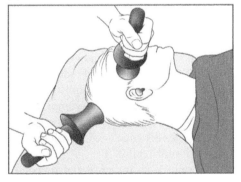

A less commonly used bilateral placement is bifrontal ECT (Figure 22.2 (b)). The electrodes are placed 5 cm above the lateral angle of each orbit on a line parallel to the sagittal plane (Letemendia *et al.*, 1993). It was hoped that it would cause less cognitive impairment than bitemporal ECT as the electrodes were placed further from the temporal lobes, but it was also believed to be more effective than low-dose unilateral ECT. It may have some modest short-term advantages for specific memory domains. However, no advantages for bifrontal ECT regarding antidepressant effect have been demonstrated (Dunne & McLoughlin, 2012).

Unilateral Electrode Placement

For unilateral ECT the d'Elia (1970) placement should be used. In right unilateral ECT, one electrode is placed at the right temple, in the same position as for bitemporal ECT and the other is positioned over the parietal lobe, just to the right of the vertex (Figure 22.2 (c)). The exact position of the parietal electrode is not critical. There must be enough distance between the electrodes to prevent the electric current shunting over the scalp. Too short a distance will result in the passage of more charge through skin and subcutaneous tissues. The patient's hair should be smoothed away from the site of the parietal electrode. It may be necessary to use more gel than on a hairless site. Supporting the left side of the head will act as a useful counterbalance to ensure good contact with temporal electrode.

Bilateral Versus Unilateral ECT

The seizure threshold (ST) for unilateral ECT is lower than for bilateral ECT. It has been suggested that this may be due to an increased density of charge in cortical areas as a result of the current traversing a shorter path (McCall et al., 1993). Switching from unilateral to bilateral electrode placement will require re-establishing the seizure threshold.

Although bitemporal ECT is effective at doses just above ST, the efficacy of unilateral ECT depends on using higher doses (Sackeim et al., 1987a, 1993). Unilateral ECT at 6 × ST is as effective as bitemporal ECT, but causes fewer adverse cognitive effects (Kolshus et al., 2017).

If patients who are responding to bitemporal ECT have clinically significant cognitive side-effects, then treatment should be switched to 6 × ST unilateral treatment, even if they may require more treatments during their course. If there is little or no response to 6 × ST unilateral ECT after six sessions, then the treatment could be changed to 1.5 × ST bitemporal ECT (Kellner & Farber, 2016; McLoughlin, 2016) although this may be more likely to be associated with cognitive side-effects.

Right versus Left Unilateral ECT

Most studies on unilateral ECT have investigated right-sided electrode placement. It has been assumed that passing current through the 'non-dominant' hemisphere would reduce recovery time and short-term memory effects. A recent review of the studies of left unilateral ECT (Kellner et al., 2017) concluded that this placement caused more verbal memory impairment than right unilateral treatment, but less than bitemporal ECT. However, patients experienced less visual and non-verbal memory impairment. The reviewers concluded that there are unlikely to be differences in efficacy between right and left unilateral ECT.

The incidence of right-sided language dominance is only 3–4% in right-handed people, but rises to 15% in the ambidextrous and 27% in left-handed people (Geschwind & Levitsky, 1968; Knecht et al., 2000). Therefore, routine clinical assessment of handedness is unlikely usefully to inform treatment decisions. Even strongly left-handed patients are likely to have left hemisphere language dominance. If a patient shows signs of post-ictal dysphasia, then the treatment with left-unilateral ECT would be justified.

What About Bifrontal ECT?

The largest study of bifrontal ECT found no difference in clinical response or cognitive side-effects between thrice-weekly 6 × ST right unilateral treatment, 1.5 × ST bitemporal treatment and 1.5 × ST bifrontal treatment (Kellner *et al.*, 2010). A systematic review of trials concluded that bifrontal ECT is not more effective than bitemporal or right unilateral ECT but may have modest short-term benefits for specific memory domains (Dunne & McLoughlin, 2012). The evidence is insufficient to support more widespread use of bifrontal ECT.

What Does Changing the Pulse Width Do?

When ECT was first introduced, the waveform used was sinusoidal (like the alternating current (AC) mains electricity supply). Present day ECT machines deliver brief pulses in a square wave (typically 0.5–1.5 ms), which is as effective as a sine wave stimulus, but causes fewer adverse cognitive effects (Sackeim *et al.*, 2007). In recent years there has been increasing interest in using 'ultrabrief' (0.25–0.3 ms) pulse width stimuli. A meta-analysis of controlled studies concluded that ultrabrief right unilateral (RUL) ECT was less rapidly effective than conventional RUL treatment and that more sessions were required to achieve remission. However, there were fewer cognitive adverse effects (Tor *et al.*, 2015).

Stimulus Dosing

Measuring Impedance

The resistance to the electrical current caused by the skin, soft tissues and skull is referred to as the impedance. The impedance needs to be checked prior to the passage of the electrical current in order to prevent a skin burn. If the impedance is too high ($> 3000\Omega$) a skin burn may result.

It is important to ensure that the patient's hair and scalp are clean. Applying a small amount of conducting gel to the electrode sites at the time of induction of anaesthesia will help to hydrate the skin and reduce its electrical impedance. If hand held electrodes are used they should be coated with a small layer of gel to ensure that there is a cushion of conducting material between the skin and the electrode. The electrodes should not be pressed against the skull so hard that this layer is squeezed out. Different methods of holding the electrodes may be used depending on comfort.

Causes of high impedance include poor contact of electrodes with the scalp, poor preparation of the scalp prior to applying the electrodes, and a faulty connection between the electrodes and the ECT machine. The operator should check that the connectors to the ECT paddles have not become disconnected.

Low impedance may be caused by the stimulus electrodes being too close together (particularly in unilateral ECT) or due to a low impedance pathway or shorting between the electrodes due to sweat or migration of the conducting gel.

Is a Seizure Necessary for ECT to Be Effective?

For ECT to be effective it is necessary to induce a generalised tonic-clonic seizure (Cronholm & Ottosson, 1996). However a seizure alone is not sufficient for antidepressant effect. The generalised seizures induced by low-dose right unilateral ECT are no more effective than sham treatment for relieving depressive symptoms (Lambourn & Gill, 1978; Sackeim *et al.*, 1987a, 1991).

When the seizure is modified by an adequate dose of muscle relaxant, some patients will have no or only minimal visible motor signs. This means that the adequacy of the seizure cannot be judged solely by observing the motor seizure. The duration of the motor seizure correlates poorly with the EEG seizure duration (see Chapter 26).

The ST is defined as 'the minimum charge required to induce unequivocal ictal EEG activity (i.e. polyspike followed by 3 Hz spike-and-wave activity)'. By convention this should last at least 15 s for motor activity and 25 s for the EEG so that a generalised seizure can be clearly documented (Freeman, 1995). ST can vary up to 40-fold between individuals (Sackeim et al., 1987b) but for the majority of patients treated with bitemporal ECT it is between 50 and 250 mC.

For bitemporal ECT, a stimulus dose of 1.5 × ST is therapeutic. In right unilateral ECT a charge of at least 6 × ST is required (Kolshus et al., 2017). Dosing of 1.5 × ST in bilateral ECT is chosen in an effort to avoid missed seizures, which are possible when patients' STs rise during the course of treatment. Doses of electricity more than 1.5 × ST for bitemporal ECT have not been proved to have greater efficacy. Although they may produce a quicker response, higher doses have been shown to be associated with more cognitive difficulties (Sackeim et al., 1993; UK ECT Review Group, 2003).

Why Should the Seizure Threshold Be Measured?

It is necessary to induce a seizure for ECT to have a therapeutic effect. The cognitive side-effects of ECT are greater if the stimulus dose is above threshold (McCall et al., 2000). Using too high a dose means that some patients will experience more cognitive side-effects, whether they are treated with unilateral or bilateral ECT. Unilateral ECT given at just ST has no therapeutic benefit, even though a seizure is produced (Sackeim et al., 1987a).

Some practitioners estimate ST from the patient's age as an alternative to the method described earlier. Older patients generally have higher STs than younger patients (Sackeim et al., 1987c). However, apart from age there are many factors that can account for the variation in ST between patients. Many studies have found that use of age-based methods to estimate dose can result in either over- or under-dosing (O'Neill-Kerr et al., 2017). Direct measurement of the ST has real advantages to maximise the clinical effectiveness of treatment and minimise the risk of adverse effects.

How to Establish the Seizure Threshold

The ST is higher with bitemporal than with unilateral ECT and often rises during a course of ECT (Krystal et al., 1998), while seizure duration may fall in parallel. However, seizure duration does not correlate well with ST or antidepressant efficacy of ECT, although subconvulsive stimulation is ineffective (Kales et al., 1997; Chung, 2002). The ST is established by attempting to induce a seizure, first with the lowest dose, then successively higher doses of charge in a procedure called 'stimulus titration'. An example of a stimulus titration protocol is shown in Table 22.1. For the vast majority of patients it is possible to establish the ST in the first treatment session. Previous ECT records may help guide treatment.

Several clinical factors are associated with increased ST:

- Older age
- Male gender

Table 22.1 Example of an ECT stimulus dosing protocol

Level	Threshold dose [ST] mC	Bitemporal treatment dose [1.5 × ST] mC	Unilateral dose [6 × ST] mC
1	25	50	150
2	50	75	300
3	75	125	450
4	100	150	600
5	150	225	900
6	250	375	Max.
7	350	550	Max.
8	500	750	Max.
9	750	1000	Max.

Max. – maximum dose of the ECT device
The first dosing column [ST] dose is used incrementally to establish the ST in the first session. In subsequent sessions the treatment dose is a multiple of the established ST, for example 1.5 × ST for bitemporal ECT and 6 × ST for unilateral ECT.

- Subcutaneous adipose tissue
- Anticonvulsant medications (including benzodiazepines)
- Propofol anaesthesia
- Bitemporal electrode placement
- Pulse width
- Recent treatment with ECT.

These factors should be taken into account when deciding on the initial stimulus dose. For example, in the protocol in Table 22.1 the initial stimulus level for a young adult female undergoing unilateral ECT would be at the lowest level, i.e. 25 mC. However, if she was over 65 years old, taking regular benzodiazepines and was about to start with bitemporal ECT, the initial stimulus could be increased by three levels up to 100 mC (see Case Vignette).

When stimulated at a subthreshold dose, the patient may grimace due to stimulation of facial muscles (a one-sided grimace often occurs during unilateral ECT) and there may be vagal stimulation causing bradycardia or brief asystole, but there will be no generalised seizure on the EEG or visible motor seizure. However, seizures may develop gradually over 10–15 s, slowly generalising to physical movements. Therefore, it is advisable to wait at least 20 s before re-stimulating to ensure that no seizure is developing. Re-stimulation should then proceed at a moderately higher dose, for example the next threshold dose level in the protocol in Table 22.1.

There should be a maximum of two re-stimulations in a titration session, so as to adequately safeguard patient oxygenation and ensure that the seizure will be modified. Anaesthetists should be made aware at the start of the treatment that the patient may require re-stimulation and may take appropriate precautions, including extra anaesthesia if they feel it is warranted. If a third stimulation is indicated, then one threshold dose level could be skipped in the protocol (Table 22.1). It has been shown in animal models

> **Box 22.1** Case Vignette
>
> A 72-year-old man is referred for ECT with a three-month history of treatment-resistant severe depression with suicidal ideation. He is on diazepam (5 mg four times daily), venlafaxine (modified release 225 mg once daily) and mirtazapine (45 mg at night). According to protocol (Table 22.1), his dose titration is started at 100 mC. He fails to have a seizure at this dose, so the dose is increased, and he is re-stimulated with 150 mC after 30 s. Again, only diffuse cortical activity similar to baseline is shown on EEG with no unequivocal ictal activity and no physical movement. The anaesthetist is satisfied with oxygenation and muscle tone through-out the procedure. The patient is re-stimulated with 350 mC and he has a successful 43 s generalised motor seizure with classical tonic and clonic phases and unequivocal 3–5 Hz spike–wave activity on EEG. He recovers uneventfully.
>
> The administering physician notes in the treatment record that stimulation should be tried at 250 mC next session as (a) the patient has been re-stimulated and his ST may thus have been elevated, and (b) the ST may well lie between 150 and 350 mC. However, at the second session, 250 mC fails to elicit a seizure, so the man is treated with 550 mC (1.5 times the initially established ST of 350 mC) at re-stimulation with good effect. It is recommended that for the third session, the initial treatment dose should be 550 mC.

(Kurinji & Andrade, 2003) that subconvulsive stimulation raises the ST; so if re-stimulation has been necessary, the ST may be overestimated. If this third stimulation results in an adequate seizure, the patient should be stimulated with the 'skipped' threshold dose level at the next session to determine whether this might be the real ST and then treated with suprathreshold ECT thereafter. If after three stimulations a seizure is not elicited, then stimulation should resume at the next daily session with the highest dose used at the last, unsuccessful, session.

What if the Seizure Threshold Is too High?

Most devices in use in the UK and Ireland allow up to 1,000 mC stimulation, whereas in the USA, the Food and Drug Administration has restricted devices used in routine clinical practice to about 500 mC. Fortunately, the vast majority of patients have STs well below this. However, it may be difficult to achieve $6 \times$ ST for unilateral ECT in older patients or those on medications with an anticonvulsive effect (see Chapter 25). It may not always be sensible to withhold such medication, as many of these medicines have a long half-life. Omitting doses before ECT may result in patients experiencing distress before their treatment. Reducing the dose before the start of a course of ECT may make a worthwhile difference to ST.

Hyperventilation (voluntary or involuntary) can prolong seizure duration and improve seizure quality, probably by producing hypocapnia. The effect on ST is not clear (Loo et al., 2010).

Xanthines

Caffeine, when given intravenously before ECT increases seizure duration without affecting ST. However, there is little evidence that this effect is of any clinical value. Experimental studies in rodents have found evidence that caffeine combined with electroshock produced hippocampal damage, which was not produced by either intervention given singly (Enns et al., 1996). Theophylline and aminophylline have been suggested as alternatives, but again there is little evidence for their utility (Loo et al., 2010).

What if the Seizure Is too Long?

Prolonged (i.e. >90 s) seizures occur in 1–2% of treatments (Benbow *et al.*, 2003; Whittaker *et al.*, 2007). The risk is highest in younger, female patients and those on high doses of medications which can lower ST (e.g. venlafaxine or clozapine). Etomidate anaesthesia is associated with longer seizure duration. Lengthy seizures should be terminated using some form of anticonvulsant medication (e.g. propofol, midazolam or diazepam emulsion). Clinics should have a protocol for managing prolonged seizures. When a prolonged seizure occurs, there should be a review of the patient's medication; consideration should be given to changing the induction agent or reducing the electric charge.

Seizure Adequacy

The pattern and duration of motor and EEG activity should be recorded (see Chapter 26). Facial flushing and piloerection may also be markers of a seizure. The treating clinician should ensure that bilateral motor and EEG effects are generated, especial with unilateral electrode placements.

If there is no motor activity detected and no evidence of a seizure on the EEG following the electric stimulus, this is described as a missed seizure. If this occurs during a treatment course (i.e. outside an ST dosing protocol) the treating clinician should consult with the anaesthetist to decide whether another stimulus should be attempted at a higher dose. A delay of at least 20 s is advised. The anaesthetist should ensure adequate oxygenation and may need to top up the anaesthetic and muscle relaxant, before the next charge is delivered, which should be at the next level in the stimulus dosing protocol (Table 22.1).

The dose for the next treatment session should be discussed with the lead consultant for ECT and appropriate adjustments made to the treatment dose.

What if the Seizure Becomes too Short during the ECT Course?

After seizures demonstrating 15 s or longer of typical 3–5 Hz spike–wave complexes, patients should not be re-stimulated. If a short seizure of 5–10 s is elicited and there has as yet been no clinical response (either because it is early in the treatment course or the patient has failed to respond because of short seizures), then the patient should be re-stimulated at the next higher level in the treatment dosing protocol (Table 22.1) to ensure an adequate treatment. For patients who have shorter seizures later in the treatment course but are having continuing satisfactory clinical improvement, then re-stimulation is not necessary but the treatment dose could be increased by one level at the next treatment session.

ST rises across a course of ECT in about 20% of patients where methohexital is used as the anaesthetic (Fink *et al.*, 2008). In order to give adequate electrical dosages, it is necessary to 'stay ahead' of a rising ST. If the seizure duration falls by 20% relative to the duration at the second session, you should increase the charge by one level. If there is an inadequate seizure at the next session, then re-stimulate at the next treatment dose. If this is successful, use this new dose level as the initial treatment dose at the following session.

Post-ECT Clinical Monitoring

Once the patient has started breathing spontaneously after the seizure and the anaesthetist is happy for them to be transferred, the patient is signed out of the treatment room (see WHO checklist above) and moved to the recovery area. They may be handed over to an experienced practitioner who has received training in the care of unconscious patients.

Physiological monitoring should continue until they are fully conscious (AAGBI, 2015). Time to re-orientation should be recorded (see Chapter 13). The anaesthetist should be immediately contactable until all patients recover full consciousness and are physiologically stable (ECTAS, 2018).

The Course of Treatment

The number of treatments required depends on the clinical response. NICE recommends that clinical status should be assessed after each ECT treatment using a formal validated outcome measure and treatment stopped when remission has been achieved, or if side-effects outweigh potential benefits. A usual course of ECT is between 8 and 12 treatments, although some patients may require more than this.

Typically around 60–80% of patients will respond to ECT (SEAN, 2016); about 53% will achieve remission (Kolshus *et al.*, 2017). Early improvement in depression (after six ECT sessions) strongly predicts high response and remission rates (Husain *et al.*, 2004; Lin *et al.*, 2016). However, 40% of patients who had not responded after six treatments still go on to achieve remission (Husain *et al.*, 2004) (see Figure 22.3). If patients are not responding or are only improving slowly, the ECT team should liaise with the referring team, to discuss ECT dosing, medications, side-effects and any other reasons for making changes to the patient's treatment. A patient who has shown no response within 12 treatments is unlikely

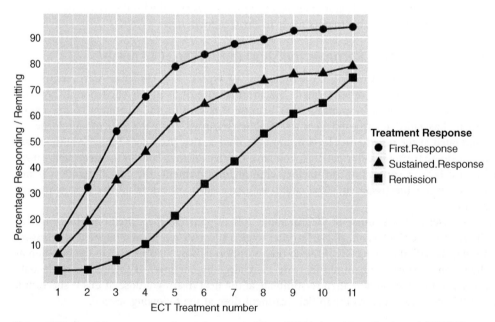

Figure 22.3 Cumulative response and remission rates to bilateral ECT (adapted from Husain *et al.* (2004)). First response was defined in this study as a 50% reduction in Hamilton Depression Rating Scale (HDRS). Sustained response was the first time that a 50% decrease in score, which was sustained to end of treatment, was measured. Remission was two consecutive HDRS scores <10.

to have a sustained response to ECT and the decision to continue will be dictated by the clinical circumstances.

Ultrabrief unilateral ECT carries the lowest risk of adverse cognitive effects, but the greatest risk that patients will not respond (Tor *et al.*, 2015). If response to treatment plateaus after three to four treatments, it is unlikely that there will be further improvement with this form of treatment; the patient should be switched to more intensive treatment (see Figure 22.3). Changing from right unilateral ECT to bitemporal ECT has been shown to improve response rates (Sackeim *et al.*, 2000), although the effect of these patients just getting more treatment cannot be ruled out.

The risk of relapse after a course of ECT is very high (over 80% – see Chapter 3). An antidepressant and/or mood stabiliser medication should be started before the end of the ECT course, if this treatment has not been continued during the ECT treatment.

Continuation and Maintenance ECT

We would suggest the term continuation ECT (c-ECT) for treatments designed to prevent relapse in the first six months after an index episode of illness, and maintenance ECT for the use of ECT to maintain remission in the longer term.

Once ECT has been discontinued there is a high rate of relapse at the end of the course. If no continuation ECT or active medication is used, about 65% of patients given ECT for depression will have relapsed within three months. Jelovac *et al.* (2013) performed a meta-analysis of published trials and concluded that, even with medication and/or continuation ECT, 50% will have relapsed within 12 months; they found that the risks of relapse are halved by continuing antidepressant treatment.

More recent studies using RUL ultrabrief therapy have confirmed that administering c-ECT in patients who had completed a course of ECT can reduce the rate of relapse. Nordenskjöld and colleagues (2013) studied 56 patients (mean age 57 years) for one year; they were randomised to receive either pharmacotherapy with venlafaxine and lithium or pharmacotherapy plus ECT. Unilateral ultrabrief (mean pulse width 0.36 ms) ECT was administered at six × ST, weekly for six weeks and every two weeks thereafter. The relapse rate for those treated with medication alone was 61%, but only 32% of those who received c-ECT relapsed.

In a study on older patients Kellner *et al.* (2016b) followed up patients over 60 years old who had responded to a course of RUL UB ECT in the PRIDE study (Kellner *et al.*, 2016a). In the continuation phase patients received open label lithium (target blood levels 0.4–0.6 mmol/l) and venlafaxine. C-ECT patients were administered RUL UB therapy according to a symptom driven algorithm (Lisanby *et al.*, 2008). All patients received at least four applications of c-ECT and thereafter the frequency of treatment was dependent on patient's symptoms. Depression scores and rates of relapse were lower in the c-ECT group. C-ECT has not been linked to adverse cognitive effects (Brown *et al.*, 2014).

It may sometimes be necessary to continue treating patients for extended periods with ECT. Criteria for maintenance ECT (m-ECT) might include:

- The patient has responded to ECT in the past.
- The patient has relapsed despite adequate antidepressant medication and/or has unacceptable side-effects to medication.
- The patient is physically fit for repeated general anaesthesia and ECT.
- The patient's attitude is conducive to having ECT.

Patients receiving ECT should have regular checks of their mental and physical health and their capacity to continue to consent to ECT.

Key Points

- The majority of ECT research to date has been on depression rather than other disorders such as mania and schizophrenia, but the general principles of ECT practice probably apply.
- Electroconvulsive therapy should normally be administered twice-weekly except where continuation or maintenance ECT are considered.
- It is not possible to predetermine the number of ECT treatments that will be required. Therefore, prescribing a set number of treatments is not warranted. The number of treatments will be determined by the patient's response, with the ultimate aim of achieving remission.
- Treating teams should be encouraged to consult with patients and liaise with the ECT team about dosage and laterality, balancing the benefits and risks for the individual patient.
- Bitemporal ECT has been used for 80 years and has a robust evidence base. It is recommended as the first-line electrode placement for severely ill patients (e.g. life-threatening catatonia) or when rapid response is required.
- In cases of informed patient preference, patients with underlying cognitive deficits, patients who have previously suffered severe confusion or memory disturbance, or those with a previous good response to unilateral ECT, it is advisable to treat with high-dose (6 × ST), RUL ECT.
- For patients who have severe cognitive difficulties or memory disturbance, ultra-brief RUL ECT should be offered as an alternative.
- For patients who fail to respond to moderate- or high-dose unilateral ECT, bitemporal ECT should be offered. This should be considered as a fresh course of ECT and the ST will need to be re-established.
- There is currently an insufficient evidence base to recommend bifrontal ECT over bitemporal ECT or recommend ultra-brief pulse over brief-pulse ECT.

References

AAGBI (2015) *Recommendations for standards of monitoring during anaesthesia and recovery 2015*. Association of Anaesthetists of Great Britain & Ireland.

Benbow, S. M., Benbow, J. & Tomenson, B. (2003) Electroconvulsive therapy clinics in the United Kingdom should routinely monitor electroencephalographic seizures. *Journal of ECT*, **19**, 217–20.

Bickerton, D., Worrall, A. & Chaplin, R. (2009) Trends in the administration of electroconvulsive therapy in England. *B J Psych Bull*, **33**, 61–3.

Brown, E. D., Lee, H., Scott D. & Cummings, G. G. (2014) Efficacy of continuation/maintenance electroconvulsive therapy for the prevention of recurrence of a major depressive episode in adults with unipolar depression: a systematic review. *Journal of ECT*, **30**, 195–202.

Buley, N., Copland, E., Hodge, S., *et al.* (2017) A further decrease in the rates of administration of electroconvulsive therapy in England. *Journal of ECT*, **33**, 198–202.

Chung, K. F. (2002) Relationships between seizure duration and seizure threshold and stimulus dosage at electroconvulsive therapy: implications for electroconvulsive therapy practice. *Psychiatry and Clinical Neuroscience*, 56, 521–6.

Cronholm, B. & Ottoson, J. O. (1996) Experimental studies of the therapeutic action of electroconvulsive therapy in endogenous depression. The role of the electrical stimulation and of the seizure studied by variation of stimulus intensity and modification by lidocaine of seizure discharge. *Convuls Ther*, 12, 172–94.

d'Elia, G. (1970) Unilateral electroconvulsive therapy. *Acta Psychiatrica Scandinavica Suppl*, 215, 1–98.

Dunne, R. A. & McLoughlin, D. M. (2012) Systematic review and meta-analysis of bifrontal electroconvulsive therapy versus bilateral and unilateral electroconvulsive therapy in depression. *World Journal of Biological Psychiatry*, 13, 248–58.

ECTAS (2018) *Standards for the administration of ECT, 14th edition*. London, Royal College of Psychiatrists.

ECTAS *6th National Report* (2016) London, Royal College of Psychiatrists.

Enns, M., Peeling, J. & Sutherland, G. R. (1996) Hippocampal neurons are damaged by caffeine-augmented electroshock seizures. *Biol Psychiatry*, 40, 642–7.

Fink, M., Petrides, G., Kellner, C., *et al.* (2008) Change in seizure threshold during electroconvulsive therapy. *Journal of ECT*, 24, 114–16.

Freeman, C. P. (ed.) (1995) *The ECT Handbook: The Second Report of the Royal College of Psychiatrists' Special Committee on ECT (Council Report CR39)*. Royal College of Psychiatrists.

Geschwind, N. & Levitsky, W. (1968) Human brain: left–right asymmetries in temporal speech region. *Science*, 161, 186–7.

Guy, W. & Bonato, R. R. (1976) 'CGI: Clinical Global Impressions'. In, *ECDEU Assessment Manual for Psychopharmacology*. National Institute for Mental Health.

Hamilton, M. (1960) A rating scale for depression. *Journal of Neurology, Neurosurgery & Psychiatry*, 23, 56–62.

Hardy, S., Cornish, J., Leyden, J., *et al.* (2015). Should nurses administer ECT? *Journal of ECT*, 31, 207–8.

Husain, M. M., Rush, A. J., Fink, M., *et al.* (2004) Speed of response and remission in major depressive disorder with acute electroconvulsive therapy (ECT): a Consortium for Research in ECT (CORE) report. *Journal of Clinical Psychiatry*, 65, 485–91.

Janakiramaiah, N., Motreja, S., Gangadhar, B. N., *et al.* (1998) Once vs. three times weekly ECT in melancholia: a randomized controlled trial. *Acta Psychiatrica Scandanavica*, 98, 316–20.

Jelovac, A., Kolshus, E. & McLoughlin, D. M. (2013) Relapse following successful ECT for major depression: a meta-analysis. *Neuropsychopharmacology*, 38, 2467–74.

Kales, H., Raz, J., Tandon, R., *et al.* (1997) Relationship of seizure duration to antidepressant efficacy in electroconvulsive therapy. *Psychological Medicine*, 27, 1373–80.

Kellner, C. H., Knapp, R., Husain, M. M., *et al.* (2010) Bifrontal, bitemporal and right unilateral electrode placement in ECT: randomised trial. *British Journal of Psychiatry*, 196, 226–34.

Kellner C. H., Husain M. M., Knapp R. G., *et al.* (2016a) Right unilateral ultrabrief ECT in geriatric depression: Phase 1 of the PRIDE Study. *Am J Psychiatry* 2016, 1101–09.

Kellner C. H., Husain M. M., Knapp R. G., *et al.* (2016b) A novel strategy for continuation ECT in geriatric depression: Phase 2 of the PRIDE Study. *Am J Psychiatry*, 2016, 1110–18.

Kellner, C. H. & Farber, K. G. (2016) The role of bilateral ECT when right unilateral ECT is inferior. *American Journal of Psychiatry*, 173, 731.

Kellner, C. H., Farber, K. G., Chen, X. R., *et al.* (2017) A systematic review of left unilateral ECT. *Acta Psychiatr Scand*, 136, 166–76.

Knecht, S., Drager, B., Deppe, M., *et al.* (2000) Handedness and hemispheric language dominance in healthy humans. *Brain*, 123, 2512–18.

Kolshus, E., Jelovac, A. & McLoughlin, D. (2017) Bitemporal v. high-dose right unilateral electroconvulsive therapy for depression: a systematic review and meta-analysis of randomized controlled trials. *Psychological Medicine*, **47**, 518–30.

Krystal, A. D., Coffey, C. E. & Weiner, R. D. (1998) Changes in seizure threshold over the course of ECT affect therapeutic response and are detected by ictal EEG recordings. *J Neuropsychiatry & Clin Neurosci*, **10**, 178–86.

Kurinji, S. & Andrade, C. (2003) ECS seizure threshold: normal variations, and kindling effects of subconvulsive stimuli. *Journal of ECT*, **19**, 31–7.

Lambourn, J. & Gill, D. (1978) A controlled comparison of simulated and real ECT. *British Journal of Psychiatry*, **133**, 514–19.

Letemendia, F. J., Delva, N. J., Rodenburg, M., et al. (1993) Therapeutic advantage of bifrontal electrode placement in ECT. *Psychological Medicine*, **23**, 349–60.

Lin, C. H., Chen, M. C., Yang, W. C. & Lane, H. Y. (2016) Early improvement predicts outcome of major depressive patients treated with electroconvulsive therapy. *Eur Neuropsychopharmacol*, **26**, 225–33.

Lisanby, S. H., Sampson, S., Husain, M. M., et al. (2008) Towards individualised post-electroconvulsive therapy care: piloting the Symptom-Titrated, Algorithm-Based Longitudinal ECT (STABLE) intervention. *Journal of ECT*, **24**, 179–82.

Loo, C. K. Simpson, B. & MacPherson, R. (2010) Augmentation strategies in electroconvulsive therapy. *Journal of ECT*, **26**, 202–7.

McAllister, M., Crabb, J., Brodie, D. & Krishnadas, R. (2011) Effect of closing ECT facilities on electroconvulsive therapy use in Glasgow. *Journal of ECT*, **27**, 131–3.

McCall, W. V., Shelp, F. E., Weiner, R. D., et al. (1993) Convulsive threshold differences in right unilateral and bilateral ECT. *Biological Psychiatry*, **34**, 606–11.

McCall, W. V., Reboussin, D. M., Weiner, R. D., et al. (2000) Titrated moderately suprathreshold vs fixed high-dose right unilateral electroconvulsive therapy: acute

antidepressant and cognitive effects. *Archives of General Psychiatry*, **57**, 438–44.

McLoughlin, D. M. (2016) Addressing crossover of high-dose right unilateral ECT to bitemporal ECT. *American Journal of Psychiatry*, **173**, 731–2.

Montgomery, S. A. & Åsberg, M. (1979) A new depression rating scale designed to be sensitive to change. *British Journal of Psychiatry*, **134**, 382–9.

National Institute for Health and Care Excellence (NICE) (2016) *Depression in adults: recognition and management.* London: NICE ISBN: 978-1-4731-2712-8.

Nordenskjöld, A., von Knorring, L., Ljung, T., Carlborg, A., Brus, O. & Engström, I. (2013) Continuation electroconvulsive therapy with pharmacotherapy versus pharmacotherapy alone for prevention of relapse of depression: a randomized controlled trial. *J ECT*, **29**, 86–92.

O'Neill-Kerr, A., Yassin, A., Rogers, S., et al. (2017) Switching from age-based stimulus dosing to dose titration protocols in electroconvulsive therapy: empirical evidence for better patient outcomes with lower peak and cumulative energy doses. *Journal of ECT*, **33**, 181–4.

Royal College of Anaesthetists (2016) Guidelines for the provision of anaesthetic services (GPAS). Royal College of Anaesthetists.

Royal College of Physicians (2015) List of equipment needed by an MDT for inpatient obesity patients. In, *Action on obesity: Comprehensive care for all*; p 20. London: Royal College of Physicians.

Sackeim, H. A., Decina, P., Kanzler, M., et al. (1987a) Effects of electrode placement on the efficacy of titrated, low-dose ECT. *American Journal of Psychiatry*, **144**, 1449–55.

Sackeim, H. A., Decina, P., Portnoy, S., et al. (1987b) Studies of dosage, seizure threshold, and seizure duration in ECT. *Biological Psychiatry*, **22**, 249–68.

Sackeim, H. A., Decina P, Prohovnik I., et al. (1987c) Seizure threshold in electroconvulsive therapy. Effects of sex, age, electrode placement, and number of treatments. *Arch Gen Psychiatry*, **44**, 355–60.

Sackeim, H. A., Devanand, D. P. & Prudic, J. (1991) Stimulus intensity, seizure threshold, and seizure duration: impact on the efficacy and safety of electroconvulsive therapy. *Psychiatric Clinics of North America*, **14**, 803–43.

Sackeim, H. A., Prudic, J., Devanand, D. P., *et al.* (1993) Effects of stimulus intensity and electrode placement on the efficacy and cognitive effects of electroconvulsive therapy. *New England Journal of Medicine*, **328**, 839–46.

Sackeim, H. A., Prudic, J., Devanand, D. P., *et al.* (2000) A prospective, randomized, double-blind comparison of bilateral and right unilateral electroconvulsive therapy at different stimulus intensities. *Arch Gen Psychiatry*, **57**, 425–34.

Sackeim, H. A., Prudic, J., Fuller, R., *et al.* (2007) The cognitive effects of electroconvulsive therapy in community settings. *Neuropsychopharmacology*, **32**, 244–54.

SEAN (Scottish ECT Accreditation Network) (2016) Annual Report 2016. NHS National Services Scotland.

Semkovska, M., Keane, D., Babalola, O., *et al.* (2011) Unilateral brief-pulse electroconvulsive therapy and cognition: effects of electrode placement, stimulus dosage and time. *Journal of Psychiatric Research*, **45**, 770–80.

Tor, P.-C., Bautovich, A., Wang, M.-J., *et al.* (2015). A systematic review and meta-analysis of brief versus ultrabrief right unilateral electroconvulsive therapy for depression. *Journal of Clinical Psychiatry*, **76**, 1092–8.

UK ECT Review Group (2003) Efficacy and safety of electroconvulsive therapy in depressive disorders: a systematic review and meta-analysis. *Lancet*, **361**, 799–808.

Whittaker, R., Scott, A. & Gardner, M. (2007) The prevalence of prolonged cerebral seizures at the first treatment in a course of electroconvulsive therapy. *Journal of ECT*, **23**, 11–13.

Woodcock, H. M., Cornish, J., Vaughan, J. J. *et al.* (2015) The development and use of a modified WHO checklist for use in ECT. *Journal of ECT*, **31**, 83–6.

Chapter 23

Anaesthesia for Electroconvulsive Therapy

Godfrey M Bwalya, Rahul Bajekal and Jonathan Waite

Introduction

Anaesthesia for electroconvulsive therapy (ECT) can be challenging for the anaesthetist with no prior experience. Most ECT facilities are located in remote, unfamiliar environments (Royal College of Anaesthetists, 2016). In the UK, the ECT Accreditation Service (ECTAS) has driven improvement in standards, addressing areas of criticism and bringing some level of uniformity (ECTAS, 2016; Bwalya *et al.*, 2011; Simpson and Lynch, 1998). In this chapter, a brief examination of the issues relating to anaesthetic practice is made.

Practice Guidelines

The Royal College of Anaesthetists (RCoA), publishes Guidelines for the Provision of Anaesthetic Services (GPAS) aimed at reducing risk and ensuring high standards of patient management (RCoA, 2016). These underpin anaesthetic practice in the UK. There is specific guidance on anaesthesia for ECT. Standards for monitoring and recovery are stipulated by the Association of Anaesthetists (AAGBI, 2015).

Role of the Lead Anaesthetist

Lead Anaesthetists for ECT require a special interest in the subject. They must fulfil the competencies for anaesthesia in a non-theatre environment (RCoA, 2010). They require support from a pool of trained anaesthetists who can provide cover. They must have a clear understanding of the benefits and risks of ECT and the relevant standards. They are responsible for assessing the patient for their risk from anaesthesia and should assist the team in making a decision whether the benefits of ECT will outweigh the risks. This involves assessing each patient's co-morbidities and whether these can be optimised before treatment begins. The anaesthetist should make a judgement as to whether the patient can be treated in the ECT clinic or will need to be anaesthetised in theatre. Consultants who work on remote sites should also meet the competencies for remote and rural anaesthesia (RCoA, 2010).

The lead anaesthetist must assist the ECT team in developing clinic protocols and provide training in anaesthetic aspects of ECT practice for other members of the clinic team.

Patient Evaluation

Pre-ECT evaluation of patients is an essential component of high quality patient management (Tess and Smetana, 2009; Sundsted *et al.*, 2014). For patients undergoing ECT, its main objectives are:

- Determining with the lead psychiatrist the indication for ECT and specific requirements for the patient.
- Where there are concerns about the patient's suitability for a general anaesthetic, jointly to consider whether there may be a safer alternative to ECT, or whether there is time to reduce the risk of anaesthesia by optimising the patient's co-morbidities.
- Checking whether there have been problems during any previous anaesthetics.
- Review of medical and psychiatric notes for co-morbidities, previous medical problems and their management (see Chapter 26).
- Review of concurrent medication, recognising the potential for interaction between anaesthetic agents and other medication (see Chapter 25).
- Physical examination, including assessment of the airway and dental or temporo-mandibular joint problems (see Chapter 24).
- Developing a plan to manage existing co-morbidities such as obesity (AAGBI, 2015).
- Requesting specialist consultation.

Investigations

The following investigations are recommended by the authors, as representatives of the Royal College of Anaesthetists and the Royal College of Psychiatrists:

For all cases:

- Full blood count
- Renal function – urea, creatinine, eGFR and electrolytes
- ECG should be performed

  - in patients over 65,
  - where the patient is taking medication which may prolong QTc or have other cardiac adverse effects,
  - where there is a history of cardiac disease.

- Chest and cervical spine X-ray should only be performed if clinically indicated
- Routine neuro-radiology is not warranted (Sajedi *et al.*, 2016), but should be performed if there is any concern over a potential organic cause for the patient's symptoms.

Monitoring

Standard monitoring should include the following (AAGBI, 2016):

- Pulse oximetry
- Non-invasive blood pressure measurement
- ECG monitoring
- Capnography
- Temperature at induction
- EEG monitoring (ECTAS, 2016).

A nerve stimulator must be available.

Anaesthesia

The goal of anaesthesia in ECT is to induce a brief period of hypnosis, covering the period of muscle relaxation and electrical stimulation (Ding and White, 2002). Anaesthesia is induced with an agent which has a rapid onset and offset with the ability to attenuate the acute physiological effects of ECT, but with minimal effect on, or facilitation of, seizure activity.

A muscle relaxant is required to attenuate the musculoskeletal manifestations of the seizure and enable airway control and facilitate ventilation and oxygenation.

To minimise the risk of dental complications, the anaesthetist should supervise the use of a flexible bite-block to distribute the force of the contracting jaw, protecting teeth and other oral structures. They should support the patient's chin and keep the jaw tight against the bite-block during the electrical stimulus; an oropharyngeal (Guedel) airway is not appropriate for dental protection.

There should be adequate pre-oxygenation before induction, followed by bag and mask valve hyperventilation with 100% oxygen, to reduce CO_2 and lower the seizure threshold until the patient has achieved adequate neuromuscular blockade and the team are ready to administer the electrical stimulus. The anaesthetist should aim to maintain airway patency and support ventilation until spontaneous respiration has resumed and the patient can be transferred to a recovery area.

A complete record of the medication administered, the results of monitoring and of any necessary intervention should be kept (RCoA, 2016). Guidance for future treatments such as changes in anaesthetic agent, muscle relaxant or other drugs should also be recorded.

Induction Agents

A list of potential induction agents with their advantages and disadvantages is given in Table 23.1.

Inhalational Induction agents

If there is a need for gas induction, sevoflurane has been suggested as a reasonable option for patients undergoing ECT. It is an option as an alternative induction agent for paediatric ECT (Franklin, 2017). However, in routine ECT practice intravenous anaesthetic agents are preferred (Hodgson et al., 2004; Toprak et al., 2005).

Alfentanil, Remifentanil, Fentanyl

Alfentanil and remifentanil can be used to increase seizure duration and reduce haemo-dynamic response (Akcaboy et al., 2005; Hooten and Rasmussen, 2008; Nasseri et al., 2009). Alfentanil (10 µg/kg) may prolong the duration of apnoea (van den Broek et al., 2004). Remifentanil (1 µg/kg) is effective without any alteration in recovery characteristics and has been used in higher doses as a sole agent in patients who are refractory to seizure induction (Sullivan et al., 2004; Hossain and Sullivan, 2008). It is not clear whether the increased duration of seizures is due to a sparing effect on the anaesthetic agent or an inherent property of the opiate. Fentanyl may shorten the duration of the seizure (Weinger et al., 1991).

Muscle Relaxants

Suxamethonium (succinylcholine) remains the relaxant of choice due to its rapid onset and offset. It is contra-indicated in conditions with neurological deficits involving spinal cord injury, peripheral nerve injury or acute muscle wasting. It must also be avoided where there are burns or hyperkalaemia. It is a known trigger for malignant hyperthermia.

Table 23.1 Induction agents

Agent	Advantages	Disadvantages
Methohexital (0.5–1 mg/kg body weight)	Longer seizure compared to propofol (Peng et al., 2014) Fewer arrhythmias compared with thiopentone in ECT (Mokriski et al., 1992) No difference in cognitive function recovery, compared to propofol and etomidate	Painful injection Hypotension Shivering Excitatory side effects Unlicensed in the UK Reduced availability
Propofol (0.75 mg/kg body weight)	Rapid onset and offset Low incidence of post-treatment nausea and vomiting Attenuation of ECT induced hypertension and tachycardia (Rasmussen, 2014) Rapid recovery (Rasmussen, 2014)	Reduced duration and intensity of seizure compared with other induction agents (Rasmussen, 2014) Increased numbers of ECT treatments (Patel et al., 2006) Higher stimulus charge required (Eranti et al., 2009)
Etomidate (0.15–0.3 mg/kg body weight)	Longer seizure duration (motor and EEG) compared to propofol or thiopental (Singh et al., 2015).	Painful injection Dyskinesia Nausea and vomiting Potential for adrenocortical suppression (Wang et al., 2011) Less attentuation of ECT induced haemodynamic changes than propofol (Erdil et al., 2009)
Thiopental (1.5 –2.5 mg/kg body weight)	Rapid onset and smooth anaesthesia Better impact on efficacy than propofol (Kumar et al., 2012) Fewer cognitive side effects than propofol (Ingram et al., 2007)	Reduced seizure duration compared to etomidate and methohexital (Swaim et al., 2006) Less attentuation of ECT- induced haemodynamic changes than propofol (Kadoi et al., 2003)
Ketamine (0.3–2.0 mg/kg body weight) (Galvez et al., 2017)	Bronchodilation (Haas and Harper, 1992) Preservation of protective reflexes (Eikermann et al., 2012)	Slow onset, delayed recovery, and increased incidence of nausea, hyper-salivation, hypertension, psychotic symptoms and ataxia during recovery (Strayer and Nelson, 2008). No advantages over other anaesthetic agents (McGirr et al., 2017)

Bradycardia can occur, particularly when a second dose is given within minutes of the first. There may be prolonged apnoea in patients with butyryl cholinesterase deficiency. The incidence of anaphylaxis is higher than with other muscle relaxants.

Non-depolarising muscle relaxants cause more prolonged paralysis, they need monitoring of both onset and duration of action with a nerve stimulator. Mivacurium, atracurium and rocuronium have been evaluated for ECT (Mirzakhani *et al.*, 2012, 2016). The action of rocuronium can be terminated by sugammadex.

Drugs to Modify the Autonomic Effects of ECT

Anticholinergic agents may be used to prevent or treat severe parasympathetic effects. Severe bradycardia can usually be prevented by glycopyrrolate (100–600 µg) (Rasmussen *et al.*, 2007) which has a theoretical advantage over atropine (300–600 µg) as it does not cross the blood–brain barrier. Sometimes higher doses or avoidance of suxamethonium are required (Birkenhäger *et al.*, 2010).

Use of a beta-blocker (Boere *et al.*, 2014) should be considered in the light of the patient's overall cardiovascular risk (Fleisher *et al.*, 2014). Esmolol has been the most intensively studied; it may cause reduction in seizure duration, but this is probably not clinically significant. Labetalol has been less well investigated; it has a longer biological half-life (Rasmussen *et al.*, 2007).

Acute Physiological Effects of ECT

The electrical stimulus (whether or not a seizure is generated) results in vagal discharge which causes bradycardia and sometimes asystole (Mizen *et al.*, 2015). If a seizure is produced there is a sympathetic response with release of catecholamines, causing tachycardia and hypertension (Bryson *et al.*, 2013). Cardiac arrhythmias may be produced which are usually self-limiting, but may require treatment (Pullen *et al.*, 2011). There is also an increase in cerebral blood flow, which can be attenuated by beta blockers, although the dose required to achieve this may cause systemic hypotension (Kadoi & Saito, 2014). The increase in blood flow can result in increased intra-cranial pressure. There is an increase in intra-ocular pressure, but patients who have had surgery for glaucoma may be safely treated with ECT (see Chapter 27).

After the seizure there may be baroreceptor-induced bradycardia; post-treatment other electrocardiographic changes or troponin elevation suggestive of sub-endocardial ischaemia have been reported (Duma *et al.*, 2017) including ST-segment deviation and T-wave inversion.

Adverse Effects of ECT

Cardiovascular

(see Chapter 14)

Hypertension may be dramatic; it sometimes requires intervention but usually settles within 20 minutes. Conduction abnormalities such as Q_T interval abnormalities are commonly found, especially in older patients (Yamaguchi *et al.*, 2011), but resolve within 10 minutes. Acute stress induced (Takotsubo) cardiomyopathy has been reported during ECT (Sharp and Welch, 2011); for further details see Chapter 14. If chest pain or pulmonary oedema occur during ECT, there should be a full cardiological assessment (Fleisher *et al.*, 2014) before resuming treatment.

Musculo-Skeletal

Suxamethonium may cause muscle pain; if this is a problem pre-treatment with paracetamol or a non-steroidal anti-inflammatory agent is usually effective.

Cognitive

(see Chapter 13)

Anaesthetic agents play some part in post treatment agitation and confusion (see individual agents above). Agitation occurs in about 10% of patients (Devanand et al., 1989). Increasing the dose of anaesthetic reduces the risk of post-ictal excitement, but increases the risk of missed or inadequate seizures (Devanand and Sackeim, 1992). Agitation can be treated by an additional small dose of propofol at the end of the EEG seizure (Tzabazis et al., 2013).

Key Points

- The anaesthetist is an essential member of the ECT team; their key role is to ensure that the patient is safely anaesthetised with minimal effect on seizure activity.
- The anaesthetist should play a leading role in assessing patients' fitness for ECT.
- Co-morbidities and decisions regarding location for treatment are best managed with a team approach.
- Anaesthetists should be familiar with techniques to ensure that therapeutic seizures are generated. This may include reducing the dose of induction agent, using an alternative anaesthetic or use of adjunctive opioids.
- Anaesthetists should ensure that standards – including monitoring – follow guidance issued by the RCoA, AAGBI and ECTAS/SEAN. They should participate in audit and the development of local protocols.
- The lead consultant should ensure that suitable training, guidance and support is provided for those giving anaesthesia for ECT.

Acknowledgements

We are grateful to David Evans and Phil Laws for helpful comments.

References

AAGBI (2015) Peri-operative management of the obese surgical patient. *Anaesthesia*, **70**, 859–76.

AAGBI (2016) Recommendations for standards of monitoring during anaesthesia and recovery 2015. *Anaesthesia*, **71**, 85–93.

Akcaboy, Z. N., Akcaboy, E. Y., Yigitbasl, B. et al. (2005) Effects of remifentanil and alfentanil on seizure duration, stimulus amplitudes and recovery parameters during ECT. *Acta Anaesthesiologica Scandinavica*, **49**, 1068–71.

Boere, E., Birkenhäger, T. K., Groenland, T. H. N. et al. (2014) Beta-blocking agents during electroconvulsive therapy: a review. *British Journal of Anaesthesia*, **113**, 43–51.

Birkenhäger, T. K., Pluijms, E. M., Groenland, T. H. & van den Broek, W. W. Severe

bradycardia after anesthesia before electroconvulsive therapy. *Journal of ECT*, **26**, 53–4.

Bryson, E. O., Popeo, D., Briggs, M. et al. (2013) Electroconvulsive therapy (ECT) in patients with cardiac disease: hemodynamic changes. *Journal of ECT*, **29**, 76–7.

Bwalya, G. M., Srinivasan, V. & Wang, M. (2011) Electroconvulsive therapy anesthesia practice patterns: results of a UK postal survey. *J ECT*, **27**, 81–5.

Devanand, D. P., Briscoe, K. M. & Sackeim, H. A. (1989) Clinical features and predictors of postictal excitement. *Convulsive Therapy*, **5**, 140–6.

Devanand, D. P. & Sackeim, H. A. (1992) Use of increased anaesthetic dose prior to ECT to prevent postictal excitement. *General Hospital Psychiatry*, **14**, 345–9.

Ding, Z. and White, P. F. (2002) Anesthesia for electroconvulsive therapy. *Anesth Analg*, **94**, 1351–64.

Duma, A., Pal, S., Johnston J., Helwani, M.A., Bhat, A. *et al.* (2017) High-sensitivity cardiac troponin elevation after electroconvulsive therapy: a prospective, observational cohort study. *Anesthesiology*, **126**, 643–52.

ECTAS (2016) Standards for the Administration of ECT, 13th Edition (edited by Buley, N., Hailey, E. and Hodge, S). Royal College of Psychiatrists.

Eikermann, M., Grosse-Sundrup, M., Zaremba, S. *et al.* (2012) Ketamine activates breathing and abolishes the coupling between loss of consciousness and upper airway dilator muscle dysfunction. *Anesthesiology*, **116**, 35–46.

Eranti, S. V., Mogg, A. J., Pluck, G. C. *et al.* (2009) Methohexitone, propofol and etomidate in ECT for depression: a naturalistic comparison study. *J Affect Disord*, **113**, 165–71.

Erdil, F., Demirbilek, S., Begec, Z., Ozturk, E. & Ersoy, M. O. (2009) Effects of propofol or etomidate on QT interval during electroconvulsive therapy. *J ECT*, **25**, 174–7.

Fleisher, L. A., Fleischmann, K. E. *et al.* (2014) ACC/AHA Guideline on Perioperative Cardiovascular Evaluation and Management of Patients Undergoing Noncardiac Surgery Circulation. *Journal of the American College of Cardiology*, **130**, e278–e333.

Franklin, A. D., Sobey, J. H. & Stickles, E. T. (2017) Anesthetic considerations for pediatric electroconvulsive therapy. *Pediatric Anesthesia*, **27**, 471–9.

Galvez, V, McGuirk, L. & Loo, C. K. (2017) The use of ketamine in ECT anaesthesia: a systematic review and critical commentary on efficacy, cognitive, safety and seizure outcomes. *World J Biol Psychiatry*, **18**, 424–44.

Haas, D. A. & Harper, D. G. (1992) Ketamine: a review of its pharmacologic properties and use in ambulatory anesthesia. *Anesthesia Progress*, **39**, 61–8.

Hodgson, R. E., Dawson, P., Hold, A. R. *et al.* (2004) Anaesthesia for electroconvulsive therapy: a comparison of sevoflurane with propofol. *Anaesth Intensive Care*, **32**, 241–5.

Hooten, W. M. & Rasmussen Jr, K. G. (2008) Effects of general anesthetic agents in adults receiving electroconvulsive therapy: a systematic review. *Journal of ECT*, **24**, 208–23.

Hossain, A. & Sullivan, P. (2008) The effects of age and sex on electroconvulsive therapy using remifentanil as the sole anesthetic agent. *Journal of ECT*, **24**, 232–5.

Ingram, A., Schweitzer, I., Ng, C. H., Saling, M. M. & Savage, G. (2007) A comparison of propofol and thiopentone use in electroconvulsive therapy: cognitive and efficacy effects. *J ECT*, **23**, 158–62.

Kadoi, Y., Saito, S., Ide, M. *et al.* (2003). The comparative effects of propofol versus thiopentone on left ventricular function during electroconvulsive therapy. *Anaesth Intensive Care*, **31**, 172–5.

Kadoi, Y. & Saito, S. (2014) Optimal dose of landiolol for preventing abrupt changes in both cardiac output and middle cerebral artery flow velocity after electroconvulsive therapy. *Journal of ECT*, **30**, 224–6.

Kumar, A., Sharma, D. K. & Mani, R. (2012) A comparison of propofol and thiopentone for electroconvulsive therapy. *J Anaesthesiol Clin Pharmacol*, **28**, 353–7.

McGirr, A., Berlim, M. T., Bond, D. J. *et al.* (2017) Adjunctive ketamine in electroconvulsive therapy: updated systematic review and meta-analysis. *Br J Psychiat*, **210**, 403–7.

Mirzakhani, H., Welch, C. A., Eikermann, M. *et al.* (2012) Neuromuscular blocking agents for ECT: a systematic review. *Acta Anaesthesiologica Scandinavica*, **56**, 3–16.

Mirzakhani, H., Guchelaar, H.J., Welch, C. A. *et al.* (2016) Minimum effective doses of succinylcholine and rocuronium during ECT: a prospective, randomized, crossover trial. *Anesthesia and Analgesia*, **123**, 587–96.

Mizen, L., Morton, C. & Scott, A. (2015) The cardiovascular safety of the empirical measurement of the seizure threshold in electroconvulsive therapy. *BJPsych Bulletin*, **39**, 14–18.

Mokriski, B. K., Nagle, S. E., Papuchis, G. C., Cohen, S. M. & Waxman, G. J. (1992)

Electroconvulsive therapy-induced cardiac arrhythmias during anesthesia with methohexital, thiamylal, or thiopental sodium. *J Clin Anesth*, **4**, 208–12.

Nasseri, K., Arasteh, M. T., Maroufi, A. et al. (2009) Effects of remifentanil on convulsion duration and hemodynamic responses during electroconvulsive therapy: a double-blind, randomized clinical trial. *Journal of ECT*, **25**, 170–3.

Patel, A. S., Gorst-Unsworth, C., Venn, R. M. et al. (2006) Anesthesia and electroconvulsive therapy: a retrospective study comparing etomidate and propofol. *Journal of ECT*, **22**, 179–83.

Peng, L., Min, S., Wei, K. et al. (2014) Different regimens of intravenous sedatives or hypnotics for electroconvulsive therapy (ECT) in adult patients with depression. Cochrane Database of Systematic Reviews 2014, Issue 4. Art. No.: CD009763. DOI: 10.1002/14651858.CD009763.pub2.

Pullen, S. J., Rasmussen K. G., Angstman, E. R. et al. (2011) The safety of electroconvulsive therapy in patients with prolonged QTc intervals on the electrocardiogram. *Journal of ECT*, **27**, 192–200.

Rasmussen, P., Andersson, J. E., Koch, P., Secher, N. H. & Quistorff, B. (2007) Glycopyrrolate prevents extreme bradycardia and cerebral deoxygenation during electroconvulsive therapy. *J ECT*, **23**, 147–52.

Rasmussen, K. (2014) Propofol for ECT anaesthesia: a review of the literature. *Journal of ECT*, **30**, 210–15.

Royal College of Anaesthetists (2010) CCT in anaesthetics: Annex D: Higher level training. Royal College of Anaesthetists. https://www.rcoa.ac.uk/CCT/AnnexD

Royal College of Anaesthetists (2016) Guidelines for the provision of anaesthetic services (GPAS). Royal College of Anaesthetists.

Sajedi, P. I., Mitchell, J., Herskovits, E. H. & Raghavan, P. (2016) Routine cross-sectional head imaging before electroconvulsive therapy: a tertiary center experience. *Journal of the American College of Radiology*, **13**, 429–34.

Sharp, R. P. & Welch, E. B. (2011) Takotsubo cardiomyopathy as a complication of ECT. *Annals of Pharmacotherapy*, **45**, 1559–65.

Simpson, K. H. & Lynch, L. (1998) Anaesthesia and electroconvulsive therapy (ECT). *Anaesthesia*, **53**, 615–17.

Singh, P. M., Arora, S., Borle, A., Varma, P., Trikha, A. & Goudra, B. G. (2015) Evaluation of etomidate for seizure duration in electroconvulsive therapy: a systematic review and meta-analysis. *J ECT*, **31**, 213–25.

Strayer, R. J. & Nelson, L. S. (2008) Adverse events associated with ketamine for procedural sedation in adults. *Am J Emerg Med*, **26**, 985–1028.

Sullivan, P. M., Sinz, E. H., Gunel, E. et al. (2004) A retrospective comparison of remifentanil versus methohexital for anesthesia in electroconvulsive therapy. *Journal of ECT*, **20**, 219–24.

Sundsted, K., Burton, M. C., Dhah, R. et al. (2014) Preanesthesia medical evaluation for electroconvulsive therapy: a review of the literature. *Journal of ECT*, **30**, 35–42.

Swaim, J. C., Mansour, M., Wydo, S. M. & Moore, J. L. (2006) A retrospective comparison of anesthetic agents in electroconvulsive therapy. *J ECT*, **22**, 243–6.

Tess, A. V. & Smetana, G. W. (2009) Medical evaluation of patients undergoing electroconvulsive therapy. *New England Journal of Medicine*, **360**, 1437–44.

Toprak, H. I., Gedik, E., Begec, Z., Ozturk, E., Kaya, B. & Ersoy, M. O. (2005) Sevoflurane as an alternative anaesthetic for electroconvulsive therapy. *J ECT*, **21**,108–10.

Tzabazis, A., Schmitt, H. J., Ihmsen, H. et al. (2013) Postictal agitation after ECT: incidence, severity and propofol as a treatment option. *Journal of ECT*, **29**, 189–95.

van den Broek, W. W., Groenland, T. H., Kusuma, A. et al. (2004) Double-blind placebo controlled study of the effects of etomidate-alfentanil anesthesia in electroconvulsive therapy. *Journal of ECT*, **20**, 107–11.

Wang, N., Wang, X. H., Lu, J. & Zhang, J. Y. (2011). The effect of repeated etomidate anesthesia on adrenocortical function during a course of electroconvulsive therapy. *Journal of ECT*, **27**, 281–5.

Weinger, M. B., Partridge, B. L., Hauger, R. *et al.* (1991) Prevention of the cardiovascular and neuroendocrine response to electroconvulsive therapy: I. Effectiveness of pre-treatment regimens on hemodynamics. *Anesthesia and Analgesia*, **73**, 556–62.

Yamaguchi, S., Nagao, M., Ikeda, T. *et al.* (2011) QT Dispersion and Rate-Corrected QT Dispersion during electroconvulsive therapy in elderly patients. *J ECT*, **27**, 183–8.

Chapter 24

Dental Issues Related to ECT

Denis Martin, revised by Basel Switzer

This chapter is designed to raise awareness of the risks of damage to dental tissue during ECT, with the possible consequences to the patient, ECT team, psychiatrists and anaesthetists, and to place dental risk into context. Although the first section of the chapter is more applicable to psychiatrists and the second section to anaesthetists, the issue of dental risk bridges both specialties. The entire chapter should be read by all staff involved with the delivery of ECT.

Dental Issues for Psychiatrists

There is a general view among psychiatrists that any dental or jaw problems associated with ECT should be managed by the anaesthetist at the time of the treatment. It is expected that the anaesthetist, during their pre-anaesthetic assessment, will identify any dental risks and work towards their safe management. This risk, however, should be seen as a shared risk.

Research from the USA (Watts *et al.*, 2011) indicates that oral (dental and tongue) injuries are the most common complication of ECT. Patients seem to accept this risk identification and management process as being part of the anaesthetist's domain and do not see it as being related to the ECT itself. The risk of dental injury (excluding soft tissue injury) is about 1–2% (Beli & Bentham, 1998) and suggests that this process has worked well. Information from the Medical Defence Union indicates that litigation following dental injury or damage is rare and this is mirrored in American psychiatry (Slawson, 1989). However, recent developments including legal issues of risk management and consent, patient attitude to dental health and technological advances in dentistry make an appraisal of dental risk management within ECT appropriate.

Although the management of dental risks during the ECT session is likely to remain with the anaesthetist, the overall management of risks from ECT are the psychiatrist's responsibility. Injury to the teeth during ECT is a well-established risk (Beli & Bentham, 1998) and therefore needs to be considered in the process of obtaining consent. See Chapter 28 for details on consenting and risk factors in ECT.

Risks to jaws, the temporo-mandibular joint (TMJ) and teeth during ECT are the direct result of the ECT and not the anaesthetic. Electroconvulsive therapy can cause dental damage by two means.

1. Bitemporal electrode placement leads to direct stimulation of the muscles of mastication during treatment. Temporalis, being beneath the electrode, is totally stimulated.

   The lateral spread of the stimulus current causes depolarisation of the masseter muscle and also the muscles of expression, which accounts for the observed grimacing of the patient. The medial pterygoids are too deep to be affected. Direct stimulation bypasses neuromuscular blockade (see Chapter 23) – as a result, the jaw muscles are stimulated to 60–75% of their maximal contractive force during the stimulus current phase.

2. Pressures on the teeth are usually limited by conscious control due to neural feedback from the periodontium, preventing excessive occlusal force. As the patient is unconscious during ECT, and stimulus is directly to the muscles of mastication, such feedback does not exist and may result in damage. The potential for damage to the teeth and jaw is greatest during the passage of the stimulus current. Once the stimulus current has finished, during the stage of the modified convulsion, all impulses to the jaw muscles from the brain via the motor branch of the trigeminal nerve are blocked by the muscle relaxant.

The primary function of the anaesthetist is to manage the anaesthetic and safeguard the patient's airway. The anaesthetist also has a role in managing neuromuscular blockade to minimise the risks due to forceful striated muscle contraction throughout the body, including protecting the teeth.

Psychiatrists need to be aware of potential dental injuries occurring during electrical stimulation. Recent technological advances, especially dental implants and modern ceramics, have allowed the development of complex restorations with excellent aesthetics. It is now possible for implants to be placed in the upper posterior jaw region by the ablation of the maxillary sinus, and in both jaws it is possible to support artificial teeth on intraosseous implants.

There may now be candidates for ECT who have a high dental awareness and possess complex dental restoration work. Any damage to these dental structures occurring during ECT will therefore, almost certainly, constitute a 'serious injury' for that individual patient, with the potential for a claim for compensation or other legal redress. This could become a significant potential risk area for ECT. It is therefore necessary to identify patients with complex dentistry in advance, in order to establish valid consent and manage the identified dental risks appropriately.

There is considerable overlap in the management of these patients and those in the 'at risk group' identified by Beli & Bentham (1998). Here, the risks were as a direct result of dental negligence, where decayed teeth and periodontal disease dominated the clinical picture. The expectation is therefore that all patients presenting for ECT with identified dental risks should be managed prospectively.

When compared to the general adult population, patients with severe mental illness have poorer oral health (Patel & Gamboa, 2012) and greater treatment needs (Kisely et al., 2011), reflected in both inpatients and outpatient settings (Patel & Gamboa, 2012; Velasco-Ortega, 2013). There is an increase in contributing factors to dental disease in psychiatric patients. Contributing factors include hyposalivation, increased sugar intake, neglect of oral hygiene, dental phobia, and limitations in ability to pay for treatment (Steifel, 1990).

The following is a risk management strategy adapted and evolved from the suggestions of Beli & Bentham (1998) and Morris (2002).

The proposed strategy is in four stages: the risks, risk awareness, risk identification and risk management.

The Risks

Electroconvulsive therapy exposes the dental tissue to the risk of damage. This includes the soft tissue as well as the teeth and dental restorations. Soft tissue trauma occurs in about

25% of cases, damage to hard tissues in 1% to 2% (Beli & Bentham, 1998). Consideration must also be given to the risk of claims for negligence and compensation. If the consent process did not address the possibility of dental damage, then that consent may be invalid.

Risk Awareness

This section provides specialist information to professionals involved with the consent process and pre-ECT assessment, to raise awareness of the existence of dental risk from ECT. Dental risk can be seen as the product of the ECT process and the dental status of the individual patient. Psychiatric patients commonly have poor dental health (Stevens *et al.*, 2010; Patel & Gamboa, 2012; Kisely *et al.*, 2011; Velasco-Ortega, 2013).

The presence of the following is related to an increase in the risk of dental damage for an individual patient:

- crowns, bridges, implants or veneers
- periodontal disease and gum recession
- heavily filled or root-filled teeth
- gaps where teeth have been lost, the presence of dentures
- loose teeth
- teeth that are painful or on which the patient is afraid to bite for fear of damage
- jaw or temporomandibular joint disease or previous jaw surgery.

Risk Identification

The assessment process should consist of a dental history taken to identify the risk factors mentioned earlier. This may need to be supplemented by information from the patient's dental surgeon or relatives. An examination of the mouth and teeth must be performed to verify the presence of any risk factors. Dentures should be checked for evidence of intraosseous fixation devices, and jaw opening and closing assessed.

The examination should be carried out by dentally experienced personnel (Morris, 2002), preferably a dentist with experience of ECT. The possibility of this role being carried out by suitably trained ECT staff should be considered.

Risk Management

For consent to be valid, all risks that may produce a significant event to the patient must be considered (see Chapter 28). It is necessary to balance the risk of dental damage against the need for ECT. The following points should be taken into account:

- Identified risks should be discussed with the patient by the consenting psychiatrist.
- Renegotiation of consent, including the identified dental risks, may be necessary in order to establish 'valid consent'.
- Liaison with the anaesthetist is essential; use of appropriate techniques by the anaesthetist at the time of treatment can minimise risk.
- Specialist dental referral may be needed for advice or the provision of specially constructed bite guards (Muzyka *et al.*, 2017). It may be appropriate to postpone ECT until this is completed.
- Prescribing unilateral ECT reduces jaw pressures by 50%, as the jaw muscles on only one side are stimulated.

- Patients who will not comply with or consent to an oral examination because they lack capacity should be managed within the framework of mental health and mental capacity legislation; legal advice may be needed. Appropriate documentation and records are essential.
- A post-treatment review of the patient's dental status, with appropriate documentation, should be performed.

Dental Issues for Anaesthetists

During the stimulus current phase of ECT, teeth with large restorations or crowns are at risk of fracture, and teeth with bridges and implants are vulnerable to being dislodged or displaced. This is due to considerable axial or non-axial forces acting on the teeth. Practical management is directed at reducing these axial or non-axial forces to safe levels. As all patients differ dentally, it is difficult to be specific in offering advice on management.

The following points are general points to consider:

- Has a dental examination been completed?
- Have any risks been identified?
- Has the consent process of the psychiatrist drawn attention to dental risks?
- Are you able to minimise the identified risks by use of a bite guard and its judicious placement in the mouth to enable evenly distributed occlusal load (Muzyka *et al.*, 2017)?
- Consider obtaining specialist advice (patient's dental surgeon or oral surgery department) and the provision of individually-made bite guards.
- Consider suggesting withholding treatment if further assessment or advice is needed.
- Consider requesting unilateral ECT – this will reduce the possible jaw pressures by 50%.
- Initiate a post-treatment dental review.

Brief Review of Specific Dental Restorations and Associated Risks

Veneers

Avoid 'point loading' on the incisal edges or contact with metal objects to minimise the risk of fracture.

Crowns

Unless a tooth has been crowned for purely cosmetic reasons, consider that beneath the crown is likely to be a heavily restored tooth, which may have been root-filled. Such root filled teeth may be brittle and more liable to fracture. There may be apical pathology, so the root may be relatively unsupported. Teeth restored by the 'post crown' procedure (where a post engages into the previously root filled root canal) are at increased risk of damage.

Bridges

These are designed to replace a lost tooth with a non-removable prosthesis. If supporting teeth are sound, there should be little increased risk with ECT. A problem exists if the supporting teeth become weakened, perhaps due to periodontal disease or decay. When the patient is conscious, the pressure applied to the bridge can be consciously limited to safe levels. During ECT, excessive pressure on the bridge may move the weakened tooth and apply damaging torsional forces to the other support tooth. It would be prudent to test all bridge 'support teeth' independently prior to ECT and off-load the bridge if concern exists.

Anterior bridges are at considerable risk if loaded during ECT, especially if the bite guard becomes pushed up behind the front teeth. The risk increases if the teeth on the bridge follow the curve of the dental arch.

Implants

Implants fill gaps in the dental arches with non-removable teeth and obviate the need for dentures. Crowns are supported on titanium implants that are inserted into alveolar bone and in time become osteointegrated into it. These implants have no periodontal membrane and therefore lack the ability to move slightly under pressure. This, together with the fact that the implant is usually much smaller than the natural root, means that they are more likely to be dislodged during ECT. They should not be loaded if at all possible.

Intraosseous Denture Supports

It is now possible to fix screws, bars or bolts into the alveolar bone or facial skeleton on which dentures can be located. The decision to be made is whether to remove the denture or give ECT with it kept in the mouth. Specialist advice should be sought on this point.

Clinical Situations that Require Different Management Strategies

The Fully Dentate Patient

Choose the thinnest bite guard possible to avoid excessive pressure on the back teeth. If the overbite (vertical overlap) or overjet (horizontal overlap) is large, do not allow the bite guard to be forced up behind the upper anterior teeth by the lower anterior teeth. This could displace the upper teeth forwards, especially in the elderly patient or in the presence of gum disease.

The Mouth with Complex Restorations

The presence of crowns, bridges and implants can cause management problems, as they may not be capable of withstanding the forces applied to the teeth during the stimulus current phase. Implants are supported by about 50% or less of the root size of the natural tooth that it replaces and must be considered to be at risk during ECT. In general, it is best to 'off-load' any of the above by the judicious placement of the bite guard.

If it is not possible to avoid such teeth, then their ability to withstand pressure could be assessed by a 'dry-run', with the teeth being loaded by jaw pressure in the patient during the pre-ECT assessment stage. It must be remembered that this is not equivalent to the loading during ECT.

Implants that are most vulnerable to axial overloading forces are posterior teeth implants, especially those in the upper jaw where they may be sited over an ablated maxillary antrum. Anterior teeth implants are vulnerable to lateral (anterior) forces and could be dislodged by the bite guard during the stimulus current phase. Consider requesting unilateral ECT and off-loading such teeth.

The Edentulous Patient

Do not allow the jaw to overclose beyond centric during treatment to avoid gum, muscle or joint damage. The articulating disc can be damaged if the joint is put under pressure in the overclosed position. Use packs or consider using the dentures to maintain the jaw in the correct position during treatment. Upper acrylic dentures may be vulnerable to midline fractures if pressure is applied to both sides of the jaws. Consider limiting the pressure to one side by using a small prop on one side only. Consider requesting the use of unilateral ECT to reduce jaw pressure.

The Partially Dentate Patient

This is the situation where one or both jaws have had teeth extracted. The resultant gaps may or may not be filled by dentures. The main issue is that solitary standing teeth are at risk of being exposed to excessive forces. It may be appropriate to consider using the dentures to support the teeth and spread the load. However, acrylic dentures may fracture, but metal-based dentures should not. An option is to request that a specially designed bite guard is constructed to spread the load on to the alveolar ridges as well as support these solitary teeth. Solitary teeth that cannot be supported should not be loaded at all.

Key Points

- Dental injuries are a common complication of ECT.
- Dental injuries are a direct result of contraction of the muscles during ECT.
- Psychiatric patients often have poor dental health.
- Modern techniques of dental restoration are costly and the resulting structures are vulnerable to damage.
- The consent process must address issues of dental risk.

References

Beli, N. & Bentham, B. (1998) Nature and extent of dental pathology and complications arising in patients receiving ECT. *Psychiatric Bulletin*, **22**, 562–5.

Kisely, S., Quek, L.-H., Pais, J., *et al.* (2011) Advanced dental disease in people with severe mental illness: systematic review and meta-analysis. *Br J Psychiat*, **199**, 187–93.

Morris, A. (2002) A dental risk management protocol for electroconvulsive therapy. *Journal of ECT*, **18**, 84–9.

Muzyka, B. C., Glass, D. & Glass, O. (2017) Oral health in electroconvulsive therapy: a neglected topic. *Journal of ECT*, **33**, 12–15.

Patel, R. & Gamboa, A. (2012) Prevalence of oral diseases and oral-health-related quality of life in people with severe mental illness undertaking community-based psychiatric care. *Br Dent Journal*, **213**, E16.

Slawson, P. (1989) Psychiatric malpractice and ECT: a review of national loss experience. *Convulsive Therapy*, **5**, 126–30.

Stevens, T., Spoors, J., Hale, R., *et al.* (2010) Perceived oral health needs in psychiatric in-patients: impact of a dedicated dental clinic. *The Psychiatrist*, **34**, 518–21.

Stiefel, D. J., Truelove. E. L., Menard, T. W., *et al.* (1990) A comparison of the oral health of persons with and without chronic mental illness in community settings. *Spec Care Dentist*, **10**, 6–12.

Velasco-Ortega, E., Segura-Egea, J. J., Córdoba-Arenas, S., *et al.* (2013) A comparison of the dental status and treatment needs of older adults with and without chronic mental illness in Sevilla, Spain. *Med Oral Patol Oral Cir Bucal*, **18**, e71–e75.

Watts, B. V., Groft, A., Bagian, J. P., *et al.* (2011) An examination of mortality and other adverse events related to electroconvulsive therapy using a national adverse event report system. *Journal of ECT*, **27**, 105–8.

Chapter 25

Interactions between ECT and Prescribed Medication

Ian M Anderson

Introduction

It is common, indeed usual in many countries including the UK, for patients receiving electroconvulsive therapy (ECT) to continue taking medication for their psychiatric disorder, and in many cases they are also being treated for one or more physical illnesses. This chapter reviews the evidence for interactions between concomitantly taken drugs and ECT, concentrating on safety issues and their management, but also commenting on therapeutic interactions where relevant. Outside the scope of this chapter are drugs specifically given as part of ECT, or administered during the session to modify seizures, reduce the likelihood of adverse effects or affect clinical outcomes.

Methods and General Considerations

A review of the literature up to end May 2017 was carried out in PubMed using the keywords (medication(s) or drug(s)) and (interaction(s) or safety or drug-interaction(s)) and (ECT or electroconvulsive), supplemented by reference lists and review articles (Dixon & Santiago, 2013; Dolenc & Rasmussen, 2005; Merk & Kucia, 2015; Naguib & Koorn, 2002; Zolezzi, 2016). Only relevant case reports are cited.

Work up for ECT includes a careful review of medication and consideration of its potential interactions with ECT, and the procedures involved in the administration of ECT. This includes taking into account the need for patients to fast before ECT and taking decisions about the timing of regular medications that would usually be given in the period before ECT. It is important to discuss any concerns with the anaesthetic team before ECT so that anaesthetic procedures and/or medication can be adjusted as necessary. Communication about any medication to be given or withheld immediately before ECT with those responsible for its administration (i.e. the ward team, patient and/or carer) needs to be clear. The anaesthetic and ECT teams should have, and review, the complete list of medication that the patient is taking before each ECT session, not forgetting to ask about herbal or complementary medicines.

Important aspects to consider in regard to interactions between ECT and regular medication are:

- the drugs used as part of ECT anaesthesia
- seizure threshold and termination
- neurochemical effects of ECT including enhancement of serotonergic 5-hydroxytryptamine (5-HT) and dopamine (DA) function (Anderson & Fergusson, 2013), and
- cardiovascular (CV) risk.

In terms of potential CV risk, greater variation in the QT interval (QT dispersion or QTD), which has been reported immediately following the ECT stimulus in the elderly (Yamaguchi et al., 2011), has been associated with an increased risk of cardiac arrhythmias. In addition, even though the ECT stimulus leads to a decrease in the rate-corrected QT interval (QTc) (Yamaguchi et al., 2011), prolonged QTc intervals are not uncommon amongst patients receiving ECT (Pullen et al., 2011) increasing their underlying CV risk. A retrospective study found that ECT is generally safe in patients with a prolonged QTc interval, but that the risk of cardiac-related events is slightly increased, although they are still rare (Pullen et al., 2011).

The evidence regarding drug/ECT interactions is patchy; for many drugs the only evidence derives from theoretical considerations or from case reports/case series. Included patients have often been treated with multiple drugs, which further hinders interpretation of the available evidence. ECT's long history means that there is considerable practical experience in its combination with medication and drug-related problems are uncommon. Although this suggests that combining ECT with standard treatments is usually safe, it also means that there can be complacency, a lack of knowledge about potential interactions and the danger that they may be overlooked. In particular there should always be a caution when ECT is given to patients on multiple medications as interactions can be difficult to predict.

Anaesthetics and Related Medication

Commonly used drugs during anaesthesia for ECT include the induction agents propofol, methohexital, thiopental, etomidate (occasionally ketamine), the depolarising neuromuscular blocker suxamethonium, and anticholinergic agents (atropine or glycopyrrolate) for bradycardia. In addition, opioids such as remifentanil may be considered to prolong seizures and to reduce haemodynamic response. For a fuller description of drugs used in the anaesthesia of ECT see Chapter 23.

Drugs used during ECT are very short-acting, and significant interactions with prescribed medication are rare; they can be difficult to distinguish from the occasional adverse effects associated with these drugs themselves and ECT itself. Sedative drugs may enhance the effect of induction agents, and neuromuscular blockade by suxamethonium may be prolonged by antimicrobials, magnesium, calcium channel blockers and drugs that decrease the activity of plasma (butyryl)cholinesterases; in contrast, resistance to the effect of suxamethonium may be seen with some anticonvulsants such as carbamazepine and phenytoin (Cammu, 2001). Use of anticholinergic drugs requires caution in patients on psychotropic drugs with significant anticholinergic actions (e.g. some tricyclic antidepressants, TCAs) and some opioid drugs can interact with monoamine oxidase inhibitors (MAOIs) leading to excitation, confusion or respiratory depression (Dolenc et al., 2004; Gillman, 2005).

Psychotropic Medication

Explanation of the types of evidence available, and their limitations, are described in Table 25.1. The evidence is summarised in Table 25.2 and discussed below.

Table 25.1 Strengths and limitations of types of evidence used in current chapter to assess drug interactions with ECT

Type of evidence	Description	Main strengths	Main limitations
Randomised-controlled trial (RCT)	Prospective, randomised comparison between treatment of interest and comparator/s, ideally including placebo or no-treatment.	Randomisation avoids selection bias and allows causal inference.	Practicalities often limit size and power to detect differences between groups or uncommon events. Other types of bias can still occur.
Non-randomised studies	Prospective but non-randomised comparison between treatment of interest and comparator/s, ideally including placebo or no-treatment.	Allows comparison between treatments in situations where randomisation is difficult or not feasible.	Patient selection bias inevitable and limits causal inference. Limited control of confounds. Other limitations as for RCTs.
Prospective	Prospective assessment of effect of treatment of interest, but without a comparator.	Allows detailed description of effects occurring with a treatment, their incidence, and potentially predictors.	Lack of comparator means that effects cannot be confidently ascribed to treatment (rather than to ECT, chance or other factor). Other limitations as for RCTs.
Retrospective	Retrospective comparison between treatment of interest and comparator/s in a defined group of patients who received ECT.	Allows use of clinical data, large data-sets are possible, useful for hypothesis generation. May detect relatively rare events.	Patient selection bias inevitable and limits causal inference. No control for confounds. Outcomes determined by availability/quality of clinical records. Reporting bias.
Case series/case report	Effects of treatment of interest in one or more selected patients.	Can identify rare events. Within-subject comparison on and off treatment of interest is possible.	Effects cannot be confidently ascribed to treatment rather than to ECT or other confounds. Lack of denominator means frequency of effect unknown. Selection and reporting bias.

Table 25.2 Evidence for psychotropic drug interactions with ECT by drug class

Class	Potential interactions Effect of drug (potential consequence)	Evidence	Comment
Antidepressants			
Tricyclic antidepressants (TCA)[1,2]	ACh antagonism (cognition), membrane effects, ion channels and NA (CV safety), 5-HT (serotonin syndrome).	*RCTs*: no effect on SD, AE; better efficacy and reduced cognitive impairment in one study (nortriptyline). *Non-RCT/retrospective*: no effect on SD, AE (fewer transient CV AE in one); unchanged *or* improved efficacy.	Combination appears safe, and with potential clinical benefit. Caution: evidence for most individual TCAs is lacking.
Selective serotonin reuptake inhibitors (SSRI)[1,3]	Seizure threshold (prolonged seizures), 5-HT (serotonin syndrome).	*RCT (cross over)*: single dose citalopram no effect on SD. *Non-RCT/retrospective*: increase in SD in most, no effect on AE; improved efficacy one study. *Case reports*: SD normal (fluoxetine, escitalopram) *or* prolonged SD (fluoxetine); spontaneous seizure (paroxetine); serotonin syndrome (fluoxetine, paroxetine).	Most evidence with fluoxetine and paroxetine, sparse/lacking for other SSRIs. Probable prolongation of SD but clinical importance unclear; caution with paroxetine, vigilance for serotonin syndrome.
Serotonin and noradrenaline reuptake inhibitors (SNRI)[1,4]	Seizure threshold (prolonged seizures), NA (CV safety), 5-HT (serotonin syndrome).	*RCT*: venlafaxine (max 257mg/d, mean 187mg/d) – no effect on SD, AE; possible better efficacy (not	Signal for potentially serious cardiovascular AEs with venlafaxine

Table 25.2 (cont.)

Class	Potential interactions Effect of drug (potential consequence)	Evidence	Comment
		statistically significant, no effect on cognitive impairment. *Non-RCT*: venlafaxine 150mg/d vs TCA – no difference on SD, CV AEs. *Retrospective*: venlafaxine (mean 225mg/d, 32%>300mg/d) – increased cognitive and CV AE. *Case series/reports*: venlafaxine – asystole (≥300mg/d), prolonged bradycardia/HT, unstable BP; duloxetine – no AEs *or* ventricular tachycardia in combination with lithium.	particularly at high doses (≥300mg/ d). Lack of evidence for other SNRIs.
Monoamine oxidase inhibitors (MAOI)[5]	NA (CV safety), 5-HT (serotonin syndrome).	*RCTs*: no effect on AE; unchanged *or* improved efficacy *Non-RCTs*: no effect on AE, CV indices. *Case reports*: prolonged ventilation needed in early reports; no effect on SD, AE, CV parameters *or* asystole followed by bradycardia in later reports.	Combination appears safe as long as drugs known to interact with MAOIs are avoided (including opioids, indirectly acting sympathomimetics).
Other antidepressants[1,6]	Seizure threshold (prolonged seizures), NA (CV safety), 5-HT (serotonin syndrome).	*Retrospective*: mirtazapine/mianserin – no effect on SD, increased transient CV AE; increased efficacy. *Case series/reports*: mirtazapine – no AE; effective for post-ECT headache: bupropion – no AE *or* prolonged seizure *or* focal status epilepticus: trazodone – ventricular arrhythmia, prolonged SD: nefazodone – no AE.	Intrinsic seizure risk and limited evidence and suggests caution with bupropion.

Antipsychotics[7]	Seizure threshold (prolonged seizures, especially clozapine), ACh antagonism (cognition), QTc effects (CV safety).	*Prospective:* no unexpected AE (including clozapine); seizure parameters not predicted by antipsychotic dose. *Retrospective:* no effect on SD *or* longer SD with low potency typical antipsychotics, no AE, no effect on QTc. *Case reports:* olanzapine, quetiapine + duloxetine – no AE.	Studies mostly investigating ECT addition in resistant schizophrenia with poor quality of AE reporting. Combination, including with clozapine, appears safe and no significant increased QTc-related risk reported.
Lithium[8]	Cognitive effects (delirium), Ach/cholinesterase (prevent suxamethonium breakdown, prolonged apnoea), 5-HT (serotonin syndrome), lithium levels (toxicity).	*RCT:* no safety concerns reported (but AE not specifically reported). *Non-RCT:* no effect on SD, apnoea, AE, lithium levels; attenuated CV response to ECT. *Retrospective:* no effect on SD, AE *or* greater post-ECT confusion. *Case series/reports:* no effect on SD, AE *or* prolonged recovery time, confusion, prolonged or spontaneous seizures, serotonin syndrome.	Lithium can usually be safely given with ECT but probable signal for increased confusion/'organic' brain syndrome/serotonin syndrome in susceptible individuals.
Anticonvulsants[9]	Seizure threshold (failed/decreased seizure), increase in suxamethonium effect (prolonged apnoea).	*RCT:* CBZ/valproate full dose vs half dose vs no drug for mania – no difference SD, ST, efficacy, cognition, suxamethonium dose. No reporting of AE. *Non-RCT:* valproate – shorter SD and lower propofol dose. *Retrospective:* lamotrigine – no effect on SD, stimulus dose; valproate, CBZ –	Lack of good evidence that regular anticonvulsants prevent therapeutic ECT seizures, but CBZ/valproate may decrease SD or inhibit seizures in some patients.

Table 25.2 (cont.)

Class	Potential interactions Effect of drug (potential consequence)	Evidence	Comment
		increased ST, decreased SD, more ECT treatments needed for clinical improvement. *Case series/reports:* CBZ/valproate – no effect on SD **or** higher doses inhibited seizures requiring lowered dose or induction agent change. lamotrigine – no effect on SD: gabapentin – no inhibition of seizure.	
Anxiolytics/hypnotics[10]	Sedation (depth of anaesthesia, recovery time) Seizure threshold/termination (failed/decreased seizure).	*RCT:* midazolam vs methohexitone for induction – no effect on SD, efficacy. *Non-RCT:* midazolam vs thiopental for induction – shorter SD with midazolam. *Prospective:* SD predicted **or** not predicted by BDZ dose, no effect on ST *Retrospective:* BDZ – no effect on SD **or** decreased SD, more ECT treatments/poorer efficacy with unilateral (UL) but not bilateral (BL) ECT: non-BDZ hypnotics – no effect on SD, clinical efficacy. *Case series/reports:* BDZ – reduced SD **or** no effect on SD compared to not taking BDZ.	Mixed evidence that BDZ may reduce SD. Mixed evidence about impairment of clinical efficacy.

Acetylcholinesterase inhibitors[11]

Prevention of suxamethonium breakdown (prolonged paralysis, apnoea).	*RCTs:* physostigmine, donepezil, rivastigmine, galantamine – no effect on SD, anaesthetic drug dose, AE; lower stimulus dose in galantamine study; all showed short-term cognitive benefit. *Non-RCT:* galantamine – no effect on AE; cognitive benefit; no effect on efficacy. *Case reports:* donepezil, rivastigmine – no apnoea, paralysis; cognitive benefit **or** no benefit.	Controlled studies assessing cognitive benefit in patients without dementia. Combination appears safe without effects on seizure parameters. Cognitive benefit demonstrated but only assessed short-term.

5-HT – serotonin; Ach – acetylcholine; AE – adverse effect(s); BDZ – Benzodiazepine; CBZ – carbamazepine; CV – cardiovascular; d – day; ECT – electroconvulsive therapy; MAOI – monoamine oxidase inhibitor(s); NA – noradrenaline; Non-RCT – non-randomised controlled trial; QTc – rate corrected QT interval; RCT – randomised controlled trial; SD – seizure duration; SNRI – serotonin and noradrenaline reuptake inhibitor(s); SSRI – selective serotonin reuptake inhibitor(s); ST – seizure threshold; TCA – tricyclic antidepressant(s).

Note: conflicting results in different studies indicated by **or**, for example cognitive benefit **or** no benefit.

1 Baghai *et al.*, 2006; Sackeim *et al.*, 2009; Serfaty *et al.*, 1996
2 Mayur *et al.*, 2000; Nelson & Benjamin, 1989
3 Caracci & Decina, 1991; Curran, 1995; Folkerts, 1995; Gutierrez-Esteinou & Pope, Jr., 1989; Klysner *et al.*, 2014; Masdrakis *et al.*, 2008; Okamoto *et al.*, 2012; Papakostas *et al.*, 2000
4 Agelink *et al.*, 1998; Bernardo *et al.*, 2000; Eraslan *et al.*, 2011; Gonzalez-Pinto *et al.*, 2002; Hanretta & Malek-Ahmadi, 2006; Heinz *et al.*, 2013; West & Hewitt, 1999
5 Dolenc *et al.*, 2004; el-Ganzouri *et al.*, 1985
6 Conca *et al.*, 1999; Dersch *et al.*, 2011; Figiel & Jarvis, 1990; Jarvis *et al.*, 1992; Kellner *et al.*, 1994; Li *et al.*, 2011
7 Braga & Petrides, 2005; Bundy *et al.*, 2010; Havaki-Kontaxaki *et al.*, 2006; Masdrakis *et al.*, 2010; Masdrakis *et al.*, 2011; Nothdurfter et al, 2006; Oulis *et al.*, 2011; Petrides *et al.*, 2015; Ravanic *et al.*, 2009; Serfaty *et al.*, 1996; Tang & Ungvari, 2002; Wang *et al.*, 2015
8 Deuschle *et al.*, 2017; Dolenc & Rasmussen, 2005; Sartorius *et al.*, 2005; Thirthalli *et al.*, 2011; Vlissides *et al.*, 1979; Volpe & Tavares, 2012
9 Hizli *et al.*, 2014; Rakesh *et al.*, 2017; Sienaert *et al.*, 2011; Sienaert & Peuskens, 2007; Virupaksha *et al.*, 2010
10 Auriacombe *et al.*, 1995; Boylan *et al.*, 2000; Bundy *et al.*, 2010; Galvez *et al.*, 2013; Jha & Stein, 1996; Krystal *et al.*, 1998; Loimer *et al.*, 1992; Nothdurfter *et al.*, 2006; Pettinati *et al.*, 1990; Serfaty *et al.*, 1996; Standish-Barry *et al.*, 1985
11 Bhat *et al.*, 2004; Henstra *et al.*, 2017; van Schaik *et al.*, 2015; Zink *et al.*, 2002

Antidepressants

The main theoretical concerns with antidepressants as a class are potential effects on seizure threshold and the cardiovascular system, together with class-specific effects.

Although there has been more evidence regarding the concurrent use of antidepressants than other psychotropics, the quality is uneven and limited with regard to individual drugs.

The oldest antidepressants, TCAs and monoamine oxidase inhibitors (MAOIs), appear to be safe in combination with ECT although with the latter there have been individual case reports of prolonged apnoea and CV effects; however their relationship to MAOI treatment is often unclear (Dolenc et al., 2004). Unless there is a compelling clinical reason to stop these drugs the usual UK practice of continuing treatment seems reasonable, as long as precautions to avoid known drug-drug interactions are taken. In fact there is intriguing, although not consistent, evidence that the combination of TCAs or MAOIs (and possibly other antidepressants) with ECT may even enhance therapeutic response (Baghai et al., 2006; Dolenc et al., 2004; Nelson & Benjamin, 1989; Sackeim et al., 2009).

Combination of selective serotonin reuptake inhibitors (SSRIs) and ECT appears safe for most patients, but they probably prolong seizure duration. The clinical magnitude and importance of this is unclear but there are rare reports of abnormally prolonged or spontaneous seizures; paroxetine appears most implicated but reporting biases may be responsible. There have been isolated reports of the serotonin syndrome with fluoxetine and paroxetine (Klysner et al., 2014; Okamoto et al., 2012) and it is prudent to have a low threshold for suspicion when using any SSRI with ECT.

Venlafaxine has been the most studied of the selective serotonin reuptake inhibitors (SNRIs), and while it appears safe at lower doses (mean doses below 200mg), there is a consistent signal for potentially serious CV adverse effects at doses of 300mg/day and above (see Table 25.2). Therefore, if venlafaxine is to be combined with ECT, lowering the daily dose to below 300mg, and possibly below 200mg, is indicated if possible. Although there is a lack of evidence for SNRIs being associated with the serotonin syndrome in combination with ECT, given their 5-HT reuptake inhibition and the case reports for SSRIs, it would seem wise to have a low threshold of suspicion for the serotonin syndrome in patients on SNRIs receiving ECT.

For other antidepressants the evidence is even more limited; case reports have implicated buproprion in increased risk of prolonged or spontaneous seizures, consistent with its known pro-convulsive risk, and prolonged seizures and CV problems have been reported with trazodone. Caution is therefore warranted with both of these drugs. Of interest, mirtazapine has been reported to relieve post-ECT headache and nausea in a case series (Li et al., 2011), presumed to be through 5-HT$_3$ receptor antagonism.

Antipsychotics

The main theoretic concerns with antipsychotics are effects on seizure threshold (especially for clozapine) and the potential for adverse cardiovascular adverse events related to QTc prolongation (see earlier in this chapter).

Although a considerable number of studies have been carried out investigating the use of ECT as an adjunctive treatment in patients on antipsychotic drugs (particularly treatment-resistant schizophrenia) (Braga & Petrides, 2005; Wang et al., 2015), good quality evidence comparing ECT alone with an antipsychotic-ECT combination is lacking (Table 25.2). From the available evidence there appears to be no appreciable signal suggesting significant interactions. A retrospective study did not identify important differences between antipsychotic classes although low potency antipsychotics may lengthen seizure duration, and atypicals shorten it (Nothdurfter *et al.*, 2006). Prospective studies of clozapine have not identified significant problems with ECT in spite of theoretical concerns about its effect on seizure threshold (Braga & Petrides, 2005; Havaki-Kontaxaki *et al.*, 2006). Some small studies have prospectively investigated the effect of ECT combined with antipsychotics on the QTc interval and found a lack of significant prolongation (Masdrakis *et al.*, 2010; Masdrakis *et al.*, 2011; Oulis *et al.*, 2011).

Lithium

Lithium has a complex effect on brain neurochemistry, a narrow therapeutic index, with central nervous system signs and symptoms occurring at an early stage of toxicity (Young & Wooderson, 2016). Concerns about, and case reports of, adverse interactions with ECT have been fairly frequent (Dolenc & Rasmussen, 2005) but largely not borne out by larger prospective and retrospective studies, and case series (Table 25.2). However it is difficult not to conclude that there is a signal for some patients to experience 'toxicity' with the combination given the reports of confusion, prolonged recovery time and seizures and serotonin syndrome.

Many patients on lithium can be give ECT without experiencing adverse reactions and the need for lithium treatment, including risks of stopping versus continuing it during the ECT course, should be carefully weighed up. Frequent monitoring of lithium levels is prudent; it is important to keep levels within the therapeutic range and maintain hydration as far as possible (e.g. by treating those on lithium early in the list). It is also necessary to monitor for signs of untoward reactions and lithium toxicity. Anecdotal concerns about lithium prolonging the effects of suxamethonium have been raised, and, although these appear less than previously suggested, it is prudent to consider careful dosing and titration of neuromuscular blockers used in initial ECT sessions.

Anticonvulsant Drugs

The obvious concern about anticonvulsant drugs is potential impact on seizure threshold and duration which could lead to inadequate or failed treatment. Carbamazepine has been reported to prolong the actions of suxamethonium, or conversely reduce the effect of nondepolarising neuromuscular blockers, but the clinical significance for ECT is unclear (Naguib & Koorn, 2002; Sienaert & Peuskens, 2007). A recent small RCT of ECT for mania randomised 48 patients on carbamazepine (CBZ) or valproate, to full dose, half dose and stopping anticonvulsants, and found no significant differences between treatment arms in seizure parameters, stimulus or ECT session drug doses, and clinical and cognitive outcomes (Rakesh *et al.*, 2017); mean seizure thresholds were highest, and durations lowest, in the full dose group but the differences were small. Of interest, a prospective study found that the most important factor determining ECT seizure adequacy was depth of anaesthesia (measured by electroencephalographic (EEG) bispectral index) and that thiopental dose and regular medication taken by the patient (including benzodiazepines which may be anticonvulsant) had little effect (Bundy *et al.*, 2010).

The limited evidence suggests that ECT can usually be administered in combination with anticonvulsant treatment without problems. There probably isn't any need to regularly adjust anticonvulsant doses although it would be reasonable to withhold the morning dose before ECT, and reduce higher doses of valproate or CBZ if there is difficulty obtaining a satisfactory seizure. Probably more important is to make sure the depth of anaesthesia is as light as possible, to change or reduce the dose of the induction agent, and possibly combine it with remifentanyl if needed (Bundy et al., 2010; Sienaert & Peuskens, 2007).

Anxiolytics and Hypnotics

Benzodiazepines (BDZ) have anticonvulsant properties and might enhance the sedative effects of induction agents. The evidence is mixed and complicated by differing dosing regimens. Overall the evidence suggests that BDZ may decrease seizure duration (Table 25.2) but the clinical implications are unclear. In retrospective studies of unilateral (UL) ECT and BDZ, two have reported poorer clinical outcomes (Jha & Stein, 1996; Pettinati et al., 1990) and one more treatments required to achieve therapeutic effect (Stromgren et al., 1980). By contrast, three retrospective studies with bilateral (BL) ECT have found no impairment of efficacy by BDZ (Galvez et al., 2013; Jha & Stein, 1996; Johnstone et al., 1982). There is a lack of good evidence with regard to other anxiolytics or hypnotics but one large retrospective study reported no effect of non-BDZ hypnotics on EEG and clinical parameters (Nothdurfter et al., 2006).

It would seem reasonable to withhold intermittently used BDZ immediately before ECT treatments if possible, but compelling evidence to stop chronic/regular BDZ administration is absent and the decision should be guided by clinical need. If clinically adequate seizures are proving difficult in patients taking BDZ then adjustment of the type of dose of induction agent, minimisation of the dose of BDZ and finally consideration of the use of flumazenil immediately before ECT can be tried. The last has been reported to be safe although breakthrough anxiety may necessitate BDZ use immediately after ECT (Krystal et al., 1998). Given the limited evidence that BDZ may interfere with clinical response to UL, but not BL, ECT (see earlier in this chapter) patients on BDZ with inadequate clinical response to the former may benefit from switching to BL ECT (as is common clinical practice in any case).

Acetylcholinesterase Inhibitors

The main theoretical concern is that acetylcholinesterase inhibitors could prevent the breakdown of suxamethonium and lead to prolonged paralysis and apnoea, particularly rivastigmine which also inhibits butyrylcholinesterase.

These drugs have been investigated in controlled trials as a treatment to ameliorate cognitive adverse effects of ECT, rather than in patients primarily taking them for dementia. They appear safe in combination with ECT and there have been no reports suggestive of interaction with suxamethonium or other significant adverse events. Short-term evidence supports statistical cognitive benefit over placebo, although the clinical importance is unclear.

Other Medication

There has been no systematic study of interactions between ECT and other medication. It has been suggested that asystole seen in a case report after the use of the β-blocker propranolol may reflect unopposed enhanced parasympathetic activity after ECT (Wulfson et al., 1984) but a case series of 32 patients receiving labetolol without an anticholinergic drug combined with ECT found no bradycardia or asystole (Dannon et al., 1998).

A randomised cross-over trial of the calcium channel blocker, diltiazem, in 18 patients, found that it shortened seizure duration, as well as resulting in the expected attenuation of ECT-related increases in heart rate and blood pressure (Wajima *et al.*, 2001). Case series and a case report have not found adverse effects from treating patients on anticoagulants with ECT (Loo *et al.*, 1985; Schmidt *et al.*, 2014), nor did a case series of 27 patients on regular corticosteroids need extra steroid cover to compensate for the physiological 'stress' of receiving ECT (Rasmussen *et al.*, 2008). Prolonged seizures have been reported with theophylline (Zolezzi, 2016); however a case series of seven patients on theophylline receiving nine courses of ECT reported only one ECT session with a prolonged seizure requiring intervention, suggesting the risk is relatively low (Rasmussen & Zorumski, 1993).

Conclusions

Avoiding and managing interactions between prescribed medication and ECT requires an understanding of the mechanisms of action of ECT and the pharmacology of the drugs involved. The evidence base provides some reassurance that interactions with commonly prescribed psychotropic medication are relatively rare and are consistent with our understanding of the potential mechanisms involved. However, the evidence available is not systematic, nor of high quality in most cases, and idiosyncratic and rare reactions are not predictable. Therefore, when a patient with ECT is on regular medication it is important to consider whether an interaction could occur, to decide whether the drug needs to be continued during the ECT course, and to have measures in place to manage interactions if they do occur.

References

Agelink M M, Zeit T, Klieser E. (1998). Prolonged bradycardia complicates antidepressive treatment with venlafaxine and ECT. *Br J Psychiatry*, **173**, 441.

Anderson I M, Fergusson G M. (2013). Mechanism of action of ECT. In *The ECT Handbook*. (eds J Waite, A Easton), pp. 1–7. Royal College of Psychiatrists Publications: London.

Auriacombe M, Grabot D, Lincheneau P M, Zeiter D, Tignol J. (1995). Use of midazolam for ECT anesthesia: effects on antidepressive efficacy and seizure duration. Preliminary findings. *Eur Psychiatry*, **10**, 312–16.

Baghai T C, Marcuse A, Brosch M, *et al.* (2006). The influence of concomitant antidepressant medication on safety, tolerability and clinical effectiveness of electroconvulsive therapy. *World J Biol Psychiatry*, 7, 82–90.

Bernardo M, Navarro V, Salva J, Arrufat F J, Baeza I. (2000). Seizure activity and safety in combined treatment with venlafaxine and ECT: a pilot study. *J ECT*, **16**, 38–42.

Bhat R S, Mayur P, Chakrabarti I. (2004). ECT-donepezil interaction: a single case report. *Int J Geriatr Psychiatry*, **19**, 594–5.

Boylan L S, Haskett R F, Mulsant B H, *et al.* (2000). Determinants of seizure threshold in ECT: benzodiazepine use, anesthetic dosage, and other factors. *J ECT*, **16**, 3–18.

Braga R J, Petrides G. (2005). The combined use of electroconvulsive therapy and antipsychotics in patients with schizophrenia. *J ECT*, **21**, 75–83.

Bundy B D, Hewer W, Andres F J, Gass P, Sartorius A. (2010). Influence of anesthetic drugs and concurrent psychiatric medication on seizure adequacy during electroconvulsive therapy. *J Clin Psychiatry*, **71**, 775–7.

Cammu G. (2001). Interactions of neuromuscular blocking drugs. *Acta Anaesthesiol Belg*, **52**, 357–63.

Caracci G, Decina P. (1991). Fluoxetine and prolonged seizure. *Convuls Ther*, 7, 145–7.

Conca A, al-Dubai Z, Konig P, Beraus W. (1999). Combining nefazodone and midazolam during ECT. *Eur Psychiatry*, **14**, 360–2.

Curran S. (1995). Effect of paroxetine on seizure length during electroconvulsive therapy. *Acta Psychiatr Scand*, **92**, 239–40.

Dannon P N, Iancu I, Hirschmann S, Ross P, Dolberg O T, Grunhaus L. (1998). Labetalol does not lengthen asystole during electroconvulsive therapy. *J ECT*, **14**, 245–50.

Dersch R, Zwernemann S, Voderholzer U. (2011). Partial status epilepticus after electroconvulsive therapy and medical treatment with bupropion. *Pharmacopsychiatry*, **44**, 344–6.

Deuschle M, Bohringer A, Meyer-Lindenberg A, Sartorius A. (2017). Electroconvulsive therapy induces transient sensitivity for a serotonin syndrome: a case report. *Pharmacopsychiatry*, **50**, 41–2.

Dixon M, Santiago A. (2013). Psychotropic drug treatment during and after ECT.In *The ECT Handbook*. (eds J Waite, A Easton), pp. 45–59. Royal College of Psychiatrists Publications: London.

Dolenc T J, Habl S S, Barnes R D, Rasmussen K G. (2004). Electroconvulsive therapy in patients taking monoamine oxidase inhibitors. *J ECT*, **20**, 258–61.

Dolenc T J, Rasmussen K G. (2005). The safety of electroconvulsive therapy and lithium in combination: a case series and review of the literature. *J ECT*, **21**, 165–70.

el-Ganzouri A R, Ivankovich A D, Braverman B, McCarthy R. (1985). Monoamine oxidase inhibitors: should they be discontinued preoperatively? *Anesth Analg*, **64**, 592–6.

Eraslan D, Genc Y, Odabasioglu G, Ergun B M, Ozturk O. (2011). Safety of electroconvulsive therapy-duloxetine combination. *J ECT*, **27**, e51–e52.

Figiel G S, Jarvis M R. (1990). Electroconvulsive therapy in a depressed patient receiving bupropion. *J Clin Psychopharmacol*, **10**, 376.

Folkerts H. (1995). Spontaneous seizure after concurrent use of methohexital anesthesia for electroconvulsive therapy and paroxetine: a case report. *J Nerv Ment Dis*, **183**, 115–16.

Galvez V, Loo C K, Alonzo A, *et al.* (2013). Do benzodiazepines moderate the effectiveness of bitemporal electroconvulsive therapy in major depression? *J Affect Disord*, **150**, 686–90.

Gillman P K. (2005). Monoamine oxidase inhibitors, opioid analgesics and serotonin toxicity. *Br J Anaesth*, **95**, 434–41.

Gonzalez-Pinto A, Gutierrez M, Gonzalez N, Elizagarate E, Perez de Heredia J L, Mico J A. (2002). Efficacy and safety of venlafaxine-ECT combination in treatment-resistant depression. *J Neuropsychiatry Clin Neurosci*, **14**, 206–9.

Gutierrez-Esteinou R, Pope H G, Jr. (1989). Does fluoxetine prolong electrically induced seizures? *Convuls Ther*, **5**, 344–8.

Hanretta A T, Malek-Ahmadi P. (2006). Combined use of ECT with duloxetine and olanzapine: a case report. *J ECT*, **22**, 139–41.

Havaki-Kontaxaki B J, Ferentinos P P, Kontaxakis V P, Paplos K G, Soldatos C R. (2006). Concurrent administration of clozapine and electroconvulsive therapy in clozapine-resistant schizophrenia. *Clin Neuropharmacol*, **29**, 52–6.

Heinz B, Lorenzo P, Markus R, *et al.* (2013). Postictal ventricular tachycardia after electroconvulsive therapy treatment associated with a lithium-duloxetine combination. *J ECT*, **29**, e33–e35.

Henstra M J, Jansma E P, van der Velde N, Swart E L, Stek M L, Rhebergen D. (2017). Acetylcholinesterase inhibitors for electroconvulsive therapy-induced cognitive side effects: a systematic review. *Int J Geriatr Psychiatry*, **32**, 522–31.

Hizli S G, Eryilmaz G, Semieoglu S, Ozten E, Gogcegoz G I. (2014). Influence of valproate on the required dose of propofol for anesthesia during electroconvulsive therapy of bipolar affective disorder patients. *Neuropsychiatr Dis Treat*, **10**, 433–8.

Jarvis M R, Goewert A J, Zorumski C F. (1992). Novel antidepressants and maintenance electroconvulsive therapy: a review. *Annals of Clinical Psychiatry*, **4**, 275–84.

Jha A, Stein G. (1996). Decreased efficacy of combined benzodiazepines and unilateral ECT in treatment of depression. *Acta Psychiatr Scand*, **94**, 101–4.

Johnstone E C, Deakin J F, Lawler P, Frith C D, Stevens M, McPherson K, Crow T J. (1982). Benzodiazepines and effectiveness of ECT. *Br J Psychiatry*, **141**, 314–15.

Kellner C H, Pritchett J T, Jackson C W. (1994). Bupropion coadministration with electroconvulsive therapy: two case reports. *J Clin Psychopharmacol*, **14**, 215–16.

Klysner R, Bjerg B B, Hansen M S. (2014). Transient serotonin toxicity evoked by combination of electroconvulsive therapy and fluoxetine. *Case Rep Psychiatry*, **2014**, Article ID 162502: http://dx.doi.org/10.1155/2014/162502.

Krystal A D, Watts B V, Weiner R D, Moore S, Steffens D C, Lindahl V. (1998). The use of flumazenil in the anxious and benzodiazepine-dependent ECT patient. *J ECT*, **14**, 5–14.

Li T C, Shiah I S, Sun C J, Tzang R F, Huang K C, Lee W K. (2011). Mirtazapine relieves post-electroconvulsive therapy headaches and nausea: a case series and review of the literature. *J ECT*, **27**, 165–7.

Loimer N, Hofmann P, Chaudhry H R. (1992). Midazolam shortens seizure duration following electroconvulsive therapy. *J Psychiatr Res*, **26**, 97–101.

Loo H, Cuche H, Benkelfat C. (1985). Electroconvulsive therapy during anticoagulant therapy. *Convuls Ther*, **1**, 258–62.

Masdrakis V G, Oulis P, Florakis A, Valamoutopoulos T, Markatou M, Papadimitriou G N. (2008). The safety of the electroconvulsive therapy-escitalopram combination. *J ECT*, **24**, 289–91.

Masdrakis V G, Florakis A, Tzanoulinos G, Markatou M, Oulis P. (2010). Safety of the electroconvulsive therapy-ziprasidone combination. *J ECT*, **26**, 139–142.

Masdrakis V G, Tzanoulinos G, Markatou M, Oulis P. (2011). Cardiac safety of the electroconvulsive therapy-paliperidone combination: a preliminary study. *Gen Hosp Psychiatry*, **33**, 83–10.

Mayur P M, Gangadhar B N, Subbakrishna D K, Janakiramaiah N. (2000). Discontinuation of antidepressant drugs during electroconvulsive therapy: a controlled study. *J Affect Disord*, **58**, 37–41.

Merk W, Kucia K. (2015). Combined use of ECT and psychotropic drugs. *Psychiatr Pol*, **49**, 1241–53.

Naguib M, Koorn R. (2002). Interactions between psychotropics, anaesthetics and electroconvulsive therapy: implications for drug choice and patient management. *CNS Drugs*, **16**, 229–47.

Nelson J P, Benjamin L. (1989). Efficacy and safety of combined ECT and tricyclic antidepressant drugs in the treatment of depressed geriatric patients. *Convuls Ther*, **5**, 321–9.

Nothdurfter C, Eser D, Schule C, et al. (2006). The influence of concomitant neuroleptic medication on safety, tolerability and clinical effectiveness of electroconvulsive therapy. *World J Biol Psychiatry*, **7**, 162–70.

Okamoto N, Sakamoto K, Yamada M. (2012). Transient serotonin syndrome by concurrent use of electroconvulsive therapy and selective serotonin reuptake inhibitor: a case report and review of the literature. *Case Rep Psychiatry*, **2012**, Article ID: 215214: http://dx.doi.org/10.1155/2012/215214.

Oulis P, Florakis A, Markatou M, Tzanoulinos G, Masdrakis V G. (2011). Corrected QT interval changes during electroconvulsive therapy-antidepressants-atypical antipsychotics coadministration: safety issues. *J ECT*, **27**, e4–e6.

Papakostas YG, Markianos M, Zervas IM, Theodoropoulou M, Vaidakis N, Daras M. (2000). Administration of citalopram before ECT: seizure duration and hormone responses. *J ECT*, **16**, 356–60.

Petrides G, Malur C, Braga R J, et al. (2015). Electroconvulsive therapy augmentation in clozapine-resistant schizophrenia: a prospective, randomized study. *Am J Psychiatry*, **172**, 52–8.

Pettinati H M, Stephens S M, Willis K M, Robin S E. (1990). Evidence for less improvement in depression in patients taking benzodiazepines during unilateral ECT. *Am J Psychiatry*, **147**, 1029–35.

Pullen S J, Rasmussen K G, Angstman E R, Rivera F, Mueller P S. (2011). The safety of electroconvulsive therapy in patients with prolonged QTc intervals on the electrocardiogram. *J ECT*, 27, 192–200.

Rakesh G, Thirthalli J, Kumar C N, Muralidharan K, Phutane V H, Gangadhar B N. (2017). Concomitant anticonvulsants with bitemporal electroconvulsive therapy: a randomized controlled trial with clinical and neurobiological application. *J ECT*, 33, 16–21.

Rasmussen K G, Zorumski C F. (1993). Electroconvulsive therapy in patients taking theophylline. *J Clin Psychiatry*, 54, 427–31.

Rasmussen K G, Albin S M, Mueller P S, Abel M D. (2008). Electroconvulsive therapy in patients taking steroid medication: should supplemental doses be given on the days of treatment? *J ECT*, 24, 128–130.

Ravanic D B, Pantovic M M, Milovanovic D R, *et al.* (2009). Long-term efficacy of electroconvulsive therapy combined with different antipsychotic drugs in previously resistant schizophrenia. *Psychiatr Danub*, 21, 179–86.

Sackeim H A, Dillingham E M, Prudic J, *et al.* (2009). Effect of concomitant pharmacotherapy on electroconvulsive therapy outcomes: short-term efficacy and adverse effects. *Arch Gen Psychiatry*, 66, 729–37.

Sartorius A, Wolf J, Henn FA. (2005). Lithium and ECT-concurrent use still demands attention: three case reports. *World J Biol Psychiatry*, 6, 121–4.

Schmidt S T, Lapid M I, Sundsted K K, Cunningham J L, Ryan D A, Caroline B M. (2014). Safety of electroconvulsive therapy in patients receiving dabigatran therapy. *Psychosomatics*, 55, 400–3.

Serfaty M A, Martin L M, Lingham R, Ferrier I N. (1996). The effect of psychotropic medication on seizure duration during bilateral electroconvulsive therapy: a retrospective study. *J Psychopharmacol*, 10, 303–8.

Sienaert P, Peuskens J. (2007). Anticonvulsants during electroconvulsive therapy: review and recommendations. *J ECT*, 23, 120–3.

Sienaert P, Roelens Y, Demunter H, Vansteelandt K, Peuskens J, Van H C. (2011).

Concurrent use of lamotrigine and electroconvulsive therapy. *J ECT*, 27, 148–52.

Standish-Barry H M, Deacon V, Snaith R P. (1985). The relationship of concurrent benzodiazepine administration to seizure duration in ECT. *Acta Psychiatr Scand*, 71, 269–71.

Stromgren L S, Dahl J, Fjeldborg N, Thomsen A. (1980). Factors influencing seizure duration and number of seizures applied in unilateral electroconvulsive therapy. Anaesthetics and benzodiazepines. *Acta Psychiatr Scand*, 62, 158–65.

Tang W K, Ungvari G S. (2002). Efficacy of electroconvulsive therapy combined with antipsychotic medication in treatment-resistant schizophrenia: a prospective, open trial. *J ECT*, 18, 90–4.

Thirthalli J, Harish T, Gangadhar B N. (2011). A prospective comparative study of interaction between lithium and modified electroconvulsive therapy. *World J Biol Psychiatry*, 12, 149–55.

van Schaik A M, Rhebergen D, Henstra M J, Kadouch D J, van Exel E, Stek M L. (2015). Cognitive impairment and electroconvulsive therapy in geriatric depression, what could be the role of rivastigmine? a case series. *Clin Pract*, 5, 780.

Virupaksha H S, Shashidhara B, Thirthalli J, Kumar C N, Gangadhar B N. (2010). Comparison of electroconvulsive therapy (ECT) with or without anti-epileptic drugs in bipolar disorder. *J Affect Disord*, 127, 66–70.

Vlissides D N, Lee C R, Hill S E. (1979). Lithium, anaesthesia and ECT. *Br J Anaesth*, 51, 574.

Volpe F M, Tavares A R. (2012). Lithium plus ECT for mania in 90 cases: safety issues. *J Neuropsychiatry Clin Neurosci*, 24, E33.

Wajima Z, Yoshikawa T, Ogura A, *et al.* (2001). The effects of diltiazem on hemodynamics and seizure duration during electroconvulsive therapy. *Anesth Analg*, 92, 1327–30.

Wang W, Pu C, Jiang J, *et al.* (2015). Efficacy and safety of treating patients with refractory schizophrenia with antipsychotic medication and adjunctive electroconvulsive therapy: a systematic review and meta-analysis. *Shanghai Arch Psychiatry*, 27, 206–19.

West S, Hewitt J. (1999). Prolonged hypertension: a case report of a potential interaction between electroconvulsive therapy and venlafaxine. *Int J Psychiatry Clin Pract*, **3**, 55–57.

Wulfson H D, Askanazi J, Finck A D. (1984). Propranolol prior to ECT associated with asystole. *Anesthesiology*, **60**, 255–6.

Yamaguchi S, Nagao M, Ikeda T, *et al.* (2011). QT dispersion and rate-corrected QT dispersion during electroconvulsive therapy in elderly patients. *J ECT*, **27**, 183–8.

Young A H, Wooderson S C. (2016). 'Mood stabilisers' and other treatments for bipolar disorder. In *Fundamentals of Clinical Psychopharmacology*. (eds I M Anderson, R H McAllister-Williams), pp. 103–23. CRC Press: Boca Raton.

Zink M, Sartorius A, Lederbogen F, Henn F A. (2002). Electroconvulsive therapy in a patient receiving rivastigmine. *J ECT*, **18**, 162–4.

Zolezzi M. (2016). Medication management during electroconvulsant therapy. *Neuropsychiatr Dis Treat*, **12**, 931–9.

Seizure Monitoring in ECT

26

David M Semple and Ryan Alexander Devlin

During ECT, a variety of observations and physiological measures should be made simultaneously, including: visible evidence of the length and quality of a motor response, blood pressure, heart rate, oxygen saturation, ECG monitoring, EEG activity and sometimes electromyogram (EMG) measurement. Here we will discuss typical observations regarding the ictal motor activity, cardiovascular response and EEG recordings.

Motor Activity

Observation

Direct observation and timing of the ECT-induced generalised seizure is useful, particularly if EEG recording is compromised by significant artefact. It is worth noting that during the electrical stimulus there is a strong motor response that is unaffected by neuromuscular blockade and due to the stimulus rather than seizure activity, including a supraphysiological clenching of the jaw, extension of the neck, and flexion of the ankles. This stops as soon as the stimulus ends and is replaced by the gradual onset of tonic muscle contraction, which is the first stage of the generalised seizure. Depending on the degree of motor blockade achieved by the use of muscle relaxant, this stage may not be obvious, but usually begins within a few seconds of the end of the stimulus. When the stimulus is just above the seizure threshold, this first stage may gradually build over tens of seconds and never fully develop into the clonic phase. The clonic phase is the second stage of the generalised seizure and is characterised by rhythmic contractions of the muscles. Again, due to varying degrees of motor blockade, this may range from very vigorous to barely visible activity. Often all that is seen are 'beats' of flexion/extension at the ankle or wrist. When it is seen, this second stage will usually last longer than the tonic stage and terminate either suddenly or with a gradual decline in intensity.

The Hamilton 'Cuff' Technique

This is a technique to allow the ictal motor response to be observed even when muscle relaxants are given. It is no longer as widely used due to the adoption of EEG monitoring as standard practice and the observation that there is little difference in seizure duration observed with EEG monitoring and the Hamilton 'cuff' technique (Lambert & Petty, 1994). It may still be used when EEG monitoring is unavailable, in patients who exhibit marked motor artefact on EEG rendering it uninterpretable, or when using an optical motor sensor (see 'Optical Motor Sensor' in this chapter). A blood pressure cuff is put around the wrist or ankle (see Figure 26.1) and inflated above systolic pressure prior to the administration of the muscle relaxant. By preventing the muscle relaxant reaching the hand or foot, motor seizure activity is more readily observed. Cuff pressure is released as soon as the seizure has occurred to reduce the risk from lack of perfusion of the distal appendage. Special care should be taken if the patient has a history of musculoskeletal problems (e.g. severe osteoporosis), vascular insufficiency or other haematological issues (e.g. sickle cell disease, clotting disorders).

Electromyography (EMG)

Motor activity in the muscles can also be directly recorded using EMG. The standard procedure is to use a single pair of electrodes three inches apart, attached to the skin overlying the muscles on the dorsum of the foot, distal to the blood pressure cuff – if the cuff technique is being used to reduce artefact (see Figure 26.1). Good skin contact is essential and the skin may be prepared using a light abrasive, e.g. NuPrep® Skin Prep Gel (Weaver and Company) and ensuring the area is dry before the electrodes are applied. Whilst EMG is more sensitive than simple observation, the electrical recordings are very likely to contain significant artefact and it cannot solely be relied upon (Krystal and Weiner, 1995). The quality of the recording depends upon good technique and this may involve adjustment of channel parameters. Although EMG recording is not standard practice for routine ECT both the Somatics Thymatron System IV (http://www.thymatron.com) and the MECTA spECTrum 5000Q (http://www.mectacorp.com) ECT machines do have additional channels that may be used to collect EMG data and display it simultaneously with the EEG recording (see Figure 26.2). This EMG data can be utilised in proprietary seizure detection algorithms to help determine the length of the motor seizure.

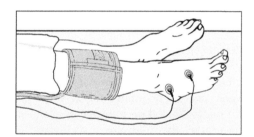

Figure 26.1 Blood pressure cuff and EMG electrode placement. (Illustration created by Adam D Semple.)

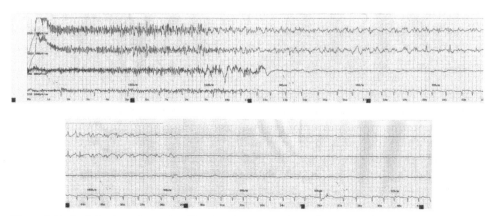

Figure 26.2 Typical 4-channel recording. This recording shows a low voltage seizure lasting around 29 seconds with muscle artefact on the EEG and ECG channels for the first 10 seconds. The EMG shows the motor seizure lasting around 12 seconds.

Optical Motor Sensor (OMS)

Available for the MECTA spECTrum Q series devices (5000Q and 4000Q), the optical motor sensor (OMS) is a photoplethysmographic sensor that may be used in place of EMG. It utilises an infrared emitter and detector to capture intra-muscular motor movement during the clonic stage of the induced seizure. The sensor is attached around a finger or toe distal to a blood pressure cuff that prevents muscle relaxant reaching the foot or hand (see 'The Hamilton 'Cuff' Technique' earlier in the chapter) and minimises possible artefact caused by arterial pulsation. During the tonic stage of the seizure no OMS activity is seen. Any movements during the clonic stage of the seizure are seen as slow waves on the spECTrum LCD monitor, chart recorder or an attached PC monitor. Provided a significant enough deflection is detected, without any artefacts, the termination of the slow waves indicates when the motor component of the seizure has ended and no OMS activity is seen postictally (see: www.mectacorp.com/optical-motion-sensor.html).

Practice Points

It is worth noting that motor activity does not terminate in all muscles at the same time and the end of the observable motor response is conventionally when all motor activity has ceased. In some centres the cessation of movement in the cuffed limb is taken as the endpoint as it can be difficult to distinguish whether other motor activity is due to a) fasciculation caused by the muscle relaxant, b) direct stimulation of the muscles of the face or c) the ECT-induced seizure.

Cardiovascular Response

Anaesthetic monitoring allows for continuous readouts of ECG, heart rate, blood pressure, capnography and pulse oximetry (see Chapter 23). Modern ECT machines also have the facility to record ECG (see Figure 26.2), and this may be part of the proprietary algorithm used to detect seizure presence and length, however, anaesthetic monitoring of ECG will usually take precedence. Initially, the patient's heart rate and blood pressure may be elevated due to anxiety. Depending upon the anaesthetic agents used, these measures may decrease to baseline levels (e.g. with propofol) or remain unaffected (e.g. with etomidate or ketamine). ECT stimulation leads to a characteristic cardiovascular response that comprises four elements. Immediately after electrical stimulus there is an initial parasympathetic response with a decrease in blood pressure and either a transient sinus bradycardia or asystole, lasting several seconds. This is followed by a sympathetic response characterised by a dramatic increase in blood pressure and heart rate, the absence of which usually indicates an inadequate ECT stimulus (Mankad et al., 2010). The induced tachycardia continues to the end of the clonic phase, when parasympathetic reactivation leads to a decrease in heart rate sometimes to the level of bradycardia. As the patient awakens from anaesthesia, sympathetic activity returns the heart rate and blood pressure to baseline levels (Perrin, 1961). There is considerable variation in how these elements appear dependent on the premorbid physical health of the patient, particularly any cardiac issues (e.g. heart block, atrial fibrillation), current prescribed medication (e.g. beta-blockers), and any pre-medication given (e.g. anticholinergics). Administration of anticholinergics such as atropine or glycopyrrolate may reduce the risk of bradyarrhythmias or asystole (Anastasian et al., 2014). ECG changes have sometimes been observed during induced seizures, typically peaked T waves, whose amplitude normalises once the seizure terminates (Khoury and Benedetti, 1989).

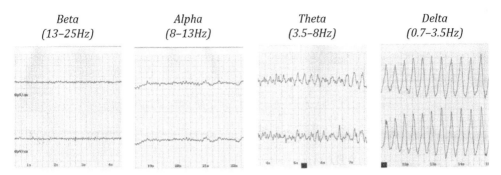

| Beta (13–25Hz) | Alpha (8–13Hz) | Theta (3.5–8Hz) | Delta (0.7–3.5Hz) |

Figure 26.3 Typical appearances of EEG bands during ECT recording.

Electroencephalography (EEG)

The EEG (Stern & Engel, 2013) is an extremely sensitive voltmeter that detects the fluctuating electrical potentials between electrodes placed on the scalp, which are the result of summated field potentials generated by excitatory and inhibitory postsynaptic potentials in vertically oriented pyramidal cells of the cortex. Typical voltages range from 30–80 μV but may be as low as 1–10 μV when suppressed postictally or as high as 1000 μV or more during a seizure. EEG signals typically consist of many different frequencies. Conventionally four frequency bands are recognised and the largest component described as the dominant frequency (see Figure 26.3).

Low voltage beta activity is associated with normal waking consciousness and may be augmented by drugs, such as barbiturates, benzodiazepines, and other anaesthetic agents. Alpha waves reflect synchronous and coherent electrical activity of the thalamic pacemaker cells and predominantly originate from the occipital lobe during wakeful relaxation with closed eyes. They are suppressed by opening the eyes, and when drowsy or asleep. Theta rhythms are seen when neural networks are being recruited, which occurs in ECT due to propagation of electrical activity following stimulus. Theta activity is observed normally when it reflects the readiness of the hippocampus and connected regions to process incoming signals (hippocampal theta) or the integration of sensory information with motor output in the cortex during spatial learning and navigation tasks (cortical theta). Delta rhythms are usually abnormal if observed in the waking state. They occur normally during stages 3 and 4 of non-REM (or slow wave) sleep and following a general anaesthetic. They may correlate to synchronous activity in cortico-thalamo-cortical distributed networks (Farzan et al., 2014).

EEG Electrode Placement

EEG monitoring is now accepted as standard for the modern practice of ECT and both the MECTA spECTrum Q series and the Somatics Thymatron System IV are capable of recording up to four channels of EEG activity although standard practice is to use only two channels reflecting activity in both hemispheres. Prefrontal and mastoid locations (see Figure 26.4) are preferred since ECT induced seizure activity is usually high in the frontal regions and the mastoid area is generally electrophysiologically inactive, making for a good reference point. It is good practice to clean and gently abrade the skin before applying the EEG electrodes (as for EMG above). Many practitioners prefer self-adhesive ECG recording pads.

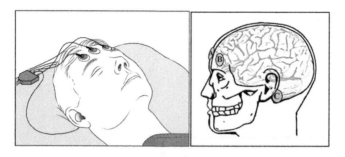

Figure 26.4 EEG electrode placement. (Illustration created by Adam D Semple.) A - Earth, B - Frontal, C - Mastoid electrodes.

5(a) Awake trace with multiple deflections due to eye blink and predominant beta frequency activity

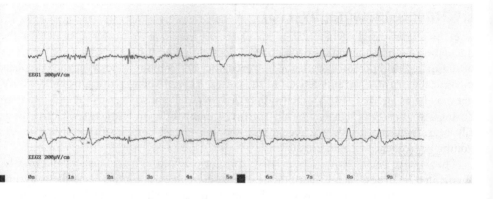

5(b) Baseline trace under anaesthesia with reduced beta and increased alpha frequency activity

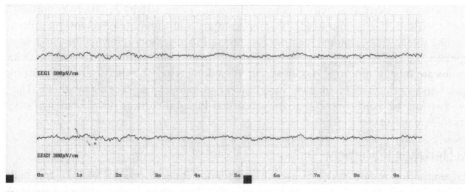

Figure 26.5 Baseline traces.

Establishing a Baseline EEG

Two baseline traces of 5–10 seconds should be recorded (see Figure 26.5). The first, with the patient awake, helps determine that the leads are correctly attached, there is a good signal with little artefact, and the machine is functioning correctly. Any problems should be quickly addressed e.g. replacing faulty electrodes or cables. The second, under anaesthesia, allows establishment of a baseline immediately before ECT stimulation for direct comparison with the ictal EEG, to determine whether a seizure has definitely occurred and post-ictal suppression is present. If the first baseline is particularly active this second baseline under anaesthesia is essential to help prevent unnecessary additional stimulations (see Figure 26.6).

Ictal and Postictal EEG Phases

Figure 26.7 illustrates typical ictal and postictal EEG phases seen during ECT. Whilst there is significant variation, a number of phases are recognised although they may not all be present on the treatment EEG (Mankad, *et al.*, 2010).

Phase 1: Electrodecremental Phase

Immediately after the electrical stimulus ends there may be a brief electrodecremental phase of low-amplitude fast activity (not seen in Figure 26.7).

Phase 2: Recruiting Rhythm

A further brief period of low to moderate amplitude activity in the alpha or beta range may be seen that is believed to be associated with the synchronising effects of thalamo-cortical projections in the early stages of seizure generalisation. Subthreshold activity may not progress beyond this phase (see Figure 26.8(b)).

Phase 3: Polyspike Activity

Higher amplitude, mixed frequency polyspike activity occurs along with tonic and early clonic motor activity. This usually lasts 10–15 seconds but may be masked with EMG artefact (see Figure 26.9(a)).

Phase 4: Theta and Delta Activity

Along with a more definite clonic phase, polyspike activity becomes more regular with polyspike and slow-wave complexes synchronised to the motor activity. They may begin at higher theta frequency before slowing to the delta range. The amplitude may characteristically increase and sometimes 2–3Hz spike and wave complexes may be seen.

6(a) very active baseline recording

6(b) end of seizure at 34 seconds with only relative suppression

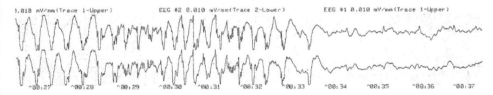

Figure 26.6 Active baseline. (Reproduced with permission from Scott, 2007.)

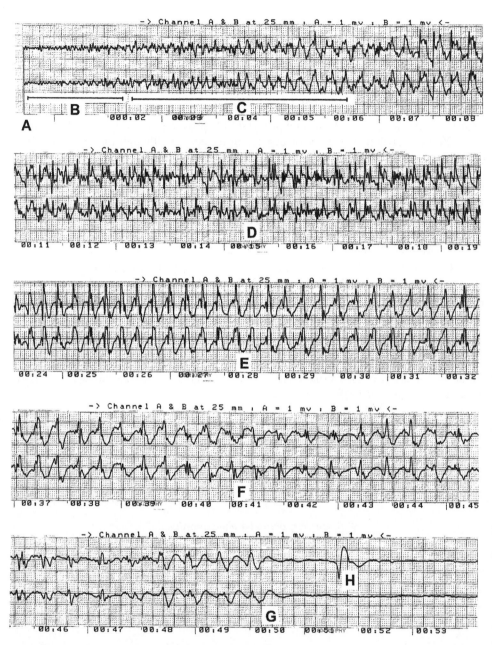

Figure 26.7 Typical treatment EEG. A - Phase 1 – end of electrical stimulation, no visible electrodecrimental activity. B - Phase 2 – recruiting rhythm, a latent phase with no visible convulsion, only low-amplitude, high-frequency activity becoming polyspike in character. C - Phase 3 – polyspike activity, increasing in amplitude and slowing in frequency. D & E - Phase 4 – theta and delta activity, occurring with the clonic phase of convulsion, becoming more classically delta frequency classic 2–3 Hz spike-and-wave activity around 25 seconds. F - Phase 5 – seizure termination, gradual loss of spike-and-wave pattern. G - Phase 6 – post ictal suppression, with low amplitude and frequency.
Note: Phase 7 – return to baseline, is not depicted but would comprise a gradual increase in activity to the pre-treatment baseline. H - Typical movement artefact from anaesthetist reapplying oxygen mask.

8(a) Baseline traces

(i) Awake, eyes open, blinking   (ii) Anaesthetised

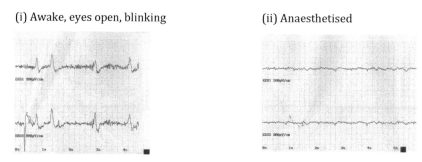

8(b) First stimulation – subthreshold, no evidence of seizure activity

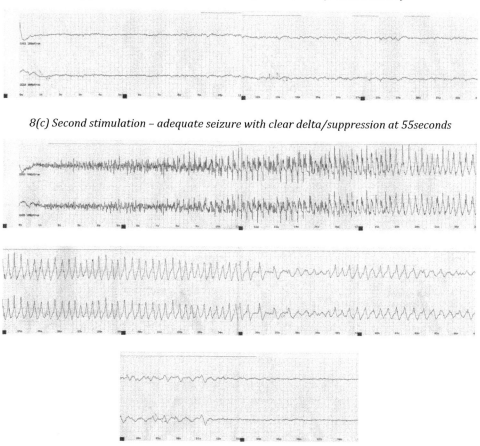

8(c) Second stimulation – adequate seizure with clear delta/suppression at 55seconds

Figure 26.8 Example of full treatment trace requiring restimulation.

Phase 5: Seizure Termination

Seizures may end in a variety of ways although the commonest are either a sudden abrupt ending with marked postictal suppression or a gradual slowing of delta activity with a reduction in amplitude to the point of suppression (see Figure 26.10).

9(a) Muscle artefact – high frequency polyspike activity on a treatment trace indicative of EMG activity rather than EEG seizure activity (i.e. inadequate treatment)

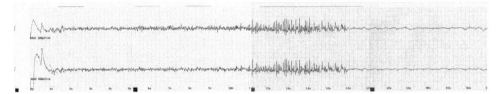

9(b) Movement artefact – poorly modified seizure making interpretation almost impossible

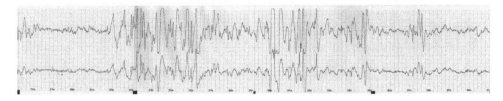

9(c) Movement artefact – caused by anaesthetist returning to patient at end of seizure

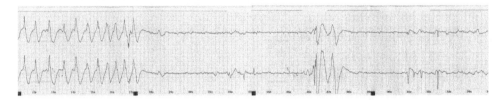

9(d) Electrode artefact – loose left (upper) electrode: right (lower) channel shows inadequate seizure with only muscle artefact

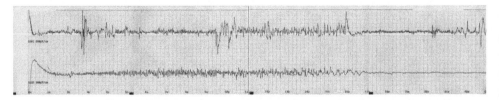

9(e) ECG artefact – magnified view of low voltage QRS complex appearing more on left (upper) EEG channel at the end of a seizure during the suppression phase

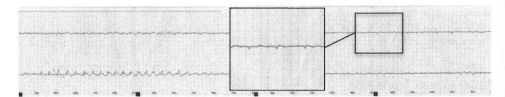

Figure 26.9 Common EEG artefacts.

10(a) Gradual slowing of delta activity, becoming more disorganised before terminating at 46 seconds with clear suppression and artefact caused by oxygen mask.

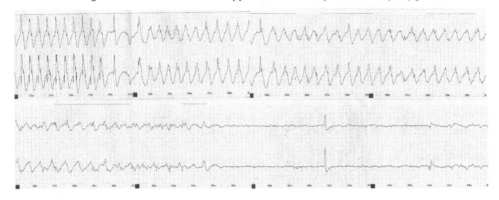

10(b) Seizure ends abruptly with marked suppression just after 01:18. (Reproduced with permission from Scott, 2007.)

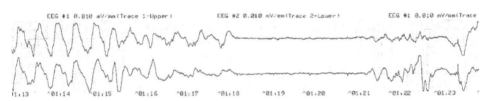

10(c) Ultra-brief seizure terminating abruptly with residual activity up to 18 seconds.

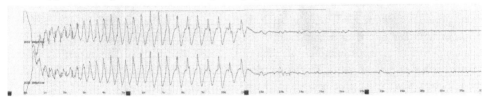

10(d) Seizure has ended (between 33 and 39 seconds) but termination obscured by artefact. (Reproduced with permission from Scott, 2007.)

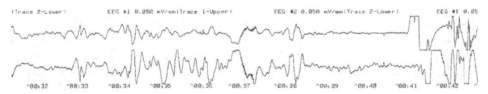

Figure 26.10 Seizure termination.

Phase 6: Postictal Suppression

This is essentially a refractory period when there is little evidence of EEG activity. When there is lack of suppression this usually means the seizure is peri-threshold and may be less effective (Krystal and Weiner, 1995; Krystal *et al.*, 1993).

Phase 7: Return to Baseline

After a few minutes the pattern of postictal suppression shows a gradual rise in both amplitude and frequency until it returns to the pre-treatment baseline.

EEG Artefacts

Familiarity with the range and variety of possible treatment EEGs will help determine the quality and length of the induced seizure (Semple, 2016). Difficulties arise particularly when artefacts appear on the trace despite the best efforts to eliminate them from the baseline measures. Artefacts fall into four main categories: muscle artefact, movement artefact, electrode artefact and ECG artefact (see Figure 26.9).

Muscle Artefact

EMG activity (see Figure 26.9(a)) appears as high frequency (>30Hz) polyspike activity superimposed on the ictal EEG, sometimes to the point of obscuring it entirely. Sometimes this reflects facial muscle activity rather than generalised seizure activity and can make it appear that a seizure has occurred even though it has not. EMG artefact caused by convulsive movements in the clonic phase will disappear from the trace when motor activity ceases, and the EEG often continues to show seizure activity for a further 20 seconds or more. Adjustment of muscle relaxant dosage will help minimise the risk of muscle artefact in subsequent treatments but cannot be guaranteed to eliminate it completely.

Movement Artefact

Significant movements due to poorly modified seizures will be seen as marked high voltage EEG deflections that can render the EEG unreadable (see Figure 26.9(b)). Lesser movement artefacts occur when the anaesthetist returns to the patient and moves their head or applies an oxygen mask (see Figure 26.9(c)). Appropriate use of muscle relaxants and ensuring team members do not cause movement of the patient until the seizure is judged to be complete will reduce the chances of these artefacts interfering with assessment of seizure adequacy. However, achieving a good quality EEG trace should not endanger patient safety and if anaesthetic intervention is required before the end of the seizure is seen on EEG, good practice is to allow the EEG to run on whilst the patient is recovered. The EEG trace can then be reviewed fully at the end of the treatment session.

Electrode Artefact

If an EEG electrode becomes loose or even detached during the treatment, the EEG in that channel may also be unreadable or absent (see Figure 26.9(d)). This is a good reason for two-channel recording, as the other channel can be used as a back-up for accurate determination of seizure occurrence. It is also one of the reasons for doing two baseline traces (see 'Establishing a Baseline EEG' earlier in this chapter).

Electrocardiographic Artefact

A common occurrence, especially when mastoid electrodes are used, is that of seeing an ECG trace particularly during the postictal suppression phase (see Figure 26.9(e)). Some clinicians use the appearance of this ECG trace as a proxy for the seizure endpoint as it is only clearly seen when suppression is marked.

Determining Seizure Adequacy

The early view that seizure adequacy corresponded to quantitative measures – 15 seconds of a motor response and/or 25 seconds of clear seizure activity on EEG (Royal College of Psychiatrists, 1989; Freeman, 1995) – has been superseded by qualitative criteria; evidence of clear bilateral tonic-clonic seizure activity and/or presence of typical EEG features: poly-spike activity, spike and wave/delta activity and postictal suppression – of no specific duration, as illustrated in Figure 26.5 and Figure 26.6 (Scott, 2005; Waite & Easton, 2013). This change in view came as a result of studies showing that marginally suprathreshold seizures had poor therapeutic benefit despite being of adequate duration (Sackeim *et al.*, 1987; 1993) and led to the search for measures of seizure adequacy relating to other elements of the treatment EEG. Systematic review of these subsequent studies (Mayur, 2006) finds strongest evidence for measures of the degree of postictal suppression, but other indices including postictal coherence and amplitude, the onset and amount of slow wave activity, and global (especially delta) EEG power may also be important. In practice, determining the end of a seizure (see Figure 26.10) and assessing delta activity and postictal suppression show good inter-rater reliability (Semple *et al.*, 2014). An EEG showing clear 'delta-suppression features', that is, the emergence of delta activity followed by evident postictal suppression, compared to a baseline trace under anaesthesia, no matter how long the seizure lasts, is likely to be adequate for the purposes of maximising the potential benefit from ECT.

Conclusion

The adoption of EEG monitoring as standard for the modern practice of ECT means that seizure quality and length can be more objectively assessed. Observation of motor activity and cardiovascular response may inform this assessment; however practitioners are becoming increasingly reliant on the EEG to determine when adjustments need to be made to treatment dosing. For example, noting a clear reduction in quality or length of the seizure on EEG may allow the ECT dose to be increased early and prevent an inadequate treatment session. Similarly prolonged or tardive seizures can be monitored rather than inferred, allowing appropriate action to be taken promptly. It is hoped that standardising and improving the practice of EEG monitoring in ECT will allow future research to address some of the unanswered questions relating to what constitutes an effective seizure.

References

Anastasian, Z. H., Khan, N., Heyer, E. J., *et al.* (2014) Effect of atropine dose on heart rate during electroconvulsive therapy. *J ECT* 30:298–302.

Farzan, F., Boutros, N. N., Blumberger, D. M, *et al.* (2014) What does the electroencephalogram tell us about the mechanisms of action of ECT in major depressive disorders? *J ECT* 30:98–106.

Freeman, C. P. (ed.) (1995) *The ECT Handbook: The Second Report of the Royal College of Psychiatrists' Special Committee on ECT*

(Council Report CR39). Royal College of Psychiatrists Publications.

Khoury, G. F., Benedetti, C. (1989) T-wave changes associated with electroconvulsive therapy. *Anesth Analg* 69:677–9.

Krystal, A. D., Weiner, R. D., McCall, W. V., *et al.* (1993) The effects of ECT stimulus dose and electrode placement on the ictal electroencephalogram: an intraindividual crossover study. *Biol Psychiatry* 34:759–67.

Krystal, A. D., Weiner, R. D. (1995) ECT seizure duration: reliability of manual and computer automated determinations. *Convuls Ther* 11:158–69.

Lambert, M. & Petty, F. (1994) EEG seizure duration monitoring of ECT. *Progress in Neuropsychopharmacolgy & Biological Psychiatry* 18: 497–502.

Mankad, M. V., Beyer, J. L., Weiner, R. D., Krystal, A. D. (2010) *Clinical Manual of Electroconvulsive Therapy* pp. 111–14. American Psychiatric Publishing, Inc., Washington, DC.

Mankad, M. V., Beyer, J. L., Weiner, R. D., Krystal, A. D. (2010) Cardiovascular Response, *Clinical Manual of Electroconvulsive Therapy* pp. 129–125, American Psychiatric Publishing, Inc., Washington, DC.

Mayur, P. (2006) Ictal electroencephalographic characteristics during electroconvulsive therapy: a review of determination and clinical relevance. *J ECT* 22:213–17.

Perrin, G. M. (1961) Cardiovascular aspects of electric shock therapy. *Acta Psychiatr Neurol Scand* 36:7–44.

Royal College of Psychiatrists (1989) *The Practical Administration of Electroconvulsive Therapy*. London: Gaskell.

Sackeim, H. A., Decina, P., Kanzler, M., *et al.* (1987) Effects of electrode placement on the efficacy of titrated, low-dose ECT. *Am J Psychiatry* 144:1449–55.

Sackeim, H. A., Prudic, J., Devanand, D. P., *et al.* (1993) Effects of stimulus intensity and electrode placement on the efficacy and cognitive effects of electroconvulsive therapy. *N Engl J Med* 328:839–46.

Scott, A. I. F. (ed.) (2005) *The ECT Handbook: The Third Report of the Royal College of Psychiatrists' Special Committee on ECT (2nd edn) (Council Report CR128)*. Royal College of Psychiatrists Publications.

Scott, A. I. F. (2007) Monitoring electroconvulsive therapy by electroencephalogram: an update for ECT practitioners. *Advances in Psychiatric Treatment* 13:298–304.

Semple, D. M., Gunn, W., Davidson, Z., Queirazza, F. (2014) Teaching therapeutic seizure criteria to psychiatrists. *J ECT* 30:220–3.

Semple, D. (2016) *Pragmatic Guidance for EEG Interpretation. (Electroconvulsive Therapy in Practice)*. Kindle Direct Publications.

Stern, J. M. & Engel, J. (2013) *An Atlas of EEG Patterns, (2nd edn)*. Philadelphia: Lippincott Williams and Wilkins.

Waite, J. & Easton, A. (eds) (2013) *The ECT Handbook (3rd edn)*. (College Report CR176). Royal College of Psychiatrists Publications.

Safe ECT Practice in People with a Physical Illness

Jonathan Waite

Physiological Effects of ECT

People with a wide range of physical illnesses are successfully treated with ECT (Tess & Smetana, 2009). Some medical problems may cause particular concern, especially cardiovascular and neurological problems.

During the passage of the electrical stimulus, both blood pressure and heart rate fall and then rise rapidly. There is a sudden, transient rise in intracranial pressure and cerebral blood flow, and cerebrovascular permeability increases. In the first seconds after the shock, parasympathetic activity, mediated via the vagus (Xth cranial) nerve, causes sinus bradycardia, sometimes with periods of asystole or electrical silence.

This is rapidly followed by sympathetic activity from the cervical ganglia causing tachycardia and increased peripheral resistance, leading to increased blood pressure. There is an increase in oxygen consumption by the myocardium, which can result in ischaemia. Contrary to popular belief, bradycardia is equally likely to occur with convulsive and subconvulsive stimuli (Mizen et al., 2015).

The parasympathetic effects of ECT can be attenuated by the use of antimuscarinic medication such as glycopyrrolate; sympathetic effects can be modified by beta-blockers. Use of these agents is considered in Chapter 23.

Coexisting Medical or Surgical Conditions

Since many medical illnesses could increase the risk associated with ECT, it is important that all people for whom ECT is being considered are fully evaluated before treatment. Any physical illness will need to be investigated and treated or at least stabilised as far as possible before ECT is begun (Tess & Smetana, 2009). The important principles here are as follows:

- When a person who is being considered for treatment with ECT is thought to present high risk, an appropriate medical opinion should be sought to fully assess the disorder and clarify the degree of risk.
- An anaesthetic opinion should be sought at an early stage. Treatment technique may be modified in liaison with the anaesthetist, to minimise any risks.
- Any underlying disorder should be fully assessed and treated before ECT.
- During the consent process, patient and family should be informed of the increased risk and any recommendations for minimising it. Risk may need to be reassessed following cardiological or anaesthetic opinion or investigation.
- High-risk patients should not be treated at remote sites, or as day patients or out-patients.

Cardiovascular Disease

The American College of Cardiology and American Heart Association (ACC/AHA) have produced guidelines on assessing and managing patients undergoing non-cardiac surgery (Fleisher *et al.*, 2014). Electroconvulsive therapy would be classified in these guidelines as a low-risk procedure; the risk of a major adverse cardiac event is less than 1% (see Chapter 14). Although ECT is unlike other procedures for which a general anaesthetic is administered, the conditions that cause higher cardiac risks during treatment are similar to those that elevate the risks associated with surgical interventions.

Arrhythmias and Cardiac Conduction Abnormalities

Patients with implanted cardiac pacemakers can be safely treated with ECT (Macpherson *et al.*, 2006). The device should be checked by an appropriately trained technician to ensure that it is functioning correctly prior to a course of ECT; if it is, no special precautions are required and it does not need to be switched off for ECT. Where a patient with an automatic implanted cardioverter defibrillator (AICD) is being given ECT, it is desirable to have a cardiology technician present in the ECT suite (Davis *et al.*, 2009). It is possible for the AICD to remain active during ECT; the benefit of shocking a life threatening arrhythmia outweighs the small risk of ECT being misinterpreted by the device and delivering a shock (Bryson *et al.*, 2015b).

If QT_c is greater than 500ms steps should be taken to investigate and manage delayed cardiac conduction. Pullen *et al.* (2011) compared the experiences of 224 patients with prolonged QT_c (>500ms) with 1216 controls. Four patients with prolonged QT_c developed tachycardia (two supraventricular, two ventricular tachycardia), compared with one control. Three of these were able to complete the course of ECT after treatment with beta blockers.

Hypertension

Hypertension is one of the greatest risks for patients receiving ECT. It is important to optimise the management of blood pressure with the referring team and/or general practitioner. Acute changes in blood pressure during ECT can be controlled with intravenous beta blocking agents such as labetalol (Boere *et al.*, 2014) – see Chapter 23. Albin and colleagues (2007) found that resting blood pressure did not change over a course of ECT.

Myocardial Infarction

It has been recommended to defer non-cardiac surgery for 60 days after myocardial infarction (Fleisher *et al.*, 2014). However, successful use of ECT without adverse effects within two weeks of acute myocardial infarction has been reported (Magid *et al.*, 2005). The ACC/AHA guidelines (Fleisher *et al.*, 2014) make recommendations about evaluation and management in such circumstances.

Pulmonary Embolism and Anticoagulation

Patients with severe depression are at increased risk of venous thromboembolic disease as a result of reduced mobility and fluid intake. Pulmonary embolism is not a contra-indication to ECT (Suzuki *et al.*, 2008). Anticoagulation and cardiac function should be carefully monitored. There were no ECT related complications in 300 patients receiving warfarin for a variety of indications (Mehta *et al.*, 2004).

Cardiac Failure

Where there is breathlessness, left ventricular function should be evaluated by echocardiography (Fleisher *et al.*, 2014). If there is significant hypertension or tachycardia during ECT in a case of cardiac failure these should be controlled on subsequent sessions using prophylactic beta blockade (Rivera *et al.*, 2011).

Cerebral Aneurysm

There are a number of accounts (reviewed by Wilkinson *et al.*, 2014) of successful use of ECT in patients with treated and untreated aneurysms. It is recommended that blood pressure should be controlled during the procedure using a short acting antihypertensive agent, such as labetalol or esmolol.

Abdominal Aortic Aneurysm

Mueller *et al.* (2009) report on eight patients with abdominal aortic aneurysms (AAAs) who underwent ECT. None of them showed signs or symptoms suggesting expansion. If AAA is suspected, ultrasound screening is suggested.

Valvular Heart Disease

Severe valvular heart disease is a relative contra-indication to general anaesthesia, but successful use of ECT in patients with severe aortic stenosis has been reported (Mueller *et al.*, 2007).

Neurological Conditions

Electroconvulsive therapy has been used safely for people with small, slow-growing cerebral tumours without raised intracranial pressure, but people who have space-occupying lesions of the brain are at high risk of neurological deterioration if treated with ECT (Krystal & Coffey, 1997). Nevertheless, people with a wide range of neurological conditions have been treated successfully with ECT (see Chapter 12).

Cerebrovascular Disease

It is advisable to delay ECT for four to six weeks after acute stroke, although ECT has been used within two weeks of a cerebellar infarct (Weintraub & Lippmann, 2000).

Parkinson's Disease

ECT is a safe adjunctive treatment for both motor and affective symptoms in Parkinson's Disease (Kennedy *et al.*, 2003). There have been several case reports of patients with multisystem atrophy showing improvement in motor function and mood after ECT (Shioda *et al.*, 2006).

Auto-immune Encephalitis

Antibody induced encephalitis may present with psychiatric or neurological symptoms. ECT has been successfully used to treat patients with anti-NMDA (n-methyl-d-aspartate) encephalitis (Gough *et al.*, 2016).

Tardive Dyskinesia

There is considerable literature on the use of ECT in tardive dyskinesia, which is contradictory and inconclusive: several case reports suggest that ECT improves this condition, while several others report that tardive dyskinesia worsens with ECT (Kennedy *et al.*, 2003).

Intracranial Foreign Objects

ECT has been used safely in patients who have undergone cranioplasty with titanium plates and other implanted devices such as aneurysm clips and electrodes, as well as bullet fragments (see Mortier *et al.*, 2012, Gahr *et al.*, 2013). The electrodes should be placed as far away as possible from any metallic object. It is sometimes possible to continue deep brain stimulation during ECT (Villa-Rodriguez *et al.*, 2014). In general it is not advisable to use ECT when a cochlear implant had been inserted (U.S. Food and Drug Administration, 2014). However, this is not an absolute contra-indication, there is a report of successful treatment of 'delirious mania' in the recipient of a cochlear implant, by using unilateral ECT on the opposite side to the implant; the implant subsequently failed (Labadie *et al.*, 2010). There are no reports of harm from a patient with a cochlear implant receiving ECT. McCrackan and colleagues (2014) applied simulated ECT to five cadavers which had been fitted with functional cochlear implants. There was no damage to the cadavers or devices after exposure to 12 unilateral applications of 288mC.

Other Medical Conditions

The anaesthetist should review and be aware of the history of all relevant medical and surgical conditions before treatment and of any conditions developing or diagnosed during treatment.

Gastrointestinal Disorders

As gastro-oesophageal reflux is associated with an increased risk of aspiration during ECT, measures to decrease or neutralise gastric acidity may be necessary, as may modifications to anaesthetic technique (Chapter 23). Gastric banding for obesity is associated with recurrent aspiration (Lubit *et al.*, 2016).

Endocrine Disorders

The patient's management of diabetes may need to be modified, although ECT does not greatly affect insulin requirements or glycaemic control (Weiner & Sibert, 1996, Netzel *et al.*, 2002). There is little information on the use of ECT in patients with thyroid disease (Saito *et al.*, 2012); no effect was found in a study of thyrotrophin releasing hormone (Esel *et al.*, 2004). ECT has been used safely in Cushing's disease (van Rooijen *et al.*, 2016).

Respiratory Disorders

Electroconvulsive therapy may exacerbate bronchospasm in patients with asthma, but serious adverse effects have not been reported (Mueller *et al.*, 2006). Barbituarate anaesthetics may cause bronchospasm and should be avoided (Pizov *et al.*, 1995).

Other Conditions

Electroconvulsive therapy has been used successfully to treat severe depression complicating chronic renal failure requiring haemodialysis (Pearlman *et al.*, 1988; Williams & Ostroff, 2005), and in a patient with hepatic impairment after paracetamol overdose (Gligorovic *et al.*, 2016). It has also been used in patients with recent burns and skin grafting – in such cases a non-depolarising muscle relaxant should be used (Iwata *et al.*, 2009).

Osteoporosis is common in older people and increases the risk of bony injury during ECT. Increased doses of muscle relaxant are recommended (up to 1.5–1.8mg/kg suxamethonium (Bryson *et al.*, 2015). A peripheral nerve stimulator is needed to assess the degree of blockade prior to administering the electrical stimulus; post-treatment apnoea will be prolonged. The use of the Hamilton cuff technique to monitor seizure duration should be avoided in patients with osteoporosis (Baethge & Bshor, 2003).

There is a rise in intra-ocular pressure during ECT, which may prove hazardous to patients with glaucoma. The rise in pressure is attenuated by surgical treatment of glaucoma (Song *et al.*, 2004).

Minimising Risk

When a person is thought to be at greater risk because of a coexisting medical or surgical condition, consideration should always be given to ways of minimising risk by modifying medical management or ECT technique. High-risk patients should not be treated at remote sites or as out-patients. Modifications to medical treatment or ECT technique will require liaison between anaesthetist, psychiatrist and any other specialist involved. Some people at high risk may best be treated in a high dependency unit, with ECG monitoring before, during and after the treatment and staff who are familiar with cardiopulmonary resuscitation and the emergency treatment of arrhythmias.

Balance of Risks and Benefits

The balance of risks and benefits to physical and mental health must be considered for each individual. The risk–benefit analysis will include:

- The severity of the psychiatric illness and the risks it poses to the individual
- The likelihood of the psychiatric illness responding to ECT
- The medical risks of ECT and the extent to which they can be minimised or controlled
- Options for alternative treatments, the likely response to and adverse effects of those treatments, and the likely outcome if the person opts for no treatment.

The patient and family will normally be fully involved in discussions about the treatment, the risk–benefit analysis and alternative treatments. Where the risk of ECT remains high, the patient and, where appropriate, the family should be informed and then involved in the careful balancing of risks and benefits. Where a person is detained under the Mental Health Act 1983 or is being given treatment under mental capacity legislation and is unable to give consent, it is good practice to involve the relatives fully during assessment and before invoking the 'second opinion' procedure (see also Chapter 28).

Recommendations

- All coexisting medical or surgical conditions should be assessed and, where possible, treated or stabilised before ECT is administered.
- When a patient is thought to be at greater risk during ECT, consideration should always be given to ways of minimising risk by modifying medical management or ECT technique (or both).
- The balance of risks and benefits to physical and mental health must be considered for each individual.

- As far as possible, patients and, where appropriate, their families should be involved in discussions about the treatment, its risks, its possible benefits and any alternative treatments.
- On the occasions when ECT is prescribed to save life, there may be no absolute contraindications to it.

References

Albin, S. M., Stevens, S. R. & Rasmussen, K. G. (2007) Blood pressure before and after electroconvulsive therapy in hypertensive and nonhypertensive patients. *Journal of ECT*, **23**, 9–10.

Baethge, C. & Bshor, T. (2003) Wrist fracture in a patient undergoing electroconvulsive treatment monitored using the 'cuff' method. *European Archives of Psychiatry and Clinical Neuroscience*, **253**, 160–2.

Boere, E., Birkenhäger T. K., Groenland, T. H. N., *et al.* (2014) Beta-blocking agents during electroconvulsive therapy: a review. *British Journal of Anaesthesia*, **113**, 43–51.

Bryson, E. O., Liebman, L., Nazarian, R. (2015a) Safe resumption of maintenance ECT 12 days after surgical repair of hip fracture. *Journal of ECT*, **31**, 81–2.

Bryson, E. O., Popeo, D. M., Briggs, M. C., *et al.* (2015b) Automatic implantable convertor defibrillator in electroconvulsive therapy. *Journal of ECT*, **31**, e32.

Davis, A., Zisselman, M., Simmons, T., *et al.* (2009) Electroconvulsive therapy in the setting of implantable cardioverter-defibrillators. *Journal of ECT*, **25**, 198–201.

Esel, E., Kilic, C., Kula, M., *et al.* (2004) Effects of electroconvulsive therapy on thyrotropin-releasing hormone test in patients with depression. *Journal of ECT*, **20**, 248–53.

Fleisher, L. A., Fleischmann, K. E., Auerbach, A. D., *et al.* (2014) 2014 ACC/AHA Guideline on perioperative cardiovascular evaluation and management for patients undergoing noncardiac surgery. *Journal of the American College of Cardiology*, **64**, e77–137. http://dx.doi.org/10.1016/j.jacc.2014.07.944

Gahr, M., Connemann, B. J., Freudenmann, R. W., *et al.* (2014) Safety of electroconvulsive therapy in the presence of cranial metallic objects. *Journal of ECT*, **30**, 62–8.

Gligorovic, P., O'Brien, J. J. & Arias, L. M. (2016) Electroconvulsive therapy in the setting of acute, deliberate acetaminophen overdose. *Journal of ECT*, **32**, e18–e20.

Gough, J. I., Coebergh, J., Chandra, B., *et al.* (2016) Electroconvulsive therapy and / or plasmapheresis in autoimmune encephalitis? *World Journal of Clinical Cases*, **4**, 223–8.

Iwata, K., Masuda, M., Soejima, K. *et al.* (2009) Combination of ECT with skin graft surgery for a schizophrenic patient with burns. *Journal of ECT*, **25**, 210–12.

Kennedy, R., Mittal, D. & O'Jile, J. (2003) Electroconvulsive therapy in movement disorders: an update. *Journal of Neuropsychiatry and Clinical Neuroscience*, **15**, 407–21.

Krystal, A. D. & Coffey, C. E. (1997) Neuropsychiatric considerations in the use of electroconvulsive therapy. *Journal of Neuropsychiatry and Clinical Neurosciences*, **9**, 283–92.

Labadie, R. F., Clark, N. K., Cobb, C. M. *et al.* (2010) Electroconvulsive therapy in a cochlear implant patient. *Otology & Neurotology*, **31**, 64–6.

Lubit, E. B., Fetterman, T. C. & Ying, P. (2016) Recurrent aspiration in a patient with gastric band undergoing electroconvulsive therapy. *Journal of ECT*, **32**, 134–5.

MacPherson, R. D., Loo, C. K. & Barrett, N. (2006) Electroconvulsive therapy in patients with cardiac pacemakers. *Anaesthesia and Intensive Care*, **34**, 470.

Magid, M., Lapid, M. I., Sampson, S. M., *et al.* (2005) Use of electroconvulsive therapy in a patient 10 days after myocardial infarction. *Journal of ECT*, **21**, 182–5.

McCrackan, T., Rivas, A., Hedley-Williams, A., *et al.* (2014) Impedance testing on cochlear implants after electroconvulsive therapy. *Journal of ECT*, **30**, 303–8.

Mehta, V., Mueller, P. S., Gonzalez-Arriada, H. L., *et al.* (2004) Safety of electro-convulsive therapy in patients receiving long-term warfarin therapy. *Mayo Clinic Proceedings*, **79**, 1396–401.

Mizen, L., Morton, C. & Scott A. (2015) The cardiovascular safety of the empirical measurement of the seizure threshold in electroconvulsive therapy. *BJPsych Bulletin*, **39**, 14.

Mortier, P., Sienaert, P. & Bouckaert, F. (2012) Is electroconvulsive therapy safe in the presence of an intracranial metallic object? case report and review of the literature. *Journal of ECT*, **29**, 231–8.

Mueller, P. S., Schak, K. M., Barnes, R. D., *et al.* (2006) Safety of electroconvulsive therapy in patients with asthma. *Netherlands Journal of Medicine*, **64**, 417–21.

Mueller, P. S., Barnes, R. D., Varghese, R., *et al.* (2007) The safety of electroconvulsive therapy in patients with severe aortic stenosis. *Mayo Clinic Proceedings*, **82**, 1360–3.

Mueller, P. S., Albin, S. M., Barnes, R. D., *et al.* (2009) Safety of electroconvulsive therapy in patients with unrepaired abdominal aortic aneurysm: report of 8 patients. *Journal of ECT*, **25**, 165–9.

Netzel, P. J., Mueller, P. S., Rummans, T. A., *et al.* (2002) Safety, efficacy and effects on glycemic control of electroconvulsive therapy in insulin requiring type 2 diabetic patients. *Journal of ECT*, **18**, 16–21.

Pearlman, C., Carson, W. & Metz, A. (1988) Hemodialysis, chronic renal failure, and ECT. *Convulsive Therapy*, **4**, 332–33.

Pizov, R., Brown, R. H., Weiss, Y. S., *et al.* (1995) Wheezing during induction of general anesthesia in patients with and without asthma: a randomized blinded trial. *Anesthesiology*, **82**, 1111–16.

Pullen, S. J., Rasmussen K. G., Angstman, E. R., *et al.* (2011) The safety of electroconvulsive therapy in patients with prolonged QTc intervals on the electrocardiogram. *Journal of ECT*, **27**, 192–200.

Rivera, F. A., Lapid, M. I., Sampson, S., *et al.* (2011) Safety of electroconvulsive therapy in patients with a history of heart failure and decreased left ventricular systolic heart function. *Journal of ECT*, **27**, 207–13.

Saito, T., Saito, R., Suwa, H., *et al.* (2012) Differences in the treatment response to antithyroid drugs versus electroconvulsive therapy in a case of recurrent catatonia due to Graves' disease. *Case Reports in Psychiatry*, http://dx.doi.org/10.1155/2012/868490.

Shioda, K., Nisijima, K. & Kato, S. (2006) Electroconvulsive therapy for the treatment of multiple system atrophy with major depression. *General Hospital Psychiatry*, **28**, 81–3.

Song, J., Lee, P. P., Weiner, R., *et al.* (2010) The effect of surgery on intraocular pressure fluctuations with electroconvulsive therapy in a patient with severe glaucoma. *Journal of ECT*, **20**, 264–8.

Suzuki, K., Takamatsu, K., Takano, T., *et al.* (2008) Safety of electroconvulsive therapy in psychiatric patients shortly after the occurrence of pulmonary embolism. *Journal of ECT*, **24**, 286–8.

Tess, A. V. & Smetana, G. W. (2009) Medical evaluation of patients undergoing electroconvulsive therapy. *New England Journal of Medicine*, **360**, 1437–44.

U.S. Food and Drug Administration (2014) Benefits and risks of cochlear implants. https://www.fda.gov/medicaldevices/productsandmedicalprocedures/implantsandprosthetics/cochlearimplants/ucm062843.htm (accessed 23 October 2017).

Van Rooijen, G., Denys, D., Fliers, E., *et al.* (2016) Effective electroconvulsive therapy in a patient with psychotic depression with active Cushing Disease. *Journal of ECT*, **32**, e20–e21.

Villa-Rodriguez, F., McGirr, A., Tham, J., *et al.* (2014) Electroconvulsive therapy in a patient with deep brain stimulators. *Journal of ECT*, **30**, e16–18.

Weiner, R. D. & Sibert, T. E. (1996) Use of ECT in treatment of depression in patients with diabetes mellitus. *Journal of Clinical Psychiatry*, **57**, 138.

Weintraub, D. & Lippmann, S. B. (2000) Electroconvulsive therapy in the acute poststroke period. *Journal of ECT*, **16**, 415–18.

Wilkinson, S. T., Helgeson, L. & Ostroff, R. B. (2014) Electroconvulsive therapy and cerebral aneurysms. *Journal of ECT*, **30**, e47–e49.

Williams, S. & Ostroff, R. (2005) Chronic renal failure, hemodialysis, and electroconvulsive therapy: a case report. *Journal of ECT*, **21**, 41–2.

Chapter 28

Capacity, Consent and the Law

Jonathan Waite

Capacity: the Principles

As health care professionals we owe a duty of care to our patients. Our patients have a right to autonomy – to make their own decisions. If we impose treatment on them against their wishes, when they have capacity to make a decision to refuse treatment, then we may be committing the tort of battery; if we fail to treat them when they lack capacity to make treatment decisions we may be found to be negligent.

These basic principles apply in all countries, but the details of the law vary in different jurisdictions. In 1995, both the Law Commission (1995) and Scottish Law Commission (1995) produced reports which contained very similar recommendations about how capacity should be assessed and how decisions could be made on behalf of people who lack capacity. These reports have been influential in developing incapacity legislation around the world.

Treating mental disorders in patients subject to mental health legislation is an exception; in these circumstances European law permits treatment of patients who have capacity against their wishes. In the UK, this exception applies only to treatment with medication, it does not hold for ECT. ECT may only be given to patients who object if they lack capacity to make this decision. It is possible to make a binding advance decision to refuse ECT and proxy decision makers (attorneys, guardians or deputies) can make a decision to refuse ECT on behalf of a patient who lacks capacity.

In an emergency, if ECT is immediately necessary to save life or prevent serious deterioration, it can be given even to a person who has capacity to refuse, or who has made an advance decision to refuse ECT, but it cannot be continued if these conditions are no longer met.

The Informal Patient: Seeking Consent

The General Medical Council (GMC) advises that:

> You must work in partnership with your patients. You should discuss with them their condition and treatment options in a way they can understand, and respect their right to make decisions about their care. You should see getting their consent as an important part of the process of discussion and decision-making, rather than as something that happens in isolation.

> In deciding how much information to share with your patients you should take account of their wishes. The information you share should be in proportion to the nature of their condition, the complexity of the proposed investigation or treatment, and the seriousness of any potential side effects, complications or other risks.

> (General Medical Council, 2008).

The information you should give would include what a reasonable patient would wish to know, not what a reasonable doctor might think was appropriate (*Chester v Afshar; Montgomery v Lanarkshire HB*).

The minimum information that the patient needs to understand is that ECT involves a course of treatment, at each treatment session a modified seizure is induced under a general anaesthetic. The physical risks are low and are comparable to any other minor procedure, carried out under general anaesthesia. There is likely to be some pain associated with insertion of cannula; there may be also be a period of nausea, headache and confusion following the procedure and muscle aches may occur. There is a possibility of dental or maxilla-facial injury (Chapter 24); some patients experience memory difficulty (Chapter 13). The benefits would be that about two-thirds of patients are 'much improved' or 'very much improved' after a course of ECT (SEAN, 2016).

If a patient is unable to understand, retain or use this information to make a decision, or cannot communicate that decision, then they lack capacity to make a decision on receiving ECT.

It is helpful for patients and carers to be provided with information obtained from different sources. Written information sheets may be useful (such as those available on the Royal College of Psychiatrists' website: https://www.rcpsych.ac.uk/healthinformation/treat mentsandwellbeing/ect.aspx); these need to be accompanied by the opportunity to discuss issues with members of the therapeutic team, family members, carers, advocates, etc. Some patients may find over-long sheets daunting; provision of information in a variety of ways (e.g. through face-to-face interview, video, audiotape, podcast or interactive DVD) may be more acceptable.

Although UK law makes no distinction between the validity of written, verbal or even implied consent, it is recommended practice to seek the patient's written consent using a standard consent form – designed specifically for ECT – which complies with national guidelines. The absence of a written statement of consent may make it very difficult to provide evidence that consent has in fact been given. In the Republic of Ireland, written consent is required. Since written consent is obtained for the course of treatment and not for each treatment session, it is important to ensure patients clearly understand that they can withdraw consent at any time, despite having signed a consent form. They should also understand how they might inform staff about a change in consent. The continuation of consent should be verbally checked before each treatment, usually by a member of staff in the ECT suite. It is good practice for consent forms to specify the maximum number of treatments to which the patient has agreed to consent. The figure can be agreed with individual patients, although a figure of 12 has been suggested as standard. Further treatment beyond the agreed figure would require new written consent. It is also good practice to record on the consent form whether the patient has specified consent for bilateral or unilateral electrode placement.

It is important that patients are broadly able to understand the implications of refusing a treatment. They must also be informed that a patient who has capacity has a right to refuse treatment for any given reason or none at all. Refusal in these circumstances does not allow for any form of coercion to persuade reluctant patients to accept ECT (e.g. 'If you don't consent then there is nothing more I will do'). The law is clear that any form of coercion (including that from families and friends) would negate the validity of the consent. It would also be unethical. Although it is unacceptable under any circumstances to use the threat of enforced treatment under mental health legislation to obtain consent, in some circumstances patients may need to understand that a possible consequence of their decision to decline ECT might be an assessment for treatment under compulsory powers. As a part of the discussion, alternative therapies to ECT should be raised and it should be made clear that a refusal of treatment will not prejudice any further care.

Assessing Capacity

If a patient is sufficiently ill for a course of ECT to be considered, it is likely that there will be some impairment in their capacity to make decisions about treatment. Clinicians who are seeking consent to treatment are under a duty to take all practicable steps to enable patients to make decisions for themselves before concluding that they lack capacity. You should discuss the proposed treatment at a time and in a place that helps them to understand and retain the information. You should aim to have a friend or relative of the patient, or a trusted member of the health care team present, to help them relax and make the decision, more than one interview may be necessary. If the patient wishes to be seen alone you should speak to someone who knows the patient well, to establish how best to communicate with the patient.

There are small differences in the definition of capacity in the different legislatures of the UK but in simple terms if a person can:

- Understand the information relevant to the decision
- Retain the information for long enough to reach a decision
- Use and weigh the information to make a decision
- Communicate their decision,

then they are considered to have capacity to make that decision. A similar definition of capacity is used in many other countries (including the Republic of Ireland).

A particular problem which may arise in treating patients with severe depression (particularly intelligent and articulate individuals) is that although the patient may be able to understand and use information to reach a decision, that decision is clouded by their feelings of futility and hopelessness. The decision which they reach is not the same as it would have been if they were not ill. It might be argued that in fact such people are not able to understand, use or weigh relevant information, hence treatment contrary to the wishes of the patient might be justified. In such circumstances it is wise to seek legal advice or the view of a clinical ethics committee.

Discussions on capacity and consent to treatment will usually be conducted by the team who prescribe ECT; it is important that they document what they have done clearly, so that the ECT treatment team can be confident that an informed choice has been made. The ECT suite at the time of treatment is generally not a good time and place to assess capacity to make decisions about treatment; where the clinic team can be sure that the patient has made a decision to accept ECT, in general the ECT team should act to facilitate implementing the decision which the patient previously made.

If a patient refuses ECT in the treatment suite, having previously consented, a member of the team with a good relationship with the patient should undertake a fresh capacity assessment, in as relaxed and calm a manner as possible, in a quiet room away from the treatment area.

- If the person has capacity there is no longer consent – any act done on that person would be unlawful. If a capacitous person removes consent, consent no longer exists and the treatment cannot continue.

- If, at this point, the person is lacking capacity as a result of stress, fear, or any other reason (which would be an impairment of, or disturbance in the functioning of, mind or brain) there needs to be a reasonable belief of lack of capacity and best interests. As in the best interests determination special regard has to be had to wishes, feelings, beliefs and values. If the person expressed their (capacitous) wishes and feelings very recently it would *probably* be fairly simple to determine that the treatment is in the person's best interests. The treatment can then go ahead.

Capacity Law

In all countries of the UK capacity legislation provides safeguards for those who care for people who lack capacity to make decisions for themselves. Each Act is prefaced by a list of principles:

- a presumption of capacity
- all practicable attempts should be made to enable the person to make a decision
- any intervention should be the least restrictive of the person's rights and freedoms.

Each Act gives a general authority to provide care and treatment and defines how capacity is to be assessed. Each explains how decisions are to be made for people who lack capacity – in their 'best interests' in England, Wales and Ireland, for their 'benefit' in Scotland. Each Act makes provision for a person or persons (proxy or proxies) to be selected to make decisions on behalf of an individual who lacks capacity. These proxies may be chosen by people for themselves at a time when they have capacity to do so ('attorneys') or appointed by the courts after the person has lost capacity ('deputies' or 'guardians'). In each country there is a system of advocacy establishing professionals whose role is to assist people who have impaired capacity, for those have no family or friends who take an interest in their welfare, or to supplement the role of informal supporters. In England, Wales and Northern Ireland there are also legal provisions to enable people, when they are competent, to make advance decisions to refuse any specified medical treatment (including ECT) on a future occasion when they are incapable. In Scotland advance statements may be made to refuse ECT under mental health legislation.

England and Wales
Mental Capacity Act 2005 (MCA)

A person who has capacity may create a Lasting Power of Attorney for personal finances and/or health and personal welfare matters (MCA ss. 9–14). People who hold Lasting Power of Attorney are generally referred to as 'attorneys', but the MCA uses the term 'donees'. Anyone with capacity may also make advance decisions to refuse specified forms of treatment, which are legally binding so long as they are correctly drawn up (MCA ss. 24–26).

The Act established the Court of Protection (MCA ss. 45–61), who may make rulings on any matter relating to mental capacity, including whether a person has capacity in respect of a particular decision, whether a treatment would be in a person's best interests, or whether an advance directive is valid and applicable. It is also possible (although unusual) for the Court of Protection to appoint a 'deputy' to make decisions on behalf of people who lack capacity (MCA ss.15–21). People who lack capacity may be entitled to the support of an Independent Mental Capacity Advocate (IMCA) (MCA ss. 35–41).

The MCA makes no specific reference to ECT, but the associated *Code of Practice* (Department of Constitutional Affairs, 2007 §10.45) cites ECT as an example of a 'serious medical treatment' for which an IMCA will need to be instructed.

Table 28.1 England and Wales

Capacity to consent	Legal status	Treatment authorisation
Capable	Informal	Written consent
	Detained	Written consent
		Capacity certified on Form T2
Incapable	Informal	Second opinion under s.5 MCA
		Only if patient is concordant with treatment
	Detained	SOAD authorises treatment certified on Form T6
	Detained – urgent	Treatment given prior to independent opinion under s.62

The Office of the Public Guardian (OPG) is responsible for administering the MCA; they maintain a register of deputies and lasting powers of attorney. It is possible to apply to search the Public Guardian registers by completing form OPG100 (https://www.gov.uk/government/publications/search-public-guardian-registers).

The donee of a Lasting Power of Attorney for health and welfare, or a court-appointed deputy may make a decision to refuse ECT, on behalf of a patient who lacks capacity. Such a refusal is legally binding. An advance decision to refuse ECT is also legally binding, providing it is 'valid and applicable'. If treatment is urgently necessary it may be possible to authorise it under s.62(1A) of the Mental Health Act – see 'Emergency Treatment' further in the chapter.

Mental Health Act 1983 (MHA)

The Mental Health Act (MHA) (see Table 28.1) regulates the compulsory admission of psychiatric patients to hospital. There are Codes of Practice for relevant professionals for England (Department of Health, 2015a) and Wales (Welsh Government, 2016). Part IV of the Act (MHA ss. 56–64) is concerned with medical treatment in hospital. It does not apply to patients detained on emergency orders (MHA ss. 5, 135 or 136), patients remanded for psychiatric reports or other detained patients (s. 35, or ss. 42(2), 73 or 74).

ECT is dealt with by s. 58A. ECT may be given under this provision to detained adult patients:

- if they consent and if either the responsible clinician or a Second Opinion Appointed Doctor (SOAD) certifies (on Form T4) that they are capable of understanding the nature, purpose and likely effects of the treatment (s. 58A(3)).
- if a SOAD certifies in writing (on Form T6) (s.58A(5)):

1. That the patient is not capable of understanding the nature, purpose and likely effects of the treatment
2. That it is appropriate for the treatment to be given
3. That giving him the treatment would not conflict with:

   (i) an advance decision which the registered medical practitioner concerned is satisfied is valid and applicable; or
   (ii) a decision made by a donee or deputy or by the Court of Protection.

The SOAD must consult a nurse and another professional (not a doctor or a nurse) who has been involved in the patient's treatment before issuing a T6 certificate. The SOAD service in

England is organised by the Care Quality Commission (CQC) and in Wales by the Health Inspectorate Wales (HIW). A SOAD visit should be requested from the CQC via the online Provider Portal; in Wales form SOAD1 from HIW should be completed.

Referring clinicians should notify the SOAD about any advance decisions and advance statements by the patient relevant to the proposed treatment and any court orders, including those of the Court of Protection. The SOAD should also be told about any attorney or deputy who has authority to make decisions on the patient's behalf about medical treatment.

Specific rules (Part 4A) apply to patients on Community Treatment Orders (CTO) (s. 17A) (Department of Health, 2015b; Chapter 24). It is permissible to give out-patient ECT to a CTO patient if they have capacity and are consenting (Department of Health, 2015b §24.7). The responsible clinician will need to complete form CTO12 to certify this. The rules for CTO patients without capacity are broadly similar to those for informal patients in England (Department of Health, 2015b §24.8–15) but see Welsh Government (2016) §17.8 for the situation in Wales.

Mental Capacity Act or Mental Health Act?

If an informal patient lacks capacity to consent but appears to adhere to treatment, then it may be preferable to give ECT under the MCA, in accordance with the 'least restrictive option' principle of the MHA Code of Practice (Department of Health, 2015a: § 1.3). Although the MCA offers fewer safeguards than the MHA it is less restrictive of a patient's freedom. Although it is not a legal requirement, it is good practice to seek a second opinion from a colleague prior to proceeding (Department of Health, 2009). If the patient does not adhere to treatment, and ECT it is still needed, it will be necessary to consider whether an assessment for detention under the MHA is necessary in order to use the explicit authority of s. 58A to treat a patient who lacks capacity and is refusing necessary treatment. It will be necessary to reassess capacity before every treatment, if capacity is regained, ECT cannot proceed without informed consent.

Emergency Treatment

A patient detained under s.2 or s.3 of the MHA may be given ECT in an emergency if it is 'immediately necessary to save life or prevent serious deterioration in the patient's condition' (MHA s. 62). Section 62 applies even if there is a contrary advance decision or an objection by a deputy or attorney. If there is concern about the validity or applicability of the advance decision to refuse ECT, consideration should be given to referring the matter to the Court of Protection for a ruling on the legality of treatment. Treatment may be continued while the Court's decision is awaited (MCA s. 26(5)). If there is concern that an attorney or deputy is not acting in the patient's best interests, this should be brought to the attention of the Public Guardian.

Some patients who have received ECT as an emergency treatment under MHA s. 62 and recover capacity may refuse further treatment, even though the clinical team feel their recovery is incomplete. There may be concern that relapse in these circumstances is likely; with a possible cycle of emergency treatment/partial recovery/refusal/relapse/emergency treatment ensuing. Since this scenario may be anticipated, good practice suggests that the consultant should discuss the possibility with the patient once they have capacity, clarifying in detail what the patient's wishes would be should their condition decline. If a patient with capacity is clear that they do not want further ECT – even if this refusal means that they will put their health at grave risk – then this is likely to be determinative.

Suggested Procedure for Consent for People under 18

There are special provisions for ECT for people under the age of 18, whether or not they are detained under the MHA (s. 58A). A person aged 16 or 17 is presumed to have capacity to consent unless shown otherwise. If the person under 18 has capacity to consent, ECT may be given only if a SOAD issues a certificate (Form T5) that the young person can and does consent to ECT and that the treatment is appropriate.

If the person under 18 has capacity but refuses to give consent, a SOAD certificate alone does not provide authority to give ECT: there must also be authority from another source. Unlike the situation in those over 18, a court may have authority to overrule this refusal, but it is likely to consider very carefully before doing so. If the young person lacks capacity to consent it is uncertain whether ECT falls within the range of treatments for which a person with parental authority (usually the parents) can give consent (see chapter 19 of the *Code of Practice* for details (Department of Health, 2015a) or chapter 33 of the *Code of Practice for Wales* (Welsh Government, 2016). Paragraph 19.41 of the *Code of Practice* (Department of Health, 2015a) expresses doubt about the appropriateness of parental consent to ECT.

Some children under the age of 16 may have sufficient understanding and intelligence to be able to consent to ECT (*Gillick v W Norfolk and Wisbech AHA* [1986]), in which case ECT can be given with their valid consent and SOAD certification. In cases of emergency when there is insufficient time to obtain parental consent or court authority, the courts have stated that doubt should be resolved in favour of the preservation of life, and it will be acceptable to undertake treatment to preserve life or prevent irreversible serious deterioration of the patient's condition (Department of Health, 2015a §19.71).

For further information on the law in England and Wales, see Fennell (2011).

Scotland

The Mental Welfare Commission for Scotland (2010) provides guidance on best practice in relation to consent to treatment for mental disorder. The relevant legislation is the Mental Health (Care and Treatment) (Scotland) Act 2003 (MHCTA) and the Adults with Incapacity (Scotland) Act 2000 (AIA). Both of these acts are relevant to patients who may require ECT (Table 28.2).

Informal Patients Capable of Giving Consent

Most patients who receive ECT in Scotland have capacity to consent to the procedure. According to SEAN (2016), in 2015, 62% of patients treated with ECT were informal patients who gave consent. The proportion of patients receiving ECT who lack capacity to consent has remained constant for several years. If a patient has the capacity to give informed consent, then the clinician should follow best practice guidelines to make joint decisions on treatment, provided there is no need to consider MHCTA 2003. When an adult with capacity decides to have ECT, then both the doctor who has explained the procedure and the patient should sign a standard consent form to record the decision. The consent form is a record that the consent has been given but it does not confirm that the consent is valid. It is best practice to record the reasons that the consent is valid in the case notes. It is also good practice for the consent to be reviewed before each treatment to ensure it remains valid. If there is a gap in treatment of greater than two weeks, then it is recommended that consent be recorded anew. The patient should be informed that they can withdraw their consent at any point. ECT cannot lawfully be given to a competent adult who refuses treatment.

Table 28.2 Scotland

Capacity to consent	Legal status	Treatment authorisation
Capable	Informal	Written consent
	Detained	Written consent Capacity certified on Form T2
Incapable	Informal	Second opinion under s. 48 AIA Only if patient is concordant with treatment
	Detained – concordant	Independent 'best interests' opinion under MHCT recorded on Form T3A
	Detained – objecting or resisting	Independent opinion recorded on Form T3B
	Urgent (includes patients detained under emergency certificates)	Treatment given prior to independent opinion. S. 47 AIA (Informal) S. 243 MHCTA (Detained)

Patients Incapable of Giving Informed Consent

The AIA 2000 may be used to authorise treatment when patients do not have capacity to understand or communicate their consent to ECT and do not show signs of objecting or resisting the treatment. If the patient is showing signs of objecting to or resisting treatment then the patient should be detained under the MHCTA. All detained patients who resist or object to ECT require an independent second opinion from a designated medical practitioner from the Mental Welfare Commission, except in very acute emergency situations.

Adults with Incapacity (Scotland) Act 2000

The AIA 2000 gives legal definitions of the concepts described earlier. The Act sets out (in s. 1) principles which can be summarised as:

- the intervention must benefit the adult
- any intervention shall be the least restrictive in relation to the freedom of the adult, consistent with the purpose of the intervention
- account must be taken of the past and present wishes of the adult
- where practicable, account should be taken of:
  - the views of relative and carers
  - the views of relevant others (guardians, attorneys, etc.).

S. 1(6) of the Act also provides definitions of 'adult' as a person who has attained the age of 16 years, and 'incapable':

which means incapable of:

(a) acting
(b) making decisions
(c) communicating decisions
(d) understanding decisions
(e) retaining the memory of decisions,

as mentioned in any provision of this Act, by reason of mental disorder or of inability to communicate because of physical disability; but a person shall not fall within this definition by reason only of a lack or deficiency in a faculty of communication if that lack or deficiency can be made good by human or mechanical aid (whether of an interpretative nature or otherwise).

(Adults with Incapacity (Scotland) Act 2000, s. 1(6))

A general authority to treat is given under s. 47 to the medical practitioner primarily responsible for the medical treatment of an incapable adult. Such treatment must safeguard or promote mental or physical health but treatment must not require the use of force or detention (unless immediately necessary and only for so long as is necessary in the circumstances). When s. 47 is used to give treatment, a certificate of incapacity should be completed. The use of force or detention is not permitted; the MHCTA 2003 should be used where a patient actively resists or opposes treatment.

S.48 of the AIA 2000 excludes from the general authority to treat special treatments such as ECT, transcranial magnetic stimulation and vagus nerve stimulation (defined in the MHCTA 2003). It sets in place a procedure whereby a designated medical practitioner second opinion must be sought. The designated medical practitioner will be provided by the Mental Welfare Commission for Scotland and will complete a prescribed form, which is lodged with the Commission within seven days of issue. The AIA 2000 has provision for proxy decision makers such as welfare attorneys, welfare guardians and those exercising an intervention order, all of whom can normally consent to treatment on behalf of an incapable adult, but they cannot consent to special treatments under Section 48 (including ECT).

Mental Health (Care and Treatment) (Scotland) Act 2003

This Act sets out, in s. 1, ten principles which are to be used by any person discharging a function under the Act. Part 16 of the Act is concerned with medical treatment:

Medical treatment' is defined in s.329 as treatment for mental disorder; for this purpose, 'treatment' includes nursing, care, psychological interventions, habilitation and rehabilitation. Medical treatment includes pharmacological interventions as well as other physical interventions such as ECT.

(Mental Health (Care and Treatment) (Scotland) Act 2003 Part 16).

Short-term Detention Certificate/Compulsory Treatment Order

Patients are initially detained under a short-term detention certificate (STDC). The STDC authorises detention and treatment under Part 16 of the MHCTA for up to 28 days; it gives the patient and their named person a number of rights, including that of appeal. Application for a compulsory treatment order requires a draft care plan. This may include ECT (the *Consent to Treatment* guidance from the Mental Welfare Commission for Scotland (2018) contains information on how to draft a care plan for ECT). All applications for a compulsory treatment order are heard by the Mental Health Tribunal for Scotland. Part 16 also applies to most people subject to mental healthcare and treatment under criminal procedures legislation.

The criteria for detention are similar for each order. They must be met for a compulsory treatment order. They must be 'likely to be met' for an STDC. Criminal procedure orders do not require the patient to have impaired decision-making ability. The criteria are:

- The presence of a mental disorder.
- Medical treatment which would be likely to prevent the mental disorder worsening, or alleviate the symptoms or effects of the disorder, is available.

- There would be significant risk to the health, safety or welfare of the patient or safety of any other person if the patient were not given medical treatment.
- Because of this mental disorder the patient's ability to make decisions about the provision of medical treatment for mental disorder is significantly impaired.
- The making of the order is necessary.

Patients detained under an STDC or compulsory treatment order may be given medical treatment for mental disorder with or without their consent. ECT can only be given to a patient under compulsion:

- If they can and do consent or
- If they are incapable of consenting and treatment is authorised by a designated medical practitioner.

If a patient does give consent, a witnessed written statement is required. This must be recorded on Form T2. The responsible medical officer must certify that:

- Consent has been given and
- Treatment is in the patient's best interests, having regard to the likelihood of the treatment alleviating or preventing deterioration in the patient's condition.

Form T2 is required irrespective of the length of time the patient has been subject to the Act (for medication Form T2 is only required after the patient has received treatment for two months). Patients can withdraw their consent at any time and no further ECT can be given by virtue of the earlier consent.

If the patient does not consent or is unable to give consent, then ECT can be authorised by a designated medical practitioner using Form T3. The process for this is very similar to that under the AIA 2000; the designated medical practitioner is provided by the Mental Welfare Commission for Scotland. If the patient is incapable of consenting, the designated medical practitioner must certify that the patient is incapable and that the treatment is in the patient's best interests.

If the patient objects or resists, the designated medical practitioner must certify this as such and that the patient is incapable of making the decision and that the treatment is necessary under the urgent medical treatment provisions of Section 243 in order to:

- Save the patient's life
- Prevent serious deterioration in the patient's condition
- Alleviate serious suffering on the part of the patient.

Should these criteria no longer be met, then no further treatment can be given under these provisions.

There may be a situation where a patient urgently requires ECT and it is not possible to arrange a visit from the designated medical practitioner. If emergency treatment is needed under the grounds specified in s. 243 of the Act, it must be reported to the Mental Welfare Commission, stating the type of treatment given and its purpose. Form T4 should be used for this. Although there is no legal requirement for a second opinion for emergency treatment, it is advisable to ask a local colleague for an opinion.

Advance Statements

Advance statements may be made under s. 275. This allows a patient to specify which type of care and treatment they would like to receive, or not like to receive, should they become mentally ill. Clinicians must have regard to the content of such statements when planning care. This does not necessarily mean that they must be followed; it is possible for the clinician to override an advance statement. In such circumstances, s. 276(8) requires the clinician to give the reasons for overriding the advance statement in writing, justified with reference to the principles of the Act. The reasons should be recorded in the case file and given to the patient, named person, welfare attorney, guardian and the Mental Welfare Commission. The Commission will scrutinise such decisions to override an advance statement.

The Act also gives any person with a mental disorder the right to independent advocacy. Advocacy workers can help patients express their views about medical treatment, including ECT.

Northern Ireland

The Mental Health (Northern Ireland) Order (1986) corresponds to the England and Wales Mental Health Act. Although there are differences in terminology, the legal principles are very similar to those underlying the England and Wales Act. Part IV of the Order relates to consent to treatment (DHSSPS, 2003).

When ECT is proposed as being the most appropriate treatment, patients, whether voluntary or detained, are asked to give their informed consent. In the case of a detained patient who is able to give valid consent to ECT, the Responsible Medical Officer (RMO) for the patient must validate this consent. A Form 22 must be signed indicating consent has been given and returned to the Regulation and Quality Improvement Authority (RQIA). Article 64 of the Order requires that for patients who cannot give informed consent to ECT or who refuse ECT, an independent second opinion is sought from a Part IV Medical Practitioner. Part IV Medical Practitioners are Consultant Psychiatrists, appointed by RQIA, to give second opinions in relation to the administration of ECT. They have to visit the patient and review the entire case history, interview the patient, discuss the treatment options with the referring consultant and provide an opinion on whether or not the treatment plan to administer ECT is appropriate. If the Part IV Practitioner agrees with the treatment plan, the decision is recorded on a Form 23. If the Part IV Medical Practitioner disagrees with the plan to administer ECT they will discuss their reasons and other treatment options with the referring consultant. In such cases the treatment plan to administer ECT will not proceed. Emergency treatment may be given under Article 68 where it is necessary to save the patient's life or prevent serious deterioration in their condition. The RQIA (2014) has produced a report on the use of ECT in Northern Ireland from 2010 to 2014.

The Mental Capacity Act (Northern Ireland) 2016 will make major amendments to the 1986 Order (Sch. 11) when it is fully implemented (the legal situation in Northern Ireland has been upset by the suspension of the Stormont Assembly and therefore the 2016 Northern Ireland Act has not come into force). It will apply equally to all patients who lack capacity and require treatment for any reason. It is specifically drafted to reduce the stigma of separate mental health legislation and to respect the rights of people with impaired capacity, enabling them to retain as much autonomy as possible and exercise their remaining decision-making capacity (Lynch et al, 2017). The principles of the Act (ss. 1-2) and its definitions of capacity (ss. 2–3) and best interests (ss. 7–8) derive (like the England and Wales Act) from the Law Commission report (1995).

Once the 2016 Act comes into force, patients will only be able to be detained if they lack capacity to make a decision about informal admission and where the degree of restraint which they require is a proportionate response to the likelihood of them coming to harm if not detained and the seriousness of the harm concerned (s. 12). Except in emergencies, detention in hospital will need to be authorised by a Health and Social Care Trust panel (Sch. 2). ECT is specified as a 'treatment with serious consequences' (s.16(1)(a)) which will require a formal assessment of capacity (ss. 13–14) and a second opinion from an appropriate medical practitioner appointed by the RQIA. They must examine the patient and any relevant health records and consult such person or persons as appear to them to be principally concerned with treating the patient (s. 18).

Republic of Ireland

The statutory basis for treating detained patients in the Republic of Ireland is the Mental Health Act 2001 (Kelly, 2007). Use of the Act is overseen by the Mental Health Commission, who publish the *Code of Practice* (2016a) and *Rules* (2016b) on the use of ECT. The *Code of Practice* provides guidance on ECT in general, whereas the *Rules* govern the use of ECT specifically for patients detained under the Irish Mental Health Act 2001. The Act was amended in 2015 to remove the power of the Commission to authorise the treatment of capacitous patients who were 'unwilling' to have ECT.

The Mental Health Commission also inspects ECT clinics and produces regular reports on the use of ECT in approved centres in Ireland (Mental Health Commission, 2016c). The *Code of Practice* and the *Rules* specify what information must be given to the patient and what information on the course of treatment is to be sent to the Commission. The *Rules* also specify cognitive and physical assessments, conditions for the administration of ECT, staffing levels in the ECT suite and documentation. The standards required are similar to those required by ECTAS and SEAN.

The majority of patients (85%) in Ireland are treated voluntarily with ECT (Mental Health Commission, 2016c) and provide valid informed consent, as assessed by the responsible consultant psychiatrist, in line with the *Code of Practice* (Mental Health Commission, 2016a). There is no mechanism for a relative, carer or guardian to give consent on behalf of the patient. Capacity to consent to ECT should ensure that the voluntary patient can:

- Understand the nature of ECT
- Understand why ECT is being proposed
- Understand the benefits, risks (including the risk of amnesia) and alternatives to receiving ECT
- Understand and believe the broad consequences of not receiving ECT
- Retain the information long enough to make a decision to receive or not receive ECT
- Make a free choice to receive or refuse ECT
- Communicate the decision to consent to ECT.

Part IV of the Act covers consent to treatment. The legislation refers to a series of up to 12 ECT treatments as a 'programme'. According to Section 59, ECT may only be administered to detained patients if the patient gives consent in writing. If the patient lacks capacity, treatment may be given where the consultant in charge of the patient's care has approved the programme of treatment, and the programme has been authorised by another consultant psychiatrist. The referring consultant fills out the first two pages of Form 16 and a second psychiatrist completes the third page.

Acknowledgements

The author thanks Dr Simon Wood, Principal SOAD, Mr Michael Sergeant, Dr Alistair Hay, and Dr Gerry Lynch for specialist advice and Dr Richard Barnes for helpful comments.

References

Department for Constitutional Affairs (2007) *Mental Capacity Act 2005: Code of Practice*. TSO (The Stationery Office).

Department of Health (2009) *Reference Guide to Consent for Examination or Treatment* (2nd edn). Department of Health.

Department of Health (2015a) *Code of Practice: Mental Health Act 1983*. TSO (The Stationery Office).

Department of Health (2015b) *Reference Guide to the Mental Health Act 1983*. TSO (The Stationery Office).

Department of Health, Social Services and Public Safety (2003) *Reference Guide to Consent for Examination, Treatment or Care*. Belfast: Department of Health, Social Services and Public Safety.

Fennell, P. (2011) *Mental Health: Law and Practice* (2nd edn). Jordan Publishing.

General Medical Council (2008) *Consent: Patients and Doctors Making Decisions Together*. General Medical Council.

Kelly, B. D. (2007) The Irish Mental Health Act 2001. *Psychiatric Bulletin*, **31**, 21–24.

Law Commission (1995) *Mental Incapacity: Law Com No. 231* HMSO.

Lynch, G., Taggart, C. & Campbell, P. (2017) Mental Capacity Act (Northern Ireland) 2016. *BJPsych Bulletin*, **41**, 353–7.

Mental Health Commission (2016a) *Code of Practice: Code of Practice on the Use of Electro-Convulsive Therapy for Voluntary Patients (Version3)*. Dublin: Mental Health Commission.

Mental Health Commission (2016b) *Rules: Rules Governing the Use of Electro-Convulsive Therapy (Version 2)*. Dublin: Mental Health Commission.

Mental Health Commission (2016c) *The Administration of Electro-Convulsive Therapy in Approved Centres: Activity Report 2014–2015*. Dublin: Mental Health Commission.

Mental Welfare Commission for Scotland (2018) *Consent to Treatment: A Guide for Mental Health Practitioners*. Mental Welfare Commission for Scotland.

Regulation and Quality Improvement Authority (2014) *Report on the administration of Electroconvulsive Therapy in Northern Ireland*. https://rqia.org.uk/RQIA/files/84/846de0ef-a242-46fe-bd62-747435981cea.pdf

Scottish ECT Accreditation Network (2016) *Scottish ECT Accreditation Network Annual Report 2016: A Summary of ECT in Scotland for 2015*. NHS National Services Scotland.

Scottish Law Commission (1995) *Report on Incapable Adults: Scot Law Com No 151)*. HMSO.

Welsh Government (2016) *Mental Health Act 1983: Code of Practice for Wales*.

Cases

Chester v Afshar [2004] UKHL 41.

Gillick v W Norfolk and Wisbech AHA [1986] AC 112 (HL).

Montgomery v Lanarkshire HB [2015] UKSC 11.

Patients', Carers' and the Public's Perspectives on ECT and Related Treatments

Jonathan Waite

ECT remains one of the most controversial treatments in psychiatry. Although its efficacy and safety are acknowledged and have been confirmed (Chapter 1) there are still attempts (based on flawed reviews of the literature) to claim that its use cannot be scientifically justified (Read & Bentall, 2010). Media accounts of ECT tend to be highly emotive and vary from lauding ECT as life changing (Seelye, 2016) to damning it as abusive (Browne, 2000).

Patients' Perspectives

Members of the general public have a strongly negative perception of ECT. These negative views have often been reinforced by media accounts by self selected subjects recounting unpleasant experiences. Studies across many nations have found that ECT is perceived as harmful or abusive (Lauber *et al*, 2005; Arshad *et al*, 2007; McFarquhar & Thompson, 2010). Images of ECT in American films have become increasingly more cruel and negative (McDonald & Walter, 2001). Chakrabarti *et al* (2010) reviewed 75 studies assessing patients' knowledge of and attitudes to ECT. They concluded that patients were mostly poorly informed, were frightened of the procedure and experienced distressing side effects. One third of patients felt coerced to have the treatment. Despite these issues, Chakrabarti *et al* concluded that the majority of patients who have experienced ECT found the treatment to have been helpful and had positive views of ECT.

Media reports on the use of ECT generally refer to guidance offered in the National Institute for Clinical Excellence (NICE) Technology Appraisal (2003). This appraisal was informed by two commissioned systematic reviews. The group tasked with assessing evidence for efficacy (UK ECT Review Group, 2003) concluded that there was evidence that ECT was an effective treatment for depressive disorders. The review of patients' perspectives on ECT – specifically their views on the benefits of treatment and adverse effects on memory – conducted by the Service User Research Enterprise (SURE) at the Institute of Psychiatry (Rose *et al*, 2003) was generally negative and emphasised adverse effects of treatment. The NICE Committee's decision to recommend ECT only when illness was life-threatening or resistant to other treatments was significantly influenced by service users' views (NICE, 2003: para. 4.3.8).

Rose *et al* (2003) reviewed 26 studies carried out by clinicians and 9 studies led by patients or undertaken with their collaboration. The proportions of patients who stated that ECT was helpful is shown in Figure 29.1. Reported rates of memory impairment were 29–55%. The studies which showed the lowest rates of satisfaction had been conducted on self-selected groups of patients who had received treatment up to 20 years previously (Bergsholm, 2012).

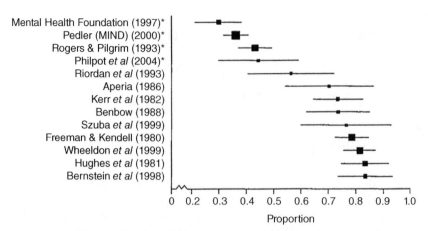

Figure 29.1 Proportions of patients who would find ECT helpful, by study. Lines indicate approximate 95% confidence intervals; size of box indicates precision. *Patient study.

The service user perspective was explored further in two further publications from the SURE group. Philpot and colleagues (2004) investigated a consecutive series of patients who had received ECT in two South London mental health trusts. The response rate was low (41%); of those who responded, 40% would not be prepared to have ECT again. Most patients (84%) complained of some memory loss which was persistent in 42%, but some felt that this was an acceptable side effect of an effective treatment.

The other study (Rose *et al*, 2004) gathered experiences of ECT from three sources: internet websites, the British Library Mental Health Testimony Archive and service user's publications. From these sources, 139 testimonies were collected. Of these, 83 were negative, 43 positive and 13 unclear. Some patients who had experienced ECT felt that the adverse effects were tolerable; others reported that they had tried to minimise symptoms to their psychiatrist in order to avoid receiving further treatment. For several patients, the main concern was about the perceived coercion which led to them receiving treatment. Of the 139 testimonies, 99 (71%) mentioned memory loss as an adverse effect of treatment; in 86 cases (62%) this was felt to be permanent. There was little variation in complaints of memory loss between people who recently received ECT and those who had been treated 50 years ago. Similar findings are reported by Johnston (1999) and Lawrence (2006).

The Royal College of Psychiatrists began to audit the quality of ECT practice in the 1970s. The first report concluded that standards of ECT practice were very poor (Pippard & Ellam, 1981). Follow-up audits (Pippard, 1992; Duffett & Lelliott, 1998) showed improvements in anaesthetic practice but only modest improvement in psychiatric aspects of treatment. As a result of the NICE report (2003) the College established the ECT Accreditation Service ECTAS (see Chapter 18).

The views of 389 patients who submitted completed questionnaires as part of the ECTAS review process have been analysed by Rayner *et al* (2009). Forty-nine respondents referred to memory loss, 21% to headaches and 10% to feelings of weakness or tiredness. Twelve patients complained of severe and persistent memory loss. Attitudes towards memory loss varied. One patient stated: 'I will never agree to receive ECT again because I have lost so much memory. Many of the memories I have lost are very valuable' (p. 383).

Other patients remarked, 'I still suffer from some memory loss, but it is nothing compared to my condition prior to ECT' (p. 384) and, 'My memory loss during and after the procedure has been disconcerting to say the least. However, on the whole, my views are positive' (p. 385). Participants were given the opportunity to add their own comments; 54 made positive remarks, whereas 17 left more negative responses.

Twelve per cent of patients who were assumed to have consented stated that they felt pressurised or forced to have ECT; others complained that they were rushed into a decision before they were ready. Nineteen patients stated that they were not given sufficient information about the side effects of treatment. The survey did not include questions on beneficial effects of ECT: of the 109 patients who entered free text comments, 79 reported beneficial effects, 22 had felt ECT had had no effect of their condition, and 7 others had initially experienced benefit but later relapsed. In addition, several patients commented on the reluctance of their psychiatrists to prescribe ECT: 'ECT is the only thing that works for me if I get really ill (suicidal). Some consultants have refused ECT for me and taken a long time to be persuaded' (p. 385).

Similar suggestions about how to improve the patient experience were found in Kershaw et al's (2007) report sent to ECTAS as part of the accreditation process. In total, 1600 questionnaires were sent out to member clinics; 389 were completed by patients. Patients generally found that helpful and friendly staff relieved their anxieties.

Rush et al (2007) working at an ECTAS accredited clinic in Dublin, received 51 responses after sending postal questionnaires to 89 consecutive patients. Only 3 found the procedure very stressful, but 47 experienced memory impairment, which persisted in 27 patients. Most found the treatment helpful but 6 would not have ECT again. The most recently published UK survey reported the findings of a study conducted by the Regulation and Quality Improvement Authority on the experiences of all patients receiving ECT in Northern Ireland between 1 July 2013 and 30 June 2014 (Maguire et al, 2016). The response was low (26%), but of these 45% had been involuntary patients. A total of 80% of respondents felt that ECT had been beneficial to them, they were satisfied with the information they had been given and the quality of the care which they had received.

Negative attitudes to ECT are not confined to UK patients. Goodman et al (1999) developed the Patient Satisfaction Survey which has been used in several subsequent publications. In their own study, patients who had received ECT were satisfied with their treatment and had more favourable attitudes to ECT than patients who had not experienced the treatment.

Koopowitz et al (2003), working in Adelaide, Australia, conducted semi-structured interviews with eight patients. Participants were between 25 and 50 years old: four had unipolar depression and four bipolar affective disorder. Their outcome from treatment varied between full remission and no response. They complained of fear of ECT, cognitive decline and memory loss. They felt that reducing waiting time prior to the procedure, improving communication between staff and patients and treating disturbed patients separately would make ECT more acceptable.

Sienaert et al (2005) conducted semi-structured interviews with 36 patients who had experienced ECT at Leuven, Belgium, using the Patient Satisfaction Survey (Goodman et al, 1999). Although many patients found the process frightening and some experienced cognitive adverse effects, the majority were satisfied with their treatment and would have ECT again. Bustin et al (2008) surveyed attitudes to and knowledge of ECT in patients receiving out-patient treatment for depression who had not experienced ECT. A total of 75 patients were recruited: 30 from Argentina, 30 from England and 15 from Canada. Most patients had a neutral or negative attitude to ECT – those who were more positive had a better level of knowledge about ECT.

Brodarty *et al* (2003) reported on attitudes to ECT in a cohort of 81 elderly patients (mean age 67.2 years) who received ECT for major depression in Sydney, Australia. Prior to treatment, they were sceptical about the possibility of benefit; patients with severe depression were most pessimistic about the likelihood of improvement. After treatment, 68.8% felt they had benefited from ECT, 6.5% felt they had become worse, and 24.7% thought their condition was the same. The treating psychiatrists were better at predicting the outcome of treatment, but they overestimated the probability of ECT being successful. Rajagopal *et al* (2013) working in Mysore, India, administered the *Patient Satisfaction Survey* (Goodman *et al*, 1999) to 50 patients and their relatives. About 65% of patients were satisfied with their treatment; nearly 75% reported that they would have ECT again if required. Only 39% were happy with the information they had received prior to ECT.

In summary, it appears that the reported experiences of patients vary with the sampling frame used and the methodology of the study, but the overall level of patient satisfaction appears to be higher in recent years. External audit by ECTAS and the Scottish ECT Accreditation Network (SEAN) in the UK appears to have had a beneficial effect on the patient experience. However, many patients remain dissatisfied by their experiences and clinics will have to continue to work to make the treatment more acceptable.

Carers' Experiences

Very little research has been published on carers' experiences of ECT. The studies have been small and have lacked a comparison group of similarly ill in-patients who have not received ECT. Sethi & Williams (2003) spoke to eight family carers of patients receiving outpatient ECT; they found that the caregiving associated with severe depressive symptoms created family distress, rather than the ECT. Smith *et al* (2009) reported on interviews with 16 people: nine patients receiving ECT and seven family members who had been involved with a course of ECT during the previous six months. Three themes emerged from discussions of the decision-making process:

- The anguish of living with a severe mental disorder
- The feelings that ECT was the last hope
- The blind trust that had to placed in the doctor.

After treatment many patients experienced relief with remission of symptoms but some experienced adverse effects including memory loss (which was more severe than expected), ataxia, mania and confusion. Those who did not improve felt more despondent. For some who did improve, remission was short lived. Participants felt that they had not been given an adequate explanation about the risks of ECT.

More positive views on ECT were expressed by the parents of young people aged under 19 years who had received ECT (Walter *et al*, 1999). Of the 28 parents interviewed, 17 felt that the treatment had been helpful, 9 thought it had made no difference and 1 believed it had been deleterious. The family members interviewed by Szuba *et al* (1991) also reported positive attitudes to ECT. Rajagopal *et al* (2013) investigated satisfaction in 50 patients who had received ECT and their relatives; about 55% of patients were generally satisfied, but relatives reported satisfaction levels of 80–100%.

Conclusions

The reported views of patients about their experiences of ECT appear to mirror the attitudes of the people who undertake the research. Staff who have a positive view on the treatment report that patients find ECT helpful, whereas investigators who are more sceptical about the effects of ECT are more inclined to emphasise negative aspects of treatment. In general relatives and carers have more favourable views on ECT than patients.

Recent surveys in Britain and Ireland suggest that peer review and accreditation by SEAN and ECTAS have led to a higher level of patient satisfaction. Routine use of patient related outcome measures such as the *Patient Satisfaction Survey* (Goodman *et al*, 1999) might lead to improvement in services.

Many patients still feel that they are coerced into accepting treatment and find the procedure frightening and stressful.

A consistent theme which emerges from all the studies conducted with service users and carers is the perceived lack of information which they received prior to treatment about the possible adverse effects of ECT, particularly the possibility of adverse effects on memory but even this seems to be finally being addressed (Maguire *et al*, 2016).

References

Aperia, B. (1986) Hormone pattern and post-treatment attitudes in patients with major depressive disorder given electroconvulsive therapy. *Acta Psychiatrica Scandinavica*, **73**, 271–4.

Arshad, M., Arham, A. Z., Arif, M., *et al* (2007) Awareness and perceptions of electroconvulsive therapy among psychiatric patients. *BMC Psychiatry*, **7**, 27–33.

Benbow, S. M. (1988) Patients views on electroconvulsive therapy on completion of a course of treatment. *Convulsive Therapy*, **4**, 146–52.

Bergsholm, P. (2012) Patients' perspectives on electroconvulsive therapy. A re-evaluation of the review by Rose et al on memory loss after electroconvulsive therapy. *Journal of ECT*, **28**, 27–30.

Bernstein, H., Beale, M. & Kellner, C. H. (1998) Patient attitudes about ECT after treatment. *Psychiatric Annals*, **28**, 524–7.

Brodarty, H., Berle, D., Hickie, I., *et al* (2003) Perceptions of outcome from electroconvulsive therapy by depressed patients and psychiatrists. *Australian and New Zealand Journal of Psychiatry*, **37**, 196–9.

Browne A. (2000) Shock therapy patients to sue. *The Observer* 23 January. https://www.theguardian.com/uk/2000/jan/23/anthonybrowne.theobserver

Bustin, J., Rapoport, M. J., Krishna, M., *et al* (2008) Are patients' attitudes towards and knowledge of electroconvulsive therapy transcultural? A multi-national pilot study. *International Journal of Geriatric Psychiatry*, **23**, 497–503.

Chakrabarti, S., Grover, S. & Rajagopal, R. (2010) Electroconvulsive therapy: A review of knowledge, experience and attitudes of patients concerning the treatment. *World Journal of Biological Psychiatry*, **11**, 525–37.

Duffett, R. & Lelliott, P. (1998) Auditing electroconvulsive therapy. The third cycle. *British Journal of Psychiatry*, **172**, 401–5.

Freeman, C. P. & Kendell, R. E. (1980) ECT: 1. Patients' experiences and attitudes. *British Journal of Psychiatry*, **137**, 8–16.

Goodman, J. A., Krahn, L. E., Smith, G. E., *et al* (1999) Patient satisfaction with ECT. *Mayo Clinic Proceedings*, **74**, 967–71.

Hughes, J., Barraclough, B. M. & Reeve, W. (1981) Are patients shocked by ECT? *Journal of the Royal Society of Medicine*, **74**, 283–5.

Johnstone, L. (1999) Adverse psychological effects of ECT. *Journal of Mental Health*, **8**, 69–85.

Kerr, R. A., McGrath, J. J., O'Kearnery, A., *et al* (1982) ECT: misconceptions and attitudes.

Australian and New Zealand Journal of Psychiatry, **16**, 43–9.

Kershaw, K., Rayner, L. & Chaplin, R. (2007) Patients' views on the quality of care when receiving electroconvulsive therapy. *Psychiatric Bulletin*, **31**, 414–41.

Koopowtiz, L. F., Chur-Hansen, A., Reid, S., et al (2003) The subjective experience of patients who received electroconvulsive therapy. *Australian and New Zealand Journal of Psychiatry*, **37**, 49–54.

Lauber, C., Nordt, C., Falcato, L., et al (2005) Can a seizure help? The public's attitude toward electroconvulsive therapy. *Psychiatry Research*, **134**, 205–9.

Lawrence, J. (2006) Voices from within: a study of ECT and patient perceptions. Available online at: http://www.ect.org/voices-from-within-a-study-of-ect-and-patient-perceptions/.

Maguire, S., Rea, S. M. & Convery, P. (2016) Electroconvulsive therapy: what do patients think of their treatment? *Ulster Medical Journal*, **85**, 182–6.

McDonald, A. & Walter, G. (2001) The portrayal of ECT in American movies. *Journal of ECT*, **17**, 264–74.

McFarquhar, T. F. & Thompson, J. (2008) Knowledge and attitudes regarding electroconvulsive therapy among medical students and the general public. *Journal of ECT*, **24**, 244–53.

Mental Health Foundation (1997) *Knowing Our Own Minds*. Mental Health Foundation.

National Institute for Clinical Excellence (2003) *Guidance on the Use of Electroconvulsive Therapy* (Technology Appraisal TA59). NICE.

Pedler, M. (2000) Shock treatment: a survey of people's experience of electro-convulsive therapy (ECT). MIND.

Philpot, M., Collins, C., Trivedi, P., et al (2004) Eliciting users' views of ECT in two mental health trusts with a user-designed questionnaire. *Journal of Mental Health*, **13**, 403–13.

Pippard, J. & Ellam, L. (1981) *Electroconvulsive therapy in Great Britain 1980*. London: Gaskell.

Pippard, J. (1992) Audit of electroconvulsive therapy in two NHS regions. *British Journal of Psychiatry*, **160**, 621–637.

Rajagopal, R. Chakrabarti, S. & Grover, S. (2013) Satisfaction with electroconvulsive therapy among patients and their relatives. *Journal of ECT*, **29**, 283–90.

Rayner, L., Kershaw, K., Hanna, D., et al (2009) The patient perspective of the consent process and side effects of electroconvulsive therapy. *Journal of Mental Health*, **18**, 379–388.

Read, J. & Bentall, R. (2010). The effectiveness of electroconvulsive therapy: a literature review. *Epidemiologia e Psichiatrica Sociale*, **19**, 333–46.

Riordan, D. M., Barron, P. & Bowden, M. F. (1993) ECT: a patient-friendly procedure? *Psychiatric Bulletin*, **17**, 531–3.

Rogers, A. & Pilgrim, D. (1993) Service users' views of psychiatric treatments. *Sociology of Health and Illness*, **5**, 612–31.

Rose, D., Wykes, T., Morven, L., et al (2003) Patients' perspectives on electroconvulsive therapy: systematic review. *BMJ*, **326**, 1363–5.

Rose, D., Fleischmann, P. & Wykes, T. (2004) Consumers' views of electroconvulsive therapy: a qualitative analysis. *Journal of Mental Health*, **13**, 285–93.

Rush, G., McCarron, S. & Lucey, J. V. (2007) Patient attitudes to electroconvulsive therapy. *Psychiatric Bulletin*, **31**, 212–14.

Seelye, K. Q. (2016) Kitty Dukakis, a beneficiary of electroshock therapy, emerges as its evangelist. *New York Times* December 31. https://www.nytimes.com/2016/12/31/us/kitty-dukakis-electroshock-therapy-evangelist.html

Sethi, S. & Williams, R. A. (2003) The family caregiving experience of outpatient ECT. *Journal of the American Nurses Association*, **9**, 187–94.

Sienart, P., de Becker, T., Vansteelandt, K., et al (2005) Patient satisfaction after electroconvulsive therapy. *Journal of ECT*, **21**, 227–31.

Smith, M., Vogler, J., Zarrouf, F., et al (2009) Electroconvulsive therapy: the struggles in the decision-making process and the aftermath of treatment. *Issues in Mental Health Nursing*, **30**, 554–9.

Szuba, M. P., Baxter, L. R., Liston, E. H., *et al* (1991) Patients and family perspective of electroconvulsive therapy: correlation with outcome. *Convulsive Therapy*, **7**, 175–83.

UK ECT Review Group (2003) Efficacy and safety of electro-convulsive therapy in depressive disorder: a systematic review and meta-analysis. *Lancet*, **361**, 799–808.

Walter, G., Koster, K. & Rey, J. M. (1999) Views about treatment among parents of adolescents who received electroconvulsive therapy. *Psychiatric Services*, **50**, 701–2.

Wheeldon, T. J., Robertson, C., Eagles, J. M., *et al* (1999) The views and outcomes of consenting and non-consenting patients receiving ECT. *Psychological Medicine*, **29**, 221–3.

Index

AACAP Guidelines for Use of ECT with Adolescents, 67, 69
abdominal aortic aneurysm, 249
Aberrant Behaviour Checklist, 50
ablative neurosurgery, 10, 144–46
  depression, 145–46
  outcome studies, 145
  technical aspects, 145
accreditation. *See* Scottish ECT Accreditation Network (SEAN), *See* ECT Accreditation Service (ECTAS)
acetylcholinesterase inhibitors, 225, 228
adolescence. *See also* paediatric ECT
  consent and, 70, 260
  guidelines for use of ECT, 67, 69
  intellectual disability and, 55
Adults with Incapacity (Scotland) Act 2000, 260–62
advance statements, 263
adverse effects of ECT
  cardiovascular, 206
  cognitive. *See* cognitive side effects of ECT
  memory. *See* memory impairment
  musculo-skeletal, 206
  non-cognitive, 121–26
  schizophrenia, 80
affective network, 14
agitation, 207
alfentanil, 204
alpha-methyl-para-tyrosine (AMPT), 18
Alzheimer's disease, 46
amino acid neurotransmitters, 14
amnesia. *See* memory impairment
anaesthesia, 202–7
  commonly used drugs, 219
  dental issues, 214

induction agents. *See* induction agents
  investigations, 203
  issues, 187
  lead anaesthetist role in, 202
  monitoring, 203
  patient evaluation, 202
  practice guidelines, 202
  pregnancy and, 64
aneurysm, 249
anterograde amnesia, 109, 111
anticholinergics, 206, 219
anticoagulation, 248
anticonvulsants, 98, 195
  interactions with ECT, 223, 227
antidepressants, 3, *See also* ketamine
  effectiveness vs. ECT, 15
  epilepsy and, 99
  functional imaging studies, 16
  inflammation and, 17
  interactions with ECT, 221, 226
  mechanism of action, 151–52
  older adults, safety issues, 45
  post-ECT relapse and, 27
  serotonin/noradrenaline effect, 18
anti-inflammatories, 15
anti-NMDAR encephalitis, 102
antipsychotics, 75, *See also* clozapine
  interactions with ECT, 223, 226
  resistance to, 68
anxiety, 155
anxiolytics, 224, 228
APR position statement, ketamine, 156
assessment
  autobiographical amnesia, 114–15
  before ECT, 121
  capacity, 256–57
  cognitive, 3, 113–15, 117, 186
atracurium, 205
audit, 6, 8, 268

autism, 53–55
autobiographical amnesia, 13, 41, 109, 112–13
  assessment, 114–15
Autobiographical Memory Interview, 115
autoimmune disorders, 102
automatic implanted cardioverter defibrillator (AICD), 248

benzodiazepines, 16
  catatonia, 86, 90–92, 100
  interactions with ECT, 228
  older adults, 46
best interests, 257
beta-blockers, 206
BFCRS score, 89
bifrontal ECT, 34, 189–90
  catatonia, 89
  electrode placement, 78
bilateral ECT, 188
  catatonia, 89
  electrode placement, 78
  emergency treatment, 28
  mania, 34
  vs. unilateral, 190
  vs. unilateral in depression, 2, 15, 25
bipolar disorder, 4, 32, *See also* mixed affective episodes, *See also* mania
  catatonia with, 87
  pregnancy and, 5
bipolar disorder depression, 4, 38–41
  cognitive side effects of ECT, 41
  efficacy of ECT, 38–40
  general treatment principles, 40–41
  recommendations, 41
  relapse rates, 41
  switch to mania, treatment and, 40, 124
  timing of ECT usage, 39
bite-guards, 204, 213, 215
bitemporal ECT, 34, 188
  catatonia, 89

efficacy in older adults, 44
electrode placement, 78
bladder effects, ketamine, 154
blood glucose levels, 187
bradycardia, 64, 193, 205, 247
brain
 networks within, 13
 tumours, 249
brain derived neurotrophic
 factor (BDNF), 14–15
brain imaging, 13–16, See also
 magnetic resonance
 imaging (MRI)
 functional, 16
 structural, 15–16
breastfeeding, 65
brief pulse (BP) ECT, 26, 191
bupropion, 18, 226

caffeine, 194
camphor, 74
capacity, 254
 assessing, 256–57
 definition, 256
 paediatric ECT, 70
 schizophrenia patients, 80
capacity legislation, 257–65
 England and Wales, 257–60
 Northern Ireland, 264–65
 Republic of Ireland, 265–66
 Scotland, 260–64
capnography, 183
capsulotomy, 10, 145
carbamazepine, 227
cardiac arrhythmia, 64, 206
cardiac failure, 249
cardiac pacemakers, 248
cardiovascular disease, 45–46,
 123–24, 218, 248–49
cardiovascular response, 236
cardiovascular side effects, 154,
 206
carers
 education/information
 provision, 173–74
 experience of ECT, 270
 information for, 58
 support from nurses, 176
 views on paediatric ECT, 71
catatonia, 85–93, 100–1
 classification and diagnosis,
 85–86
 co-administration of
 benzodiazepines, 90–91
 continuation/maintenance
 treatment, 91

current usage of ECT, 86
duration of ECT treatment,
 90
efficacy and effectiveness of
 ECT, 87–89
electrode placement, 89, 92
frequency of ECT, 89
history of, 86
intellectual disability and,
 53–55
NICE guidelines, 5, 86
NMS and, 101
paediatric ECT, 69
recommendations for ECT, 92
types of, 53
Catatonia Rating Scales, 53
cellular pathology, 14
cerebral aneurysm, 249
cerebral tumours, 249
cerebrovascular disease, 249
challenging behaviour, 55–56
checklist for ECT treatment,
 178, 187
chemically induced seizures, 74
childhood. See also paediatric
 ECT
 intellectual disability and, 55
chlorpromazine, 75, 77
 mania treatment, 32–33
cholinesterase inhibitors, 46
cingulotomy, 10, 145
Clinical Global Impression
 (CGI) scores, 102
clinical governance, 6, 181
clozapine, 68
 adverse effects, 80
 catatonia, 101
 ECT augmentation, 77
 psychosis in Parkinson's
 disease, 97
 treatment resistance to, 81
cochlear implants, 250
coercion, 255, 268
cognitive assessment, 113–15,
 117, 186
 in depression, 3
cognitive control network, 14
cognitive impairment, 2
 dementia with ECT, 103
 ketamine, 153
cognitive side effects of ECT,
 109–17, 207
 bilateral vs. unilateral, 25
bipolar disorder depression,
 41
immediate, 110–11

prevention, 115–16
subacute and longer term,
 111–13
types of, 109
compulsory treatment order,
 259, 262–63
consent
 before ECT, 121
 dental risks and, 212–13
 informal patients, 260
 informed, 2, 260
 intellectual disability and, 58
 paediatric ECT, 70, 260
 rTMS, 6
 seeking, 254–56
 written, 255
continuation ECT, 27, 197
 catatonia, 91
 schizophrenia, 79–81
cortex, 13
cortical connectivity, 16
Court of Protection, 257, 259
C-Reactive Protein (CRP), 15
cuff technique, 234, 236, 251

deep brain stimulation (DBS),
 10, 140, 143–44
default mode network, 13, 16
delirium, 102–3, 111
delta activity, 239
delusions, 27
dementia, 102–3
 behavioural disturbance
 with, 102
 depression with, 103
 ECT challenges, 46
 psychosis with, 103
dental issues, 211–16
 bite-guards, 204, 213, 215
 bridges, 214
 crowns, 214
 dentures, 216
 for anaesthetists, 214
 implants, 215
 intraosseous dental supports,
 215
 risk management strategy,
 212–14
 veneers, 214
depression, 24–29, See also
 bipolar disorder
 depression, See also
 antidepressants
 ablative neurosurgery, 145–46
 bipolar disorder, 4, 38–41
 capacity and, 256

depression (cont.)
DBS, 144
dementia, 103
different populations, 28
efficacy of ECT treatment,
24–26
emergency treatment with
ECT, 28
epilepsy and, 99
ketamine treatment, 7–8
memory impairment and,
114
NICE guidelines on ECT
usage, 2–3
NMD treatment, 9
older adults, 44
Parkinson's disease and, 97
pathophysiology of, 13–15
predictors of response to
ECT, 27
pregnancy, 5, 63–64
RCP position statement, 3
relapse, post-ECT, 27–28
rTMS, 6, 130
single neurotransmitter
theories of, 13
tDCS treatment, 8–9
treatment-resistant, 28, 131,
149
types that respond to ECT, 27
unilateral vs. bilateral ECT, 2,
15, 25
VNS, 143
vs. schizophrenia ECT usage,
75
detained patients, 70, 261,
264–65
diabetes, 250
diazepam, 194
disorientation, 110
dopamine antagonists, 99
dose of electrical stimulus, 25
Down syndrome, 57
drug abuse/dependence, 153
drug interactions with ECT,
218–29
by drug class, 221
types of evidence used, 220

eating disorders, 155
ECT Accreditation Service
(ECTAS), 67, 75, 161–63,
171, 202, 268
Standards, 161, 168, 178
ECT clinics
inspection, 161–62

managing, 179–80
nurse-administered ECT,
180
service delivery, 168–69
service standards, 171
ECT treatment suite, 183–85
capacity assessment, 256
equipment, 183–84
nursing care in the, 177–78
rationalisation and closure,
184–85
treatment room, 183
waiting area, 183
EEG monitoring, 237–45
artefacts, 244
electrode placement, 237
establishing a baseline EEG,
238
ictal and postictal phases,
239–44
electrical current, dosage of, 15
electrically induced seizures, 75
electrocardiography (ECG),
203, 244
electrode artefact, 244
electrode placement, 188–90,
237
bilateral vs. unilateral, 78
catatonia, 89, 92
mania, 34
electrodecremental phase, 239
electromyography (EMG), 235
emergency treatment, 28, 259
encephalitis, 102, 249
epilepsy, 74–75, 98–99, 141
esketamine, 150–51
esmolol, 206
ethics, 9, 57
etomidate, 195, 205

falls, 125
families. See carers
fentanyl, 204
first-line treatment
depression with ECT, 29
ECT as, 3
flumazenil, 90
flupentixol, 79
frequency of ECT, 26, 69, 78,
89, 92, 186
functional MRI (fMRI), 13, 16,
129

gamma-aminobutyric acid
(GABA), 14, 16–17, 85
glaucoma, 206, 251

glutamate, 14, 16–17, 85, 151
glycopyrrolate, 206
grimacing, 193, 211

Hamilton cuff technique, 234,
236, 251
Hamilton Depression Rating
Scale (HDRS), 24, 196
herpes simplex virus, 102
hippocampus, 15–16, 19
Huntington's disease, 100
hypertension, 248
hyperventilation, 46, 194, 204
hypnotics, 224, 228

ictal EEG phases, 239–44
impaired executive function,
109, 112
impedance, measuring, 191
implanted pulse generator
(IPG), 140–41
incident mania, 34
induction agents, 90, 204, 219
inflammation, 15
ECT and, 17
informal patients, 254–56, 260
information
different formats, 173
different sources of, 255
for carers, 58
nurses as a resource for, 173
sharing with the patient,
254–55
informed consent, 2, 260
intellectual disability, 50–59
autism and catatonia, 53–55
case series/reports, 51, 53,
55–56
challenging behaviour and,
55–56
diagnostic issues, 50
mood disorders and, 51–53
observations on the use of
ECT, 56–57
prevalence of psychiatric
disorders, 51
recommendations, 58
self-injurious behaviour, 68
syndromes associated with, 56
interleukin-6 (IL-6), 15, 17
intracranial foreign objects, 250
Irish Mental Health Act 2001,
265

ketamine, 7–8, 17, 149–57, 205
clinical effects, 149–50

clinics and guidance, 155
ECT and, 152
formulations and licensing,
154–55
glutamate and, 14
registries and monitoring,
156
side effects, 7, 152–54

Lasting Power of Attorney,
257–58
lead consultant, 168–69, 185
lesion neurosurgery. *See*
ablative neurosurgery
Lewy Body Dementia, 46
lipopolysaccharide (LPS), 17
lithium, 3
cognitive side effects, 110
interactions with ECT, 223,
227
vs. ECT in mania treatment,
32–33
lorazepam, 53, 55, 86, 91

MADRS (Montgomery-Asberg
Depression Rating Scale),
167
magnetic resonance imaging
(MRI), 13–14, 16, 130
maintenance ECT, 28, 197
catatonia, 91
schizophrenia, 80
malignant catatonia, 86, 88–89,
92, 101
malignant hyperthermia, 204
mania, 4
ECT and concomitant
medication, 34
efficacy of ECT treatment,
32–33
electrode placement and
stimulation parameters, 34
incident to ECT treatment, 34
recommendations for ECT,
35
side effect of ECT, 124
switch to bipolar depression,
treatment and, 40
mechanism of action of ECT,
13–14
memory impairment
adolescents, 69
anterograde amnesia, 109, 111
autobiographical, 13, 41, 109,
112–15
patients' experience of, 268

Mental Capacity Act (Northern
Ireland) 2016, 70, 264
Mental Capacity Act 2005, 58,
257–65
Mental Health (Care and
Treatment) (Scotland) Act
2003, 260, 262
Mental Health (Northern
Ireland) Order (1986), 264
Mental Health Act 1983, 258–59
mental capacity, 80
paediatric ECT, 70
methohexital, 195, 205
mirtazapine, 24, 194, 226
mivacurium, 205
mixed affective episodes
ECT and concomitant
medication, 34
efficacy of ECT, 33
recommendations for ECT,
35
monitoring
anaesthesia, 203
ECT, 186
EEG, 237–45
ketamine, 156
post-ECT, 195–97
seizures, 234–45
monoamine oxidase inhibitors
(MAOIs), 222, 226
monoamines, 18–19
Montgomery-Åsberg
Depression Rating Scale
(MADRS), 38
mood disorders, 68
intellectual disability, 51–53
Mood, Interest and Pleasure
Questionnaire (MIPQ), 50
mortality rate, 121–23
movement artefact, 244
movement disorder, 96–97, 103
multiple sclerosis, 101
muscle artefact, 244
muscle relaxants, 192, 204, 234
musculo-skeletal side effects, 206
myocardial infarction, 248

neuroleptic malignant
syndrome (NMS), 69, 86,
101
neuromodulation, 140
neuropsychiatric disorders,
96–104
neurosurgery for mental
disorder (NMD), 9–11,
140–46

neurotransmitters, 14
neurotrophic hypothesis,
depression, 14
NICE guidelines
antenatal and postnatal
mental health, 5
bipolar disorder, 4
challenging behaviour and
learning disability, 56
cognitive assessment, 186
ECT, 161
ECT in catatonia, 5, 86
ECT in depression, 2–3
ECT in pregnancy, 63
ECT in schizophrenia, 75
rTMS, 6, 130, 135
schizophrenia, 4
tDCS for depression, 8
VNS, 11, 143
NICE Technology Appraisal
2003, 4, 267
NMD (neurosurgery for mental
disorder), 9–11, 140–46
N-methyl-D-aspartate
(NMDA) receptor, 14, 151
NMS (neuroleptic malignant
syndrome), 69, 86, 101
non-cognitive side effects of
ECT, 121–26
assessment before, 121
cardio-pulmonary, 123–24
mania, 124
mortality rate, 121–23
prevalence of, 125
prolonged seizures, 124
suicide, 124
non-memory cognitive side
effects, 111–12
noradrenaline, 18
nortriptyline, 24
number of ECT treatments, 26,
196–97
nursing, 173–81
administered ECT, 180
clinical governance, 181
ECT lead nurse, 163
ECT nurse specialist, 179–80
ECT treatment suite, 177–78,
185
education/information role,
173–74
inpatients and day patients,
173–74
preparing patient for ECT,
177
recovery care, 178

nursing (cont.)
supportive role, 176
theatre environment, 179
training and development,
180

obsessions, 98
obsessive-compulsive disorder
(OCD)
DBS treatment, 143
ketamine, 155
NMD treatment, 9
oesophageal reflux, 250
older adults, 44–47
efficacy of ECT, 44–45
practical considerations, 46
recommendations for ECT,
47
rTMS in, 134
safety issues, 45–46
optical motor sensor (OMS),
236
organic catatonia, 100
osteoporosis, 251

paediatric ECT, 67–71
catatonia, 69
consent, capacity and legal
considerations, 70–71, 260
epidemiology, 67
indications for use, 67–68
mood disorders, 68
NMS, 69
patients, carers and clinicians
views, 71
prognosis, 70
psychotic disorders, 68
side effects, 69–70
Parkinson's disease, 18, 96–98,
143, 249
patients
anaesthetic evaluation, 202
detained, 70, 261, 264–65
experience of rTMS, 134
incapable of informed
consent, 260
informal, 254–56, 260
information/education
provision, 173–74
inpatient and day patient
care, 174–76
patient-centred services, 165
perspectives of ECT, 267–70
preparation for ECT, 177
recovery care and discharge,
178

selection for rTMS, 131–32
support from nurses, 176
views on paediatric ECT,
71
pentylenetetrazol, 74
pharmacotherapy. See also
individual drug groups, See
also drug interactions with
ECT
anaesthetics commonly used,
219
relapse post-ECT and, 27
vs. ECT in bipolar
depression, 38–39
vs. ECT treatment, 33
physiological effects of ECT,
206
polyspike activity, 239
Positive Behaviour Support,
56
positron emission tomography
(PET), 15
post-ictal delirium, 102, 111
post-ictal suppression, 243
postnatal period, 63
ECT in the, 64–65
key points, 65
post-traumatic stress disorder
(PTSD), 155
predictors of response to ECT,
27
prefrontal cortex, 14
pregnancy, 63–64
ECT during, 5, 63–64
key points, 65
rTMS in, 134
prescribing ECT, 186
propofol, 69, 90, 205, 207
puerperal psychosis, 64
pulmonary disease, 123–24, 248
pulse width, 26, 191

quinolinic acid, 17

RCP Best Practice Guide to
ECT Training, 168–70
RCP Diagnostic Criteria for
Psychiatric Disorders for
Use with Adults with
Learning Disabilities, 50
RCP position statement
ECT in depression, 3, 29
ketamine, 7, 156
NMD, 9, 144–45
tDCS treatment, 9
recruiting rhythm, 239

relapse
bipolar disorder depression,
41
post-ECT, 27–28, 197
remifentanil, 204, 219
remission rates, 27, 196
repetitive TMS (rTMS), 6, 129–
36
administration, 132–33, 135
administration, training for,
134–36
contraindications, 131
efficacy in depression, 130
guidance and approvals, 130
patient selection, 131–32
patients' experience of, 134
safety, 133
vs. ECT, 132
vs. ECT in depression, 25
resting motor threshold
(RMT), 133
resting state fMRI, 13
resting state network
connectivity, 16
retrograde amnesia. See
autobiographical amnesia
risk-benefit analysis, 251
risperidone, 87
rocuronium, 206

safety
guidance pre-surgery, 178
older adults and, 45–46
rTMS, 133, 136
schizophrenia, 74–82
adverse effects and risks of
ECT, 80
continuation ECT, 79–81
current ECT usage, 75
duration of acute treatment,
78–79
ECT recommendations, 81
efficacy and effectiveness of
ECT, 75–77
electrode placement, 78
frequency of treatment, 78
history of treatment, 74–75
intellectual disability and,
57
legal considerations of ECT,
80
maintenance ECT, 80
NICE guidelines, 4
speed of response to ECT,
77
treatment-resistant, 4, 76, 81

Scottish ECT Accreditation Network (SEAN), 161, 164–67, 170–71
patient-centred, 165
Standards, 165
second opinion doctors, 70, 80, 258
second-line treatment
depression with ECT, 29
ECT as, 3
seizure monitoring, 234–45, See also EEG monitoring
adequacy of seizure, 245–46
cardiovascular response, 236–46
motor activity, 234–36
seizure threshold, 190
definition, 192
establishing, 192–94
measurement, 192
too high, 194
seizures, 98, See also epilepsy
adequacy of, 195
adolescents, 69
chemically induced, 74
ECT effectiveness and, 15, 191–92
ECT in depression, 16
electrically induced, 75
older adults, 45–46
prolonged, 124, 195
termination, 241
too short, 195
selective serotonin reuptake inhibitors (SSRIs), 221, 226
self-injurious behaviour, 55, 68, 91
serotonin (5-HT), 18
serotonin and noradrenergic reuptake inhibitors (SNRIs), 221, 226
service delivery, 168–69
service standards, 171
Service User Research Enterprise (SURE), 267–68

sevoflurane, 204
short-term detention certificate (STDC), 262–63
sine wave ECT, 26
smoking, 45
staffing, 185–86, See also nursing, See also lead consultant
standardised Mini Mental State Exam (sMMSE), 113
status epilepticus, 99
stigma, ECT, 173
stimulation parameters, 34
stimulus dosing, 191–95
protocol, 193
stimulus titration, 192
stroke, 100, 249
Subjective Memory Assessment, 113
subjective memory difficulty, 109, 113
suicide, 124
ECT efficacy, 27
ketamine effect on, 150
schizophrenia, 81
sulpiride, 77
suxamethonium, 204, 206
systemic lupus erythematosus (SLE), 100

tardive dyskinesia, 103, 250
theophylline, 194, 229
theta activity, 239
thiopental, 205
tonic-clonic seizure, 191
training course, rTMS, 134–35
administration, 135
efficacy and safety, 136
setting up the machine, 135
training, nursing, 180
training, psychiatrists, 168–71
service delivery, 168–69
service standards, 171
supervision, 170
transcranial direct current stimulation (tDCS), 8–9

transcranial magnetic stimulation (TMS). See repetitive TMS (rTMS)
traumatic brain injury (TBI), 104
trazodone, 226
treatment-resistant depression, 28, 131
ketamine effect on, 149
treatment-resistant schizophrenia, 76, 81
augmentation strategy, 4
tricyclic antidepressants (TCAs), 221, 226
tryptophan depletion, 18

UK, ECT usage, 1
ultrabrief pulse (UBP) ECT, 26, 191
unilateral ECT, 190
catatonia, 92
cognitive side effects, 115
depression, 29
electrode placement, 78
mania, 34
right vs. left, 190
vs. bilateral, 190
vs. bilateral in depression, 3, 15, 25

vagus nerve stimulation (VNS), 11, 140–43
depression, 143
outcome studies, 142–43
technical aspects, 141–42
valproate, 17, 35
valvular heart disease, 249
venlafaxine, 24, 44, 194, 226

warfarin, 248
WHO checklist for ECT treatment, 178, 187
written consent, 255

xanthines, 194

Young Mania Rating Scale (YMRS) scores, 34